CLAUSEWITZ IN ENGLISH

CLAUSEWITZ IN ENGLISH

The Reception of Clausewitz In Britain and America 1815–1945

CHRISTOPHER BASSFORD

New York Oxford
OXFORD UNIVERSITY PRESS
1994

Oxford University Press

Oxford New York Toronto
Delhi Bombay Calcutta Madras Karachi
Kuala Lumpur Singapore Hong Kong Tokyo
Nairobi Dar es Salaam Cape Town
Melbourne Auckland Madrid

and associated companies in
Berlin Ibadan

Published by Oxford University Press, Inc.,
200 Madison Avenue, New York, New York 10016

Oxford is a registered trademark of Oxford University Press

Library of Congress Cataloging-in-Publication Data
Bassford, Christopher,
Clausewitz in English : the reception of Clausewitz in
Britain and America, 1815–1945 /
Christopher Bassford.
p. cm. Includes bibliographical references and index.
ISBN 0-19-508383-0
1. Military art and science—United States—History.
2. Military art and science Great Britain—History.
3. Clausewitz, Carl von,
1780-1831—Influence. I. Title.
U43.U4B37 1994 355.02′0941—dc20 93-19001

2 4 6 8 9 7 5 3 1
Printed in the United States of America
on acid-free paper

To my parents,
Philip James Bassford,
and Marynelle H. Bassford,
who deserve so much more.

Acknowledgments

Owing to the broad time-span covered in this book and its inclusion of both British and American sources, I have been more than usually dependent on the assistance of a great many specialists. It is one of the great pleasures of working in the historical profession that its practitioners are generally happy to share their knowledge without reservation, and my correspondents have, with very rare exceptions, been enthusiastically helpful. Such errors as this book still no doubt contains are, of course, my own.

I am particularly indebted to John B. Hattendorf, Ernest J. King Professor of Maritime History at the United States Naval War College, and to Professor Michael Howard, now at the Institute for Advanced Study at Princeton. Professors Hattendorf and Howard both have great reputations for charm and for being helpful to younger scholars, virtues amply demonstrated in their assistance to myself. Both plowed through the great bulk of my early manuscript in draft form, and their comments, encouragement, suggestions, and leads to new sources have been critical to whatever progress I have made.

I owe special thanks as well to Professor Alan D. Beyerchen of Ohio State University; Dr. Evelyn Cherpak, head of the Naval Historical Collection at the Naval War College; Major Alan Harfield of the Army Museum's Ogilby Trust; Douglas Hendry, Public Record Office at Kew; Virginia Murray, of the John Murray Company, London; Professor Peter Paret, Institute for Advanced Study; Professor Barry Steiner, California State University at Long Beach; Professor Hew Strachan, Corpus Christi College, Cambridge; Richard Taylor and Patricia Methven of the Liddell Hart Centre for Military Archives, King's College London; Dr. C.M. Woolgar, University of Southampton; and R.C. Snelling, British Library.

The faculty and staff of Purdue University have also been most supportive. Professors Robert E. May, Gordon R. Mork, and Randy Roberts, of the Department of History, have all lent a willing ear and often a helping hand. The staff of the Interlibrary Loan Office, Ruth Rothenberg, Mary Sego, Roger Strater, and Kathy Garner, have assisted me in a manner far beyond the call of duty. The chief bibliographer of Purdue's HSSE Library, E. Stewart Saunders, has also given me great support.

For more specific assistance I must thank Louise Arnold, U.S. Military History Institute; Professor Martin Blumenson; Professor Brian Bond; Fred Baumann, Library of Congress Manuscripts Division; Professor Henry S. Bausum, *Journal of Military History*; L. James Binder, *ARMY* magazine; Michael Bott, Archivist, University of Reading; Thomas W. Branigar, Eisenhower Library; Major Mark Clodfelter, USAF; Professor Gordon A. Craig; Professor Martin van Creveld; Professor Daniel Crosswell; Professor Lorenzo Crowell; Captain Antulio J. Echevarria II, USAR; Keith Eiler, Hoover Institution; Professor Robert M. Epstein; Professor Norman Gash; Professor Felix Gilbert; Major-General John David Carew Graham, Royal Parachute Regiment; Professor Arthur Groos; Eric Grove; Joanna Hitchcock, Princeton University Press; Professor I.B. Holley; Hermione Jolles; Claire L'Enfant, Routledge publishing; D.J. Lyon, National Maritime Museum (U.K.); M.G. Little, Royal Marines Museum; Professor Jay Luvaas; Lars Mahinske of the *Encyclopaedia Britannica*'s research department; Major Michael Matheny, USA; Colonel Lloyd Matthews, USA; Dr. Joachim Niemeyer, the Militärgeschichtliches Forschungsamt; Professor Peter Novick; Sumiko Otsubo of Ohio State University; Professor Mark Peattie; Joan Phillips, Air University Library at Maxwell Field; Professor William B. Pickett; Richard L. Popp, University of Chicago archives; Carlos Rivera of Ohio State University; J.R. Russell, National Library of Scotland; Elizabeth Sage, University of Chicago Library; Professor Donald M. Schurman; Judith A. Sibley, West Point Library; John Slonaker, U.S. Army Military History Institute; Dr. Richard P. Stebbins; Professor Jon T. Sumida; Dr. Detlev F. Vagts; Gore Vidal; and Professor Harold Winton.

Most of all, of course, I must thank my friend and advisor Professor Gunther Rothenberg of Purdue University, without whose encouragement I would long ago have abandoned this project and whose rigorous demands have given it whatever quality it possesses.

As with every major project I have undertaken for a long time now, my deepest appreciation goes to my wife, Sunyong Bassford, who has been unfailingly supportive while nonetheless insisting that I remain in touch with the rest of the planet.

Financial support for this project was provided by David Ross grants from Purdue University and by an Olin Postdoctoral Fellowship in Military History and National Security Studies from the Ohio State University. I am also thankful for the practical support of my friends, colleagues, and superiors here at the United States Marine Corps Command and Staff College in Quantico, Virginia, and for their tolerance for the more-than-occasional distraction from daily business that this project entailed. Thanks are due as well to the Trustees of the Liddell Hart Centre for Military Archives, King's College London, for permission to quote from materials in their possession, and to the Controller of Her Majesty's Stationery Office for permission to quote from documents held by the Public Records Office.

Contents

CLAUSEWITZ IN ENGLISH

1

Introduction

Bernard Brodie liked to characterize Carl von Clausewitz's military classic *On War* (*Vom Kriege*, 1832) as being "not simply the greatest book on war but the one truly great book on that subject yet written."[1] This is hyperbole, of course. Nonetheless, if any one work can be said to form the basis for modern military thought, *On War* is the book. First published in Germany in 1832, it has been the bible of many thoughtful soldiers ever since the elder Moltke attributed his stunning victories in the wars of German unification to its guidance. Since 1976, when Peter Paret and Michael Howard published their magnificent new English translation, the interest in it of soldiers and scholars has grown almost exponentially; indeed, "Clausewitz studies" have become something of a cottage industry for military intellectuals. By the 1980s, the philosophy of Clausewitz (1780–1831) had become a major, direct influence on American military doctrinal writing and even on national policy (if we are to consider the "Weinberger Doctrine" as official policy), as well as on the writing of most sophisticated military history. Most unusually for a book of its abstract nature, the new translation of *On War* has sold over forty thousand copies.[2]

Inspired in large part by the efforts of Paret, Howard, and Brodie, a great deal has been written in English about Clausewitz over the past few decades. There have been new biographies, new attempts at analysis, and reissues of old (and often hoary) condensations. Clausewitz's own thoughts have been traced to their sources. Their influence in many countries—most particularly Germany itself—has been examined in great detail.[3]

For various reasons, however, the latter efforts have tended to ignore the history of the study of Clausewitz in English, particularly that before World War I. This peculiar state of affairs has many roots. Clausewitz's students tend naturally to focus on Germany, where Clausewitz wrote and where his disciples have most eagerly identified themselves as such. In contrast, the Anglo-Saxons are often perceived as hopelessly parochial in the military realm. British and American strategic successes often appear to owe little to any military–theoretical sophistication on the part of the leadership. They can more easily be ascribed to geopolitical, economic, and demographic advantages sufficient to counterbalance the persistent military naiveté of these two nations. The dissertation from which this book is derived is entitled "The Reception of Clausewitzian Theory in Anglo-American Military Thought, 1815–1945." It was suggested by more than one commentator that the term "Anglo-Saxon Military Thought" was an oxymoron. Because much British writing on Clausewitz during the interwar period was hostile and seemed to indicate little real understanding of his ideas, it has generally been assumed that Clausewitz had had no positive impact on that nation. In this view, Clausewitz exercised no meaningful influence in either country until after World War II, perhaps not even until after Vietnam.

There is some truth to this opinion, especially in regard to the Americans. It would be absurd to claim that Clausewitz exercised any sweeping influence in Great Britain—much less the United States—before 1945, although perhaps not much more absurd than claiming that he had exercised any such sweeping influence on the military behavior of Germany, his own homeland. Nonetheless, this book demonstrates that the Anglo-American study of Clausewitz has had a longer history, has involved a larger readership, and has assumed quite a different character from what such disparate historians as Basil Liddell Hart, Russell Weigley, and Peter Paret have thus far suggested. A number of Clausewitz's works, both historical and theoretical, have been examined by British readers since the mid-1830s. Significant commentaries on Clausewitz were made in the 1840s by members of the duke of Wellington's circle (including the duke himself), by instructors at the British army's Staff College at Camberley after 1860, and by members of the "Wolseley ring," the clique of military reformers surrounding General Sir Garnet Wolseley, from the 1870s on. Clausewitz was a significant and direct influence on British military thought in the period preceding World War I.

On War also had a noteworthy influence on important individual American soldiers and writers after about 1910, but recent attempts to demonstrate an interwar appreciation of Clausewitz at the institutional level are flawed. It was the inexorable pressures of World War II that forced the creation of a genuine class of military intellectuals in America and made Clausewitz a significant intellectual influence on some. It was the uncertainties of the atomic era and the Cold War that made Clausewitz's conceptions appear fundamental to the American military intellectual community in general. It was only the crisis of self-confidence wrought by Vietnam that made them institutionally acceptable to the armed forces themselves.

Thus Clausewitz has had a pervasive—if ambiguous—impact on Anglo-American military thought for a long time. The uses made of Clausewitz's concepts by Anglo-Saxon writers have, however, been different and less obvious than those by German and French commentators. Also, at various times and for various reasons, some British and American writers have deliberately obscured the influence that Clausewitz has had on their thinking. These considerations account for some of the underestimation of his audience. Some of the misunderstanding of Clausewitz's reception in English also derives from a generalized contempt for Anglo-American military thinking or institutions (a failing particularly but not exclusively of German expatriate writers) and from a misunderstanding of his message (a failing particularly of native popular writers and military historians). The former factor led to an easy assumption that the philosopher had been ignored. The latter factor caused some historians—basing their analyses on little reading of Clausewitz or on a too-credulous reading of his critics—to look for his influence in a doctrine of unremitting, offensive, amoral, mass warfare. Particularly damaging were Liddell Hart's unreasonable attacks, which left a generation of military commentators confused about the relationship between the philosopher's theories and those of his alleged "misinterpreters."

In fact, most of the British and American military commentators who actually read *On War*, at least those who recorded their impressions, understood Clausewitz in sensible if not necessarily "correct" ways. The oft-cited "misinterpretations" of Clausewitz originated with authors, mostly French or German, who understood but consciously and explicitly rejected key portions of his argument. Native British proponents of total war and the unremitting offensive (Douglas Haig, James Thursfield) were also quite aware of the conflict between Clausewitz's arguments and their own.

The ideas of Clausewitz run like a subterranean river through all of modern military thought. The reception of Clausewitz's ideas in Great Britain and in the United States is thus an important and often revealing aspect of the evolution of military thinking in both countries. If this study has no other value, it can at least serve as a bibliographical guide to English-language studies involving Clausewitz. A historical examination of the various uses and interpretations made of the philosopher's works may also help our understanding the actual messages that those works convey. It is, after all, changing historical circumstances rather than the actual content of his work that have led to Clausewitz's being called in different eras the "apostle of total war" and "the preeminent military and political strategist of limited war in modern times."[4] Beyond that, the manner in which Clausewitz's ideas have been received in the English-speaking countries may offer some broader lessons concerning the manner in which such ideas are transmitted, rejected, ignored, or implemented. The relevant factors include personal and national character, institutional and private values, rational calculation and irrational lashing out, careerism and national interests, and personal and international antagonisms.

The aim of this book, therefore, is to survey the reception given Clausewitz by military commentators in Great Britain and the United States up to 1945, and to examine the manner in which their views fit into the larger context of Clausewitz's worldwide reception up to the present day. Such a survey must include certain works by foreign writers, particularly those whose discussions of the philosopher are available in English translation. The primary emphasis, however, is on works written in English.

It is also important that the reader understand what this study is not. It is not an attempt to discover the practical uses to which Clausewitz's teachings have been put on the battlefield or in doctrine. Indeed, this research has made me skeptical of any attempt to determine the "practical" influence of theory. There is a close relationship between theory and practice, but it certainly is not a simple "cause and effect" relationship running in either direction. Neither does this book attempt to interpret the broad military views or actions of Anglo-American military writers or leaders as being somehow "Clausewitzian" or otherwise. Nor is it a history of Anglo-American military theory, education, or practice, although it throws a useful light on those subjects. Rather, this is a study of the rarefied world of individual military thinkers, not of practical warfare or even of military institutions.

In titling this work, I have chosen to use the term *reception* rather than *influence* for reasons important to explain. *Influence* is rather hard to define. One can be influenced by a book without agreeing with it, without reading it, or without even being aware of its existence. A great book's influence often comes second- or thirdhand via other writers, diluted and inextricably mixed with their own, often contrary, ideas. This has certainly been the case with Clausewitz. To avoid these complexities, I have focused very narrowly on the manner in which British and American commentators on military affairs, be they soldiers, journalists, historians, political scientists, propagandists, or some combination thereof, have specifically and explicitly discussed Clausewitz and his ideas.

I do not argue that the writers to whom I refer had necessarily any great practical influence on military organization, doctrine, or events, since this is in most cases impossible to determine in any meaningful way. In many cases they probably did not. Rather, I am interested in the nature of their interpretations and in the reasons why they settled on particular views. I focus on writers like Francis Egerton, Lord Ellesmere, simply because they were English speakers who had something to say about Clausewitz: They reflect at least something of the wider culture. Other writers that I discuss clearly did have influence, although the practical impact upon policy of a Spenser Wilkinson or a Colonel Repington, even of a major military figure like William Robertson or Dwight Eisenhower, is surprisingly difficult to gauge.

Neither is it my purpose to examine Clausewitz's writings themselves, beyond the broad description of the man and his ideas provided in Chapter 2 for the convenience of the reader. To condense or summarize *On War*, even in the belief—in my view erroneous—that parts of it are "obsolete," is unavoidably to distort it. Its form and method are as important as its specific arguments. Although the commentaries of other writers are in some cases nearly indispensable to its interpretation, the reader who wants to gain a genuine understanding of Clausewitz cannot escape the task of actually reading *On War*.

Because this is a work of intellectual history, there are some special structural problems to be explained. First of all, this book treats a large number of different individuals whose relationship to one another was often tenuous at best. The subject naturally lacks the kind of organic unity to be found in any discrete event. As Peter Novick has pointed out, writing intellectual history is much like "nailing jelly to the wall."[5] My treatment therefore tends to be topical and episodic, although I have tried throughout this study and in its conclusions to delineate whatever trends and interconnections appear to be indicated by the sources.

To impose some order, this book is basically organized around a few key historical events. Part I covers the period from 1815 to 1873, the first date being chosen because that is the point at which one of Clausewitz's writings first appeared in English, the second because of the near-simultaneity of Germany's emergence as the world's leading military state and the appearance of the first complete English translation of *Vom Kriege*. The two latter events may or may not be connected. Personally, I suspect that the timing was coincidental, but the sources do not permit a firm conclusion either way. Part II covers the period between this first translation and the outbreak of World War I. The Great War sparked changes in the way that Clausewitz was interpreted, in some degree because it marked a decisive change in the way that Western society looks at war in general. Part III ends in 1945 because the explosion of American nuclear weapons over Japan in that year marked what was perceived at the time as—and what may have been in fact—a decisive change in the nature of war itself. It certainly had a great impact on the way in which *On War* was subsequently used and interpreted. The advent of nuclear weapons also led to the growth of an entirely new class of military intellectuals, particularly in the United States, so 1945 also marks a convenient cutoff point for the main body of this study. Clausewitz's reception after 1945 is so large and complex a story that continuing the detailed approach of the main treatment would be impracticable.

Unfortunately for the writer of intellectual history, individual human beings are not so easily periodized. Although the nature of the era often determined a writer's acceptance of some particular aspect of Clausewitz's theory, sometimes it did not. As an example of the latter case, Julian

Corbett stood almost alone as a limited-war theorist in the period just before World War I. The interwar theorist Hoffman Nickerson wrote in a period of mass armies, which he loathed. He nonetheless considered Clausewitz—generally associated with such armies—to be a guiding light. Some writers on Clausewitz lived through these key events without ever changing the way they treated him in print. Basil Liddell Hart is a good example: Even in 1963 his public attitude toward Clausewitz was determined almost exclusively by the events of 1914–18. Dwight Eisenhower discovered Clausewitz in the 1920s. He formed his views at that time and did his most important work as a soldier before 1946, but the sources for his interpretation of *On War* derive mainly from his time as president, 1953-1960. Whether Eisenhower perceived the coming of the atomic era as a strategic sea change is debatable. It did not, in all likelihood, change his interpretation of *On War*. Other writers, most notably J. F. C. Fuller, continuously evolved in their views on the philosopher.

The point is that there is no way in which to neatly compartmentalize neatly within the rigid framework dictated by historical events the various writers with whom this book deals. Operating under the belief that a rigid consistency is the hobgoblin of little minds (a belief that Clausewitz shared), I have therefore dealt with each writer on a case-by-case basis. In most cases I have elected to deal with an individual's entire career more or less in one continuous narrative, even when that takes us outside the boundaries of our periodization.

I have also found it necessary to take issue with a number of historians who have written on this topic. In such cases I have dealt with them within the period at issue rather than in the period during which the historian himself was writing. The latter approach—which might, strictly speaking, be more logical—would make for endless redundancies. For example, I have discussed the modern historian Hew Strachan in Part I because our views of Clausewitz's reception in that period differ, as do our understandings of his message. Similarly, I have taken issue with Liddell Hart over the influence of Clausewitz on the British army in the period before World War I and with Russell Weigley's 1962 interpretation of the views on Clausewitz of Robert M. Johnston, who died in 1920.

For such inconsistencies I can offer no apologies. Whatever value this study might have would be sharply reduced by any attempt to force it into a rigid structure. For added measure, I have added in the Conclusions a chapter that brings the story up to the present day, in the firm belief that the present is prologue to the past.

2

Clausewitz and His Works

The bibliography of this book is replete with works that seek to explain or condense Clausewitz's theories. Some are more successful than others. A few are brilliant. None is acceptable as a substitute for Clausewitz's own work; none can capture *On War*'s richness and complexity. Further, all attempts to do so (including the one given here) are distorted by the impact of contemporary concerns and by idiosyncratic personal interpretations. *On War* itself is often misleading for much the same reason: Clausewitz placed great stress on some points simply because they were antagonistic to the fashions of his own time, leaving later readers somewhat confused about the importance of those points to his overall scheme. The issue of moderation in war, his comments on the idea of the "bloodless victory," and his sometimes contradictory comments on the value of intelligence and surprise are examples. Nonetheless, it is appropriate here to provide a short survey of the man and his works, one molded by an acute awareness of the widespread confusion regarding both.[1]

Clausewitz's personality—important to any interpretation of his work—has been treated in a great many different ways. To the British military historian Michael Howard he was a "soldier's soldier" who wrote a practical military philosophy aimed at practical military men. Peter Paret, a German émigré to America who has emerged as the most prominent of contemporary Clausewitz scholars, presents him as a somewhat aridly brilliant intellectual. Clausewitz's detractors have portrayed him as a bloodthirsty military dilettante, and generations of bored soldier-students in Germany as well as Britain and America have treated

him as a stuffy old pedant, author of a dry and tiresome tome best left
to college professors.

In fact, Clausewitz was a complicated man of both action and thought
who left a complicated legacy. Sensitive, shy, and bookish by nature, he
could also be passionate in his politics, his love for his wife, and his longing
for military glory. Frequently in combat,[2] he regularly displayed coolness
and physical courage. He was untouched by scandal in his personal life,
and his intellectual integrity was ruthless. His keen analytical intelligence
was accompanied, perhaps unavoidably, by a certain intellectual arrogance.
The latter quality is amply demonstrated by the many sarcastic comments
that appear in *On War*. These characteristics may account for the fact that,
while he rose to high rank in the Prussian service, he almost always served
as a staff officer rather than as a commander. His assignments, however,
frequently put him near the center of military–political events.

The works most important to Clausewitz's reception in the English-
speaking world are *On War* itself and its distant precursor *Principles of
War* (written in 1812), along with two historical studies: *The Campaign
of 1812 in Russia* (partly written in 1814 and finished after 1824) and
The Campaign of 1815 in France (completed after 1827).[3] The two latter
works can be regarded as intermediate steps in the evolution of Clausewitz's ideas; they contain or reflect important elements of his maturing
theories but are basically straightforward studies of Napoleonic campaigns
in which Clausewitz himself had participated.

In 1812, Clausewitz resigned from Prussian service in principled
protest of Prussia's collaboration with Napoleon in the coming war with
Russia. He then took service with the Russian czar's armies. Before
leaving Berlin, Clausewitz wrote "The most important principles of the
art of war to complete my course of instruction for his Royal Highness
the Crown Prince" (usually entitled in English the *Principles of War* or
"Instruction for the Crown Prince"). He presented it to the sixteen-
year-old Prussian crown prince Friedrich Wilhelm (later King Friedrich
Wilhelm IV, r. 1840–58), whose military tutor Clausewitz had become
in 1810. The *Principles* represented, in appropriately simplified form,
Clausewitz's theoretical development up to 1812. It was, however, only
a rather primitive precursor to his later magnum opus, *On War*. Although
some of the more important theoretical concepts of *On War* are fairly
well developed (e.g., "friction,"), many are present only in embryo, and
others are entirely absent. The *Principles of War*'s subject matter is largely
tactical.

In particular, and in great contrast with the later work, *Principles of
War* is not notably sophisticated in historical terms. It is based almost
entirely on the experience of Frederick the Great and the more recent
wars with revolutionary France and Napoleon. Unfortunately, it has often
been treated as a précis of Clausewitz's mature theory, which it most
emphatically is not.

On War (based on unfinished manuscripts and published posthumously in 1832) is a hefty work. It has often been printed in three separate volumes, and the newest single-volume English-language edition runs about 580 pages (not counting the accompanying commentaries). It is internally divided into eight books: (1) On the Nature of War, (2) On the Theory of War, (3) On Strategy in General, (4) The Engagement, (5) Military Forces, (6) Defense, (7) The Attack, and (8) War Plans.

Books 1, 2, and 8 are generally considered the most important, as well as the most nearly finished. Other sections are often left out of abridged versions, especially Books 5, 6, and 7, allegedly because they are tactical in nature and thus obsolete. This sometimes leads to serious misunderstandings of Clausewitz's arguments, for it is precisely in these books that he works out the practical implications of his ideas. For those who preferred to paint Clausewitz as the "apostle of the offensive," it was especially convenient to leave out Book 6, "Defense," for it is by far the largest. To be understood, the work really has to be approached as a whole.

Precisely who was to benefit from reading *On War* is a trifle perplexing. Clausewitz's practical purpose in writing it was to give "military analysts" a clear conceptual scheme for understanding war, in hopes of improving both its actual conduct and the literature discussing it. He hoped that such an understanding would improve the judgment of military commanders, but he also believed that "military genius" was more a matter of temperament and character than of intellect. Perhaps because of his awareness of his own character, he felt that intellectuals generally made poor commanders. Only a self-conscious intellectual, however, was likely to plow through a book like *On War*. The book seems in fact to be aimed more at historians, military educators, and staff officers than at actual commanders, perhaps in the hope of some sort of "trickle up" effect.

On War certainly was not intended to provide a practical guide to commanders in the field, some sort of military "cookbook." Such a purpose, which underlies a great deal of military doctrinal writing, was alien to Clausewitz's approach to military theory: "Given the nature of the subject, we must remind ourselves that it is simply not possible to construct a model for the art of war that can serve as a scaffolding on which the commander can rely for support at any time." Since theory could not be a guide to action, it must be a guide to study; it is meant to assist the student in his efforts at self-education and to help him develop his own judgment, "just as a wise teacher guides and stimulates a young man's intellectual development, but is careful not to lead him by the hand for the rest of his life." His studies of educational theory had convinced Clausewitz of the limits of intellectualizing: Knowledge, he knew, was not ability. "These truths certainly need to be authenticated by experience." Reality (experience) always took precedence over the kind of abstract "truth" that can be transmitted by mere writing. Theory must never conflict with reality, and thus must be essentially descriptive of war, never prescriptive of action. "No theory, no general, should have anything to do with psychological and philosophical sophistries."[4]

Unfortunately, it is clear that many would-be readers of *On War* have made it no further than halfway through the first chapter and given up on what seems to be an exceedingly abstract philosophical treatment of the problem.[5] These first few pages set up an abstract theoretical ideal-ization of war, what Clausewitz called "absolute war." This term represents a philosophical abstraction, a "logical fantasy" impossible to achieve in reality. Absolute war is war in a pure form, violence at its most extreme, unrestrained by intelligent forces. It occurs for no particular reason and takes place in one near-instantaneous maximum effort by both warring parties. It aims at the utter overthrow of the enemy through the destruc-tion of his physical means to resist.

This discussion of war in the abstract, however, takes up only a small section of the first chapter (about five out of fifteen pages) and is not typical of the overall work. In the rest of the book, Clausewitz deals with "real war," that is, the gritty reality of war as we actually experience it. He explores why it is so different from his own idealization, from the faulty constructs of other intellectuals, and from the pontifications of "pedants" (the latter group a particular object of scorn). Real war is constrained by limits in the form of the ever-present social and political context, of human nature, and of the restrictions imposed by time and space. These factors forbid that the absolute should ever come to pass.

Because Clausewitz's classification of the varieties of war is so often misunderstood, it is necessary to nail home this point. The spectrum of war does not run smoothly from "absolute" to "limited." Rather, we have on the one hand absolute war, an abstraction that never actually occurs. On the other we have "real" war, which is always limited by practical factors. Real war occurs along a spectrum from the mere threat of force to conflicts that are unlimited in the sense that at least one of the antag-onists is unwilling to accept any outcome other than the complete over-throw of his adversary.

Of all real-world possibilities only thermonuclear war, which Claus-ewitz naturally did not envision, could closely match the absolute concept. One might argue that such a war has never occurred simply because it is equally unrealistic, in the sense that, although it may have become tech-nologically feasible, there seems to be no comprehensible political motive that would impel a state to launch it. The Cold War's nuclear strategists were unable to provide a credible political scenario to explain the nuclear exchanges they described, and the nuclear powers were always careful to avoid creating a situation that might make such mutual suicide seem desirable or necessary to any individual state among them.[6]

It is also important to note that Clausewitz's concept of absolute war is distinct from the later concept of "total war." Total war was a prescrip-tion for the actual waging of war typified by the ideas of General Erich von Ludendorff (1865–1937), who actually assumed control of the Ger-man war effort during World War I. It requires the total subordination of politics to the war effort—an idea that was anathema to Clausewitz—

and the assumption that total victory or total defeat are the only options. The concept of total war involves no suspension of the effects of time and space, as did Clausewitz's idealization. Clausewitz sometimes wrote as if Napoleon had approached or even achieved the absolute, but this is mere rhetorical excess and clearly inconsistent with his careful definition.

To understand *On War*, to distinguish it from Clausewitz's earlier works, and to differentiate his ideas from those of his competitors, one must understand Clausewitz's evolving attitude toward history. Alone, his historical studies of Napoleonic campaigns would probably not have altered his approach to theory, but as time went on he also made detailed studies of earlier and quite different wars. These included, among other things, seventeenth-century campaigns like those of Gustavus Adolphus and Turenne, the War of the Spanish Succession (1701–14), and east European wars with the Turks. Thus *On War* reflects a much wider range of historical experience and a much more sophisticated approach to history as a discipline than did the earlier *Principles of War*. Much of the misappreciation of Clausewitz's basic theories derives from the fact that he generally worked out their practical significance in a contemporary European context, but the underlying theory has universal implications.

Clausewitz's approach to history became increasingly historicist. That is, he saw history in relative terms, rejecting absolute categories, standards, and values. The past had to be accepted on its own terms. The historian must attempt to enter into the mind-sets and attitudes of any given period, the "spirit of the age." History is a dynamic process of change driven by forces beyond the control and often beyond the comprehension of any individual or group. This historicism is particularly obvious in two key themes of *On War* that are missing in the *Principles*. These are the famous notion that "war is a continuation of policy with an admixture of other means" (i.e., organized violence) and the recognition that war can vary in its forms depending on the changing nature of policy and of the society within which it is waged.

Both insights derived from Clausewitz's relentless criticism of his own evolving ideas. Clausewitz's earlier theoretical musings emphasized the quest for "decisiveness" in warfare. These derived from the experience of the French Revolution and its sequels, but this approach clearly could not explain the relatively indecisive and limited warfare of earlier periods. Unless, that is, earlier generations of soldiers were to be dismissed as fools, and Clausewitz ultimately rejected this solution. He therefore determined that war could legitimately take on the near-absolute form in which it had been waged by the revolutionary armies and Napoleon or assume a much more limited character, depending on its sources and motivations.

> Most former wars were waged largely in [a] state of equilibrium, or at least expressed tensions that were so limited, so infrequent, and feeble, that the fighting that did occur during these periods was seldom followed by important results. Instead a battle might be fought to cele-

brate the birthday of a monarch (Hochkirch), to satisfy military honor (Kunersdorf), or to assuage a commander's vanity (Freiberg).

In our opinion it is essential that a commander should recognize these circumstances and act in concert with their spirit.

Clausewitz suspected that the example of the Napoleonic wars would serve as a model for future conflicts. Much of *On War* is therefore concerned with hard-fought struggles aimed at achieving a real political decision, the actual "overthrow" of the enemy, and thus with military strategies aimed at actually disarming the enemy through the destruction (physical and/or moral) of his armed forces. This was unlimited war.

On the other hand, Clausewitz also saw the possibility that war would revert—or evolve—into forms more closely resembling those of the pre-revolutionary era. He called these weaker forms of war "limited wars" and characterized them in various ways: "wars in which no decision is sought," wars of limited aims; wars to seize a slice of enemy territory (either for its own sake or as a bargaining chip for use in attaining some other end).[7] Although the concept is clearly present and clearly important, it is by no means fully developed. That may be an advantage, of course. Leaving the concept open-ended makes it easy to adapt to changing circumstances.

Clausewitz's rewriting of his draft manuscript for *On War* was largely a matter of reworking it to incorporate these insights. This process was never completed, cut short by his untimely death from cholera at the age of fifty-one. *On War* is therefore essentially two very different books superimposed. In some sections the earlier contempt for the limited form still shines through,[8] but the theoretical justification for waging such wars, though not fully explored, is undeniably present. The historian in Clausewitz had triumphed over the purely empirical soldier.[9]

Indeed, much of *On War* is devoted to discussions of the place of war in history, the practical uses of military history to the soldier, and the difficulties of both reading and writing it. Clausewitz's most important technical contribution to the field of military history was his discussion of "critical analysis."[10] Clausewitz distinguished carefully between the historian and the military critic, even though he recognized that the two roles often went together. Historical research, he maintained, has nothing to do with either theory or criticism. It is the discovery, interpretation, and arrangement of equivocal facts. Critical *analysis* is the tracing of effects back to their causes. Criticism proper is the investigation and evaluation of actions taken (or "means employed"), the consideration of alternative courses of action, the realm of praise and censure. In such evaluation, actions must be analyzed both on their own level (i.e., tactical, operational,[11] strategic, political) and as they interact at other levels. Theory provides the framework for analysis and judgment.

Clausewitz insisted that history not be abused. There were four ways in which historical examples could legitimately be used in conjunction with theory: to explain an idea, that is, to give dimension to an abstract concept; to show the application of an idea; to demonstrate the mere possibility of some phenomenon; and to deduce a doctrine (this being by far the most difficult). He was highly skeptical that the last could be achieved in most cases and demanded the most exacting rules of evidence. Very little of the existing literature met these requirements, particularly in the case of ancient history, for which so much of the detail and context had been lost.

Given the difficulty of producing a truly useful historical study and the ease with which shallower efforts could mislead students, Clausewitz advocated that military educators rely on the in-depth examination of one campaign (the more recent the better) rather than on broader but less exacting histories. This concept underlies the later historical researches of the German general staff. But although it may contribute to a staff officer's technical virtuosity, this insistence on depth rather than breadth may constitute a weakness in Clausewitz's pedagogical views. It tends almost inevitably to leave students less sensitive to the changeability of the "spirit of the age." Hans Delbrück, on the other hand—generally considered to be the founder of modern, professional, "scientific" military history—emphasized the wider implications of Clausewitz's theories. His work was never popular with the German general staff.

Before discussing further the actual content of Clausewitz's theories, it is useful to take note of three other important writers with whom his ideas are often contrasted. While it falls outside the scope of this book to deal directly with Moltke, Jomini, and Sun Tzu, the reader should be aware of their importance. All of these writers differ from Clausewitz in noteworthy aspects, though none is truly his antithesis.

The ancient Chinese sage Sun Tzu lived, if such an individual existed at all, sometime during the "Warring States" period of Chinese history (453–221 B.C.).[12] Sun Tzu's book is generally considered the most important of the Chinese military classics and has had a significant if unmeasurable impact on the modern Japanese as well as on the military theories of Mao Tse-tung and subsequent writers on revolutionary warfare.

Sun Tzu is often offered up as the antithesis of Clausewitz, particularly on the issue of the "bloodless battle." His admonitions that a good general gains victory without battle and that no nation ever benefited from a long war are widely perceived as a direct contradiction to *On War*'s emphasis on combat. In actuality, Sun Tzu and Clausewitz are more complementary than antithetical, and there are many direct parallels.[13] Sun Tzu's understanding of history as a dynamic process and his subordination of military to political considerations certainly parallel Clausewitz's. Both stress the destruction of the enemy's will rather than merely of his physical forces. Sun Tzu discussed the tactics and strategies of actual combat at great length, and much of his discussion of "bloodless struggle" refers to political and psychological matters rather than actual war. Winning an interstate struggle without combat might be desirable from Clausewitz's point of view, but even though war is a continuation of politics, by Clausewitz's definition it involves the admixture of violence. Much of Clausewitz's emphatic rejection of the idea was prompted by the fanciful musings of earlier theorists of a warfare based exclusively on bloodless maneuver. There may be a direct connection of sorts here, for Sun Tzu's work was translated into French in 1772 and was popular with writers of the late Enlightenment.[14] The idea also appears, however, in earlier European works like those of Maurice de Saxe (1696–1750), who has likewise been contrasted with Clausewitz.

If there is in fact any fundamental difference between the two writers (beyond Sun Tzu's extreme brevity, which most readers applaud), it can probably be traced to their differing approaches to the balance of power mechanism. Sun Tzu accepted the traditional Chinese ideal of uniting "all under heaven," despite the fact that the China he discussed was split into warring states in many respects as unique as those of modern Europe. The Warring States period ended, in fact, in the unification of China. Clausewitz thought the idea of unifying Europe's diverse peoples to be an absurdity, as one might expect in an opponent of Napoleon.

Antoine-Henri Jomini, later Baron de Jomini, was a French-speaking Swiss (1779–1869). Originally headed for a career in banking, young Jomini got carried away by the excitement of the French Revolution and joined the French army in 1798. He returned to business in Switzerland after the Peace of Amiens (1802), where he began writing on military subjects. His *Traité de grande tactique* was first published in 1803. He continually revised, enlarged, and reissued it into the 1850s.[15]

Rejoining the army in 1804, Jomini was accepted as a volunteer staff member by one of Napoleon's marshals. He served in the Austerlitz and Prussian campaigns, then in Spain. He finally received an actual staff commission in the French army at the behest of Napoleon a while after Austerlitz (1805). He served for a while as chief of staff to his long-time mentor, Marshal Ney. Unfortunately, Jomini's arrogance, irrascibility, and naked ambition often led to friction with his fellows and eventually to a falling-out with Ney. Eventually, however, Jomini was promoted to brigadier general and given a succession of fairly responsible staff positions, mostly away from actual troops. Following his recovery from the rigors of the Russian campaign, he was reassigned to Ney in 1813 but shortly thereafter arrested for sloppy staff work. His ambitions thwarted by real or imagined plots against himself, Jomini joined the Russian army in late 1813. He spent much of the remainder of his long career in the Russian service.

During his actual military career, "Jomini . . . [had been] a very minor figure, seldom mentioned in orders or dispatches, practically ignored in the memoirs of the officers who had served with him." Nonetheless, he became by far the best known military commentator of his day, and maintained that position through zealous self-promotion. His most famous work, *Summary of the Art of War*, was written, like Clausewitz's *Principles of War*, for a royal prince to whom he was military tutor.

Although long since retired, he advised Czar Nicholas during the Crimean War and Napoleon III during his Italian campaigns. Even during Jomini's lifetime, of course, there were many prominent military men who viewed his work with great skepticism. Napoleon himself is alleged to have said to his marshals, "You all think you understand war because you have read Jomini's book! Is it likely that I should have permitted its publication if it could accomplish that?"[16]

Ironically, in his maturity Jomini grew wary of the revolutionary passions that had originally inspired him to take up the sword himself. Perhaps his dependence on one of the most conservative governments in Europe had some influence on his attitude. His prescriptions seem therefore to be aimed at professional soldiers leading professional armies in wars more similar to those of the ancien régime than to those in which he had fought as a young man.

Jomini's military writings are easy to unfairly caricature. They were characterized by a highly didactic and prescriptive approach conveyed in an extensive self-defined vocabulary of strategic lines, bases, and key points. His fundamental prescription was simple: Place superior power at the decisive point. He constantly stressed the advantages of interior lines. Indeed, Clausewitz's own sweeping critique of the state of military theory appears to have been aimed in large part at the Swiss:

> It is only analytically that these attempts at theory can be called advances in the realm of truth; synthetically, in the rules and regulations they offer, they are absolutely useless.
>
> They aim at fixed values; but in war everything is uncertain, and calculations have to be made with variable quantities.
>
> They direct the inquiry exclusively toward physical quantities, whereas all military action is intertwined with psychological forces and effects.
>
> They consider only unilateral action, whereas war consists of a continuous interaction of opposites. . . . Anything that could not be reached by the meager wisdom of such one-sided points of view was held to be beyond scientific control: it lay in the realm of genius, *which rises above all rules.*
>
> Pity the soldier who is supposed to crawl among these scraps of rules, not good enough for genius, which genius can ignore, or laugh at. No; what genius does is the best rule, and theory can do no better than show how and why this should be the case.[17]

These passages immediately follow Clausewitz's sneers at the "lopsided character" of the theory of interior lines, comments unquestionably directed at Jomini.

Jomini was no fool, however. His intelligence, facile pen, and wide experience of war made his writings a great deal more credible and useful than so brief a description can imply. Once he left Napoleon's service, he maintained himself and his reputation primarily through prose. His writing style—quite unlike Clausewitz's—reflected his constant search for an audience. He dealt at length with a number of practical subjects (logistics, sea power) that Clausewitz largely ignored. Elements of his discussion (e.g., his remarks on Great Britain and sea power and his sycophantic treatment of Austria's Archduke Charles) are clearly aimed at protecting his political position or expanding his readership. And, one might add, at minimizing Clausewitz's. Jomini evidently perceived the Prussian writer— whose death thirty-eight years before his own was a piece of rare good fortune—as his chief competitor.

The fundamental differences between Clausewitz and Jomini are rooted in their differing concepts of the historical process and of the nature and role of military theory. Essentially, Jomini saw war as a stage for heroes, a "great drama." He saw the revolutionary warfare in which he himself had participated as merely the technical near-perfection of a fundamentally unchanging phenomenon, to be modified only by superficial matters like the list of dramatis personae, technology, and transient political motivations. He drew his theoretical and practical prescriptions from his experiences in the Napoleonic wars. The purpose of Jomini's theory was to teach practical lessons: His target audience is not in doubt, being clearly "designed for officers of a superior grade." Accordingly, Jomini's tone was thoroughly didactic and utilitarian, often pedantic. His writing thus appealed more readily to military educators, and his key work, *Summary of the Art of War* (*Précis de l'art de la guerre*, 1838), became, in various translations, popularizations, and commentaries, the premier military–educational text of the mid-nineteenth century.[18]

Much of the oft-commented-on contrast between Jomini and Clausewitz can be traced to such factors, and to the frequent abridgment of *On War*, which makes it appear much more abstract than Jomini's work when in fact they often discussed the same practical subject matter.[19] Despite his insistence that theory must be descriptive rather than prescriptive in nature, Clausewitz frequently lapsed into didactic discussions of common military problems, particularly in Books 6 and 7.

It is also important to remember, but frequently forgotten, that the *Summary* was written after Jomini had read *On War*. Clausewitz's comments therefore do not reflect the modifications that Jomini made afterwards to his original argument, for the *Summary* contains many adjustments clearly attributable to Clausewitz's influence. These include Jomini's comments on the importance of morale, the impossibility of fixed rules (save perhaps in tactics), the need to assign limits to the role of theory, the skepticism of mathematical calculations (and a denial that Jomini's own work—despite all the geometrical terminology and diagrams—was based on such), the disclaimer of any belief that war is "a positive science," and the clear differentiation between mere military knowledge and actual battlefield skill.[20]

This recognition of the validity of many of Clausewitz's points did not lead Jomini to adopt the philosopher's style, for at least three reasons. First, he correctly distinguished his own work from Clausewitz's by pointing to its explicitly didactic purposes. Despite his agreement that war was essentially a political act, he pointed to the practical implications of this different focus: "History at once political and military offers more attractions, but is also much more difficult to treat and does not accord easily with the didactic species."

Second, and in common with a number of Clausewitz's later detractors, Jomini found the Prussian's approach to be intellectually arrogant, overly metaphysical, and simply too damned difficult to digest. He stressed simplicity and clarity over a "pretentious" search for deeper truths. Further, he objected to what he saw as Clausewitz's extreme skepticism (*incrédulité*) of all military theory—save that in *On War*.

Third, there was a personal element in Jomini's critique of Clausewitz. Clearly, on some level he did greatly admire Clausewitz's work. Jomini regretted that the Prussian had not been able to read his own *Summary*, "persuaded that he would have rendered to it some justice." He was thus deeply wounded by the criticisms in *On War*. He expressed his bitterness in a number of hyperbolic sneers ("The works of Clausewitz have been incontestably useful, although it is often less by the ideas of the author, than by the contrary ideas to which he gives birth") and in accusations of plagiarism ("There is not one of my reflections [on the campaign of 1799] which he has not repeated"). These insults, because they refer to the Prussian by name, have more meaning to readers unfamiliar with *On War* than do the *Summary*'s concessions on theoretical issues.

It is often assumed, therefore, that Jomini and Clausewitz are opposites. In fact, their differences are as often stylistic as real, but then, in intellectual matters, style and substance are often the same thing.

Unlike Jomini, the great German soldier Helmuth von Moltke (1800–91) was a self-confessed disciple of Clausewitz. Austere but remarkably tactful, Moltke was that rarity, an intellectual and staff officer who made his mark as a great commander.[21] He was selected as chief of the Prussian general staff in 1857 and remained in the job until 1888. It is for his work in this position that he is chiefly remembered today. Before Moltke brought it to prominence by masterminding the great Prussian victory at Königgrätz, so obscure was the position of chief of the general staff that one general receiving his orders is said to have asked, "Who is this Moltke?" Working (not always harmoniously) with Otto von Bismarck as chancellor and Albrecht von Roon as minister of war, Moltke did a great deal to create the German military model that, after Prussia's victories over Austria (1866) and France (1870–71) and the ensuing unification of Germany, came to dominate military organizations throughout the world. Moltke's military behavior and his explicit discussions of military theory reveal a mind thoroughly grounded in the concepts of *On War* but much more concerned with organizational matters. He left an intellectual and organizational legacy, however, that seems to many to contradict that of his master.

On the issue of the political control of war, Moltke argued that "strategy can direct its efforts only toward the highest goal that the available means make practically possible. It best supports policy in working solely to further political aims, but as far as possible in operating independent of policy. Policy dare not intrude itself in[to] operations."[22] In other words, the political leadership could dominate only at the beginning and end of a war; in the meantime, the role of the military leadership was to reduce the enemy to helpless acquiescence in the political goals of the victorious state. Military leaders must, in this view, be allowed to do their jobs without political interference. Moltke evidently believed that this view was in complete accordance with Clausewitz, quoting one of the latter's letters to Müffling: "The role and right of military science, as regards policy, is principally to take care that policy does not demand things contrary to the nature of warfare, nor, through ignorance of the operation of the instrument commit errors in the utilization thereof."

Moltke's attitude concerning the relationship of the military commander to the political leadership actually reflected not so much a disagreement with Clausewitz as a fundamental problem in the Prussian—and later the German Empire's—constitution. Under Napoleon, of course, political and military responsibility had been collocated, and in parliamentary governments the dominance of the political leadership was largely uncontested. In Prussia, the relationship was quite unclear. As Moltke wrote to the kaiser, the political and military chiefs were two parallel, "mutually independent agencies under the command of your majesty."[23] Also, the evolution not only of the army but also of the Prusso-German state apparatus itself meant that they came to represent distinct (and sometimes antithetical) social classes rather than the nation. Unfortunately, Moltke's argument is easily taken out of this specific context.

A classic clash between the military and political spheres occurred in late 1870, as Moltke's army moved on Paris after the destruction of the French field armies at Sedan and Metz. Bismarck, the kaiser's chancellor and chief political officer, wanted Paris brought under attack as soon as possible. His concern was not so much the conduct of the war itself (although he was eager to influence France's internal political struggle) as worries that a protracted war might lead to some outside intervention disastrous to Prussian policy. Moltke resisted Bismarck's demands, citing technical military reasons. There was doubtless some truth to these, but Moltke was also motivated by institutional concerns to resist the chancellor. He had perhaps a political motive as well: Like many Germans, Moltke wanted to see the power of France—the incorrigible aggressor—permanently smashed. He feared that Bismarck was aiming at a less-than-maximized victory of the sort he had imposed on Austria in 1866.

In the event, the kaiser eventually overruled Moltke and placed the control of war policy in Bismarck's hands. (The constitutional issue nonetheless outlasted Bismarck's tenure in office.) In this context, the relation-

ship between Moltke's and Clausewitz's views on the political guidance
of war is difficult to characterize.

In seeking out the fundamental nature of Clausewitz's own mature
theories, perhaps the best place to start is with some of the most common
*mis*conceptions of his argument. Such misconceptions are almost always
the product of writers who either never read *On War* (or read only the
opening paragraphs or perhaps a condensation or secondary treatment)
or who sought intentionally (i.e., for propaganda purposes) to distort its
content. The book's specific arguments are very clearly put forth and rarely
difficult to comprehend, though admittedly hard to absorb in their en-
tirety. The first of these misconceptions is the notion that Clausewitz
considered war to be a "science."[24] Another (and related) misconception
is that he considered war to be entirely a rational tool of state policy. The
first idea is drastically wrong, the second only one side of a very important
coin.

To Clausewitz, war (as opposed to strategy or tactics) was neither an
"art" nor a "science." Those two terms often mark the parameters of
theoretical debate on the subject, however, and Clausewitz's most ardent
critics (Jomini, Liddell Hart, the young J. F. C. Fuller) tended to be those
who treated war as a science. As Clausewitz argued, the object of science
is knowledge and certainty, whereas the object of art is creative ability. Of
course, all art involves some science (e.g., the mathematical sources of
harmony) and good science always involves creativity. Clausewitz saw
tactics as more scientific in character and strategy as something of an art,
but the conscious, rational exercise of "military strategy," a term much
beloved of theorists and military historians, is a relatively rare occurrence
in the real world. "It has become our general conviction," he said, "that
ideas in war are generally so simple, and lie so near the surface, that the
merit of their invention can seldom substantiate the talent of the commander who adopts them."[25] Most real events are driven by incomprehensible
forces like chance, emotion, bureaucratic irrationalities, and intraorganizatio-
nal politics, and many "strategic" decisions are made unconsciously, often
long before the outbreak of hostilities. If pressed, Clausewitz would have
placed war making closer to the domain of the arts, but neither definition
was really satisfactory.

Instead, war is a form of social intercourse. The Prussian writer occasionally likened it to commerce or litigation, but more usually to politics.[26] The distinction is crucial: In both art and science, the actor is
working on inanimate matter (or, in art, the passive and yielding emotions
of the audience), whereas in business, politics, and war the actor's will is
directed at an animate object that reacts and, furthermore, takes independent actions of its own. War is thus permeated by "intelligent forces."
War is also "an act of force to compel our enemy to do our will," but it
is never unilateral. It is a duel, a contest between independent wills, in
which skill and creativity surely play important roles but are no more
prominent than personality, chance, emotion, and the various dynamics

that characterize any human interaction. Thus when Clausewitz wrote that war may have a grammar of its own, but not its own logic, he was pointing out that the logic of war, like that of politics, is the logic of social intercourse, not that of art or science.

Writing in German, Clausewitz used the word *Politik*, and his most famous phrase has been variously translated as "War is a continuation of 'policy'—or of 'politics'—by other means." He also assumed, for the purpose of argument, that state policy would be rational, that is, aimed at improving the situation of the society it represented. He believed along with most Westerners of his era that war was a legitimate means for a state's advancement of its interests. This is often taken to mean that war is somehow a "rational" phenomenon, and Clausewitz has been convicted of advocating the resort to war as a routine extension of unilateral state policy.

In fact, the choice of translation for *Politik*—"policy" or "politics"—is indicative of differing emphases on the part of the translator, for the two concepts are quite different. Policy may be defined as rational action undertaken by a group that already has power, in order to maintain and extend that power. Politics, in contrast, is simply the process (comprising an inchoate mix of rational, irrational, and nonrational elements) by which power is distributed within a given society.[27] And war is an expression of—not a substitute for—politics. Thus, in calling war a "continuation" of politics, Clausewitz was advocating nothing. In accordance with his belief that theory must be descriptive rather than prescriptive, he was merely recognizing an existing reality. War indeed is an expression of both policy and politics, but "politics" is the interplay of conflicting forces, not the execution of one-sided policy initiatives.[28]

The actual word that Clausewitz used in his famous formulation is *Fortsetzung*, literally a "setting forth." Translating this word as "continuation," though technically correct, evidently implies to many that politics changes its essential nature when it metamorphoses into war.[29] This is an impression contrary to Clausewitz's argument. War remains politics in all its complexity, with the added element of violence. The nonrational and completely irrational forces that affect and often drive politics have the same impact on war.

On the side of the rationality argument, it is certainly true that Clausewitz argued, didactically, that a state contemplating the resort to war should do so with a clear idea as to what it means to accomplish and how it intends to proceed toward that goal. The connection of war to rational political goals meant that war could not be a generic commodity; the conduct of wars would have to vary in accordance with their political objects. His definition of "strategy"—that it was "the use of combats for the purpose of the war"—has been criticized for overemphasizing the need for bloody battle, but its key point is "the [political] purpose of the war."

If war was to be an extension of policy, that is, a tool of policy, then military leaders must be subordinate to political leaders and strategy must be subordinate to policy. Like the Moltke–Bismarck contretemps demonstrated, this poses practical organizational problems. As with many of Clausewitz's teachings, his solution was not a simple prescription but a dualism: The military instrument must be subordinated to the political leadership, but political leaders must understand its nature and limitations. Politicians must not attempt to use the instrument of war to achieve purposes for which it is unsuited.

Exactly whose responsibility it is to determine just where this line is located is a constitutional matter of some importance. Clausewitz did little to clarify it. In his original manuscript, Clausewitz stated "If war is to be fully consonant with political objectives, and policy suited to the means available for war, . . . the only sound expedient is to make the commander in chief a member of the cabinet, so that the cabinet can share in the major aspects of his activities." This was altered in the second German edition (1853) to say "so that he may take part in its councils and decisions on important occasions."[30] Whether the change resulted from well intentioned editorial intervention (for the original edition is full of inconsistencies, obscurities, and obvious editorial errors) or more sinister motivations is unclear, as are its practical ramifications. This minor editorial subversion, if subversion it was, certainly was not the cause of later German strategic errors, as some have implied.[31]

This constitutional question aside, it is clear that Clausewitz demanded the subordination of military to political considerations throughout a conflict. As he said in 1831, "He who maintains, as is so often the case, that politics should not interfere with the conduct of a war has not grasped the ABCs of grand strategy."[32]

Policy considerations also can demand actions that may even seem irrational, depending on one's values. Clausewitz's desire that Prussia turn on Napoleon before the 1812 campaign would have demanded virtual state suicide in the short run, but he felt that the state's honor—and thus any hope for its future resurgence—required it. Clausewitz saw both history and policy in the long run, and he pointed out that no strategic decision is ever final; it can always be reversed in another round of struggle. This side of Clausewitz is uncomfortable for modern Anglo-American readers because it reflects a romantic view of the state as something that transcends the collective interest of its citizens. It provides a philosophical basis for apocalyptic policies like Hitler's and Japan's in World War II. Most modern readings of Clausewitz, including my own, tend to skate over such aspects of *On War*. They are simply too alien to the spirit of our age to have much meaning.

So much for the rational control of war. On the other hand, Clausewitz lived during the transition from the Enlightenment to the age of Romanticism, and his worldview reflects elements of each. His vision of war thus falls also very much into the domain of the nonrational and even the irrational, "in which strictly logical reasoning often plays no part at all and is always apt to be a most unsuitable and awkward intellectual tool."[33] Because the flow of military events is so thoroughly conditioned by the specifics of every situation, from its politics and personalities to the terrain and even the weather, the course of war is never predictable.

One of the most important requirements of strategy in Clausewitz's view is that the leadership correctly "estimate the character of the war." This is often understood as meaning that leaders should rationally decide the kind of war that will be undertaken. In fact, the nature of any given war is beyond rational control: It is inherent in the situation and in the "spirit of the age." Good leaders, avoiding error and self-deception, can at best merely comprehend the real implications of a resort to violence and act accordingly.

Further, a war often takes on a dynamic beyond the intentions of those who launched it, for the conduct of war always rests—in unpredictable proportions—on the variable energies, interests, abilities, and character of Clausewitz's famous trinity of the people, the army, and the government. Political leaders may easily misjudge or lose control of passions in their own state. Further, their opponents have similar such uncertainties as well as wills and creativities of their own.

In 1976, Russell Weigley—one of the most creative, interesting, and influential of modern American military historians—attacked Clausewitz for missing this very point. Weigley had clearly developed his own recognition that war tends to escape rational control, but he denied Clausewitz any understanding of that fact, so central to the Prussian's argument. Quoting Gerhard Ritter, he wrote that

> what Clausewitz failed to see or at least to acknowledge is that war, once set off, may very well develop a logic of its own because the war events themselves may react on and alter the guiding will [note the singular case]; that it may roll on like an avalanche, burying all the initial aims, all the aspirations of statesmen.

In fact, the Prussian writer had clearly noted that "the original political objects can greatly alter during the course of the war and may finally change entirely *since they are influenced by events and their probable consequences.*"[34] Like so many of Clausewitz's critics, Weigley—via Ritter—was engaged in reinventing the wheel. It is clear that Clausewitz's war is, despite all that intellect and reason can do to modify it, a game of chance outside the bounds of rational control.

> Would Prussia in 1792 have dared to invade France with 70,000 men if she had had an inkling that the repercussions in case of failure would be strong enough to overthrow the old European balance of power? Would she, in 1806, have risked war with France with 100,000 men, if she had suspected that the first shot would set off a mine that was to blow her to the skies?[35]

Thus Clausewitz was hardly one to urge that the resort to war be taken lightly or routinely, nor to claim that its result would necessarily further the unilateral policy goals of the party who launched it.

Another source of unpredictability was what Clausewitz called "friction," stemming from war's uncertainty, chance, suffering, confusion, exhaustion, and fear. Friction stems from the effects of time, space, and human nature; it is the fundamental and unavoidable force that makes war in reality differ from the abstract ideal of "absolute war." Events take time to unfold, with all that that implies. Purely military or political courses of action are deflected by countless delays and distractions. Strategic intelligence and battlefield information are often misleading or flatly wrong, and even the wisest order is subject to loss, delay, misinterpretation, poor execution, or willful disobedience. Every individual human being is a friction-producing cog in the machine of war, producing a delicate machine of endless complexity and unreliability.

> Everything in war is very simple, but the simplest thing is difficult. . . . Action in war is like movement in a resistant element. Just as the simplest and most natural of movements, walking, cannot easily be performed in water, so in war it is difficult for normal efforts to achieve even moderate results.[36]

It is perhaps no accident that slang terms like SNAFU and FUBAR originated in a military context. Much of what Clausewitz called "military genius" revolved around willpower; an iron will and a powerful sense of purpose are indispensable for overcoming the forces of friction.

To some extent, of course, the causes of this difficulty are inherent in any large organization; Clausewitz saw it as unique to war because European armies were the first truly large, modern organizations. Clausewitz never had to convince the Social Security Administration that no, he had not died and was thus still eligible for benefits.

Much of what Clausewitz called friction was, however, peculiar to war, particularly something that may seem obvious but escapes many theorists and armchair war planners: War is dangerous, and danger (either physical or moral) has an impact on the behavior of the participants. Under its influence, "the light of reason is refracted in a manner quite different from that which is normal in academic speculation . . . . [and] the ordinary man can never achieve a state of perfect unconcern in which his mind can work with normal flexibility."[37]

Jomini, whose military experience was as great as Clausewitz's, understood perfectly well the practical importance of such factors. To him, however, they were unpredictable and therefore extrinsic to theory, whereas to Clausewitz they were so much a part of the fabric of war that theory must consider them as intrinsic.

This insistence on the unpredictability of war raises some important issues. Clausewitz's writings are sometimes cited in support of various attempts at mathematically modeling war,[38] but although much of Clausewitz's logic sounds vaguely mathematical and many of his individual propositions could no doubt be expressed in numbers, Clausewitz pointedly refrained from doing so. In essence, his explanation for this restraint is very similar to that of modern Chaos theory and nonlinear analysis as it is applied in such varied fields as physics, biology, and economics.[39] In demonstrating why long-range weather prediction is bound to fail, for instance, nonlinear theorists cite the so-called butterfly effect: "A butterfly stirring the air today in Peking can transform storm systems next month in New York"; that is, tiny differences in input quickly become overwhelming differences in output. (A more dignified term for this effect is "sensitive dependence on initial conditions.")[40] Chaos theorists have demonstrated how even a few variables imperfectly known can reduce a system to a chaotic state. In war, there is an inherently unknowable number of largely unquantifiable variables, all of which may interact with one another in an unpredictable way. The very parameters of any equation of war are unfathomably variable.

Nonlinear theory performs three valuable functions relating to Clausewitz's ideas: It confirms his assessment of the predictive approach to military theory; it provides a clear scientific validation of his worldview; and it gives the historian metaphors useful in comprehending the real world in which Clausewitz sought to root his own theory.[41] Like the nonlinear theorists, Clausewitz insisted on keeping in view the whole phenomenon under discussion rather than attempting to draw conclusions from those few unrepresentative subcomponents that might lend themselves to linear mathematical analyses. He focused on real-world experience, on concrete phenomena, rather than on simplified and inherently unrealistic models.[42] "Just as some plants bear fruit only if they don't shoot up too high, so in the practical arts the leaves and flowers of theory must be pruned and the plant kept close to its proper soil—experience."[43] Clausewitz's historicist belief that war can change its nature depending on the "spirit of the age" echoes the chaoticists' "paradigm shifts." Their observations of "symmetry at different scales" parallels Clausewitz's similar "ends and means" analyses of tactics, strategy, and politics, the same phenomena expressed at different scales in terms of time and space. The Prussian theorist would agree that mathematics had a place in war, as did other kinds of arts and sciences, but using math as a basis for theory or prediction was a laughable absurdity.

The significance of butterflylike individual inputs and unique variables is particularly clear in Clausewitz's discussion of friction, of the significance of individual actions by any of the individual participants—of whatever rank—in military and political events, and of the impact of factors like terrain, always unique.

> [Military] events are proof that success is not due simply to general causes. Particular factors can often be decisive—details known only to those who were on the spot. There can also be moral factors which never come to light; while issues can be decided by chances and incidents so minute as to figure in histories simply as anecdotes.[44]

Note that Clausewitz's emphasis on the triumph of specific over general factors is most true of contests between near-equals, which he generally assumed to be the case in European conflicts. In struggles between opponents markedly unequal in either moral or material terms, as in, say, the recent United Nations war against Iraq, general factors tend to be more decisive. This emphasis on the particular and the specific permeates Clausewitz's mature theories. Frustrated readers seeking in his writings an answer to some particular problem sometimes bemoan this facet of his argument as an evasive "Well, that depends . . . ," but that is just the point. The greatest familiarity with the most correct theory does not permit the decision maker to skip the details. For good measure, Clausewitz heightens the frustration by noting that the details are very often missing or wrong.

So what, then, was Clausewitz's strategic prescription? Various writers have argued that Clausewitz was the advocate of a particular style of war, held by some to be that of "total" or "absolute" war (terms that represent quite different concepts) and by others to be that of "limited" war. In fact, the mature Clausewitz advocated neither. Rather, he called for state policy to choose a form of war, consistent with its goals and the situation, from somewhere along the continuum between those two extremes. Although the younger Clausewitz of the "Instruction for the Crown Prince" tended toward a didactic prescription of decisive battle, the mature Clausewitz of *On War* did not. To seek decisive battle did not, after all, make sense for a party who could expect to lose, and Clausewitz sought a theory of universal applicability. Readers easily detect that Clausewitz had some emotional attachment to war in its more powerful form as a result of his own experience with it, but intellectually he was quite clear on the validity of either. The philosopher's students are shown how to analyze a military problem but are left on their own as to what to do about the ones they actually face.

Other writers have claimed that Clausewitz was an advocate of concentric attacks, in contrast with Jomini's advocacy of "interior lines." In fact, Clausewitz spent more time discussing concentric operations in part simply because Jomini had already done so good a job explaining the opposite approach. The choice of either would depend, as always, on the specific situation.

Clausewitz did provide some guidance in choosing military objectives. Perhaps most important was the concept of focusing one's military efforts on the enemy's "center of gravity" (*Schwerpunkt*). He often used this term in tactical discussions merely to denote the main line of attack. When applied to strategy, however, it assumes a more narrow definition. The center of gravity was the most important source of the enemy's strength. Normally it would be the enemy's army in the field, but it could be his capital or something less concrete, like an alliance or even public opinion. The correct choice, as usual with Clausewitz, would have to be consistent with the character of the situation and appropriate to the political purposes of the war. To seek for an all-purpose strategic prescription in Clausewitz's discussion of the "center of gravity" will, accordingly, lead to the usual frustration. The prescription simply is not there.

A superficial reading of *On War* may, however, leave the reader somewhat confused on this point. After all, Clausewitz's definition of strategy emphasizes battle, and he states clearly, time after time, that "there is only one means in war: combat." The subtlety that one must be aware of here is that by "combat" Clausewitz means not only the *actual* bloody clash of armed men on the field of battle but also *potential* or merely *possible* clashes.[45] The distinction is crucial: Clausewitz likened actual bloodshed to the occasional cash transaction in a business normally operating on credit. He did not say that a bloodless war of maneuver (à la Sun Tzu or Saxe) is impossible, merely that maneuver by itself is meaningless; it must be backed up with the credible threat of battlefield success. An effective maneuver may create a situation in which the enemy is convinced that if it comes to battle, he will lose more than he is willing to risk. The maneuvering party must still be prepared for the possibility that his bluff will be called. The battle of Blenheim, 1704, is a good example. The Franco-Bavarian leaders thought that they had maneuvered Marlborough's army into a position from which it must, according to the conventions of the time, retreat. Instead, Marlborough attacked and inflicted one of the greatest setbacks that French arms were to suffer before May 1940.[46]

This argument was part of a larger one that any kind of moderation or limitation in war must be based on a realistic expectation that it will be reciprocated and that such expectations are often unrealistic. Clausewitz used an interesting metaphor to make this point: "He must always keep an eye on his opponent so that he does not, if the latter has taken up a sharp sword, approach him armed only with an ornamental rapier."[47] Dealing with "absolute" war in the abstract, Clausewitz pointed out that "to introduce the principle of moderation into the *theory* of war itself would always lead to logical absurdity." (Italics added.)

This argument has much to do with Clausewitz's bloodthirsty reputation. One of the accusations made against Clausewitz is that his sanctions against "moderation" in theory led directly to the later German practice of military *Schrecklichkeit* (frightfulness). In fact, Clausewitz did not mean that moderation was absurd in practice, because the social conditions within civilized states and the relationships between them often made moderation an element of policy. He failed to develop this point very far, however, and the accusation that it served to justify later German atrocities—to say that it "caused" them would certainly be going too far—is one of the hardest of all the indictments against him to evade. The theoretical point is hard to deny, but the language in which it was expressed is harsh.

> Kind-hearted people might of course think there was some ingenious way to disarm or defeat an enemy without too much bloodshed, and might imagine this is the true goal of the art of war. Pleasant as it sounds, it is a fallacy that must be exposed: war is such a dangerous business that the mistakes which come from kindness are the *very* worst.

The maximum use of force is in no way incompatible with the simultaneous use of the intellect.

Clausewitz's position is easier to understand if we consider the military transition that Europe was forced to undergo at the end of the eighteenth century. As had happened to a great extent in Europe under the ancien régime, a society might well ritualize war into a mere game for social reasons, in the name of humanitarianism, or in the hope of economizing on the waste of resources. To accept such a conventionalization of war was, in Clausewitz's view, to fall into a trap. "The fact that slaughter is a horrifying spectacle must make us take war more seriously, but not provide an excuse for gradually blunting our swords in the name of humanity. Sooner or later someone [i.e., some revolutionary or alien invader] will come along with a sharp sword and hack off our arms."[48] The conventionalization of war in prerevolutionary Europe had created the ideal situation for a Napoleon to exploit.

Unfortunately, Clausewitz's not-unreasonable conviction that the state must always be prepared for a life-and-death struggle fed easily into the unreasoning paranoia that helped lead Germany's leaders to launch World War I. That Clausewitz himself was touched by such an attitude is heavily suggested in other essays he wrote.[49]

The popular forces unleashed by the French Revolution, the event that triggered Clausewitz's fears, were, however, too powerful to be put back into the bottle. French successes had created a precedent that others would undoubtedly try to repeat. Clausewitz was therefore interested in the role of popular passions and public opinion in both politics and war. As a professional officer in an army with a venerable and glorious tradition, he was also sensitive to the quite different military virtues represented by such armies. All of these considerations fell generally under the heading of "moral factors," and Clausewitz's work is famous for its emphasis on them: "One might say that the physical seem little more than the wooden hilt, while the moral factors are the precious metal, the real weapon, the finely-honed blade."[50] They applied at the individual (usually discussed under the rubric of "military genius"), the organizational, and the societal levels.

Curiously, even though Clausewitz's emphasis on moral factors has always been noted, many of his later critics argued that he had reduced strategy to the simplistic act of bludgeoning the enemy to death with overwhelming numbers. This accusation should not be dismissed out of hand as some modern analysts have done.[51] Clausewitz's method of argumentation on this point illustrates the ease with which his ideas can be distorted by sloppy reading or hostile editing. In discussing the armies of modern Europe, Clausewitz did indeed stress numbers:

> Here we find armies much more alike in equipment, organization, and
> practical skill of every kind. There only remains a difference in the
> military virtues of Armies, and in the talent of Generals which may

fluctuate with time from side to side. . . . From this we may infer, that
it is very difficult in the present state of Europe, for the most talented
General to gain a victory over an enemy double his strength. Now if
we see double numbers prove such a weight in the scale against the
greatest Generals, we may be sure, that in ordinary cases, in small as
well as great combats, an important superiority of numbers but which
need not be over two to one, will be sufficient to ensure the victory,
however disadvantageous other circumstances may be. . . . The first rule
is therefore to enter the field with an Army as strong as possible. This
sounds very like a commonplace, but still it is really not so.

It is clear that Clausewitz regarded the raising of the largest possible armies
as an important factor in national strategy (and the ability to raise troops
was in large part clearly a function of popular support for state policy).
The number of troops "is determined by the government . . . with this
determination the real action of the War commences, and it forms an
essential part of the Strategy of the War." Tactically, Clausewitz stressed
concentration of superior force at the decisive point, as do virtually all
military writers: "In tactics, as in strategy, superiority of numbers is the
most common element in victory."

This point is fundamental to Clausewitz's outlook on strategy, but translation problems sometimes obscure his point, as in Clausewitz's famous
characterization of war as a "duel." Used in all of the English translations,
it is not a very good substitute for the original German *Zweikampf*, literally
"two-struggle." A duel with sword or (particularly) pistol is based more
clearly on skill than on raw strength and lacks the dynamic character, the
multiple points of contact, and the mutability of a wrestling match, Clausewitz's actual imagery.[52] His original metaphor provides a much better
graphic image into which to fit the term "center of gravity."

His argument was not, however, that the victor would necessarily be
the side with the most men but that there was no excuse for going into
combat with less than the maximum available power:

> If we strip the combat of all modifications which it may undergo
> according to its immediate purpose and the circumstances from which
> it proceeds, lastly if we set aside the valour of the troops [*dem Wert
> der Truppen*] . . . there remains only the bare conception of the combat
> . . . in which we distinguish nothing but the number of the combatants.
> This number will therefore determine victory. Now from the number
> of things above deducted to get to this point, it is shown that the
> superiority in numbers in a battle is only one of the factors employed
> to produce victory; that therefore so far from having with the superi-
> ority in number obtained all, or even only the principal thing, we have
> perhaps got very little by it, according as the other circumstances . . .
> happen to vary. . . . There remains nothing, therefore, where an abso-
> lute superiority is not attainable, but to produce a relative one at the
> decisive point, by making skillful use of what we have . . . to regard
> [numerical superiority] as a necessary condition of victory would be a
> complete misconception of our exposition.[53]

A partial reading of Clausewitz's views on surprise can be just as misleading. His bald statements that it "would be a mistake . . . to regard surprise as a key element of success in war" and that "surprise has lost its usefulness today" are characteristically misleading if taken out of context, which often seems to be the case.[54] Also controversial is his argument that surprise often favors the defense. Overall, Clausewitz actually strongly emphasized the concept of surprise, suggesting that—defined as "the desire to surprise the enemy by our plans and dispositions, especially those concerning the distribution of forces"—it "lies at the root of all operations without exception, though in widely varying degrees depending on the nature and circumstances of the operation." He clearly appreciated its psychological impact and felt that almost the only advantage of the attacker rested in surprise.

Clausewitz obviously believed in the practical utility or necessity of war, and he was very conscious of its offer of individual "glory." As a Prussian nationalist he had little sympathy for the claims of subjugated peoples such as the Poles. He was, however, no advocate of a policy of conquest. Although he is often portrayed as the "high priest" of Napoleon, this view ignores the fact that he was both a passionate Prussian patriot and a die-hard opponent of the French emperor. Clausewitz was detached enough to admire Bonaparte as a professional soldier, but his experience of the Napoleonic wars convinced him of the power of both nationalism and of the balance-of-power mechanism. In his view, those forces would generally lead to the destruction of any would-be Alexander or Napoleon, at least in the European context. Thus, the wars he describes are often those of Napoleon, but his strategic biases are essentially conservative and antirevolutionary; the approach he takes is not Napoleon's but that of the emperor's most capable enemy, Scharnhorst. To call Clausewitz the "codifier of Napoleonic warfare" as his critics (and some of his supporters) often have, is to miss this important point.[55]

The clearest evidence of Clausewitz's faith in the balance-of-power mechanism lies in his analysis of the dynamic relationship of the offense and the defense.[56] He has been portrayed by various writers as a proponent of one or the other form, but as in so many important aspects of his theory, his actual position was instead to set up a dualism: Defense is the stronger form of war, but it has a negative object (self-preservation); offense is the weaker form, but it alone has a positive purpose (increasing one's strength through conquest). Any realistic military theory must embrace both.

The sources of the fundamentally greater strength of the defense are many. In a sense, the defensive form's superiority is self-evident: Why else does the weaker party so often resort to it? At the tactical level, Clausewitz was impressed by the power of entrenchments—and alarmed at the "pedants'" tendency to dismiss them—and by the defender's frequent ability to choose his own ground. He was also interested in fixed fortifications, although he warned against overreliance on them and made some careful observations on their correct use. In most battles, however, both sides use both offensive and defensive methods, and losses tend to be fairly equal until one side or the other breaks. Therefore he strongly emphasized the pursuit, which permits the infliction of disproportionate losses on the loser.

Much more important were the strategic aspects of defense. However strongly an offensive may start out, it inevitably weakens as it advances from its original base. The need to provide garrisons, the maintenance of lines of supply and communications, and the greater physical strain on troops in the attack all degrade the aggressor's force. Meanwhile, the defender falls back on the sources of his strength. Every offensive, however victorious, has a "culminating point." If the defender has enough time and space in which to recover (and Russia offered an excellent example), the aggressor will inevitably reach a point at which he must himself turn into the defender. If he pushes too far, the equilibrium will shift against him. The aggressor, in his own retreat (often through devastated territory), cannot draw on the defender's usual sources of strength, physical or psychological.

Moreover, public opinion is more likely to favor the strategic defender; any significant conquest by one aggressor state will threaten the rest. Eventually, the conqueror reaches a "culminating point of victory" at which his successes provoke sufficient counteraction to defeat him.

The essence of the defense is waiting: waiting until the attacker clarifies his own intentions; waiting until the balance of forces shifts; waiting for any improvement in the defender's situation, whether from the culminating process just described above, from outside intervention, from mobilization of his own resources, or from some chance development. Time is almost always on the side of the defender.

Waiting, however, does not imply mere passivity, and a passive defense is not at all what Clausewitz was describing. His vision of any effective defense was profoundly active. If the defense functions essentially as a shield, it is best "a shield made up of well-directed blows."[57] Defense must, even at the strategic level, shift at some point to the offense; it is the "flashing sword of vengeance." Thus it is easy to find in *On War* isolated quotations that seem to glorify the offensive. It is nonetheless the *interaction* of the two forms that concerned Clausewitz.

The dynamic relationship between defense and offense is just one of a larger group of concepts that might collectively be labeled the "dynamics of war." These would include the emphases on friction and morale, the diminishing force of the offensive, and the "culminating point of victory"; in short, all of the factors that prevent war from being a linear process and that create the unpredictable seesawing between opposing wills and powers that characterizes our real-world experience of war.

Last but not least among the factors to be considered in understanding his ideas is Clausewitz's political position. Many of Clausewitz's basic historical, political, and military views derived from the influence of Scharnhorst and other Prussian military reformers. In broad terms, their argument was that the French Revolution had achieved its astounding successes because it had tapped the energies of the people. If the Prussian state was to survive, much less prosper, it had to do the same. This meant sweeping social and political reforms in the Prussian state and army, both of which had ossified under the successors of Frederick the Great. To conservatives, Scharnhorst's circle appeared to be dangerously radical, but although Clausewitz's works reflect a strong reform impulse, neither he nor his mentors desired a social or political revolution. Clausewitz's stance on the power of the defense and the workings of the balance of power and his lack of sympathy for the would-be conqueror demonstrate his fundamental moderation. He did in fact have a great enthusiasm for the British parliamentary model, a radical notion in Prussia, but his

> insistence on what would one day be called 'the primacy of foreign policy' set him at odds with those who believed constitutional government was a political goal surpassing all others. It also made his point of view anathema to those who considered the preservation of the social hierarchy an objective rivaling the safety of the state.[58]

Thus Clausewitz was not a liberal or a revolutionary or a Nazi. Trying to place him and his theories somewhere on an anachronistic left–right political spectrum is a futile exercise. His politics can be understood only in reference to the specific situation of Prussia in the Napoleonic and restoration periods.[59]

There are, of course, many other aspects of Clausewitz's life and work that are worthy of examination, but these are the matters that have surfaced most often in English-language discussions.

I

Clausewitz in English to 1873: Present But Not Accounted For

Writing about England between 1815 and 1854, the British historian Hew Strachan said recently that "it was not that Clausewitz was dismissed: he was simply unheard of." This statement embodies the conventional wisdom on the subject, and the same is often said of the entire English-speaking world in the period before 1873: "The earliest English translation, which introduced the title *On War*, was prepared by J. J. Graham in 1873"; "In fact, it is doubtful whether he was known at all [in the United States] before the [Civil] war."[1]

This view is, however, something of an exaggeration.[2] It is unquestionably true that books by other foreign writers on war, even some by other Germans, were much more widely read and appreciated. Nonetheless, Clausewitz's name was in fact known to British military writers in this period, and important elements of his theoretical argument became available in the English language within a few years of their publication in Germany. At least two of his historical works were read, in English, within the highest circles of the small British military community in the 1840s. These works were by no means devoid of their author's more abstract theoretical views. Clausewitz's writings, both historical and theoretical, were discussed at the British army's Staff College at Camberley during the 1860s, even before the German military model achieved preeminence in Europe.

As for the appearance of an English translation of *On War* in 1873, the conventional wisdom seems to be just as wrong when it assumes that its publication was motivated by Helmuth von Moltke's great successes and his praise of Clausewitz and that it ushered in a period of intensified interest in the Prussian theorist. Aside from its timing, there is no internal or external evidence to indicate that its translator was motivated by contemporary events at all, nor was its publication the cause or result of any widespread fascination with its contents. Although the Anglo-Saxons certainly took a great interest in the German military model after 1870, there is no evidence for a sharpened interest in Clausewitz in particular before the 1890s.

The translation of *Vom Kriege* in 1873 should therefore be seen not as the beginning of Clausewitz studies in English but as an important expression of a long-standing interest in his thought.

For reasons inherent in the nature of Clausewitz's ideas, however, their influence is difficult to trace beyond the occasional quotation from or reference to their author. The influence of Clausewitz's great rival Jomini is easy to detect because his followers naturally adopted Jomini's extensive and distinctive strategic vocabulary. Clausewitz, in contrast, explicitly renounced the creation of such a technical jargon in the field of strategy, and his ponderous but penetrating style of argumentation does not—save for a few choice and often misleading lines—lend itself to quotation. The one quotation from *On War* with which most of us are familiar, and which has been the focus of much recent writing on Clausewitz, is his famous statement that "war is a continuation of politics by other means." This aspect of the Prussian thinker's multifaceted philosophy was not, however, the focus of Clausewitz's nineteenth century Anglo-Saxon readers.

Nonetheless, the evidence suggests that the standard assumption concerning Clausewitz's influence in the English-speaking world in this period, that is, that there was none, is based upon false expectations regarding the nature of such an influence and upon persistent misapprehensions of his actual teachings. Writers in this field have sought—and failed—to find his influence in the areas of strategy and practical doctrine. The core of Clausewitz's military theory, however, lies in its historicist philosophy, its analysis of the nature and the dynamics of war, and its pedagogical aims and methods. These elements did in fact strike a chord with some British thinkers.

All this is not to say that the British before 1873 (or after, for that matter) were in any sense "Clausewitzians" or to make any sweeping claims for the influence of Clausewitz's theories. Other writers and theorists were clearly more influential. Clausewitz nonetheless did have a place in British military thought. Strachan's comment could more accurately be applied to the United States, but even then it would not be entirely true. Clausewitz's name would have been familiar to any well-read American military man in the 1850s or 1860s. There is, however, far less reason to suppose that the name would have conveyed any meaning.

3

Clausewitz in Great Britain Before 1873

There were some signs of a mutual interest between Clausewitz and Great Britain even during his lifetime. His writing first appeared in English in 1815, in *The Life and Campaigns of Field-Marshal Prince Blücher*. This contains what Peter Paret has described as a "free rendering" of Clause-witz's study of the campaign of 1813. It was attributed to Gneisenau, how-ever, and reveals neither the name of its true author nor any recognizable elements of his theoretical method.[1] Clausewitz actually visited England in 1818. In 1819, he made an attempt to gain an ambassadorial appointment to London; he also wrote an essay urging the use of the British parliamen-tary model in Prussia. His diplomatic ambitions were frustrated, however, probably because his part in the reform of the Prussian army and in the events of 1812/13 had left him politically suspect not only in Berlin but also among conservatives in British diplomatic circles.[2]

The posthumous publication of Clausewitz's *Vom Kriege* did, how-ever, receive some early notice in the English-speaking world. In 1835, a substantial review article entitled simply "On War" appeared on both sides of the Atlantic. In England, the unsigned review was printed in the *Metropolitan Magazine*. This was a London monthly edited by Captain Frederick Marryat, a former naval officer better known today as an inno-vative writer of children's literature. It was picked up in America by the *Military and Naval Magazine of the United States*, published in Wash-ington, D.C.[3] The appearance of this article alone contradicts the common assumption that Clausewitz's major work was unknown in the English-speaking world before the Franco-Prussian War.

The anonymous but enthusiastic author of this review presented a fairly accurate description of Clausewitz's argument and fully appreciated its importance:

> To such of our readers as may be acquainted with the German language, we cannot too strongly recommend the perusal of this posthumous production of General von Clausewitz; than which, few publications connected with the elementary principles of war were ever more deserving of attention—none more essentially calculated to elevate the author to the highest rank amongst strategists and philosophers.

The writer went on to recommend the work's translation and use in the military college at Sandhurst.

It is interesting to note the specific aspects of Clausewitz's discussion that drew our reviewer's attention. He mentioned in passing Clausewitz's discussion of the relationship of war to policy but fixed most strongly on the dynamics of war (particularly "friction"), the role of violence, and the nature of "military genius." There were also intelligent discussions of Clausewitz's views on the nature of theory and the role of personal experience in comprehending it; the uses (and abuses) of military history, and definitions of strategy and tactics. The writer was by no means uncritical. In particular, he berated Clausewitz for placing "patriotism amongst the fugitive portions of valor" in his discussion of moral forces: The courage and patriotism of British soldiers were not dependent on circumstances.

The article reveals a few things about its anonymous author. He presents himself as a man of some military experience. Perhaps more important, he shows a marked dissatisfaction with the negative effects of English social precepts as carried over into the armed forces: "Indeed, the baneful influence of patronage, interest, and wealth, whether in the army or navy, is generally so exclusive as to render merit, in inferior ranks, a mere dead letter, and often to stifle all feelings of legitimate ambition." (In a footnote, the editors expressly disavow support for this statement.) In short, our earliest Anglo-Clausewitzian was a "military reformer," a type that appeared frequently in the ranks of Clausewitz's readers in Great Britain.

It was suggested by a contemporary that the anonymous reviewer might have been Major North Ludlow Beamish (1797–1872), the historian of the King's German Legion.[4] The suggestion was a logical one. Beamish, too, called for reforms (in the British cavalry), and his later work vociferously attacked the practice of purchasing commissions. Unfortunately for this supposition, his 1855 edition of Bismark's cavalry manual, revised with a great deal of material from as late as the Crimean War and heavily footnoted with references to Jomini, Archibald Alison, and the Archduke Charles, makes no reference to Clausewitz.[5] Beamish was thus almost certainly not the enthusiastic reviewer of 1835.

That Beamish was the reviewer was suggested by a man who would otherwise have been himself a very likely candidate for authorship, the reform advocate Colonel John Mitchell (1785–1859).[6] Mitchell's father, a British diplomat, had enrolled his young son in the Ritterakademie in Prussia in 1797. He was commissioned in the British army in 1803 (Fifty-seventh Regiment) and served in the West Indies. He participated in the disastrous Walcheren expedition of 1809 and then served Wellington in the peninsula from 1810 to 1812. In 1813 he joined the quartermaster general's staff, served in the campaign of 1814 in the Low Countries, and joined in the occupation of Paris. Owing to his great linguistic abilities, he was frequently employed by Wellington in negotiations with the allies. On half-pay from 1826, Mitchell was promoted to lieutenant-colonel in 1835 and to major-general in 1854. He wrote profusely on military subjects. A cultivated man, Mitchell also wrote a book entitled *The Art of Conversation, with Remarks on Fashion and Address*, under the pseudonym of Captain Orlando Sabertash.

Mitchell's views on military reform can be divided into two broad categories: tactical and organizational. His tactical ideas had little future. He believed in the dominance of shock over firepower, emphasizing the *arme blanche* of the cavalry. Somewhat inconsistently, however, he disparaged the bayonet and called for its abandonment. Although Mitchell's attitude toward the latter weapon was grounded in his practical observation that formed units virtually never used their bayonets in actual combat, it is curious that he should have ignored its moral effect. In every other respect he was intensely conscious of moral and psychological factors.

These factors are predominant in the organizational aspects of his theories, which were as radical as—if ultimately more realistic than—his tactical concepts. Mitchell sought to capitalize on what he saw as the splendid qualities of the common British soldier. He called for a new and closer relationship between officers and men, the abolition of the degrading system of punishments by which discipline was enforced, and the elimination of the pernicious effects of "interest" in the army. In pursuit of the last goal, he advocated the end of promotion by purchase and its replacement by a purely merit-based system. In these aims he was certainly both visionary and prophetic. Promotion by purchase was not ended until 1871.

Mitchell embarked on his public quest for reform around 1830, and his views seem to have been fully formed by 1838.[7] His major theoretical work, published in that year, was *Thoughts on Tactics and Military Organization*. He opened with a chapter entitled "Causes of the Slow Progress of Military Science," which noted that although England might at any moment be called on to wage war in any quarter of the globe, there was not "a single work on military science" in the English language. Pursuing the question as to why this should be so, Mitchell paused to give the floor to Clausewitz:

> The late General Clausewitz tells us in a very able, though lengthy, and often obscure book on War, that "war comes not within the province

of the arts and sciences, but is simply an action of ordinary life; a conflict of great interests that ends in blood, and differs in this last respect only from other conflicts. The principal difference [between art and war] consists in this," says the General, "that war is not deliberate action directed against dead matter or substance, as in the mechanical arts; nor is it deliberate action directed against a living, yet suffering and yielding object, as in the arts intended to influence the minds or feelings of men . . . but it is action directed against re-action. How little this kind of action comes within the province of arts and sciences is evident, and it proves how dangerous and detrimental to armies must have been the constant striving to govern them, by laws resembling those to which dead matter is subject. And yet it is exactly after the mechanical arts, that men have attempted to model the art of war."[8]

Rather curiously, despite this observation, Mitchell continued to call for a British study of "military science."

This was the only explicit reference to Clausewitz in Mitchell's *Thoughts on Tactics*, although he shortly thereafter discussed war as a duel and the question as to whether generals are born or made. In these discussions he clearly seems to be drawing on the same source. Indeed, one could read a Clausewitzian influence into many sections of this book, but this is the only place where firm connections can be demonstrated. Mitchell's three-volume *The Fall of Napoleon* (1845) also made many respectful if sometimes puzzled references to Clausewitz, drawing on both *Vom Kriege* and the campaign studies of 1812, 1814, and 1815. During the Crimean War, Mitchell used Clausewitz's discussions of the campaign of 1812 in explaining Russian vulnerabilities, calling the Prussian writer "in the estimation of many, the highest authority that can be quoted on a Military subject."[9]

In another article, Mitchell made an argument for the utility to Britain of a military theory aimed at the deeper fundamentals of war:

It would, of course, be impossible to calculate how far [our] total disregard of military science may have influenced our military enterprises; but it is a curious circumstance, that though generally victorious when contending against adversaries who met us with the usual arms of disciplined foes, and fought us according to the conventional mode of European warfare, our most signal defeats were sustained from undisciplined adversaries, who knew little or nothing of our modern tactics, and struck, by chance or good management on their part, at the weak points of our conventional and only method of fighting. . . . Might it not be said, that, believing our system of tactics to have attained absolute perfection, we had neglected to examine the original principles of the science, and had never compared its strength and efficiency with the different modes of fighting which might be brought against us? . . . The work of Clausewitz, *Vom Kriege*, published at least eight years ago, and forming, it may almost be said, an era in military science, has never been translated or noticed among us—never noticed in any of the leading reviews of [a] country the soldiers of which must at all times be prepared to encounter every description of enemy, from the trained armies of Europe to the fierce swordsman of Persia; and from the stealthy rifleman of America to the wild horseman of Lahore.[10]

Strachan found it ironic that "Clausewitz's outstanding British pupil" should imbibe his wisdom in the area of tactics rather than in strategy. This is somewhat unfair to Mitchell, because his book is, after all, about tactics. His overall reform argument, on the other hand, was based on a moral and psychological perception that far transcended mere tactics. It is unfair as well to Clausewitz, because his book likewise is about far more than strategy. Mitchell's comments on the Prussian writer's theories, just excerpted, certainly have more than tactical implications. The first describes a concept that is one of the central pillars of Clausewitz's philosophy of war.

Strachan also sees Mitchell as strategically unsophisticated, largely because of the latter's contemptuous attitude toward Napoleon. Mitchell's critique of Napoleon was not, however, rooted in a purely military judgment. In that area Mitchell was certainly far more critical of the emperor than is customary, but it was Napoleon's moral and political errors, which in fact led to the collapse of the empire, that drew his deeper scorn. There is, after all, something to be said for judging strategists by the ultimate outcome of their efforts.[11] Since Napoleon held both the political and the military reins, our judgment of him as a strategist should embrace both aspects.

Mitchell never explicitly discussed Clausewitz in terms of the relationship of war to policy and politics, but he did bring up both the intimate connection between Britain's military weaknesses and its constitution and the requirement that the British army remain utterly apolitical. He apologized for even touching on the subject of politics in a military work but justified his temerity in this regard by his own scrupulously evenhanded contempt for both Whigs and Tories.[12] Such comments help explain the general lack of attention paid by British writers to this aspect of Clausewitz's thought.

The extent to which the Prussian military philosopher had actually shaped Mitchell's overall views is unknowable, of course. Mitchell had embarked on his reform efforts before *Vom Kriege* was published, and neither Mitchell nor other British military writers of this period were in the habit of footnoting the sources of each of their insights and inspirations.

Clausewitz's writings also drew some attention closer to the heart of Britain's military community. On 24 September 1842, the duke of Wellington addressed a memorandum to Francis Egerton, earl of Ellesmere, concerning Clausewitz's study of the Waterloo campaign of 1815.[13] It is an interesting document not only because it refers to Clausewitz but also because it is the only personal response that Wellington ever made to any of the many studies of that famous battle.

Although chiefly remembered as a literary figure and as a patron of the arts, the politically prominent Ellesmere (1800–57) held a (probably honorary) commission as a captain in the Staffordshire yeomanry and served as secretary at war for a brief period in 1830. Ellesmere wrote, edited, and translated several works on military history and on contemporary military events.[14] He was a friend and admirer of the duke. His military interests may in fact be more a reflection of this relationship than of his own inclinations. Ellesmere served as Wellington's mouthpiece in several disputes over military policy and history. In this role he was probably a valuable pressure valve for the duke, who took great pains in his own signed works never to cause offense.

Around 1839, another of Wellington's friends, the third Lord Liverpool, had been introduced to Clausewitz's collected works by a German friend.[15] Charles Cecil Cope Jenkinson (1784–1851) was the son of the Tory prime minister Lord Liverpool (in office from 1812 to 1827). He had spent time as a youth in the Royal Navy, served as attaché at Vienna, and fought in the Austrian army at Austerlitz. Afterward he entered Parliament, joined the cabinet in 1807, and became undersecretary of state for war and the colonies in 1809. Liverpool was initially interested only in the German author's role in General von Yorck's defection, with his Prussian corps, from Napoleon's to the allied camp in 1812. He grew absorbed, however, in the philosopher's other works and became quite enthusiastic about the theoretical arguments contained in *On War*. Liverpool told the duke about *On War*, which he called a "work of exceeding interest."

Wellington, however, had no interest in theory—or mere "reveries," as he called it. He was concerned only with Clausewitz's discussion of the Waterloo campaign, particularly his analysis of Marshal Grouchy's operations.[16] Liverpool offered some defense of the theoretical aspects of *On War* but made no headway. He then provided the duke with a manuscript translation of *The Campaign of 1815 in France*.[17]

Clausewitz's study pays more attention to the Prussian than to the British role in the campaign, not because of national prejudice but because he considered the Prussian forces to have taken a more active role. They had met the first French assault and later, after Wellington's defensive action, they had exploited his victory by conducting the pursuit. Although complimentary in many respects, Clausewitz was critical of Wellington's passivity, his dispositions, and the dispersion of his forces (particularly the detachment of some eighteen thousand troops to cover other possible French approaches via Hal and Tubize; these men were effectively eliminated from the Anglo-Dutch order of battle at Waterloo). Clausewitz also implied that the duke was overconcerned with his own line of retreat and had made no offensive plans to exploit any defensive success. His key observation, however, was that "Lord Wellington had never personally commanded against Bonaparte and perhaps therefore he was not sufficiently aware that the lightning bolt of a major battle would be forced on him" by the emperor, who always sought thus to reach a decision.[18]

The Campaign of 1815 was completed around 1827, that is, before Clausewitz had fully developed the great insights of *On War*. This is an important point to keep in mind when considering Wellington's response.

Wellington turned the manuscript over to Colonel John Gurwood (his literary assistant) and Lord Ellesmere, directing that they check the translation before he read it.[19] After reading it, the duke responded in a memorandum that was drafted in part by Egerton and was evidently well known in nineteenth-century Britain.[20] Despite the widespread interest in Clausewitz since 1976, this exchange has fallen into obscurity. Historians to whom I have mentioned it have responded with surprise.[21] One modern British historian who is aware of it nonetheless dismissed it, noting in his bibliography that "Germans who have written about the campaign are too much interested in pleading their own causes."[22]

Wellington's discussion of Clausewitz's Waterloo study was elaborate, which is especially interesting because his policy was normally to ignore critics. In general, the duke was unhappy with all unofficial accounts of the campaign and discouraged all attempts to write them, being convinced that a satisfactory account was impossible. "The battle of Waterloo is undoubtedly one of the most interesting events of modern times, but the Duke entertains no hopes of ever seeing an account of all its details which shall be true."[23]

> Surely the details of the battle might have been left in the original official reports: Historians and commentators were not necessary. . . . We find the historians of all nations, not excepting . . . the British, too ready to criticize the acts and operations not only of their own Generals and armies, but likewise of those of the best friends and allies of their nation, and even of those acting in co-operation with its armies. This observation must be borne in mind throughout the perusal of Clausewitz's History."[24]

Wellington persisted in this attitude right up to his death. His rigidity in this matter is curious, since he was himself an avid reader of military history and he knew well the inherent imperfections of the genre. He once pointed out that a battle was rather like a ball, full of interesting incidents that none of the participants could later put into anything like chronological order, much less reconstruct into a coherent story.[25] It was only with regard to his own battles that he complained of historians' futile attempts to do so. One motive may have been his concern about resurrecting "certain dishonourable incidents" involving British officers.

Although he disputed some important points, Wellington seems to have had a high opinion of Clausewitz as a historian. At least, the memorandum contains none of the vitriol that Egerton, writing at the duke's behest, cast at the historian Archibald Alison and at Clausewitz's competitor Antoine-Henri Jomini.[26] Wellington himself credited the German writer with many insights, saying, for instance, that his account of events on 17 June 1815 was "as nearly as possible, an accurate representation of what passed." He also took pains to show that he had always given proper credit to the Prussians for their role in the campaign.

The most interesting portions of the memorandum concern Clausewitz's criticisms of Wellington's initial defensive dispositions in the period before Napoleon took the offensive. Part of this discussion is technical, involving the disposition of the Anglo-Dutch and Prussian armies and the order of battle. Wellington defended his decisions on the grounds that Napoleon's route of advance could not be predicted and was, in the event, not the best choice.

More important from any theoretical point of view, Wellington went well beyond the merely technical into an examination of the deeper strategic and political reasoning behind his actions. His treatment became, in fact, quite theoretical. Wellington noted Clausewitz's sensitivity to the interplay between war and politics and objected that his criticisms of allied defensive dispositions were rooted in his preference for an offensive strategy aimed merely at the fighting of a "great battle." He felt that alternative dispositions (which he remarks that Clausewitz was "too wise" to describe in any detail) would have uncovered the Netherlands and his communications with England without, in fact, making such a decisive battle any more likely. Here, Wellington seems to have misconstrued Clausewitz's description of Napoleon's intention as the Prussian theorist's own desire.

The duke felt that the Prussian writer, in criticizing his army's relative passivity, had ignored the overall strategic dispersal of the allied armies and Napoleon's possession of the local initiative. Wellington saw no value in seeking such a "great battle . . . even under the hypothesis that the result would have been a great victory." His object was the preservation of the allied forces in Belgium for use in crushing Napoleon through coordinated actions that, because of the alliance's sheer numerical superiority, would have been far more sure—and less costly—in their result. The moral effect of a defeat, on the other hand, might have imperiled the entire allied cause. Clausewitz's desire for decisive battle did not, in this case, accord with the political aims of the alliance.

> The Historian [Clausewitz] shows in more than one passage that he is not insensible of the military and political value of good moral impressions resulting from military operations. He is sensible of the advantage derived by the enemy from such impressions. He is aware of the object of Buonapart to create throughout Europe, and even in England, a moral impression against the war, and to shake the power of the then existing administration in England. He is sensible of and can contemplate the effect of the moral impression upon the other armies of Europe, and upon the governments in whose service they were, resulting from the defeat or even want of success of the Allied armies under the command of the Duke of Wellington and Prince Blücher. But he is not sensible of, and cannot calculate upon, or even consider the effect of, the moral impression resulting from the loss of Bruxelles and Ghent, the flight of the King of the Netherlands, and of

the King Louis XVIII., the creatures of the treaties of peace, and of the acts of the Congress of Vienna; and this with the loss of the communications of the army under the Duke of Wellington with England, Holland, and Germany, without making the smallest effort to save any of these objects.

Wellington's criticism of Clausewitz is thus an appreciation of the very contradictions that Clausewitz himself had later discovered in his own work, a discovery that had led to his major revisions in *On War* and to his development of the more comprehensive theory that marks his greatness as a military philosopher. Decisive battle need not be the goal of the wise strategist: Decisions must instead be made in full accordance with the specific political situation. This does not necessarily invalidate Clausewitz's criticisms, of course, many of which have since been accepted even by British writers.[27]

The English translation of *The Campaign of 1815* was never published. Wellington's good friend Francis Egerton was, however, the anonymous translator of Clausewitz's *Campaign of 1812 in Russia*, which was published by John Murray in 1843.[28] The earl included a decent biographical sketch of the author in a long and thoughtful preface. Wellington wrote Egerton an entirely positive letter discussing its contents, although it is uncertain whether he actually had read the book. Once again, the duke's interest was largely personal, excited by Ellesmere's observation that elements of the Russian plan of defense had been fashioned after Wellington's own defense of Torres Vedras.[29]

This study of the 1812 campaign—which, like most of Clausewitz's published works, is somewhat unfinished—is sometimes dismissed as a mere recounting of its author's experiences in Russia with no theoretical significance. In fact, however, it is a useful demonstration of Clausewitz's critical approach to the writing of military history and contains an assessment of Napoleon's 1812 strategy more extensive in some respects than that given in *On War*. It also contains some important elements of Clausewitz's larger theory. The concept of "friction," for instance, is implicit in his discussion of his own role in bringing about the Convention of Tauroggen (Yorck's decision to defect with his corps from the French camp), but it is also explicitly discussed as a theoretical concept. A great many other aspects of Clausewitz's analysis of the dynamics of war also appear, particularly his concept of the "culminating point" of the offensive.[30]

Another of Clausewitz's historical studies formed the main basis for an 1852 article by C. E. Watson (Seventh Royal Fusiliers), "The German Campaigns of Gustavus Adolphus." Watson was impressed by Clausewitz's theoretical arguments concerning defensive war, although he did not describe those arguments in detail.[31]

None of Clausewitz's campaign studies was published in French before Jean Colin's translation of *The Campaign of 1796 in Italy* appeared in 1899.[32] *Vom Kriege*, however, was translated into French in 1849–51 by a Belgian artillery officer named Jean Baptiste Charles François Neuens. (Another French translation appeared in 1886–87.)[33] Nicolas Édouard Delabarre-Duparcq was professor of the art of war at St. Cyr. His 1853 *Commentaire sur la traité de la guerre de Clausewitz* was based on Neuen's work.[34]

A long and unsigned English review of Duparcq's commentaries appeared in the pages of the *United Service Magazine* in 1854.[35] The reader must labor under the triple handicap of reading a British writer's review of a French commentary on a French translation of a work that is not entirely clear in the original German. The British writer did not help things when he indiscriminately mixed his own comments on England's military reform problem and his own views of both Duparcq and Clausewitz with Duparcq's original observations. It is nonetheless an interesting document that is worthy of some detailed attention.

Indicating that there was indeed a British awareness of Clausewitz in this period, the reviewer opened with a comment that is as applicable in its implications today as it was in 1854: "General von Clausewitz's work on *Warfare* is known, at least by name, to most military men."[36] He noted the initial enthusiasm that had greeted the work in Germany, as well as a certain disappointment with it and a subsequent loss of interest. At the time of his writing, however,

> it has appeared, owing to the events of the late wars being now read with less party bitterness, that Von Clausewitz was far more correct than was at first allowed. Of his numerous critics, De La Barre Duparcq . . . appears the most impartial and judicious in his remarks; and in laying these before our readers, we shall be doing them no little service.

The review was critical in several areas, but like virtually all British discussions of Clausewitz before 1914, it maintained a respectful tone throughout.

We cannot know what subtle, perhaps unconscious lessons Duparcq and others took from reading Clausewitz themselves,[37] but their published comments would have helped shape the general perception of a military audience that was aware of his reputation but not his message. This review certainly did not paint Clausewitz as a bloodthirsty ogre or as a mere proponent of mass and the offensive, views that became widespread after World War I. It touched on quite a few of the many facets of his work and attempted to grapple with several of the subtle questions that Clausewitz raises.

Duparcq (or his reviewer) praised Clausewitz unreservedly on several points. He accepted his comments on the unwisdom of moderation in war arising from feelings of humanity, although he understood this simply as being, in the long run, the more humanitarian approach; he did not discuss Clausewitz's deeper understanding of the role of violence in war. He accepted as well Clausewitz's rejection of theories rooted in mathematical calculation, his portrayal of war as a game of chance, and his insistence on the role of personal experience in understanding military theory. The reviewer described attack and defense in a manner that prefigures Hans Delbrück's later discussion of the strategy of attrition, but he expressed frank puzzlement concerning Clausewitz's skepticism of the maneuver warfare of the eighteenth century. He endorsed the Prussian's emphasis on the power of moral factors in warfare but had great difficulty in distinguishing between the effects of "morale" and purely physical factors like firepower. The brief discussion of Clausewitz's definition of war as an instrument of policy is especially curious. The point was not disputed, but its author was criticized for not enumerating all of the various political motives that may underlie specific wars. The reviewer therefore provided a list similar to Jomini's.[38]

This British reviewer was by no means a reactionary or even particularly conservative; indeed, he commented on the many blunders of the British army, on the rigidities of organization brought about by too great an attention to social class and "interest," and on the shortcomings of British officers resulting from stagnation and oversupervision in small and scattered garrisons. Such comments reflect the reformist attitudes that drove most of the British writers interested in Clausewitz.

In general, "theorizing never has been the characteristic of Englishmen; it is held, perhaps, in too great disrepute."[39] The reviewer also had a skeptical attitude toward the application of theory to war. He regarded most theory as mere verbiage and made scathing references to Jomini's attempt to create a whole new strategic vocabulary. He found Clausewitz's approach refreshing, but he grasped it only in part: He had accepted Clausewitz's pedagogical ideas but not their deeper historicist basis. He clearly agreed with Clausewitz that it is the specifics of every situation rather than some sort of strategic recipe that must determine a commander's actions:

> Clausewitz well assimilates theory in this respect to a "wise preceptor, who confines himself to directing and facilitating the intellectual development of his pupil, and does not attempt to keep him in leading strings through life." It is good to see a military writer allow that his theory is not infallible—that, far from being a universal law, it is merely a guide.

The reviewer failed, however, to grasp the larger historicist argument that underlies this approach, saying "war is almost always based upon identical circumstances; and at bottom its means are pretty nearly the same, unless we take into consideration the mechanical progress of weapons, and the genius of the commander." In general, the reviewer resisted any kind of systematic approach to war that would have limited his own freedom to pick and choose among ideas. Rather than becoming a self-conscious disciple of Clausewitz, as would many of the later German military writers, he saw his works as a mother lode of intriguing ideas to add to the stockpile. He remained determinedly eclectic and idiosyncratic. In this approach he reflects a pattern visible in almost all British military writers.

Clausewitz's *Campaign of 1815* surfaced again in a book by Colonel Charles Chesney, R.E. (1826–76). In 1858 Chesney was appointed professor of military history at Sandhurst, and in 1864 he was appointed professor of military art and history at the British army's new senior educational center, the Staff College at Camberley. He succeeded Edward B. Hamley, the author of a highly Jominian treatise on war.[40]

Chesney gained considerable recognition with *Waterloo Lectures*, published in 1868.[41] He had set out to write a balanced and factual account of the Belgian campaign, in contrast with those by "so-called national historians, who willfully pander to the passions of their countrymen at the expense of historical truth." In particular, he sought to give proper credit to the Prussians. He drew heavily on Clausewitz's campaign study (among many other works) and also discussed its writer's importance in Germany. He evidently placed a great deal of faith in Clausewitz's judgment, going so far as to side with Clausewitz against Wellington on certain specifics of the campaign.[42]

Chesney observed that his lectures on Waterloo "commenced the course of Military Art and History" at the Staff College between 1864 and 1868. If so, those of his students who remained awake—Chesney's reputation as a lecturer was excellent, but that of his students as students was not—would have become familiar with the Prussian writer's name and significance in Germany, as he cited Clausewitz's *Feldzug von 1815* at least thirty times.[43] They would also have become familiar with the Prussian's approach to the writing of military history, if not with his broader theories.

Chesney himself, however, was clearly familiar with those broader theories. He had read *On War* (albeit in French) and evidently had drawn a great deal from it, chiefly in the area of critical analysis. His major focus on the single campaign of Waterloo, while reflecting British national pride, is also very much in line with Clausewitz's pedagogical theories, as is his strong emphasis on developing the student's capacity for independent thought.[44]

Chesney's work clearly preceded the Franco-Prussian War and was evidently based on research and teaching that predated Prussia's startling military emergence in the Seven Weeks' War of 1866. Thus we can see that there was some interest in Clausewitz in a significant place (the Staff College) even before Prussia/Germany's rise to military preeminence and before *Vom Kriege* was translated into English in 1873.

Chesney also served on the Royal Commission on Military Education from 1868 to 1870. He was an official observer of the Franco-Prussian War and later worked with the secretary of state for war, Edward Cardwell, in pursuit of the latter's famous military reform program. Chesney continued to use Clausewitz in his lectures after leaving Camberley in 1868. Speaking before the Royal United Service Institution in 1871, he discussed Bismarck's strategy, the training of the Prussian general staff, and Clausewitz's theories linking war and policy.[45] He raised the specter of a Germany always ready and willing to resort to the sword in pursuit of political goals, an approach that he saw as a natural extension of Clausewitz's subordination of war to national policy.

Chesney's main concern, however, was organizational, in line with the emphases of the Cardwell reforms:

> Following out the maxims of Clausewitz, as propounded in his warlike philosophy, they have subdivided their responsibility out so completely in time of peace, that when war comes all they have to say by telegraph is "War is declared! prepare!" and everybody makes ready at once . . . instead of personages in high office striving to get every paper referred to their own tables to be there, if possible, decided upon, they put as many things as they can fairly away from them, and make their subordinates responsible for their proper work, by steadfastly discouraging all *unnecessary* appeals to higher authority.

Chesney's greatest interest in the German model was thus the Germans' successful decentralization of authority, which often proved so elusive in the British and, some would argue, American armies. Chesney's concern was the essence of what we have lately come to call *Auftragstaktik*,[46] which became a major focus of British military reformers in the period following the South African War of 1899–1902 and of American reformers following the Vietnam War.

4

Clausewitz in America

There is little reason to question that the foreign military writer best known in the United States in the decades before the Civil War was Antoine-Henri Jomini. Jomini himself occasionally mentioned Clausewitz. Although these references were usually critical, Clausewitz and Archduke Charles of Austria are virtually the only other theorists mentioned in the text of his *Summary of the Art of War*.

A detailed assessment of the impact of Clausewitz and Jomini on each other will probably have to await Jomini's biographer, but Jomini's *Summary*, the book for which he was best known in the United States, was obviously written in part as a reaction to *On War*. He made a number of adjustments in his presentation in order to adapt to what he evidently perceived (but would not acknowledge) as legitimate points in Clausewitz's argument. Thus Jomini's American and British disciples, if they read their master closely, were already receiving an indirect Clausewitzian influence.

The full extent of Jomini's critique (and thus also advertisement) of Clausewitz is often missed because the standard English translation today is the 1862 Mendell/Craighill version, in which there are only two direct references to him. Neither conveys very much beyond Jomini's disdain.[1] The translation with which most American officers trained before the Civil War would have been familiar is the Winship/McLean translation of 1854.[2] This version contained the extensive bibliographical note by Jomini, missing in the later translation, that discussed Clausewitz in more—and highly pejorative—detail. In itself, that discussion still does little to clarify Clausewitz's thoughts, but it is so prominent that one would think that it would have drawn some attention to his book. Evidently not. Perhaps Jomini's description of *Vom Kriege* as "pretentious . . . a learned labyrinth . . . metaphysical and skeptical" was enough to dampen any incipient interest.

The foremost American expert on Jomini was probably Henry Wager Halleck, Lincoln's chief of staff during the Civil War. "Old Brains," as Halleck came to be known, had translated Jomini's *Life of Napoleon* and was intimately familiar with the *Summary*.[3] Halleck was definitely aware of Clausewitz and presumably had some notion of his ideas. His greatest source of inspiration may, however, have been neither Jomini nor Clausewitz, but the Archduke Charles. Halleck's work on the law of war shows no sign of either Clausewitz's name or influence, despite many areas to which his arguments are relevant.[4] On the other hand, Clausewitz's works are listed three times in the chapter bibliographies in Halleck's 1846 *Elements of Military Art and Science*, which repeat none of Jomini's negative remarks.[5] He might also have seen Duparcq's commentary on Clausewitz; he certainly was aware of Duparcq's *Eléments d'art et d'histoire militaire*, since he had lent his name to advertisements of an 1863 translation.[6] Clausewitz's discussion of civil–military relations might not have sat well with him, however: "We must regard . . . particularly the civil and military authorities in the [enemy] state, for if the latter be made entirely subordinate, we may very safely calculate on erroneous combinations."[7]

Despite Jomini's clear dominance in this period, there has been considerable speculation about an early Clausewitzian influence in America. Colonel Thomas Griess, for example, in his 1968 dissertation on Dennis Hart Mahan, observed that certain elements in Mahan's thinking about the relationship between war and policy seemed to go beyond those of his usual guide, Jomini. He questioned whether Mahan might have been influenced by Clausewitz, but this discussion was clearly speculative.[8]

There have also been many suggestions that Lincoln was familiar with Clausewitz's theories, largely because those theories seem to many to be so compatible with his management of the Northern war effort. Nathaniel Wright Stephenson had Lincoln reading Clausewitz in his 1922 biography. So did Carl Sandburg in 1939. Even the fiction writer Gore Vidal, in his novel *Lincoln*, shows the president studying and applying Clausewitz's ideas.[9] Few of these suggestions are accompanied by evidence, however, and some are highly ambiguous.[10] T. Harry Williams accused "the modernist" interpreters of the Civil War of having "insinuated into interpretations of the war the idea that his victorious strategy was inspired by the theories of Clausewitz."[11]

These suggestions have been rejected by others, again without evidence, based on the assumptions that *On War* was unknown in the English-speaking world until 1873 and that Lincoln did not read French or German.[12] Vidal got around the latter problem by having John Hay translate. (Hay was Lincoln's personal secretary and later was secretary of state, from 1898 to 1905.) Hay's own published works, however, make no certain reference to Clausewitz (although Hay's and John G. Nicolay's biography of Lincoln, published in 1890, makes some intriguing statements, discussed later). There were also several German-born generals prominent in the Union army. Julius Stahel (Számvald) was actually Hungarian, a former lieutenant in the Austrian army. Sigel had been a lieutenant in the army of the Grand Duchy of Baden; Schimmelfennig a Prussian engineer officer; and Steinwehr, a lieutenant in the army of Brunswick. Among them, the only likely candidate as purveyor of Clausewitzian ideas to Lincoln is Carl Schurz (1829–1906).

Schurz, a native Prussian, did indeed mention in his memoirs that he had studied both Clausewitz and Jomini, evidently as a young revolutionary in Germany and again in 1861.[13] He had participated as a student in Bonn in the revolution of 1848. Shortly thereafter he came as a refugee to the United States, where he soon joined the anti-slavery movement. As a delegate to the Republican convention of 1860, he supported Lincoln. He was rewarded with a posting as minister to Spain in 1861. From Spain, he offered the president the benefit of his military knowledge: "Some things I know by the personal experience gathered in a campaign before the enemy and of others I have acquired a knowledge by study."[14] He soon returned and became a brigadier general of volunteers, fighting at Second Bull Run, Chancellorsville, Gettysburg, and Chattanooga. Schurz definitely had strong interests in both politics and war, particularly revolutionary war. He had reformist social views, which—as we have seen in the British case—often accompanied an openness to Clausewitz's ideas. He certainly had access to Lincoln.

"Schurz," wrote the British military commentator F. N. Maude to a correspondent in 1928, "was in frequent conference with Lincoln on politico-military matters just when McClellan was starting for the peninsula. This of course is not conclusive proof, but to my mind it helps to account for Lincoln's clear grasp of the fact that war is a phase of political action." Maude also saw Clausewitz's hand in a dispute between Lincoln and McClellan in which the president forced his general to organize corps-level headquarters: Although McClellan was "familiar with the army corps as the French then understood it . . . he apparently was not familiar with Clausewitz's reasoning on the maximum number of divisions that can be handled, as such, through a single headquarters without the imposition of corps headquarters."[15]

In the absence of better evidence, however, this argument tells us less about Lincoln, Clausewitz, Schurz, and the strategy of the Civil War than it does about the inherent uncertainties in the transmission of ideas. McClellan's reluctance to establish intermediate headquarters appears to have been in actuality a question of timing and personalities rather than of military theory. As for war and politics, the statement that "war is a continuation of politics by other means" is important not because Clausewitz said it but because it reflects a fundamental reality. That reality would have been obvious to a professional politician in the throes of a political crisis that had led to war.

What is surprising is not this insight but that Lincoln should have had the self-confidence and strength of will to pursue it over the resistance of men with what must have seemed far better credentials than his own. Although such strength of character is consistent with Clausewitz's view of "military genius" (which has much more to do with personality than with intellect), we can be sure that it did not come out of any book, and most assuredly not at second hand. Lincoln hardly needed to read Clausewitz to have taken the approach he did, any more than Grant needed to read him to be a near-perfect exemplar of Clausewitz's concept of the ideal general. Lincoln's own writings on military subjects are couched in Jominian terms.

Grant's generalship is frequently called Clausewitzian, as often in a reproachful tone as in praise. Although the term is correct insofar as it is applied to Grant's temperament and Clausewitz's description of military genius, most such comparisons have emphasized the concept of absolute war and likened it to the brand of total war waged by Grant and Sherman in 1864–65. However, Grant's subtle perception of the interrelationship of war and politics provides a much better basis for connecting his ideas with those of Clausewitz. "If [to Grant] the Civil War was politics by other means, then Reconstruction was in some sense a continuation of the struggle to achieve through political means the aims for which the war was fought."[16]

U.S. Army War College historian Jay Luvaas has poked some fun at *post hoc ergo propter hoc* attempts to impute Union strategy to the Prussian philosopher's influence. For demonstration purposes, he invented a letter from Grant indicating that his actions had been influenced by conversations with a staff officer of German origin, who had quoted Clausewitz at some length. Luvaas's point, of course, was to demonstrate the difficulty of tracing the transmission of intellectual concepts, especially ones that are essentially common sense and thus liable to frequent reinvention.[17]

The close parallels between Clausewitz's more extreme notions and W. T. Sherman's conduct of war have often been noted.[18] (B. H. Liddell Hart, who admired Sherman and continually attacked the Prussian, naturally made no such comparison.)[19] The intellectual Sherman would seem a much better candidate for that kind of speculation than either Lincoln or Grant, but it seems that no one has ever suggested that he had read *On War*.

In John Hay's and John G. Nicolay's biography of Lincoln, published in 1890, there is one passage that comes tantalizingly close to establishing some kind of a connection between Clausewitz's views and those of Lincoln's closest circle. Discussing the disaster of the first battle of Bull Run, Hay and Nicolay observed that

Historical judgement of war is subject to an inflexible law, either very imperfectly understood or very constantly lost sight of. Military writers love to fight over the campaigns of history exclusively by the rules of the professional chess-board, always subordinating, often totally ignoring, the element of politics. This is a radical error. Every war is begun, dominated, and ended by political considerations; without a nation, without a government, without money or credit, without popular enthusiasm which furnishes volunteers, or public support which endures conscription, there could be no army and no war—neither beginning nor end of methodical hostilities. War and politics, campaign and statecraft, are Siamese twins, inseparable and interdependent; and to talk of military operations without the direction and interference of an Administration is as absurd as to plan a campaign without recruits, pay, or rations.

Applied to the Bull Run campaign, this law of historical criticism analyses and fixes the responsibilities of government and commanders with easy precision. When Lincoln, on June 29, assembled his council of war, the commanders, as military experts, correctly decided that the existing armies—properly handled—could win a victory at Manassas and a victory at Winchester, at or near the same time. General Scott correctly objected that these victories, if won, would not be decisive; and that in a military point of view it would be wiser to defer any offensive campaign until the following autumn. Here the President and the Cabinet, as political experts, intervened, and on their part decided, correctly, that the public temper would not admit of such a delay. Thus the administration was responsible for the forward movement, Scott was responsible for the combined strategy of the two armies, McDowell for the conduct of the Bull Run battle, Patterson for the escape of Johnston, and Fate for the panic; for the opposing forces were equally raw, equally undisciplined, and as a whole fought with equal courage and gallantry.[20]

This passage clearly reflects the practical experience of the war, and it is easy to ascribe the close parallels to Clausewitz's exposition on war and politics to the very nature of the idea being expressed. The reference to a "law of historical criticism" and the ensuing analysis, however, is so redolent of Clausewitz's discussion of "critical analysis" that some firm connection is easy to suspect. But such a suspicion must remain only that, for there is no clear reference to the Prussian theorist. In any case, by 1890 Clausewitz's works were readily available in English. There is no evi- dence that this analysis reflects the conscious thought process of Lincoln's cabinet in 1861.

Nonetheless, Halleck's references, Schurz's knowledge, Jomini's com- ments on Clausewitz (especially as reported in the 1854 translation), the 1843 translation of Clausewitz's study of the Russian campaign, Wel- lington's "famous" response to Clausewitz's *Campaign of 1815*, the French translations and commentary, Mitchell's work in England, and the appear- ance of the 1835 article on Clausewitz in Britain and in the *Military and Naval Magazine of the United States* make untenable the assumption that

Clausewitz's name and important aspects of his theories were inaccessible to American political and military figures in the Civil War era. Thus a Clausewitzian influence on Lincoln or on others in his circle remains a real possibility. In the absence of conclusive evidence one way or the other, the question must remain open.

5

The English Translation of *On War*

The specific reasons that Colonel J. J. (James John) Graham (1808–83) undertook to publish a translation of *Vom Kriege* in 1873 are unknown.[1] There is no contemporary evidence—other than its timing, which may well be coincidental—that the translation of *Vom Kriege* was motivated by German military successes or by Moltke's praise of Clausewitz. There is no internal evidence that the events of 1870–71 were the motivating factor or any evidence of an interest in Moltke; in fact, neither Graham nor the contemporary reviewers even mentioned Moltke.[2] The assumption of a link between Moltke's influence and the translation of Clausewitz derives from F. N. Maude's frequent discussion of Moltke in his introduction and notes to the 1908 edition. Graham may have begun his work much earlier. It is in fact conceivable (although it cannot be demonstrated) that Graham was the author of the 1835 review of *On War*. There are similarities in style; Graham was in England at the time; and he held the same social views as those expressed by the anonymous reviewer. Further, even though Graham's 1873 work certainly had long-term importance, sales of the book were minuscule. There is thus no reason to conclude that the timing of this publication represented any great upsurge in British interest in Clausewitz's ideas.

Graham himself is an obscure character, surprisingly so. His father, his son, and at least one of his grandsons were generals, but J. J. was put on half-pay in 1842 and never returned to active service in the British army. He entered Sandhurst in 1822, served in the West Indies as deputy judge advocate, and evidently served briefly as an engineer. From 1832 to 1835 he took civilian employment as secretary and treasurer to the South-Eastern Railway Company in England and then returned to the army as a captain in the Seventieth (Surrey) Regiment of Foot. He was involved in a colonization scheme in Canada in 1851, apparently aimed at settling British veterans there. In June 1854 he was promoted to lieutenant-colonel on the unattached list (i.e., he was not attached to any British regiment) and then served as military secretary to Sir Robert Hussey Vivian, commander of the British "Turkish Contingent" in the Crimean War. For the latter service he was awarded the Turkish Medal and also the Sultan's Order of the Medjidie, Third Class. He sold his commission in 1858.[3]

Graham's book *Elementary History of the Progress of the Art of War* (1858) is a rather sophisticated work.[4] Perhaps it was too sophisticated, particularly for the distinctly anti-intellectual tastes of the British army in this period. His other major work, *Military Ends and Moral Means* (1864), is a classic statement of the reformist critique of the British army. Its title amply conveys his concern with moral factors in war, and his organizational proposals are much like those of John Mitchell. By this time, however, such views were becoming widespread. In reading Graham's earlier work, one is tempted to see a Clausewitzian influence, but this is a hazardous approach to be avoided as a matter of policy unless there is a proven prior connection. Neither of his two substantive books mentions Clausewitz explicitly. Graham cited Jomini several times with approval but was by no means dogmatically attached to his teachings. Like most British military writers, Graham was decidedly eclectic.

From a business point of view, the publication of *On War* was a failure. Only 254 copies were printed in 1873. Of these, 21 went to Graham, and 32 were sent out as free review copies. Of the rest, 192 were still languishing in the publisher's hands in 1877. For some unknown reason, Trübner printed a further 440 copies in that year, and 572 were still in the warehouse in 1885.[5] The book drew no substantial audience and Graham's material rewards thus appear to have been few. He was appointed a Military Knight of Windsor in 1877, but this was not much of an honor and was unrelated to his publishing ventures. "Military Knights" was a new term for an ancient order that had been called the "Poor Knights" until around 1833. Not actually a knighthood, membership was granted as a form of relief for indigent retired officers.[6] Graham evidently lived the rest of his life in quarters provided at Windsor. He died there in 1883.

Whether Graham's work was a success as a translation is worthy of more debate. Peter Paret has frequently criticized Graham's work, and his dismissive views appear to have been widely accepted. In his "Bibliographical Survey" (1965), Paret wrote that "the many inaccuracies of the Graham–Maude translation have often been noted," referring to the 1908 reissue of Graham's work "edited" by F. N. Maude. He cited as evidence a 1908 review in the *Journal of the Royal United Service Institution*.[7] That review, however, made reference only to some typographical errors in the original 1873 edition and complained mildly that Graham had adhered too closely to the German phrasing. The criticisms were of Maude's claims to have edited the work when in fact the text was identical to Graham's. The only other complaint was about the expense of the new edition, given its "great importance to the Army." There were very few criticisms made of Graham's work before the 1960s, and Paret cannot be regarded as an entirely impartial commentator, since he was already at work on a new translation.[8]

By 1976 Graham's translation of *Vom Kriege* into Victorian English had clearly outlived its usefulness, and the highly readable translation of *On War* published by Paret and Michael Howard in that year was a great achievement.[9] In saying that, however, it is not necessary to denigrate the Graham version. Although it certainly contains some obscurities and errors, Graham's edition is superior to the most recent translation in at least one regard: It has a useful index.[10] At some points it also more accurately reflects the sometimes lurid language of the German original.[11] Graham took none of the liberties with Clausewitz's ideas that T. Miller Maguire did in his 1909 translation.[12] His adherence to the German sentence structure may not make for easy reading, but it was evidently rooted in the somewhat self-effacing personality that also led him to avoid any intrusive commentary (like Maude's) or insertion of his own views into Clausewitz's work. Paret has correctly noted elsewhere that a translation is inevitably an interpretation as well,[13] but his consciousnes of this truth may have led him to color the work with too much of his own cool intellectualism. As Michael Howard put it, in clarifying the German text, "We may occasionally have overdone it, like overcleaning a picture."[14]

The most reasonable criticisms of the Graham translation are not so much of the translation itself as of the third German edition from which Graham worked, which had been corrupted to some degree by its German editors. This criticism applies as well to all of the other translations made before 1976.

Graham's work also includes as an appendix Clausewitz's "Instruction for the Crown Prince," which is absent from the newer translation. Although this is sometimes denigrated as being mere instructions for a child, it is useful to remember that the child was the heir apparent of the Hohenzollern dynasty. That family demanded a high degree of military professionalism from its sons, as well it might, since the fortunes of Prussia were uniquely dependent on the military talents of its ruling house. Unfortunately, although the "Instruction" is a valuable document in that it provides clues to the evolution of Clausewitz's ideas, it has more often served as a source of confusion for readers who believe it to be an accurate summary of the larger and later work, *Vom Kriege.*

Despite competition, the Graham translation would remain the standard English version for over a century. Roger Ashley Leonard's 1967 *A Short Guide to Clausewitz on War* was based on it, as was Anatol Rapoport's

1968 abridged edition of *On War*.[15] Graham's was an achievement that merits some respect.

In any case, the Graham translation is also a historical document in its own right. Historians should not make the mistake of citing the most recent translation, however excellent it may be, when discussing figures whose understanding of Clausewitz would have come from Graham.

6

Assessment, 1815–1873

The publication of On War in English was one small reflection of the broad new interest in the German military system motivated by the outcomes of the wars of 1864 and 1866, and especially the humiliation of France in 1870–71. There may be some truth to the view that it was Moltke's praise that drew British attention to Clausewitz, but this translation was also the logical outcome of a long-standing interest in Clausewitz in Britain. Nonetheless, the publication of Graham's work did not immediately lead to any noteworthy surge in Clausewitz studies.

Most of the occasional bursts of enthusiasm for Clausewitz, like most bursts of military reform, have been motivated by military embarrassments or defeats. Certainly this has been the case in the post–Vietnam War United States. Why did the specifically British humiliations of the Crimean War (1853–56) not stimulate a British interest in Clausewitz? To this I would answer speculatively that the relatively low military prestige of Prussia in the 1840s and 1850s and the continuing active self-promotion of Jomini, who lived on until 1869, would have helped to keep Clausewitz in the background. In any case, with the exception of the Crimean War there was little enough stimulus for any British interest in military writing. As Egerton put it in 1851, "The literature of England has been pronounced to be scantily supplied with the article of military history. The deficiency may be traced to an absence of demand arising from causes by no means to be regretted, and which every Englishman must wish should be perpetual."[1] Of course, Ellesmere was dismissing in a rather cavalier fashion the constant colonial warfare waged by Victorian Britain, which kept its unit-level officers the most experienced soldiers in Europe.

Works in French were also much more accessible to British military men than were works in German, and *On War* was available in French after 1851. It is worth noting here that almost all of the English translations of Jomini's works were done by Americans, among whom a knowledge of any foreign language would have been less common. That German was still an exotic language even to the British editors who ran the 1835 review may be evidenced by the fact that both words of the book's title were misspelled, as "*Von Kiege.*"

It would be an error, however, to overstress the respect in which Jomini was held in England. Much of what is frequently considered Jominian is in fact derived from Archduke Charles's work. A committee of the Corps of Royal Engineers, writing in the 1840s, took Jomini severely to task for a perceived anti-British bias.[2] Certainly Jomini was much better known and more widely read than Clausewitz, but even though the Swiss theorist took Wellington's side in the debate over Waterloo,[3] Egerton—writing on behalf of and evidently at the instigation of the duke—referred to "the pompous charlatanerie of Jomini." John Mitchell also expressed disappointment in Jomini's works, which, he noted, were "very far below" his reputation.[4] Neither Egerton nor Wellington (nor any other pre–World War I British writer that I am aware of) ever sounded any similar note concerning Clausewitz, even when disputing his conclusions or complaining of the mental effort required to read his major work.

The fact is that most British writers on war were extremely eclectic, drawing freely on their own experiences and on whatever authors they happened to have read. They were most impressed by their own home-grown heroes: Marlborough, Wellington, and Napier, who were themselves by no means unsophisticated. They were skeptical of any "theoretical" approach to the study of war for many of the same reasons that Clausewitz was skeptical of Jomini and his less advanced predecessors, Lloyd and Bülow. Given the confusion that has always arisen from Clausewitz's own work, perhaps they had a point.

Jomini did, however, make considerable efforts to come to terms with the question of sea power and with Britain's unique strategic role, sharing an appreciation of those factors with Napoleon III. Since Clausewitz almost completely ignored these concerns, his work may not have seemed as relevant. (A number of later writers—most notably the Englishman Julian Corbett, the German Baron Curt von Maltzahn, and the American George Meyers—would nevertheless find it profitable to adapt Clausewitz's ideas to the naval arena.) Although there was a tremendous amount of interest in Britain in the land campaigns of the American Civil War,[5] it would be the major British effort on land in South Africa (1899-1902) that would modify this navalist orientation. (British strategy naturally remained predominantly maritime.) Beside that, the greater British failures in the Crimea were largely logistical and managerial in nature. Tactical and strategic mistakes were less striking, even if they prompted some stirring poetry. The need for a Clausewitz simply was not widely felt in Britain before the humiliations in South Africa.

Another factor that might have made Clausewitz less interesting to British military men was his concern with the "nation in arms." It is ironic, of course, that an officer of the conservative king of Prussia should be the one to base his theories on the most radical legacy of the revolutionary period, whereas Napoleon's own staff officer and interpreter, Jomini, should aim his theories at the professional officer corps of essentially eighteenth century–style armies. Most of the Britons who cited Clausewitz showed some streak of social radicalism. Wellington was obviously an exception (although his friends Ellesmere and Liverpool showed at least some openness to both *On War* and reform arguments), but his interest in Clausewitz's work stemmed from essentially personal concerns. The sources of the duke's military conservatism are complex, however. It certainly was not rooted in any blind faith in the military capacity of the British officer corps, as his own sardonic comments show: His greatest hope was that the list of British generals would be as frightening to the enemy as it was to himself.

These various factors may account for the dominance of conservative military thought in Britain before 1870. On the other hand, we have seen that there was, in fact, a fair degree of attention paid to Clausewitz in England between 1835 and 1873. His work certainly was known within Britain's small and close-knit military community, and in important places like Wellington's circle and the Staff College, well before the Franco-Prussian War. Clausewitz's studies of the campaigns of 1812 and 1815 (not to mention the "free rendering" of his work on the campaign of 1813) appeared in English long before they were translated into French. These studies were by no means free of their author's more abstract theoretical concepts, some of which were discussed quite explicitly. As historical works they were praised by Mitchell, Liverpool, Ellesmere, and Chesney and were given a somewhat more ambiguous endorsement by Wellington himself. They clearly had an influence on Chesney's historical writing and teaching at the Staff College. Given the importance of Clausewitz's pedagogical and historical views to his overall military theory, these campaign studies must be considered significant, but *On War* was known also.

Thus Clausewitz may have played a greater role in British military thinking than has been recognized, particularly in terms of the writing and teaching of military history.

Why then is it the conventional wisdom that Clausewitz's work was ignored? I suspect that there are two fundamental sources of this misperception. The first is the eclectic nature of British military thought and its skepticism regarding "theory." As Mitchell said, "Had Clausewitz written in England, indeed, the chances are that not five copies of his work would ever have sold, and that he himself would have been abused as a theorist by persons of such high intellect as to suppose the word a term of reproach."[6] There was as well perhaps a nationalistic reluctance of British authors to align themselves too closely with any foreign thinker on war, especially the militarily unfashionable Germans. No clearly "Clausewitzian" influence appears because Clausewitz was rarely cited by name and his influence was thoroughly diluted and always transformed by each writer's particular experience and idiosyncrasies. This, rather than slavish acceptance and repetition, is, after all, what Clausewitz had prescribed.

Detecting the actual influence of Clausewitz remains a problem even when dealing with modern writers. It is hard enough to pinpoint Clausewitz's impact on British authors whom we know to have read him; it would be harder still to find it in the work of those who kept this fact to themselves. Although Clausewitz is more frequently mentioned by name today, most references are very general. It is rare to find any actual quotation from his works other than the ubiquitous (and often misunderstood or misrepresented) "War is a continuation of policy by other means."

Today, of course, Clausewitz is a name to conjure with. Such would not have been the case in England before the Franco-Prussian War. Most writers on the British army in this period have noted its intense parochialism and anti-intellectualism. Reference to any foreign book, especially a theoretical work like *On War*, might have raised hackles in many quarters. A failure to name it does not necessarily, therefore, imply a lack of reading. It is hardly likely, however, that any intelligent man could read *On War* without picking up something from the experience.

Second, modern students of war have tended to impose their own preconceptions concerning the nature of any likely Clausewitzian influence on a period before these conceptions had jelled. Strachan, for instance, writes that the evident British lack of interest stemmed from the "unacceptability of Clausewitz's emphasis on battle as strategy's central object and his belief that generals, far from embracing limited warfare as the Jominians wished, were only restrained from total war by political expediency." I would argue that this is a view of Clausewitz that is based on only one facet of his work, and a selective perception of that. (In any case, battle is only the means, not the object, in Clausewitz's view of strategy.) This attitude is derived in some measure from Basil Liddell Hart's later misrepresentation of Clausewitz as the "Mahdi of Mass" and the apostle of total war. The tendency to seek Clausewitz's influence in this or that "strategy" betrays a curiously lingering desire to use his theories in a prescriptive, Jominian manner. *On War* prescribes no strategy.

British rejection of the centrality of battle in Clausewitz's definition of strategy might simply be due to a failure to grasp the subtlety of that theorist's view of the role of violence in war: Clausewitz postulated no requirement for decisive battle, demanding only an awareness of the possibility. On the other hand, it may result from the fact that British military operations—owing to the maritime form of British power projection, the nature of the coalition warfare in which Britain was usually involved, the salient economic elements thereof, and the scarcity of British military manpower—almost always emphasized delay and attrition over offensive combat. (Marlborough was an exception, of course, but the high human cost of his victories was also a factor in his political demise.) Placing battle at the center of their definition of strategy would have called for a greater degree of subtlety than is usual—or wise—in practical doctrine. British definitions would not reflect Clausewitz's until after the South African War.

One of the central themes in Clausewitz's works is their emphasis on the specific: To be useful, all military analysis must be based on local, temporary, personal, and political factors and placed firmly in the context of what Clausewitz called "the spirit of the age." Most of the early British writers who paid attention to Clausewitz also demonstrated a strong sensitivity to Britain's unique strategic situation. Certainly Mitchell did, and the 1835 reviewer strove to find Clausewitz's relevance to Britain. To see Clausewitz in this recognition of Britain's peculiar military position would be unjustified, but no more so than many other writers' attempts to find a Clausewitzian influence in this doctrine or that strategy. The predispositions of his readers are probably the major element in any theorist's popularity. Still, the same recognition appears clearly in later British writers who were definitely influenced by *On War*, notably Colonel G. F. R. Henderson (1854–1903), General Sir Frederick Maurice (1841–1912), and the historian and journalist Spenser Wilkinson (1853–1937), in an age when there were stronger pressures to adapt to continental military models.

In contrast, the relationship between war and policy—today considered so central to Clausewitz's thought—was accepted as such a commonplace by British thinkers that this aspect of the theory in *On War* drew little attention. Mitchell's and Wellington's discussions demonstrate some of the reasons why. Although they seldom thought to challenge the constitutional subordination of the military to the political authorities, the disdain, contempt, and sometimes outright hostility of Britain's soldiers concerning politicians and politics tended for a long time to dampen interest—or at least public discussion among soldiers—concerning this facet of Clausewitz's thinking. It would not become a major focus in the English-speaking world until civilian strategists (like Spenser Wilkinson, Liddell Hart, and Bernard Brodie) began to play a larger role in the development of military theory. Nonetheless, Wellington's critique of Clausewitz's *Campaign of 1815* shows that the duke had as subtle an appreciation of the relationship of war and policy as the philosopher ever developed.

In any case, Clausewitz was clearly known and discussed in Britain. There is no corresponding evidence of any American interest in Clausewitz. Indeed, it is difficult to find any significant American reference to him before World War I. One can only speculate on the reasons for this, but they may lie in the differing ethos of the British and American officer corps. British army officers tended to play the role of enthusiastic amateur. They were often men of affairs with outside interests and often outside incomes. The small coterie of American West Pointers, on the other hand, tended toward a very narrow professionalism. For them, the "cookbook" approach of Jomini must have seemed much more utilitarian, and Clausewitz's insistence on bringing politics into strategy would have been even more repellant to the American soldier than to the British. Clausewitz's interest in popular warfare would have stimulated the suspicions of a small professional officer corps whose interests (both patriotic and selfish) were always threatened by the widespread but largely fallacious American faith in the militia tradition.

To seek such explanations may be digging too deep, however. The language barrier, the military obscurity of Germany before 1866, Jomini's rude comments, and the anti-intellectualism general among military officers may well have been the decisive factors.

In any case, the slowness with which Anglo-American military thinkers came to appreciate Clausewitz should not be taken as proof of their backwardness. Even in Germany, Jomini's approach would remain dominant until the era of Moltke. The original printing of fifteen hundred copies of *Vom Kriege* had still not sold out twenty years later.[7] Such diverse German military thinkers as Karl Wilhelm von Willisen and Friedrich Wilhelm Rüstow were disciples of Jomini, and as late as the 1880s, Albrecht von Boguslawsky was arguing that there was no essential conflict between the thought of the Swiss theorist and that of Clausewitz.[8] Boguslawsky was still publishing German translations of the *Summary* in 1885. Otto von Bismarck, that seemingly most Clausewitzian of statesmen, observed in 1889 that "to my shame I have to confess that I have never read Clausewitz and have known little more about him than that he was a meritorious general."[9]

II

To the First Golden Age of Clausewitz Studies in English: 1874–1914

The standard interpretations of Clausewitz's reception in Great Britain and the United States between 1873 and 1914 are somewhat contradictory: First, there is the belief that the study of Clausewitz began only after the German triumph over France in the Franco-Prussian War of 1870/71. Second, there is an assumption that Moltke's praise of Clausewitz then led to intense study of his work; the publication of Graham's translation in 1873 is taken as evidence of this development. Third, there is the rather contrary assumption that Clausewitz remained largely unappreciated until World War I, a view stated very emphatically by Michael Howard's student Azar Gat in 1989. In the United States and Great Britain "on the eve of the First World War," said Gat, "Jomini's dominance remained unchallenged."[1] Russell Weigley traced British and American interest in *On War* only to the period of World War I itself.[2]

Finally, and in contrast with Gat's opinion, is Basil Liddell Hart's view:

> One is inclined to find [the source of Britain's errors leading to the carnage of the First World War] . . . in the military mode of thought inspired by Clausewitz. That we adopted it is only too clear from an analysis of our pre-war military textbooks, of the strategical memoranda, drawn up by the General Staff at home and in France during the war, and of the diaries and memoirs of the dominant military authorities published since the war. They are full of tags that can be traced to Clausewitz, if often exaggerated in transfer.[3]

Liddell Hart's views were echoed more recently by Weigley: "The first English-speaking generation to read Clausewitz got the impression that he believed victory is the only object of war, that when the guns begin firing, diplomacy abdicates to military strategy."[4]

Several of these assumptions were challenged in the previous chapter. The first is obviously inaccurate. There is little evidence to support the second; there is no sign that the 1873 translation was motivated by Moltke's comments or of a significantly heightened interest in Clausewitz before the 1890s. Gat's view that Jomini was unchallenged—and that his theories were dominant in 1914—is flatly wrong. Clausewitz was well known in Great Britain in the decade and a half before World War I, and a good case could be made that his theories had come to dominate British military thought after the South African War of 1899–1902. Liddell Hart's statement, however, is at best misleading. He has confused the broad impact of the German military model (and the ideas of certain French thinkers) with the direct influence of *On War* in Britain. Many of the French and German theorists most influential in Germany, Britain, and the United States before 1914—and those most directly involved in the kind of thinking that Liddell Hart condemned—had explicitly rejected key aspects of Clausewitz's thought. Weigley's argument is disputable on two counts: The World War I generation was not the first to read Clausewitz, and those who read *On War* (rather than only secondary sources) seem to have gotten no such false impression.

In the United States, it was primarily the German military model, rather than Jominian thought, that dominated American military thinking after 1871. Still, direct references to Clausewitz by American soldiers were few, far between, usually at second hand, and generally unclear, although *On War* seems to have been known to intellectual circles in the American navy.[5] Part II is therefore concerned almost exclusively with Great Britain.

7

Prelude: The Study of Clausewitz Before the South African War

The first major research question that arises concerns the attention that Clausewitz received in the wake of the Franco-Prussian War of 1870/71. The conventional wisdom is that interest was greatly stimulated at that time by Moltke's statements concerning the importance of Clausewitz in shaping his own strategic conceptions. It is difficult, however, to find much contemporary evidence to support this view. The focus on German military thinking that certainly does appear in England in this period is on organizational matters like the Prussian reserve system and the general staff, not strategy or military philosophy.[1] In several English-language studies of military education done about this time, no mention is made of any theorist, not Jomini or Clausewitz or anyone else. It seems significant in this regard that Moltke's own works on strategy were never translated into English; the German general staff's compilation of his *Precepts of War* was (partially) translated only in 1935, and this translation was never published.[2] As another example, Wilhelm Blume's *Campaign 1870–1871* was published in Berlin in 1872 and translated into English the same year; his *Strategie: Eine Studie* never appeared in English.[3] Although Clausewitz dealt at some length with the concept of the "nation in arms," organizational topics like staffs and reserve systems are conspicuously absent in *Vom Kriege*. This may be one reason that Graham's 1873 translation sold so poorly.

The British soldier-writer Colonel F. N. Maude, R. E., claimed to have been introduced to Clausewitz as a very young man by a German officer immediately following the war of 1870/71. Other observers (most notably the American generals Philip Sheridan and William B. Hazen) gave no evidence of this.[4] Emory Upton (1839–81), probably the most important military theorist in the post–Civil War United States and an admirer of the German general staff, never mentioned Clausewitz. About the only quantitative measure of interest available is sales of Graham's translation: By December 1880, only 39 copies had actually been sold, although a total of 92 had been distributed in one way or another. In the next five years another 30 were sold. In 1885, 350 unbound copies were "sold as waste." The remaining copies sold at the rate of 10 to 20 per year through the end of the century.[5] The book would not reissued until 1908.

Of course, many of these copies of *On War* may have gone to libraries, and the British community of military intellectuals was a small one. Some would have read *On War* in the original German or perhaps in one of the French translations. It is thus hard to judge just how large or significant Clausewitz's British readership was. It seems clear that there was no noteworthy surge of interest in *On War* as an immediate result of the new German military preeminence in Europe, only a slowly spreading awareness of its teachings and of the differences between Clausewitz's approach and Jomini's.

A key question, although one not susceptible to a clear answer, is at what point Clausewitz began to supersede Jomini as the preeminent military theorist in England and the United States. It is perhaps worth noting in this regard that the ninth edition of the *Encyclopædia Britannica* (1878–88) gives Jomini an article of his own, whereas Clausewitz has none; in fact, the German writer is not even listed in the index. Nonetheless, he is discussed in the articles "Battle" and "War." In the first, he is described as "the greatest of all theoretical writers on war" and, in the second, as "the most profound of all military students."[6]

The articles were written, respectively, by Colonel Charles Chesney, R. E., and Colonel J. F. Maurice, R.A. Each held at some point in his career the position of professor of military history at the Staff College. That both writers were from technical branches may also be significant. Their comments in the *Britannica* are in themselves hardly proof that the Staff College was a hotbed of Clausewitzian studies, but they are interesting. Products of the Staff College overwhelmingly dominated the British army by 1914.[7]

Charles Chesney was discussed in Chapter 3. His statement in the *Britannica* regarding Clausewitz echoes similar observations in his earlier *Waterloo Lectures*. His brother, Sir George Tomkyn Chesney (1830–95), wrote a fascinating and highly alarmist article in 1871 describing—from a vantage point fifty years in the future—a successful German invasion of Britain. Such studies were something of a staple in British popular military writing; such invasion books date back at least to Henry Lloyd (1720–83) and probably to the period of the Armada. But George Chesney's stands out. It reads in places somewhat like H. G. Wells's *War of the Worlds*.

Chesney's description of the price of defeat is staggering, with Britain shorn of its empire, commerce, and industry and reduced to utter pauperism and insignificance. Chesney blamed the hypothetical defeat on Britain's heroic but thoroughly unprofessional land forces.[8] The Chesneys thus appear to be solidly in the reformist tradition of the English readers of Clausewitz.

Although a number of authors showed some interest in Clausewitz in the 1880s and early 1890s (notably F. N. Maude, G. F. R. Henderson, and Spenser Wilkinson), the English military writer most prominent at the time, Sir Edward B. Hamley (1824–93), was clearly a disciple of Jomini and Archduke Charles. Hamley had been Chesney's predecessor as professor of military history at the Staff College and was commandant from 1870 to 1877. His most important book, *Operations of War* (1866), was frequently revised and updated. It was standard reading at the Staff College until World War I and would still be on the reading list at the U.S. Naval War College as late as 1934.[9] Hamley himself, however, became a laughingstock in the army as a result of his pompous and inept attempts to function as the "strategist" for Sir Garnet Wolseley's Egyptian campaign of 1882.

Despite Hamley's apparent intellectual dominance, a significant Clausewitzian influence could be found operating at Camberley even after Chesney's retirement in 1868. Colonel (later Major-General) John Frederick Maurice (1841–1912) was professor of military art and history at the Staff College from 1885 to 1892, and author of the 1888 *Britannica* article on "War" just cited. He has been characterized as "one of the most articulate spokesmen for the Wolseley Ring," the reformist military clique that struggled for control of the British army from 1873 to the South African War. He was, in fact, Sir Garnet Wolseley's best friend, his "second pen."[10]

Maurice seems to have had an engaging personality and, in the earlier part of his career, was a highly capable field officer with considerable combat experience in colonial expeditions. As he aged, however, he grew impractical, argumentative, and absentminded to the point of becoming a figure of fun. In 1897, a sympathetic but realistic Wolseley asserted that Maurice was "incapable of weighing [his] own capacity" for command but "much abler with his pen . . . than ever."[11]

Maurice first came to prominence in 1871 when, as a subaltern and instructor in tactics at Sandhurst, he won the £100 Wellington Prize essay competition on the subject "The System of Field Manoeuvres Best Adapted for Enabling Our Troops to Meet a Continental Army."[12] (Colonel Wolseley won second prize.) At what point Maurice first read Clausewitz is unclear; although the bibliography for this essay listed many works in German, *On War* was not included. It is therefore open to speculation whether the many "Clausewitzian" elements in his analysis reflect the influence of *On War* (either directly or via other writers) or a predisposition to the acceptance of its arguments. Such elements include his views on the chain of command, his focus on the destruction of the enemy's will to fight, and his ideas concerning the relationship between the offensive and the defensive. Despite his admiration of the German army and his knowledge of its many offensive successes in the just-concluded war with France, he maintained a healthy skepticism of both the German organizational model and of purely offensive prescriptions. Maurice recommended pursuit of the strategic offensive, but by means of defensive tactics.

Maurice enlarged his 1888 *Britannica* article and added a long bibliographical discussion. He then published it in 1891 as a book entitled simply *War*, "one of the best known of his purely military works" and "one of the most famous works on the subject of war published in England during the nineteenth century."[13] Although Maurice repeated his high praise for *On War* in a number of places, a cursory examination of the book would indicate that it is essentially a Jominian work; the definitions of strategy and tactics come straight out of Hamley's *Operations of War*. It is clear that Maurice, like the earlier English writers discussed by Hew Strachan, rejected the centrality of battle in Clausewitz's definition of strategy.

A closer examination, however, reveals some rather un-Jominian features in his thought. Maurice raised the question as to whether strategy, like tactics, changed over time. In an extensive discussion, he concluded that it did,[14] crediting the changes not only to technological developments but also to evolution in "the very spirit, discipline, and organization by which [armies] are held together." This distinctly Clausewitzian perception was accompanied by explicit references to Clausewitz on the role of military theory and the purpose of military education. Throughout, Maurice stressed the importance of considering the specifics of each case. He also echoed Clausewitz in his skepticism regarding complex stratagems and maneuvers. Although not a "Clausewitzian" as modern writers have defined the term, Maurice was definitely drawing heavily on the philosophy of *On War*, which, judging by his critical comments concerning Graham's translation, he had studied in German.[15]

Maurice's comments on the uses of military history appear to have been drawn directly from *On War*. He stressed the superiority of a "close and intimate study" of one campaign over a broad superficial coverage, the role of theory in educating an officer's judgment, and the need for his student staff officers to develop a capacity for independent thought. In this latter aspect he was quite different from Hamley.[16] Military history was, he wrote, "worthless except in so far as it places the man who reads it in the position of those whose actions he is studying, and therefore enables him to profit by their experience, and to learn both from their failures, their misfortunes, and their successes."[17]

8

In the Wake of the South African War

The event that cleared the way for Clausewitz's real rise to eminence in Britain was the South African War of 1899–1902. The poor British performance in this war led to many important military improvements, most notably the famous "Haldane Reforms" of Richard Burton, first Viscount Haldane, appointed secretary of war in 1905. Undertaken were such important and concrete reforms as the creation of a true general staff, replacement of the old post of commander in chief by a genuine chief of the general staff, integration of the old "volunteers" with the regular army in a new "territorial" force, and the creation of a modern and deployable field army, which appeared in 1914 as the British Expeditionary Force (BEF) in France. The widespread reformist mood included serious dissatisfaction with prevailing military theories. Both the nature of war itself and the particular matter of "strategy" became prime subjects of debate.[1]

The resulting interest in Clausewitz was soon reinforced by praise for the Prussian thinker issuing from Britain's allies in the Far East, the Japanese commanders victorious over Russia in the war of 1904/5. Clausewitz was well known in Japan. *Vom Kriege*'s publisher, Dümmlers Verlag, sent an advanced copy of the fifth edition to the Japanese general Count Tamemoto Kuroki (1844–1923) in 1904. Kuroki, victor over Russia in the battle of the Yalu, responded that Clausewitz's work had already been translated into Japanese and had been a significant influence on Japan's conduct of the war. Just which work of Clausewitz—and which translation—Kuroki was referring to is problematical. Some Japanese officers being trained in Germany became familiar with Clausewitz around 1887.[2]

Indications of the Japanese faith in Clausewitz reached England by a number of routes, but probably the most widely read report appeared in the London *Times* on 23 March 1905, written by the *Times*'s military correspondent and entitled "À la Clausewitz."[3]

The correspondent was Colonel Thomas à Court Repington, a former student of Maurice's at the Staff College. Spenser Wilkinson later characterized him as "the best staff officer in the Army." A soldier of great promise, he had been widely seen as a potential chief of staff.[4] Repington seems to have been more than a bit rash and indiscreet, however. In particular, he had the poor sense to get involved with a married woman. The ensuing scandal led to his resignation in 1902, after which he found his new niche as one of Britain's best-informed—and best-connected—military correspondents. It would be Repington who would break the news of the "shell shortage" in May 1915.

In the 1905 article, Repington lavished praise on Clausewitz. It is clear that he was referring to Clausewitz's "Instruction for the Crown Prince" rather than *On War*. Most Britons did not make much distinction, since the "Instruction" appeared as an appendix in the Graham translation. Repington's works of the next few years, however, show a great familiarity with *On War* and with Clausewitz's report on the catastrophe of 1806.[5] Repington traced the influence of Clausewitz in Japan to the training provided to the Japanese army by the German military scholar Major (later Major General) Klemens Wilhelm Jakob Meckel (1842–1906), who served in Japan from 1885 to 1888.

The broad interest in Clausewitz reached into some unlikely places. The future "Lawrence of Arabia," T. E. Lawrence (1888–1935), read *On War* in 1906 or 1907. At the time, he was a civilian student of archaeology at Oxford. Although he later expressed disillusionment with the Prussian's theories, he felt at the time that "Clausewitz was intellectually so much the master of them all that unwillingly I had come to believe in him."[6]

In this, Lawrence was hardly unique. Another example: Claude Auchinleck (1884–1981), commissioned a junior officer in 1904 and eventually to be a field-marshal, victor at the first battle of Alamein (1942), later recalled having read Clausewitz in about 1910. "I had a notebook full of [notes] culled out of his book which I read with avidity!"[7]

Clausewitzian terms and ideas came to abound in British military literature. The *United Service Magazine* began a monthly series on Clausewitz that ran from March 1907 to March 1909. The Graham translation of *On War* was reissued in 1908 with an introduction by Maude. In contrast with the poor sales of Graham's original edition, however, the new version sold 573 copies in its first year.[8]

There was a veritable avalanche of publications on Clausewitz in the following year. Clausewitz finally got an *Encyclopædia Britannica* article of his own in 1910 (unsigned, probably Spenser Wilkinson's work), in which *On War* was described as "an exposition of the philosophy of war which is absolutely unrivalled." (Interestingly enough, the same period

saw several translations of the *Sun Tzu*, at least one of which was characterized as "equivalent to a précis of Clausewitz—and infinitely more interesting.")[9] In August 1914, the Times Book Club tried to cash in on
the war fever through prominent ads for "war books." The first one listed
was "Clausevitz (*sic*) On War." The next four were by Goltz, E. A. Altham,
and W. H. James. Each of these books contained discussions of Clausewitz.
Jomini appeared nowhere on the list.[10]

This post–Boer War burst of enthusiasm for Clausewitz in Britain is
interesting because its motivation by the embarrassments in South Africa
creates a definite parallel with the interest in Clausewitz and German
military ideas in general that is so evident in the post–Vietnam War United
States. Second, it is useful to note the particular aspects of Clausewitz's
thought that drew attention. These were primarily his pedagogical ideas,
his moral/psychological emphasis, and his views on the dynamics of war
(friction, chance, and the interplay of attack and defense). The famous
line that "war is a continuation of policy by other means" was discussed
but was not the major focus of concern.

The relationship of war and politics was, however, the subject of a
short but sharp curricular debate within the general staff that occurred at
a meeting at the Staff College in 1908.[11] The meeting was attended by
the chief of the general staff, General Sir Neville Lyttelton, and by such
luminaries as Major-General Douglas Haig and Brigadier-General Henry
Rawlinson. The source of the dispute was Assistant Director of Military
Operations Colonel Count Gleichen's perception that Sir Henry Wilson,
then head of the college, was encouraging the students to debate issues
of politics and policy that were outside their competence and, indeed,
outside the proper interests of any British soldier. These issues "could
really only be decided after a very long study by the higher political
people." He suggested that "it would be better to turn the students into
good Staff officers than to make excursions into the realm of politics."

Rawlinson, a former head of the Staff College himself, defended the
inclusion of political aspects, which, he said, antedated his own administration of the school. He had, in fact, extended the practice "in order to
encourage students to think out large questions, partly, perhaps, political,
but chiefly military and naval." Brigadier-General (later Field-Marshal)
William R. Robertson sided with Gleichen, arguing that students

> ought . . . to keep clear of political matters. In practice, the policy to
> be adopted in any given contingency, was usually furnished by the
> Foreign Office to the War Office, and if not furnished it was assumed[!],
> but it was never discussed by the General Staff. Their duty was to
> consider and advise how a certain policy could best be carried out.

He noted, however, that "strategy must be in harmony with policy, and
therefore the policy . . . must be laid down . . . before a useful strategical
paper can be prepared."

Colonel Launcelot E. Kiggell (who would be the Staff College commandant in 1913/14 and Douglas Haig's chief of staff in 1917) then defended the school's practices by saying that he "had for some time past tried to study war and had tried to teach it, and the more he had tried, the more he had become convinced that politics were at the back of all strategical problems." It was "not possible to separate strategy from politics, and indeed Clausewitz based his whole theory of war on the fundamental principle that strategy must be based on policy."[12]

Since Wilson's training methods went unchanged,[13] it might be said that this Clausewitzian argument prevailed.

"Wully" Robertson (1860–1933) was a most unusual character. The son of a village tailor, he rose by dint of sheer hard work to become chief of the Imperial General Staff CIGS) from 1915 to 1918. His nickname was derived from his conspicuous lower-class accent, which he intentionally retained despite his rise in the army and in society. He evidently had cause later to reconsider the rather passive conception of the relationship of soldiers to political leaders that he had expressed in 1908. After the war, Robertson said

> There can be no question that, with us, whatever may be the case with other countries, the supreme control in war must be civil. . . . [The responsibilities of the national war leadership] cannot be properly discharged unless those holding ministerial office have, by previous study, made themselves acquainted with the principles upon which the business of war should be conducted. . . . It follows that soldiers who exercise high command should, without in any way becoming what are termed political generals, know something about politics and try to understand the way in which ministers look, and must necessarily look, at political things.
>
> The time may come when a policy is proposed which . . . [military leaders] feel convinced will, if pursued, have disastrous results, and they then have to choose between acquiescing in it, thereby jeopardizing the interests of the nation, and saying in unmistakable terms that they can be no party to it. . . . A minister once tried in the course of conversation to persuade me that the duty of a professional adviser begins and ends with giving his advice. . . . I was unable to agree with him as to the *chief* professional adviser, holding that he had a duty to the country as well as to ministers, and I said so, though I admitted that only special circumstances would justify the conclusion that duty to ministers conflicted with duty to country and must accordingly take second place.[14]

Robertson (a "Westerner") attributed his removal as CIGS in February 1918 (by Lloyd George, an "Easterner") to his perseverance in these principles. Robertson's argument nicely balances Clausewitz's subordination of strategy to policy against his requirement that politicians respect the nature of the military instrument.[15]

Whether this change of heart can be ascribed to Clausewitz's influence or simply to Robertson's war experience is unknowable, but Robertson's familiarity with Clausewitz is demonstrable, as his private papers include a set of notes from *On War*. These six typescript pages appear among the texts of several lectures that Robertson gave at the Staff College before 1914, where he was Commandant from June 1910 to October 1913. They consist of extracts and summarizations of sizeable portions from *On War* and address the role of military theory; the nature of military genius, and friction in war.[16] Robertson had clearly read at least these sections with some care, in the period between his two rather different statements on the relationship of military to political leaders.[17]

A number of other prominent general staff officers actually published discussions of Clausewitz in the years leading up to World War I. Repington has already been mentioned. Colonel (later Brigadier-General) J. E. Edmonds (1861–1956) was another staff officer and later author of the official histories of operations in France and Belgium. Only months before the outbreak of World War I, he published an intelligent, positive article on Clausewitz and the Jena campaign in the general staff's periodical, *Army Review*.[18] Lieutenant-Colonel W. H. James published *Modern Strategy* (an examination crammer) in 1903. It provided, among other points, a short but perceptive discussion of Clausewitz's views on the relationship of attack and defense.[19] Major-General Edward A. Altham had been head of the Strategical Section at the War Office. His 1914 *The Principles of War Historically Illustrated* (which Michael Howard describes as giving "a clear account of the strategic and tactical thinking of the British General Staff on the eve of the First World War")[20] cited Clausewitz four times; Jomini's name did not appear (though Hamley's did, once). Altham used only bits and pieces of Clausewitz's thought. Still, since he was a general staff officer and had at one time been head of the Strategical Section at the War Office, his references to Clausewitz must be regarded as significant. The works of other general staff types like Repington, Edmonds, and James show a much broader and deeper understanding of Clausewitz.[21] Douglas Haig quoted Clausewitz on occasion.[22]

The British concern with Clausewitz in this period was only one aspect of a much wider concern with the German military model which, in turn, was only a part of a larger debate over the impact of modern technology and political organization. In most cases, Clausewitz was a distinctly secondary issue. Mixed in with—and usually eclipsing—strictly Clausewitzian ideas was a continuing concern with organizational issues like the problem of a general staff, the reserve system, and—in another striking parallel with the present American reform debate—a lively and acrimonious discussion of what we now hear called *Auftragstaktik*, the German system of decentralized tactical responsibility and mission-oriented orders.[23] The issue of personnel stability and cohesion, a hot topic in the U.S. Army since Vietnam, was also a component of this British debate. In the British case, however, it appears only in reference to the higher staffs that would have to be created upon mobilization; stability at unit level has always been the norm in the British regimental system. This aspect of the debate was a major consideration in the eventual creation of the British general staff, which was in place by 1906.

Jehuda Wallach has suggested that the British interest in Clausewitz, which he says developed only on the very eve of World War I, was aimed narrowly at understanding the German conduct of war.[24] Although this certainly was a motivation, it is clear that British readers of *On War* tried as well to apply its concepts to Britain's own situation.

It is much harder to find contemporary evidence of any American interest in Clausewitz, although there were many indirect sources of his influence. For the most part this indirect influence came through the writings of German authors, who dominated the curriculum at the Command and General Staff School and the Army War College. The most important such writer was General (later Field Marshal) Freiherr Colmar von der Goltz (1843–1916), whose 1883 *Das Volk in Waffen* was translated in England in 1887. A later work, *The Conduct of War*, was translated in 1896 by the American lieutenant Joseph T. Dickman, then an assistant instructor in the art of war at the U.S. Infantry and Cavalry School at Fort Leavenworth, Kansas.[25] Both books are thoroughly permeated by references to Clausewitz, but Goltz differed from the earlier writer in some key areas (to be discussed later).

The few actual references to Clausewitz by Americans in this period are, for the most part, unenlightening. John Bigelow (who graduated from West Point in 1877) listed *On War* in the bibliography of his essentially Jominian *The Principles of Strategy* (1894), but there is no internal evidence of its influence.[26] The United States' war with Spain, successful though it was, sparked reform efforts culminating in the establishment of the Army War College and a general staff, but the reformers made scant mention of Clausewitz. The newly commissioned Lieutenant (later Brigadier General) John McAuley Palmer found Graham's *On War* on his commander's shelf in 1892. He later recalled his immense surprise at reading that war is a continuation of politics by other means. "This truth was so startlingly simple that I could not grasp it at first. But it gradually dawned upon me that here was a fundamental military concept which I had never heard about in my four years at West Point."[27]

There was, however, at least some interest at the level of individual officers. George Patton purchased a copy of *On War* during his honeymoon trip to England in 1910 and finished reading it the same year. Unfortunately, Patton chose T. Miller Maguire's peculiar and truncated translation, either by mischance or because the more accurate but much longer Graham version might have interfered with more pressing honeymoon pursuits.[28] He wrote a letter to his wife complaining that it was "as full of notes of equal abstruceness as a dog is of fleas."[29] Patton would persevere in his pursuit of Clausewitz, however, and in 1926 he would finally acquire the Graham/Maude edition.

9

Major British
Military Writers

One of the first major writers to deal frankly with the lessons of the war in South Africa was G. F. R. [George Francis Robert] Henderson.[1] Colonel Henderson was a highly charismatic professor of military history at Camberley (1892–99). Succeeding Maurice, he got the job as a result of the success of his writings on the American Civil War.[2] One of Henderson's greatest qualities was an ability to admit that he had been wrong, something that he had ample opportunity to do after the experience in South Africa invalidated many of his earlier predictions on the impact of modern weaponry on tactics. Henderson showed great promise as instructor, leader, and staff officer. Unfortunately, he died in 1903 as a result of illness contracted during the war.

Peter Paret and Michael Howard have expressed diametrically opposite views of Henderson's attitude toward Clausewitz. Paret has argued that "of all British writers, Colonel G. F. R. Henderson, without ever devoting a special study to Clausewitz, entered most fully into his thought."[3] He is probably referring to Henderson's strong emphasis on the psychological and moral aspects of war.[4] Howard, in contrast, says:

> The general contemptuous ignorance in which Clausewitz was held by British soldiers was probably well summed up by the most admired of all the teachers at the Staff College, Colonel G. F. R. Henderson, who, in a lecture at the Royal United Services Institution in 1894 on "Lessons of the Past for the Present," had mentioned Clausewitz only to say, sarcastically and inaccurately: "Clausewitz, the most profound of all writers on war, says that everyone understands what moral force is

and how it is applied. But Clausewitz was a genius, and geniuses and clever men have a distressing habit of assuming that everyone understands what is perfectly clear to themselves."[5]

Paret's view is probably closer to the mark. Henderson's presentation of Clausewitz was evidently phrased so as to make his underlying ideas acceptable to a readership not enamored of "Teutonic philosophizing." Perhaps for the same reason, his direct references to Clausewitz are few, but his intellectual debt to Clausewitz is obvious. In the 1902 supplement to the *Encyclopædia Britannica*, for example, Henderson's contributions included the articles "War" and "Strategy." Clausewitz's name does not appear at all, but a great many of his arguments do: "War . . . is a political act, initiated and controlled by government. . . . All war is simple, but the simple is most difficult. . . . War is assuredly no mechanical art. Broadly speaking, it is a war between the brains and grit of the two commanders."

Most surprisingly, Henderson's definition of strategy (and evidently official British infantry doctrine) had finally come to accept the centrality of battle: "Strategy, according to the official text-book of the British infantry, is the art of bringing the enemy to battle. . . . It will also be observed that the end of strategy is the pitched battle." In this, Henderson had overshot Clausewitz, for in the philosopher's view, the end (goal) of strategy was peace, which was to be gained through victory, in the pursuit of which battle was the primary tool.[6] This is a significant deviation and may reflect Henderson's aversion to politicians, frequently expressed and often aimed at Lincoln. This aversion tends to negate his theoretical acknowledgment of the supremacy of the political over the military.[7]

Henderson's approach to military history and theory is, however, also reminiscent of Clausewitz. His detailed battle studies do explicitly refer to Clausewitz and *On War*, although the Prussian writer was not mentioned as often as were his more recent German expositors like Goltz and Verdy du Vernois.[8] Henderson never attempted to provide a military "cookbook" on the order of Hamley's, and although he clearly sought to impart theoretical lessons, he did so in the course of his historical studies rather than in overtly theoretical works. His battle studies stress the need for initiative at all levels and the role of theory in educating an officer's judgment. Henderson's undogmatic approach to the peculiarities of Britain's military problems stresses the specific:

> It is as useless to anticipate in what quarter of the globe our troops may be next employed as to guess at the tactics, the armament, and even the color . . . of our next enemy. Each new expedition demands special equipment, special methods of supply and special tactical devices, and sometimes special armament. . . . Except for the defence of the United Kingdom and of India, much remains to be provided when the cabinet declares that war is imminent.[9]

Whether Henderson's attitude on this last point reflects Clausewitz's specificity or his own common sense, it reveals one very real reason that many in Britain were so reluctant to adopt the continental military model that modern writers have so often seen as the test of a "Clausewitzian" understanding of war. The imperial mission always inhibited preparation for warfare on the continent, both psychologically and in all the practical matters that Henderson pointed out.

Another aspect of Henderson's approach that both echoes Clausewitz and contradicts commonly held ideas as to what constitutes a "Clausewitzian" approach is his belief in the importance and power of the defense. In a period increasingly falling under the spell of the "ideology of the offensive," Henderson stressed "the importance of the spade." He clearly understood the dynamic relationship between the two modes of warfare, however. In his study of the battle of Spicheren he faulted the French commanders for failing to recognize "the power of the offensive."[10] Again, whether this view was based on or enhanced by his direct study of Clausewitz or derived entirely from his practical study of the American Civil War is impossible to determine. Nonetheless, it is clear that Henderson was familiar with Clausewitz and that his views were, in important particulars, consistent with the message of *On War*.

Colonel F. N. (Frederick Natusch) Maude, R. E. (1854–1933), was for many years the book review editor for the *Journal of the Royal United Service Institution*. He seems to have been a bit eccentric: He was the inventor of a smoke-eating machine and a proponent of a "science of organization" called "andrology."[11] His *Who's Who* entry reads "Recreations: nil." Maude was associated with the mystic Aleister Crowley, who introduced the young J. F. C. Fuller to him around 1906 to 1908. Maude's garrulous and argumentative books were critical of just about everyone. A fervent admirer of the German military system, he saw Germany as England's deadliest natural enemy. A relentless reformer, he was critical of the British army but harsh on the "half-baked" ideas of most other military reformers.[12] An energetic proponent of the study of Clausewitz, Maude pointedly rejected key portions of *On War* (notably its argument on the power of the defense). In his reformist views, however, he seems to have been a fairly typical British Clausewitzian.

Maude first discovered *On War* in 1872, but he later admitted that it had taken him a long time to fully appreciate the work.[13] He saw its essence in its analysis of the dynamics of war, particularly chance and "friction": "The whole result of his system is finally concentrated in Clausewitz's well-known phrase, 'In war everything is simple, but to secure this simplicity is difficult.'"[14] Despite his admiration for *On War*, Maude always insisted that its author had never understood Napoleon,[15] which may reflect a lack of appreciation of Clausewitz's actual relationship to the French emperor. Nonetheless, when Maude urged the younger Fuller to study Napoleon, he also recommended Clausewitz.[16]

Maude edited Graham's by-then scarce translation of *On War* and reissued it in 1908. Beyond enlarging the type and breaking the work into three volumes, Maude's contributions were few, but they exercised a great influence on the way the book was perceived by a new generation of readers: He added a series of footnotes pointing out technological and organizational changes since Clausewitz's day and discussing Moltke's role. He also added a short introduction, hostile to Germany but immensely respectful of Clausewitz, which presents the book in a social Darwinist light; the later image of Clausewitz as a believer in war for its social benefits derives largely from Maude's footnotes.[17] The Graham/Maude edition would long be the standard English version of *On War*. Its immediate financial success has already been described. It would be reprinted in 1911, 1918, 1940, 1962, and 1966 and provide the basis for most subsequent condensations and abridgments.

Another but less complete translation of *On War* appeared in book form the very next year, produced by one of the most prolific—if sometimes unsophisticated—Clausewitz enthusiasts of this period, T. Miller Maguire (1849–1920).[18] It had initially appeared in 1907–9 as a series in the *United Service Magazine* (owned at one time by Frederick Maurice). Like some others who have attempted to produce condensed versions of *On War*, Maguire ("Inner Temple, Barrister-at-Law") was neither a soldier nor a historian. He had a doctorate in law. On the other hand, Maguire was a frequent lecturer on military topics, speaking at the Royal United Service Institution, the Aldershot Military Society, and the Royal Artillery Institution. He was also a fellow of the Royal Historical Society.

Maguire wrote or edited a large number of books on military subjects. Most of these appear to have been well received, but he was widely regarded as a "crammer," whose works were designed to provide a relatively painless preparation for various military examinations. He frequently referred to Clausewitz's work but did it a great disservice by constantly harping on the "great difficulty" of reading it. In this he was no doubt sincerely relating his own experience. Still, magnifying the unreadability of the original could not have hurt the sales of a crammer's "easy-reading" condensation, even though Maguire's condensation is, in places, nearly impenetrable.

Maguire's daughter did the actual translation and assisted him in preparing his version of *On War*. The book is interesting for its attempts to adapt Clausewitz to the analysis of the American Civil War, but Miss Maguire's introduction inevitably arouses some skepticism of her father's work: "I may say that my father, T. M. Maguire, has helped me in various ways, principally by supplementing the original paragraphs with some remarks of his own, with which, he says, Clausewitz would have agreed, had not that man of genius died in 1831."[19] Her father's own dedication of the book to General Sir Horace Smith-Dorrien, which is unusually obsequious even for the period, and his preface, in which he says the translation was made "without any slavish acceptance of all of [Clausewitz's] principles and details," do nothing to enhance the book's credibility as a guide to the original's contents.

A much better condensation of Clausewitz appeared in the same year as Maguire's (1909): Major Stewart L. Murray's *The Reality of War: An Introduction to Clausewitz*, based on the Graham translation and prefaced by a note from Spenser Wilkinson.[20] Murray (Gordon Highlanders), had become interested in *On War* around 1893. In writing about Clausewitz in 1909, he was responding to a perceived demand in the army: He had earlier been requested to give a lecture on Clausewitz to the officers of the Second Division, whose interest had been stimulated by the Japanese victories in Manchuria.[21] The book evidently sold well, since a second edition appeared in 1914.

Murray was typically eclectic:

> Let not any critic affirm that I have treated war in this book as if unaware of "The influence of sea-power upon history." . . . In my book "The Future Peace of the Anglo-Saxons," I have given ample evidence to the contrary. I am as much a disciple of Mahan as of Clausewitz. Only this book is an introduction to Clausewitz and not to Mahan.

Murray took a very cheery view of the difficulties of Clausewitz's book, arguing that its unfinished nature was "really an advantage," since it left the reader "unhampered by too complete a crystallization of his ideas." In contrast with many other readers, Murray liked *On War* because "it is a book which 'any fellow' can read," being free of the pedantries and dogmatism of writers like Jomini and Hamley. He felt that *On War* was essentially adapted to British officers because Clausewitz had been "a gentleman of fine character." Nonetheless, he advised readers to take the book in small doses.

The Reality of War stressed that technological changes, however great they had been, could never outmode the Prussian thinker, *"the chief exponent of the moral and spiritual forces in war. . . .* Their chief apostle. . . . "[22] The overall message that Murray and Wilkinson put forward, however, was that Clausewitz's theories were basically common sense. To understand and absorb them was to make them one's own. Clausewitz was not an authority to be cited as the arbiter of great decisions, but a personal guide in the forming of one's own judgments. This certainly was the spirit in which writers like Henderson and Repington accepted *On War*, and it helps to explain why their direct references to it were so few.

Arguably the most influential English military writer in this period was the ubiquitous political and military correspondent Spenser Wilkinson (1853–1937), who in 1909 became the first Chichele Professor of Military History at Oxford. As Liddell Hart later put it, "Spenser Wilkinson's influence was so pervasive over so long a period of time that it is not easy to assess, or to summarize. . . . One might term Wilkinson the human germ that ultimately caused an intellectual pandemic."[23] (The "germ" simile notwithstanding, Liddell Hart's assessment of Wilkinson was entirely positive.) Wilkinson was cited as an important influence as early as Maurice's 1888 *Britannica* article "War," and he remained a respected voice well into the interwar period.

Like most of the British Clausewitzians, Wilkinson was a zealous
military reformer. Indeed, he regarded his entire adult life as having been
spent in pursuit of the creation of a large, modern, national British army
and of a professional officer corps, based generally on the German model.

> In 1874, when I was twenty-one and at Oxford, I found myself puzzled
> by the existence of large armies on the Continent and of a small one,
> said to be inefficient, at home. I determined to find out what it meant,
> so I began to read books about war. They were full of technicalities
> which I did not understand, so hoping to get the practical knowledge
> which would explain them I became a private in the University Volun-
> teer corps. I learned my drill and began to understand the books but
> found the corps a sham. I got up a Kriegsspiel club and read more
> books, English, French and German. Four or five years later I was
> offered a commission in the best of the Manchester corps and accepted
> it thinking it would be a better chance to learn. By 1880 I had got a
> company and made my position as a practical officer; at the time I was
> called to the Bar and beginning to get briefs. I knew then as much
> about war as could be got from textbooks; was satisfied that the Army
> was not what it should be and determined to give ten years of my life,
> so far as the necessity for getting a living would allow, to the attempt
> to get the army put right.[24]

Wilkinson's reforming instincts were rooted deep in his family background. His father had been a crusading liberal and a member of the
Union and Emancipation Society. These instincts were also a pervasive
feature of Wilkinson's powerful personality and were not limited to military matters. His duties as a journalist at the *Morning Post* in London
(for which he wrote from 1895 to 1914) included the role of drama critic.
His autobiography recounts with relish the many suggestions made to—
and, he claimed, accepted by—Sarah Bernhardt on the subject of her
acting.[25]

Although Wilkinson was a civilian trained as a lawyer, he entered
journalism in 1882 (having been invited by the *Manchester Guardian*
to write editorials on the Egyptian campaign), thinking that that profession would serve both his mission in national defense and his need
to make some money. His energetic campaign to give the nation a
military education, particularly his 1890 *The Brain of an Army*, was
instrumental in the creation of the British general staff. He was also one
of the founders of the Navy League. Wilkinson was closer than Chesney
or Maurice to being an advocate of the continental military model
(although he did not support peacetime conscription), but his strategic
vision was still very much an "imperial" one, so much so that he has
been miscast by many subsequent writers as a doctrinaire member of the
"Blue Water" school.[26]

Wilkinson knew and talked to virtually everybody of influence. He was
also the brother-in-law of Sir Eyre Crowe, permanent undersecretary in the
Foreign Office. He carried on a very active correspondence with many in-

fluential soldiers and politicians. For example, his papers contain more than one hundred pages of correspondence with Field Marshal Lord Roberts (the last commander in chief of the British army—the post was abolished in 1904), some of which concerns very sensitive political and military matters and is marked "private and confidential." Roberts (1832–1913) was clearly an avid reader of Wilkinson's writings. Other correspondents included such figures as the elder Moltke (in German), Jean Colin (in French), General Ian Hamilton (who would command the ill-fated Gallipoli expedition), Lord Haldane, Admiral Fisher, and Lord Kitchener.

Wilkinson, who was a thoroughgoing Clausewitzian, was prone to evangelize on Clausewitzian themes to his correspondents and partners in conversation.[27] His papers contain a detailed abstract of *On War*, written in English but evidently based on reading in German.[28] His arguments were, from an early date, always informed by a broad and deep understanding of *On War*.

One of Wilkinson's correspondents and admirers was the prominent politician Sir Charles W. Dilke (1843–1911). Dilke, a Radical politician often touted as a future prime minister, saw his political career destroyed by a scandalous divorce case in 1886. He had become widely known as a defense expert by the time he returned to the House of Commons in 1892. In an 1893 letter to Arthur Balfour, then leader of the opposition to Gladstone, Dilke wrote concerning Wilkinson that

> I owe to him the clearing of my own mind [on military issues], and believe that he is probably the best man on such questions who ever lived, except Clausewitz. . . . Admiral Colomb, and Thursfield of *The Times*, who are really expositors of the application to our naval position of the general principles of military strategy of Clausewitz, helped me by their writings to find a road.[29]

Wilkinson would be widely hailed as "the British Clausewitz" in reviews of his books published during World War I.[30]

Wilkinson's installation as the first Chichele Professor of Military History at Oxford in 1909 represented in some respects the institutionalization of Clausewitz's influence in Britain. Creation of the chair was itself the culmination of a long campaign, spearheaded by Wilkinson, for the national study of military history.[31] His inaugural lecture at Oxford, entitled "The University and the Study of War," is largely a distillation of themes from *On War*.[32] It was Wilkinson who put Clausewitz's magnum opus on the compulsory reading list for military history specialists at Oxford. There it remained until it was removed by—ironically—Michael Howard at some point in the 1970s.[33]

Wilkinson's work early became influential on the other side of the Atlantic as well. A. T. Mahan was familiar with his books, and Elihu Root read his *The Brain of an Army* as part of his self-education in military affairs. Wilkinson had handed a copy to General William Ludlow, whom Root had appointed chief of a board studying the general staff idea.

Ludlow took it to Berlin, confirmed its accuracy, and passed it on to Root. Root later wrote Wilkinson to say

> I do not forget, although I dare say a great many people do, what a great part your little book "The Brain of an Army" played in bringing it to pass that both countries had some sort of an institution of that kind already in existence when the sudden emergency came.[34]

10

German, French, and British Interpretations

Translations of various French and German writings, particularly Colmar von der Goltz's *The Nation in Arms* (translated in 1896) and Rudolf von Caemmerer's *The Development of Strategical Science During the Nineteenth Century* (1905), were widely read in Britain and the United States. Virtually all of these German works contain numerous references to *On War* and a great degree of influence by Clausewitz. Those French and German writers who rejected Clausewitz (Lewal, Rüstow, Willisen) were rarely translated. Caemmerer was particularly sophisticated and balanced in his understanding of Clausewitz's work.[1] Goltz was probably the most widely read. Friedrich von Bernhardi's two-volume *On War of Today*, another heavily Clausewitzian tome, was translated and published in England in 1912 and 1913.[2]

Hans Delbrück, whose important theories on strategic analysis were based on an extrapolation from Clausewitz's work, was known in England and occasionally lectured there. Little of his work was translated before the war, however, and reviews in English of his German-language works did not do much to connect the two theorists. Delbrück was rarely cited in prewar discussions on military affairs.[3]

The translated writings of Goltz, Meckel (the German adviser to the Japanese army general staff),[4] Blume, Bernhardi, Verdy du Vernois, and even Boguslawsky (who held on to Jomini longer than most) are permeated by the words and ideas of Clausewitz, to the point that they either did not bother to list him in their indexes or, like Bernhardi, merely wrote "Clausewitz, Karl von, *passim*." They sought not to extend the scope of

Clausewitz's theory but to apply what they conceded to be the universally valid precepts of *On War* to the specific political, social, and technological situation in which they found themselves. As Goltz stated,

> Everything important that can be told about the nature of war can be found stereotyped in the works which that great military genius has left behind him. . . . I have, accordingly, not attempted to write anything new, or of universal applicability about the science of warfare, but have limited myself to turning my attention to the military operations of our own day.[5]

This does not mean that they all agreed with one another, of course, or even that they accepted every aspect of the master's thought. The two areas in which they were most prone to disregard Clausewitz's views were, first, the relationship between military strategy and policy and second, the relationship between the attack and the defense.

Most of the translated German military writers followed Moltke in rejecting the idea that Clausewitz's subordination of strategy to policy meant the complete domination of the military by the political leaders. Caemmerer, however, rejected Moltke's argument and actually sided with Bismarck on the famous issue of the bombardment of Paris in 1870/71.[6]

Caemmerer also had an interesting interpretation of what Clausewitz was talking about when he discussed "limited war."[7] His analysis was based on Clausewitz's memorandum, written during the winter of 1830/31, on the then-imminent possibility of a war with France under circumstances far less favorable than those described by "The Plan of a War Designed to Lead to the Total Defeat of the Enemy," in Book 8, Chapter 9, of *On War*.[8]

In Caemmerer's view, the purpose of "war with a limited object" was not to pursue limited policies but, rather, to enable a state lacking the resources to overthrow its enemy to seek instead an achievable alternative military objective. The purpose was still the destruction of the enemy's will to fight through the destruction of his armed forces, but an attack with a limited object sought to encounter those forces in a way that would minimize their strength, even though this would also minimize the immediate gains to be won. The idea of Clausewitz's 1830 war plan against France—which would necessarily have had to be undertaken with much smaller forces than those envisioned in *On War*'s "Plan of a War Designed to Lead to the Total Defeat of the Enemy"—was to defeat the French in Belgium. There the French would be unable to draw on the great resources available to any nation defending its own territory. Victory over the French army in Belgium, however, would not be an end in itself. By weakening the French army, it would prepare the way for greater victories.

Caemmerer's views on Clausewitz's meaning for the term "limited war" tied into his conception of what it was that Clausewitz had been trying to achieve in writing *On War*. Caemmerer denied that the philosopher had sought to produce a historical theory that could encompass all historical modes of warfare. He particularly disagreed with Delbrück's attempt to apply Clausewitz's limited-war concept to the maneuver warfare of the eighteenth century. (Delbrück had developed the ambiguity of Clausewitz's unlimited-/limited-war dichotomy into a theory of the "two poles" of war, annihilation and attrition, using the latter "pole" to reinterpret—while still justifying—the strategy of Frederick the Great.) Caemmerer argued instead that Clausewitz—first and above all a practical soldier and only secondarily a historian—had had a purely didactic purpose. In this view, Clausewitz had in fact sought to write a prescriptive manual on war and had had no intention of rehabilitating the often indecisive warfare of the earlier era.[9]

This interpretation of limited war has been adopted by few others and is decidedly out of fashion today, but it was the view that Spenser Wilkinson and Stewart Murray chose to follow in *The Reality of War*.[10]

Caemmerer was again in the minority among German military writers in upholding Clausewitz's analysis of the dynamic relationship between attack and defense: "The defensive is the stronger form with the negative object; the attack is the weaker form with the positive object."

> It is strange! We Germans look upon Clausewitz as indisputably the deepest and acutest thinker on the subject of war; the beneficial effect of his intellectual labors is universally recognized and highly appreciated; but the more or less keen opposition against this sentence never ceases. And yet that sentence can as little be cut out from his work *On War* as the heart from the body of man. Our most distinguished and prominent military authors are here at variance with Clausewitz. General Meckel says: "The resolution to act on the defensive is the first step to irresolution."[11] General von Blume declares: "The strategic offensive is therefore the most effective form of conducting war; it is the form which alone leads us to the final aim, whatever may be the political object of the war, whether positive or negative." General von der Goltz thinks, in his *The Nation in Arms*, that "the idea of the greater strength of the defense is, in spite of all, only a delusion"; and he concludes that part of his work with the sentence: "To make war means attacking."[12]

Goltz's views were essentially those of an even more important German soldier, Alfred von Schlieffen.[13] Even Clausewitz's own editors railed against him on this point:

> We can scarcely help putting a large question mark after [Clausewitz's description of the weaknesses of the offensive mode]. . . . Clausewitz, the man of "moral forces" par excellence, quietly ignores . . . that high spirit of enthusiasm, that self-assured, manly pride, that instinctive confidence of the common soldier, all of which, spurring him to extraordinary achievement, spring from the consciousness of belonging to the attacking party.[14]

Caemmerer thought that the most telling point in favor of the defense, reflecting Clausewitz's belief in the efficacy of the balance-of-power mechanism and his essentially conservative views on the nation-state system, was that the nation defending its native soil can far better reckon on allies than the strategic assailant can.[15] This was obviously not the German general staff's opinion.

British students of Clausewitz were also divided, albeit rather more evenly, over his views on attack and defense, particularly at the tactical level. That the British should better appreciate the power of the defense is not too surprising, given their experience in South Africa and their interest in the American Civil War. Henderson was a strong believer in the spade even before the Boer War, as Maurice had been. Repington's views on attack and defense, forcefully expressed both before and during World War I, are those of *On War*.[16] Wilkinson and Murray cited Caemmerer approvingly on the subject of defense, although they emphasized (as did Clausewitz) the active defense (or "defensive offensive") and were more convinced of its superiority in strategy than in tactics.[17] F. N. Maude, on the other hand, was an unremitting proponent of what has been called the "ideology of the offensive."

Douglas Haig was an important—perhaps crucial—example of the latter view, insisting on the superiority of the attack because it alone could yield positive results. In general, Haig held Clausewitz in high regard. In 1910 he wrote Kiggell complaining that few at the War Office or Camberley itself understood either "what war really is, nor Clausewitz's fundamentals."[18] The extent to which Haig (the "educated soldier")[19] had actually studied Clausewitz is hard to determine, although he appears to have had more than a passing knowledge of *On War*. His occasional references to the Prussian writer seem to indicate that his knowledge was indirect or at least that he did not have ready access to a copy of Clausewitz's book: "Clausewitz describes Napoleon's conception of war somewhat as follows. . . . "[20] Haig clearly had read Caemmerer, however, and quoted him frequently and precisely in the same work.

On the subject of attack versus defense, however, Haig was evidently most impressed by a short study done by Captain (later Brigadier-General and Haig's intelligence chief in France, 1916–17) John Charteris, R.E., at the Indian Staff College in 1907, "The Relative Advantages of Offensive and Defensive Strategy."[21] Charteris had been assigned to answer a question phrased as follows: "Clausewitz says 'The defensive is the stronger form of war than the offensive.' Mahan says 'War once declared must be waged offensively, aggressively. The enemy must not be fended off but smitten down.' Reconcile these apparently contradictory maxims."

Charteris's answer was a curious one. He understood Clausewitz's argument quite well—better than that of Mahan (whose name he misspelled throughout). He agreed that despite changes in technology, the task of the invader was still more difficult than that of the defender. Assuming that policy would demand positive results, however, he nonetheless fixated on the weaker form with the positive aim. Charteris reconciled Clausewitz and Mahan by stating that "a rapid mobilization and a prompt assumption of the offensive leads most directly to decisive results." Given the writer's clear understanding of Clausewitz's argument, it is hard to avoid the suspicion that this was "the school solution." Haig's failure to grasp the subtlety of Clausewitz's own argument may be a symptom of shallow reading—or no reading—or merely of a psychology that insists on a clear hierarchy of values.

At the strategic level, aggressive wars of conquest on the continent (i.e., against European defenders) had few if any proponents in Britain, and the strategic value of the moral high ground was generally assumed. Wilkinson stated the argument most explicitly when he argued that Britain's very existence as a great power depended on the rest of the world's acceptance that the *Pax Britannica*, maintained by the Royal Navy on the high seas, was for the benefit of all. He saw morality as a fundamental aspect of morale: "A nation cannot be called to arms except for the assertion of some cause which appeals to the hearts and consciences of the mass of its citizens. For a nation, therefore, to go to war, except in behalf of a cause which makes that appeal, is to court defeat."[22]

In the British military community as a whole, there was great disagreement over the issue of attack versus defense. On balance, the majority probably held to the inherent dominance of the offensive, although Tim Travers has argued that this view was shifting in the period after 1912: "It seems possible that, if the outbreak of war had been delayed for another two years or so, the British army might well have moved toward both more realistic and more imaginative tactics."[23] This debate was driven by differing views on the nature of discipline, morale, and the impact of technology, and, on the side of the inflexible partisans of the attack, a belief that a defensive stance must "paralyse the spirit of enterprise."[24] A better understanding of the dynamic relationship between attack and defense would certainly have contributed to a better appreciation of the tactical problems that were to appear on the Western Front, but the Clausewitzian interpretation appears to have been more widely accepted by theorists in Britain than elsewhere.

In regard to war and policy, it is difficult to find a British writer willing to divorce strategy from rational political calculation, although Henderson's contempt for Lincoln (and, by extension, all politicians) somewhat belies his explicit acceptance that war is "a political act, initiated and controlled by government." He lamented, of course, that the political authorities in England were so habitually ignorant of the military component of their responsibilities. Most British writers merely accepted as a given the right of political leaders to meddle in operations, while bemoaning their excessive tendency to do so.[25] The narrow range of opinions on this matter in the army's leadership was demonstrated at the 1908 conference at Camberley cited earlier.

Stewart Murray provided one of the few extended British discussions of this topic in *The Reality of War*. He and Wilkinson attempted to carve out a "middle way," which conceded that Moltke's fears of political meddling were understandable and held that "during actual operations the statesman should exercise the greatest possible restraint, and avoid all interference, except when demanded by overwhelming political necessity." This is, in essence, to side with Clausewitz against Moltke, since it is the statesman who must exercise the restraint, not the soldier.[26]

About the same time that Caemmerer was translated into English, Ferdinand Foch was publishing his *Des principes de la guerre* in France; this was certainly influenced by Clausewitz, albeit with considerable distortion in line with the extreme French emphasis on morale and on the *offensive à outrance*. There has been much debate concerning Foch's influence on the controversial Field Marshal Sir Henry Wilson. Foch's book was not, however, published in English until 1918.[27]

A more scholarly voice was that of Jean Colin (1864–1917), commandant of the École de guerre. Considered by Paret as "the most knowledgeable and profound student of Napoleonic war,"[28] Colin was also a profound student of Clausewitz. It was he who translated Clausewitz's *Der Feldzug von 1796 in Italien* into French in 1899. (The next year saw five more of the campaign studies published in French.) Colin's most influential book was probably *Les transformations de la guerre* (1911), which was translated by L. H. R. Pope-Hennessy in 1912 (and dedicated to Spenser Wilkinson).[29] In it, Colin noted Clausewitz's skepticism regarding surprise and complex maneuvers and speculated that his attitude concerning these points had underlain the successful Prussian strategy in 1866 and 1870/71. He saw this as an important predictor of German behavior on the battlefield:

> Clausewitz, who reminds men continually of the dangers, the uncertainty, the friction amidst which decisions are taken and operations carried on, advises men to avoid everything that is complicated, fragile, or ambitious. His disciples will deliberately avoid the wide Napoleonic manoeuvres; they will seek neither to prepare turning movements from afar, nor to combine their marches skillfully so as to conceal their object or to be able to change their dispositions according to circumstances. . . . [E]verything is of the most extreme simplicity.[30]

Although Clausewitz appears throughout the book, the most interesting discussion comes under the heading "War and Policy" in the chapter "War in the Twentieth Century," in which Colin discussed Clausewitz's ideas on limited war. "Can a war undertaken with serious chances of success have a more or less limited object? Is it possible to fix a restricted objective for a general? Can any general propose to himself anything short of the ruin of the enemy's armies?"[31] Although he accepted the concept as one with theoretical validity, he doubted that limited war had been a real possibility even in the era when *On War* was written. "At all events it no longer seems to be possible in the twentieth century for European wars." The national passions of Europe and the material conditions of modern war made victory the only issue in war. "Therefore, the indications which a government should give to a general on the political object of war are reduced to a very small affair."

Although Colin rejected the limited war aspects of Clausewitz's theories, he was a careful student of *On War*. He and Foch correctly understood Clausewitz's definition of "economy of force," which states that all portions of a nation's available military power should be employed simultaneously, in some manner, against the enemy. None should be idle. This concept is sometimes referred to as a "concentration in time."[32] Referring directly to Clausewitz's definition but perhaps taking it too literally, Colonel Foch said in 1900 that "we must make use of all our troops, whatever their kind. What folly to reserve the less good men for the despairing struggle of the last hour! . . . In future, as in the past [a reference to the *levée en masse*], we must employ all the living forces of the nation . . . together and in the same battle."[33]

Colin also accepted Clausewitz's arguments concerning relationship of the attack and defense: "It is absolutely certain, as Clausewitz and Moltke say so clearly, that the defender derives a very real superiority from his form of action." The attacker must therefore seek sources of countervailing strength. Such strength could come from numbers or additional artillery. More ominously, Colin found another, ultimately more important source of offensive superiority in morale: "If the defender and the assailant differ notably in moral worth, success is to the more energetic, and this without it being necessary to call in the help of a flank attack." In a manner similar to Clausewitz's, Colin noted that "we shall rarely, if ever, find very marked differences in moral qualities and technical skill between European armies," but for Foch and others among the French commanders of 1914, this wish became father to the belief.[34]

For these views, rooted in the acceptance of some aspects of Clausewitz's theory and the rejection of others, it is these French thinkers who most deserve the sobriquets later bestowed by Liddell Hart on Clausewitz: the "Mahdi of Mass" and the "apostle of the offensive."

11

The Sea Power Theorists

German naval writers were also interested in Clausewitz, of course, and even though the predominant naval theorists of the era were Anglo-Saxons, German naval writings sometimes found their way into English. Rear-Admiral Baron Curt von Maltzahn (1849–1930), appointed professor of naval strategy at the German naval academy in 1898 and director in 1899, published an article on Clausewitz and naval warfare in June 1905. It was promptly translated and circulated at the Royal Navy's War College at Portsmouth as "What Lesson Has General von Clausewitz's Work, 'On War,' for the Naval Officer?"[1]

Maltzahn's analysis was no doubt of great interest to his British readers, not least because of his emphasis on England as both model and enemy. His discussion drew on many British examples, including the Pitts and the Peninsular War. In particular, he drew parallels between the ideas of Clausewitz and Horatio Nelson, emphasizing their common focus on the destruction of the enemy's armed forces. Maltzahn represented England as a nation that saw both war and commerce as weapons to be used in pursuit of policy, implying a moral equivalence between the two. His view of the Anglo-German naval race could only have been seen as a naked threat: "In the case of England, the rendering the enemy defenceless, that is, gaining the command of the sea, approximates so closely to the object of war that it to some extent takes the place of that object 'as something not strictly pertaining to war.'" In other words, England could be rendered subservient to Germany's will merely by depriving her of superiority at sea.

Maltzahn argued that "we only need to take up the thread of [Clause-witz's] argument . . . to apply it direct[ly] to naval war." He placed the emphasis of naval warfare on destruction of the enemy fleet, although he acknowledged that not all battles must have that purpose. Like Caem-merer, he sided with Bismarck against Moltke on the relationship of war and policy, stating explicitly that "not only the 'main outlines of the war' . . . but also the actual conduct of the war 'comes under the political, and not the military authorities.'" On the issue of attack and defense, however, he contended that the nature of the sea, as an area belonging to neither side in peacetime, permitted no distinction between the strategic offense and defense; the latter started at the enemy's shoreline. The lack of terrain features meant that there was no tactical difference, either.

Clausewitz also appeared prominently in the 1898 American trans-lation of an important Russian work on naval theory: S. O. Makarov's book on naval tactics. Makarov was an energetic military reformer, as was typical also of those Britons who cited Clausewitz. Makarov's many references clearly derive from the *Principles of War*, not *On War*. The most striking impression he drew from the Prussian author was the importance of seeking "death with honor"; that is, it is better to go down to defeat in a manner that creates the basis for a national renewal than to survive in a manner that calls into question the state's *raison d'être*. He was also impressed by Clausewitz's insistence on boldness and taking the initiative.[2] Practicing what he preached, Makarov was killed in battle with the Japanese in 1904 while trying to inspire his sailors by example.

The influence of Clausewitz can also be found in Anglo-Saxon naval writers of this period. Clausewitz may in fact have penetrated both the British and American navies long before he became well known in the U.S. Army. In Britain, prominent navalists like Admiral Philip Howard Colomb, James Thursfield, and (above all) Julian Corbett drew on Clause-witz. In the United States, *On War* was the very first book on the Naval War College's recommended reading list as early as 1894 (although its position there may be an accident of alphabetization).[3] By 1910, books by Clausewitz, Wilkinson, and Corbett were high on this list.[4]

The American Alfred Thayer Mahan, the dominant naval writer of the era and an original theorist in his own right, made few references to Clausewitz and drew heavily on Jomini. Nonetheless, by the 1890s Mahan—who did not read German—had become familiar with at least the broad outlines of Clausewitz's thought.[5] Mahan's interest is further evidenced by his marginal notes in a copy of Major Murray's 1909 *The Reality of War*.[6] Although he called Clausewitz "one of the first of authorities" and occasionally drew on specifically Clausewitzian themes, he found him to be in essential agreement with Jomini in all significant respects.[7] Mahan therefore continued to put forth his arguments in largely Jominian terms.[8] One of the points that most impressed him about Jomini was the Swiss theorist's grasp of the tight connections between war and foreign policy.

This is a major theme in Mahan's own work, as he sought always to integrate naval operations with "diplomacy."

Mahan was also influenced by his chief British competitor, the naval theorist Julian Stafford Corbett (1854–1922). Originally a lawyer and then a war correspondent for the *Pall Mall Gazette* and a historical novelist, Corbett published his first scholarly work on naval history in 1898.[9] He began lecturing in the Royal Navy's War Course in 1902. In 1903 he became Ford Lecturer in English History at Oxford.

Corbett was essentially a historian, and a better one than Mahan, who based his work on secondary sources. Corbett worked principally with primary sources and did not have a high opinion of Mahan's abilities as either a historian or a strategist. He had as well a strong interest in tactics and contemporary policy. Less well known than Mahan, he was influential enough to be knighted in 1917 for his work as secretary of the Historical Section of the Committee of Imperial Defence. He early became an important member of Admiral Fisher's circle. Corbett's biographer, Donald M. Schurman, suggests that Corbett's most important influence on Fisher was to keep him reminded of the human, moral, and intellectual side of war.[10] During the war, Corbett would draft the general instructions to Admiral Jellicoe, commander in chief of the Grand Fleet.[11] Corbett's thinking may in fact have been a major influence in forming Jellicoe's cautious and almost certainly correct policy of "not losing the war in an afternoon."[12] Corbett's strategic ideas (which stressed the strengths of the defense) would actually be blamed by many traditionalists for the Royal Navy's "failure" at Jutland. Afterward, Corbett would write the controversial official history of the naval war.

Corbett was a brilliant if somewhat erratic thinker, and his work shows a continual evolution making it difficult to summarize. He was not a Blue Water theorist, however, and his work stressed the limitations as well as the importance of naval power; it was the coordination between land and naval strategy, rather than independent naval action, that most interested him. Ultimately (by around 1910) it was Fisher's resistance to the creation of an efficient naval staff and to inter-service planning that alienated him from the flamboyant first sea lord.[13] Corbett rejected the idea, common in the Royal Navy after Copenhagen and Trafalgar, of the invariable dominance of the offensive. This made him a controversial figure in many naval circles, where it was felt that his analysis tended to denigrate Nelson and the Nelsonian tradition. In a prefatory note to his official history of naval operations in the Great War, the lord commissioner of the admiralty disclaimed responsibility for its arguments: "Their Lordships find that some of the principles advocated in this book, especially the tendency to minimize the importance of seeking battle and of forcing it to a conclusion, are directly in conflict with their views."

When dealing with an original and progressive mind like Corbett's, it is often difficult to discern the impact of other thinkers. Nonetheless, Corbett's work unmistakably bears a strong Clausewitzian stamp. Mahan certainly perceived Corbett as a Clausewitzian: "Corbett relies mainly on Clausewitz."[14] Donald Schurman suggests that he was introduced to Clausewitz around 1906 by Captain (later Admiral) Edmond Slade, director of the Royal Navy's war course and later director of Naval Intelligence.[15] Corbett's lecture series in the Naval War College's strategy course began with a talk on the need for strategic theory; the second lecture was entitled "The System of Clausewitz" and the fifth lecture was "Limited and Unlimited War."[16]

These lectures provided a coherent analysis of naval history from the Armada through the Spanish-American and Russo-Japanese wars. This analysis was based almost entirely on Clausewitz's concepts of limited war, the strengths of the defense, and war as a continuation of policy. Curiously, despite his belief in the power of the defensive mode, Corbett rejected the notion of convoys. Put into practice in World War I, this rejection had disastrous results.

Corbett's seminal theoretical work, usually called the "Green Pamphlet" (1906), contained many adaptations from *On War* in both its overall military theory and the specifically naval arena.[17] His next historical book, *England in the Seven Years' War* (1907), certainly contained a strong measure of Clausewitz's thought.[18]

In his most important work, *Some Principles of Maritime Strategy* (1911), Corbett's theory reached its highest expression. It is very obvious that this work was founded on that of Clausewitz and, to a much lesser extent, Jomini. The limited and defensive war components were somewhat toned down in response to the climate of opinion in the navy, but they were still very much in evidence. Barry D. Hunt has recently provided a most perceptive analysis of Corbett's evolution of Clausewitzian themes, although he was incorrect in seeing Corbett's reading of Clausewitz as unusual for his generation.[19]

Although Corbett's views of the nature and uses of military theory and his basic analysis of the nature of war echo Clausewitz, the most interesting of his derivations from *On War* concern the dynamic relationship of the offense and defense at sea and the concept of limited war, especially as it applies to naval powers and to Great Britain in particular. Part I of *Some Principles* is largely devoted to the concept of limited war, which Corbett considered to be Britain's traditional way of war.[20] Corbett's analysis is too complex to review here, but the very fact that he considered defensive maritime strategy not only possible but sometimes advisable even for Great Britain distinguishes him from most naval writers, and his belief in the continuing possibility of less than unlimited war among even the European powers marks him as nearly unique in his period. Corbett's work on limited war theory would later catch the attention of the American naval writer and military theorist Bernard Brodie, who would contribute heavily to the post-Korean War renaissance in Clausewitz studies.[21]

There is another figure whose connections to Corbett are tantalizing to the historian of strategic ideas: Winston Spencer Churchill. Churchill and Corbett moved in the same naval circles, of course. In *The World Crisis*, Churchill referred to Mahan's book on sea power as "the standard work" but to Corbett's as providing "the best accounts."[22] During World War I, Reginald Brett, Lord Esher, wrote Maurice Hankey that "all sorts of lessons, some of inestimable value, can be gleaned from [Corbett's book]. No one, except perhaps Winston, who matters just now, has ever read it."[23] Unfortunately, while Churchill's interest in and familiarity with Corbett's work are amply attested,[24] we have little more than conjecture with which to determine just what piqued his curiousity and what lessons he drew from it. Although there have been suggestions that Churchill's strategy in World War II drew heavily on Corbett's Clausewitz-inspired ideas about war fought with limited resources,[25] insofar as I have been able to discover, Churchill never committed any relevant thoughts to paper.

Corbett was not without competitors even in Britain. Wilkinson, whose interests had hitherto been almost exclusively connected with land warfare, decided in the period between 1891 and 1894 to become an expert on naval affairs as well. His mentor in this effort was Admiral Lord Charles Beresford, Jackie Fisher's most virulent opponent, although his interest was probably prompted by Dilke.[26] In 1894 he published a work called *Command of the Sea*, and in 1895 he published *The Brain of the Navy*.[27]

In August 1909, when reviewing the Naval Prize essay of the previous year, Wilkinson praised the essay but was scathing in his criticism of the influence upon it of Corbett's strategic thinking as expressed in his work on the Seven Years' War:

> Mr. Corbett and his disciple appear to me to have completely misunderstood the meaning of the doctrine expounded by Clausewitz, whose fundamental idea was that it is very dangerous to go into a war with the idea that you will not have to fight, that once you are engaged in a fight there is no safety short of knocking your opponent down, and that the most dangerous mistake you can possibly make is to assume in advance without very substantial reason that there is any limit to the risks you run.

He also denigrated Corbett's faith in the defensive form of war at sea, basing his critique on Clausewitz's dualistic exposition on the dynamic relationship of offense and defense. Unfortunately, Wilkinson was convinced, Corbett's derivations from Clausewitz thoroughly dominated the Admiralty.[28]

This conviction was probably misplaced. The prize essay was indeed almost pure Corbett and Clausewitz, and it dealt at length with the issue of limited war. In fact, all three winners drew on Corbett; but the top two were primarily Mahanian and ignored Corbett's "Green Pamphlet." All three also drew on Clausewitz but, in the case of second prize only via Wilkinson's own work.

Three years later, Wilkinson was extremely critical of Corbett's *Some Principles of Maritime Strategy*, feeling that he had misread or misused Clausewitz's ideas. "I am unable to follow Mr. Julian Corbett, whose instinct seems to lead him on paths of his own." The main thrust of Wilkinson's critique was aimed at Corbett's limited-war ideas and his "desire to resuscitate this part of the theory of Clausewitz." Wilkinson, citing Colin and Goltz, argued that the idea of war with a limited object could no longer be pressed in regard to European wars. In particular, Wilkinson wrote, "it would be suicidal for any Power to go to war with Great Britain" without the intent of actually destroying her command of the sea. That, he said (citing Maltzahn among others as evidence), was exactly what Germany intended to do. Therefore, since "Clausewitz makes it very clear that the condition of limited war is that it should be limited on both sides," Corbett's theories had no relevance to the current situation and certainly should not be taught to impressionable naval officers.[29]

Corbett received a more balanced treatment from another reviewer, Major (later Major-General) L. H. K. Pope-Hennessy, in the *Edinburgh Review*. Pope-Hennessy, who had seen considerable combat in colonial campaigns and would see more both in Europe and in Mesopotamia during the coming Great War, also assessed Corbett's (and Mahan's) arguments by reference to Clausewitz.[30] He took a much more positive attitude toward Corbett's work as a whole but also took sharp issue with him over the possibility of limited war.

These blunt denials of the concept of limited war so soon after it had been amply demonstrated in the Spanish-American (and, arguably, the Russo-Japanese) War can only be explained by the growing British fixation on war with Germany. Obviously vexed, Corbett scrawled across his copy of this review, "I have never suggested it applied to war with Germany."[31]

Wilkinson and Pope-Hennessy made other points, but what is probably most important for our purposes is to note that this sophisticated clash among several of Britain's best known military writers, conducted in the pages of the popular press, was carried on almost entirely in explicitly Clausewitzian terms. Rather curiously, Wilkinson considered his own and Maltzahn's views, both of them coming from overt and sophisticated Clausewitzians, to be "substantially identical" with those of Mahan.[32]

The violence of Wilkinson's attack seems hard to explain on purely theoretical grounds, although a personal animus would be out of character. Corbett's association with Fisher may have been a factor. Wilkinson was frustrated by Fisher's refusal to create an effective naval staff, a goal that his *Brain of the Navy* made quite personal for him. He may not have been aware of Corbett's unhappiness over the same issue. Wilkinson as historian might have found Corbett's analysis to be of great interest, but Wilkinson as Cassandra, intensely aware of Europe's accelerating slide toward catastrophe and of Britain's unpreparedness for it, did not.

Wilkinson's work on naval power has led some modern writers to lump him in with the Blue Water school of strategists.[33] This is a misleading characterization of Wilkinson, who actually lost his job at the *Morning Post* in part for failing to support what he considered to be excessive naval appropriations bills. His editor complained that Wilkinson was "not half strong enough" on the naval bills even after "hours of talking to every evening."[34] The topic does, however, lead us to one of the key strategic debates of the day, in which Clausewitz's theories were used as ammunition.

It is impossible to draw a sharp line between the Blue Water theorists and the army's soldiers, as some have done. Most military men seem to have agreed that the navy was Britain's first line of defense, and there were various shades of opinion regarding the relationship of British naval power to such military problems as the defense of India, a continental war against Germany, and the defense of Britain itself against invasion. There was, however, an extreme school of Blue Water theorists. One of its key ideas was that possession of an undefeated "fleet in being"—in some versions even a defeated one—was an absolute bar to any overseas invasion of its possessor because of the threat it would pose to any landing operation. No nation could launch a seaborne invasion without itself first achieving "command of the seas." Opponents of the naval extremists called this the "dinghy theory," since the Blue Water types had allegedly argued that "not even a dinghy" could break through the Royal Navy's cordon around Britain and therefore that no large land forces would be required to defend the home island. (Actually the argument was that no invasion force more significant than a raid of five thousand to ten thousand men could be put ashore.) In the extreme Blue Water view, mere possession of uninterrupted sea-lanes from Britain to her vast colonial possessions—even those that, like India and Canada, were menaced by strong land powers—guaranteed them from hostile seizure.

Although he certainly saw Britain as primarily a naval power and the navy as Britain's first line of defense, Wilkinson flatly rejected these views. Repington's reactions to "the extravagant claims of Blue Water fanatics" were much the same, and his critique of the Blue Water school was couched in explicitly Clausewitzian terms:

> The master error of the Blue Water extremists is their failure to realize the predominant part played by chance in the passionate drama of war. From the first moment of contact between belligerent forces Chance reigns as the uncrowned King of War. . . . "There is no human affair," says the greatest of German military writers, "which stands so constantly and so generally in close connexion with chance as war. . . . " So far as I understand it, the Japanese disregarded both [Blue Water] theories at the outbreak of their last war and were not a penny the worse. These theories are based on the false assumption that belligerents are not prepared to take risks. . . . The absolute and the mathematical nowhere find any sure basis in the art of war. To think that the whole secret of war is in the formula—superior numbers at a given spot at a given time—is a restriction overruled by the force of realities. All these ideas

direct attention to material forces, whereas all military action—as we have seen at Mukden and Tsu-shima—"is penetrated by intelligent forces and their results." "Pity," says Clausewitz, "pity the theory which sets itself up in opposition to the mind."[35]

Corbett's belief in the power of the naval defense, however, which was rooted in Clausewitz's analysis of attack and defense, did serve to support the Blue Water view of the unlikelihood of a successful amphibious invasion of Britain. When Repington launched an invasion scare in 1906–8, he postulated a German "bolt from the blue" descent on an unsuspecting England. Corbett gave his friend Captain Slade a memorandum analyzing the roles of the army and navy in frustrating previous threats of invasion.[36] Slade then delivered the critical arguments that led the government's investigating committee to conclude that Repington's expressed fears were without foundation—as indeed they were, having been put forward with the principal purpose of gaining an increase in the army's budget. Thus Corbett's argument, made from about 1906 on, may have helped cause the army to focus on its continental rather than its home defense missions.

Neither Repington, a known reader of *On War*, nor Slade, who was certainly familiar with Corbett's work, made any direct reference to Clausewitz when testifying before the committee. It is worth noting, however, that the testimony by Wilkinson's correspondent Field-Marshal Lord Roberts and by Lieutenant-Colonel Lord Lovat did include intelligent references to Clausewitz.[37] Roberts clearly assumed that the Committee of Imperial Defence knew who Clausewitz was.

Lord Roberts's discussion was particularly interesting. In the context of a one-on-one war between Britain and Germany, Roberts found the threat of a German seaborne invasion of the British Isles to be quite credible, if not imminent. It had been pointed out as a fundamental problem with the kind of surprise-invasion scenario that Repington had put forth that such a "bolt from the blue" could occur only during a period with no obvious political tension of the sort that customarily precedes wars. It would thus be a war with no political cause and hence unlikely. Roberts disputed this interpretation:

> There have been discussions on the question whether Germany, or any other Power, could be so base as to attack us by surprise, but these discussions, as a rule, confuse two totally different things, namely, attacks without *warning* and attacks without *cause*. There have been instances in Prussia's history when she has attacked an enemy both without warning and without cause, but it is not necessary for our argument that we should assume their recurrence. According to German teaching, when a cause for war arises, it becomes the business of German statecraft to provide that war breaks out in conditions most favourable to the success of the national arms. The exact relations between policy and war were defined in the clearest manner by the organ of the German Great General Staff in a remarkable paper entitled

"Politik und Kriegführung,"[38] published before Moltke's death, and bearing the impress of his style. The paper reached the conclusions I have stated, and they imply that, when Germany finds a cause for war, she will not announce the fact from the housetops, but will keep it to herself, and strike when her hour comes.

As an example, Roberts mentioned Japan, "who is Germany's disciple in these matters," and the course that led from the three-power intervention against Japan in China in 1895 to the Russo-Japanese War of 1904/5.

> I consider, Gentlemen, . . . that it is imperative upon Germany, from the point of view of legitimate defence, to take the initiative and strike the first blow in a war with us, because she thoroughly understands that if we have the initiative, she might never be able to strike at all. The Germans are, I understand, in possession of our plans for capturing their maritime trade, and they know that this maritime trade will be destroyed, and their merchants ruined without any compensating gain, if we are allowed to strike first. The greater our naval strength in proportion to that of Germany, and the greater the harm that we can do her, the greater becomes her need of taking the initiative in war. This doctrine is preached by Clausewitz in relation to strategy and to tactics in land warfare, and it embodies the German theory, at least on this vital matter, a theory with which I am in entire accord. We cannot safely assume that a virile and a military nation of 60,000,000 people will suffer war at our hands and not wage it. The converse must be true, and this Committee will judge whether we or the Germans are most likely to seize that initiative which appears to be indispensable for the success in arms for either. . . . Even if the success of invasion cannot be mathematically demonstrated, is that a reason why it should not be attempted? To this Clausewitz has replied that "reasonable an operation will always be if we can do nothing better, and if we employ such means as we possess to the best advantage." In war the greater the risk the greater as a rule the advantage; and the fact that the attempt is bold and even hazardous, may in large measure increase its chances of success.[39]

Thus Clausewitz was an influence on major figures on both sides of this important issue.

Other navalists were strongly influenced by Clausewitz. Wilkinson's friend Charles Dilke saw British Admiral Colomb as an expositor of Clausewitz's ideas (and Dilke was in a position to know), although it is hard to pinpoint the influence of *On War* in Colomb's published works.[40] Dilke also identified the *Times*'s naval writer, James R. Thursfield (1840–1923), as a Clausewitzian. Thursfield was the leading editorial writer for *The Times* after 1881. A journalist by profession, he was also a naval historian and a popularizer of Mahan's works. Thursfield was a great proponent of the "moral factor" in war. He showed

> how the moral factor in all cases and at every epoch dominates and controls the material; how the "animus pugnandi," . . . the desire to

get at the enemy in "anything that floats," transcends every other weapon in a nation's armoury; how, if that spirit is present, all other difficulties can be surmounted, and how without it the thickest armour, the biggest all-shattering guns shrivel in battle to the measure of mere useless scrap iron.[41]

In this emphasis, of course, Thursfield was rather overshooting *On War*, and he was clearly a proponent of the "ideology of the offensive" in naval terms. Although his definition of war as a conflict of wills and as a continuation of state policy by other means was taken from Clausewitz, he was unable to conceive of less than total war. In his view the subjection of the enemy's will could not be achieved without the destruction of his means of waging war:

> Many commentators on war distinguishing, with Clausewitz, between "limited" and "unlimited" war, would further insist that the forms of war must vary with its object. I cannot follow this distinction. . . . The only limitation of your efforts that you can tolerate is that they should involve the least expenditure of energy that may be necessary to make your policy prevail. But that is a question of the economics of war; it is not a question of "limited war" or of "war for a limited object." Your sole purpose is to bend the enemy to your will. . . . The only sure way of obtaining this object is to destroy his armed forces.[42]

In naval as in military matters, then, the proponents of total war and the ideology of the offensive were forced explicitly to break with Clausewitz.

12

Assessment, 1873–1914

The reputations of Britain's World War I military leaders have lately been emerging from under the cloud cast by the "Colonel Blimp" caricature that developed during and after the war. It seems increasingly possible even to accord them enough sophistication to have appreciated Clausewitz at some level. The performance of Britain's small professional army in 1914, as personified in the British Expeditionary Force (BEF), was impressive. Its leaders, with a few notable exceptions, were certainly not stupid men, and whatever errors they made were matched or exceeded by their counterparts in virtually every other European army. It was the British army and nation that stood up best to the moral, political, and military stresses of the long struggle, and it was British arms that led the victorious campaign of late 1918. After all, in "ninety-five electrifying days from 8 August to 11 November 1918, the British Army in France fought nine great battles, equal to or exceeding any of its operations in the Second World War, capturing as many guns and prisoners as the French, Americans and Belgians put together."[1]

That Britain's professional military leaders were exposed to Clausewitz's thought, and quite heavily at that, has been demonstrated already in our discussions of Maude, Murray, Maguire, and Wilkinson, by the uses made of Clausewitz by men who were instructors and commandants at the influential Staff College at Camberley, like Chesney, Maurice, Henderson, and Kiggell, by general staff officers like Repington and Edmonds, and by navalists like Colomb, Thursfield, and Corbett. Lord Roberts clearly had some familiarity with Clausewitz, and it can be demonstrated that at least one wartime chief of the Imperial General Staff (Robertson) had read *On War*. Given the frequency with which Clausewitz was cited by officers of the general staff and in the theoretical literature of the period, it is odd that he remains unmentioned in major examinations of British war planning.[2] Perhaps this area needs to be reexamined. Such an examination remains, however, outside the scope of this book.

It is certainly incorrect to assert, as did Azar Gat, that in the United States and Great Britain "on the eve of the First World War, . . . Jomini's dominance remained unchallenged."[3] By the beginning of World War I, the importance of Clausewitz was well established among British staff officers and military theorists, although significant references by Americans remained scarce. The attention paid to Clausewitz by crammers like James and Maguire is perhaps the surest proof that Clausewitz was widely discussed. This is not to say that Britain's military writers—much less her soldiers—should be characterized as "Clausewitzians," for all of these writer remained far more eclectic than their continental counterparts. It does mean, however, that Britain was by no means the military–intellectual backwater that it is widely assumed to have been.

It is true that many of the British writers just cited complained at great length about the ignorance of—and hostility to—military theory in Britain. Although this accusation is almost certainly correct when applied to Britain's political leadership, it becomes more problematical when applied to the military leadership. It is true that theory was always suspect in British eyes, a point frequently noted by both natives and foreigners.[4] This is not necessarily a bad thing given the usefulness of most of the military theory that has appeared over the years. Many of the complaints, however, were motivated by ignorance of—and hostility to—the particular theories held by the complainer. In any case, military theory is rarely popular reading in any country, even among military professionals.

The relationship of theory to practice is always problematical, but Britain's military errors during the war can probably be better ascribed to organizational weaknesses (i.e., the newness of the general staff, the influence of class and the old-boy network on promotions, the disruption in leadership occasioned immediately before the war by the "Curragh mutiny," and the smallness of Britain's professional military cadre in the face of massive wartime expansion) than to either stupidity or theoretical naiveté.

What role did Clausewitz's theories play in Britain's conduct of the war? Throughout his writing career, Basil Liddell Hart argued that Clausewitz had had a deep and pervading influence on British military thought: "Our pre-war military textbooks, . . . the strategical memoranda, drawn up by the General Staff at home and in France during the war, and . . . the diaries and memoirs of the dominant military authorities published since the war . . . are full of tags that can be traced to Clausewitz."[5]

There are, however, several problems with this interpretation. The first is the problem of correctly identifying those "tags." It is all too easy to see Clausewitz behind every doctrinal bush, and so I have rejected that approach. Clausewitz specifically refused to create a strategic jargon of the sort that makes Jomini's influence so easy to detect, and his complex phrasing does not lend itself to quotation. Many of Clausewitz's British students sought with varying degrees of success to express his ideas in their own terms; often one has to be very sensitive to detect the echoes of Clausewitz even in the writing of so thoroughgoing a Clausewitzian as Wilkinson. If one listens too hard, however, one can hear Clausewitz's voice in almost any argument. Clausewitz's own particular terminology would occasionally appear in wartime writing. For example, Repington's fervent insistence on the "Westerner's" point of view, that is, that resources should not be dribbled away in peripheral operations in places like Gallipoli and Syria, would be couched in terms of the "centre of gravity." His analysis of operations on the Western Front discussed "continuity of operations, tensions and rest."[6] These are analytical terms, however, not strategic prescriptions. Those peripheral operations could equally be described in a positive manner using Clausewitz's definition of "economy of force." Corbett, an avid Clausewitzian, was an Easterner, the position later approved by Liddell Hart.

Second, Liddell Hart grossly overestimated the extent to which Clausewitz was read and the degree to which his ideas were accepted. He claimed that following the Franco-Prussian War of 1870/71, Clausewitz's "gospel was accepted everywhere as true—and wholly true. All soldiers were quick to swallow it."[7] Such was certainly not the case.

Liddell Hart himself systematically misrepresented the ideas of Clausewitz and refused to distinguish clearly between the ideas of *On War* and its alleged misinterpretation by the author's "disciples." Why and how he did so is a problem for Part III of this book. What seems clear, however, is that what Liddell Hart was referring to was the broad influence of the German model and of Foch's school, not that of the native British readers of Clausewitz. He claimed to see Clausewitz in the ideologies of total war and of the offensive as expressed by writers like Goltz, and he refused to acknowledge that in these matters Goltz (and British thinkers like Maude, Haig, and Thursfield) had neither "wholly accepted" nor misunderstood *On War*. Instead, they had consciously and explicitly rejected key aspects of Clausewitz's teachings. Liddell Hart's comments on Wilkinson, foremost of the native British Clausewitzians, were always positive, and his own views of British strategy were suspiciously similar to Corbett's.

To what extent then, can the mind-set with which Britain and America entered the slaughterhouse of World War I be attributed to the specific influence of *On War*? This is an exceedingly complex problem, and one that I frankly think is beyond the historian's ability to determine. Beyond the fundamental question of the influence of any military theory on actual practice and the fact that the most widely accepted ideas are those most rarely explicitly discussed, Clausewitz's direct influence must be distinguished from the broad influence of German military writing, organization, and practice. Further, we must distinguish between Clausewitz the mature theorist—the writer of *On War*—and Clausewitz the young military instructor, author of the "Instruction for the Crown Prince."

At the doctrinal level, it is easy to find attempts to use Clausewitz's writings, especially his "Instruction for the Crown Prince," as the basis for lists of "principles" and for tactical prescriptions of all kinds. The "Instruction" was readily available in English after 1873; it was a focus of the attention to Clausewitz created by the Russo-Japanese War; it would be the basis for a trench-going pocketbook by the American Robert M. Johnston, published in 1917. It would not be at all surprising to find elements deriving from the "Instruction" in the *Field Service Regulations* or other doctrinal materials. That work was much more categorical than *On War* was in prescribing the destruction of the enemy's army as the objective of strategy. Henderson's discussion of the infantry textbooks appears to show a definition of strategy derived (but significantly different) from *On War*'s. General Haig's edition of the *Field Service Regulations* refers to "centres of gravity" and uses some other specifically Clausewitzian terminology.

As John I. Alger points out in his history of the "principles of war," however, attempts to attribute doctrinal lists of "principles" to Clausewitz are "most misleading."[8] No matter how often Clausewitz's name may have been invoked in support of them, he was not their source. Although Clausewitz occasionally discussed "principles," he did so in a manner quite different from the prescriptive laundry lists so common in later British and American doctrinal materials.

Because of the broad readership enjoyed by Clausewitz and even more by others who cited his works, it would be foolish to reject entirely the suggestion that the thoughts contained in *On War* contributed to the disasters of World War I, at least in terms of style. Its abstract discussion of "absolute war" unquestionably served to reinforce a tendency toward total war that was already present. As Michael Howard puts it,

> Clausewitz could hardly be blamed for those distorted notions of the offensive which sent nearly a million young Frenchmen to their deaths in 1914 and 1915. But in the grinding battles of attrition of 1916 and 1917 and the arguments used to justify them, one can clearly trace a Clausewitzian philosophy both of tactics and of strategy. The skepticism for strategic maneuver; the accumulation of maximum force at the decisive point in order to defeat the enemy main force in battle; the conduct of operations so as to inflict the greatest possible number of losses on the enemy and compel him to use up his reserves at a greater rate than one was expending one's own; the dogged refusal to be put off by heavy casualties; all these familiar Clausewitzian principles were deployed to justify the continuation of attacks on the Western Front by British commanders who almost self-consciously embodied those qualities of calm, determination and perseverance which Clausewitz had praised so highly.[9]

The problem with this view is that it is impossible to sort out cause from effect and inspiration from predisposition. After all, Clausewitz had set out to write a descriptive theory of war, heavily influenced by the nationalistic warfare of his own era. If subsequent wars matched his description, that in itself tells us only that he was an accurate observer of the phenomenon he discussed. It may well be that Clausewitz's description of military genius had caught on and helped determine key personnel decisions or organizational values, but this would be impossible to demonstrate given the Byzantine manner in which personnel decisions are made and group norms set.

It is much easier to argue that World War I took its nature from the "spirit of the age" than from the pages of the philosopher's book and that the broad current of events was unaffected by his particular ideas, especially in regard to the participation of the British and the Americans. Societies fight the wars for which they are equipped, politically, technologically, and psychologically. For example, the limited war aspects of Clausewitz's theories were well understood by some, in the abstract, but they seemed simply irrelevant to most in the prevailing atmosphere created by mass armies, general staffs, and unrestrained nationalism. The most likely conduit for any Clausewitzian influence at high levels in British government would have been the writings and agitations of Spenser Wilkinson. Wilkinson's worldview was certainly rooted in Clausewitz, perhaps to as great an extent as that of any writer in English since. When it came to practical prescriptions for immediate problems, however, Wilkinson—like Goltz—adapted to the irresistible spirit of the age. He drew on his own practical experience as a volunteer officer and on his broad and deep understanding of history and politics. Clausewitz had undeniably educated his judgment, but his judgments were his own. So, too, were the actions of those to whom he offered his advice, as Wilkinson's bitter wartime frustration with the British government and constitution indicates.[10]

The relationship of war and policy and whether the British pursued a rational connection of the sort Clausewitz described is a perplexing question because the meaning of the phrase is so open to debate. Few if any British theorists rejected the connection, however, and Britain did go to war for what were traditional and rational strategic reasons, that is, to prevent the Low Countries from falling into the hands of a strong power and, in pursuit of Britain's policy of centuries, to prevent the establishment of a European hegemony by any single continental nation. The British insistence on total victory may also be considered rational in the light of Brest Litovsk and what Fritz Fischer has revealed about the thinking of the German leadership.[11] Britain's actions, however, would almost undoubtedly have been the same had Clausewitz never written a word.

It has been pointed out with monotonous regularity by the modern proponents of the view of Clausewitz as a "prophet of limited war" that the unyielding determination with which all of the powers pursued an increasingly meaningless victory is antithetical to the rational relationship that Clausewitz suggested be maintained between military and political goals. Unfortunately, the alternative course for any of the individual participants in the war, save possibly Germany, is unclear.[12] But the British perception (as enunciated by Lord Roberts) that Germany was consciously intent on war and pursuing a rational strategy à la Clausewitz no doubt served to support prewar British suspicions of German intentions. Translated "Clausewitzian" analyses by German writers like Admiral von Maltzahn would have reinforced that impression. The primary factor there, however, was undoubtedly the bellicose behavior of Germany and the bizarre pronouncements of the kaiser.

On the specific subject of limited war, the only important British proponent of the idea was Corbett, although he was a significant exception. Murray's *Reality of War* considered it briefly but preferred to interpret the matter in the same manner as Caemmerer did's. This is quite different from most recent interpretations and has nothing to do with Corbett's. Thursfield rejected the possibility as nonsensical.

In the event, Wilkinson's and Jean Colin's viewpoint turned out to be the operative one. "Limited war," as it is usually understood (based on Clausewitz's discussion in *On War*), presupposes a desire for limitation by both sides, as was to be the case in Korea in 1950–53. In the atmosphere of 1914–18, there could be no "limited war" in this sense. A "limited" grab for a thin slice of territory meant an unlimited swipe at the prestige of its owner. No government could stand that would sustain such an attack on its sovereignty and the national honor. No individual actor (theorist, leader, or nation) can stem such a tide, as Wilkinson and Colin had realized.

Colonel Charles Edward Callwell, who would be director of Military Operations in 1914/15, noted this reality in 1905 when he said that

> a nation which is inspired by patriotic instincts prizes all portions of its territory without regard to their actual intrinsic value, that a blow aimed at some remote province or island belonging to it inflicts a grave, even if it be in a sense an imaginary, injury upon that nation, and that the effect of capturing places from an enemy which are strategically insignificant may exert a remarkable influence over the fortunes of the belligerents and over the result of the contest.[13]

Thus the concept of limited war was seriously examined. Nonetheless it was rejected, based on its examiners' assessment of the "spirit of the age."

On the relationship of the attack and the defense, there is nothing but a number of isolated phrases in Clausewitz's works that can be used to support the "ideology of the offensive" that permeated all European armies on the eve of war. (Such isolated phrases include, of course, the one echoed by Jackie Fisher in his celebrated statement that "moderation in war is imbecility!" Where Fisher picked up this tidbit from Clausewitz— if, indeed, he did not think it up himself—is unclear. Fisher seems never to have mentioned Clausewitz in print, and it seems unlikely that this particular idea would have been transmitted by Corbett.) That "ideology" may have been rooted in organizational pressures,[14] in social Darwinist thought, in practical ignorance deriving from the long European peace; in hubris originating in the easy slaughter of countless native warriors in the colonial wars, or perhaps even in the theories of Jomini, who always stressed the attack. It was not rooted in *On War*, as its proponents clearly realized. The Western Allies never, in the course of the war, accepted Clausewitz's view that the defensive is the stronger form of war with a negative purpose, perhaps because they were never able to accept that theirs was the negative goal. Their relentless pursuit of the offensive in the face of overwhelming evidence of its futility remains one of the great mysteries of history.

To conclude, however, that Clausewitz had no impact at all on the British conduct of World War I would mean accepting that all of the fervent discussion of Clausewitz carried out by the likes of Chesney, Maurice, Henderson, Maguire, Maude, Murray, Corbett, Repington, and— above all—the influential Wilkinson, had had no consequences. Such a conclusion is obviously unsatisfactory to any academic with aspirations to influence.

With that in mind, we should note that Britain's soldiers were probably the least wedded of any of the great powers' to the "ideology of the offensive" in its most extreme forms. They had profited by their experience in South Africa to a considerable extent. After all, it was not the British who went to war in red trousers. The role of theory in this appreciation of the defense, as opposed to that of practical experience, cannot be determined. Still, the British military thinkers were clearly more evenly divided in their views on the relevant aspect of *On War* than were their continental counterparts, the great majority of whom rejected it. At sea, Jellicoe's cautious handling of the Grand Fleet may well reflect Corbett's interpretation of Clausewitz's theories on offense and defense as they applied to naval warfare.

The area in which the influence of Clausewitz in Britain is most visible is in the British approach to military history and military analysis. The teaching of military history at Camberley was certainly influenced by Clausewitz, starting in the 1860s. That tradition, started by Chesney, was continued by Maurice, Henderson, and others. The creation of the Chichele chair in military history at Oxford in 1909 was the culmination of a long campaign by the likes of Maude, Repington, and Wilkinson for the national study of military history, and Wilkinson's inaugural address was little more than a condensation of key themes from *On War*. Henry Wilson's teaching of military problems at Camberley before the war involved political issues, and L. E. Kiggell's defense of that practice was explicitly Clausewitzian. The British army examination in military history in 1914 was to have been on the subject of the Jena campaign, on which Clausewitz was one of the major commentators. A prominent general staff officer (Edmonds) published a study of Clausewitz and the 1806 campaign just four months before the outbreak of the war.

That *On War* had little impact is nonetheless probably true in the sense of a direct translation of Clausewitz's theories into action, and for reasons that are best explained by Clausewitz himself. The very nature of Clausewitz's theory argues against any obvious practical impact, because it is essentially descriptive, not prescriptive. Clausewitz is very helpful in describing a given situation or in explaining why it exists or existed, and this is of no small value. His usefulness is far less obvious in explaining what specifically to do about it, and this limitation was in fact found appealing by the determinedly empirical, pragmatic, and anti-theoretical British military writer.

It is no doubt true that specific passages in Clausewitz's works contributed to certain specific actions: The German plans for the invasions of France in 1870 and 1914 surely descend in no little degree from his "Plan of a War Designed to Lead to the Total Defeat of an Enemy." This can be attributed to the fact that Clausewitz was a Prussian staff officer whose work involved practical projects against France.

Other passages, particularly Clausewitz's rejection of moderation in principle, were also cited in justification of certain atrocious behavior. Again, there is no reason to think that these actions would not have occurred anyway. They certainly had their precedents in the atrocities perpetrated in the wars that had inspired Clausewitz himself to write.

It is possible that the most significant (direct) influence of Clausewitz on British thinking derived from the idea of specificity, that each situation had to be considered on its own terms. To be useful, his concepts must be incorporated into the unconscious repertoire of its user and applied in the specific light of specific situations that Clausewitz did not pretend to foresee. His discussion on that point was always attractive to British thinkers, as it appealed to their instinctive skepticism of theory. The eclectic spirit of Britain's military theorists and their persistence in considering the imperial—rather than the continental—military problem is a better reflection of this aspect of Clausewitz's thought than a heavy-handed adaptation of the arguments of continental theorists like Foch and Bernhardi would have been. Most of the British military writers who actually read Clausewitz for themselves used his theories properly as a basis for analysis rather than as a source of prescriptions.

Thus it may be that the most significant impact of Clausewitz's thinking was exactly the opposite of what most modern students of war would expect to see and in many cases do not, thus accounting for the widespread assumption that Clausewitz had gone unread. Far from encouraging the British to adopt the continental model—mass conscript armies and the like—and to seek decisive offensive battle on the fields of Europe, the British perception of Clausewitzian theory may have encouraged them in their natural tendency to focus instead on the unique aspects and specific problems of the British Empire. Until the continental commitment that slowly evolved after 1904, in the face of a strategic situation radically altered by the emergence of the German naval threat, those specifics would have led Britain to reject the continental model. Even Wilkinson rejected peacetime conscription. (His correspondent Lord Roberts, on the other hand, was the leader of the movement favoring it.) Clausewitz's analysis of the dynamics of war was prominent in the arguments of those who rejected the ideology of the offensive, and its proponents were forced explicitly to reject that aspect of his theories. Thus the pre-war influence of Clausewitz should perhaps be seen in Britain's resistance to the rush toward Armageddon rather than in the embrace that Liddell Hart described.

As to the wider question—implicit in Liddell Hart's complaints—of whether Clausewitz's thought in *any* of its derivatives was influential in bringing on the slaughter of World War I, the question is pointless. The various lines of thought descending, evolving, and in many cases radically mutating from Clausewitz's original arguments make absurd any clear cause-and-effect argument of this kind. Beyond the problems in describing Clausewitz's hydra-headed legacy, it seems clear that Britain's actions, at least, can be more easily explained by reference to traditional British attitudes that were, in themselves, by no means irrational or even necessarily wrong.

Nonetheless, our discussion has demonstrated that Clausewitz's many-faceted theories had penetrated British military thought to a greater degree and in a rather different manner than has heretofore been suspected. Jakob Meckel was therefore quite right when he wrote to Stewart Murray that "everyone who nowadays either makes or teaches war in a modern sense, bases himself upon Clausewitz, even if he is not conscious of it."[15]

III

The Apostle of
Total War: 1914 –1945

The period between the South African War and World War I had been,
in Britain at least, the first golden age of Clausewitz studies in English.
As a result, elements of Clausewitz's thinking were incorporated into most
subsequent English-language military writing, but often in incoherent bits
and pieces that were often themselves misunderstood or distorted and, in
many cases, not associated with their author's name. A more sophisticated
understanding certainly existed, more widespread in Great Britain than in
the United States until the 1940s, although its practical impact is (as
always) difficult to gauge. But even though the European war of 1914–18
sent Clausewitz's great rival Jomini into near eclipse, reaction to the war's
slaughter and futility led many to an emotional rejection of Clausewitz as
well.

As a result, two contrasting images of the military philosopher began
to emerge in the English-speaking world. The first was largely negative,
the image of Clausewitz as "the apostle of total war," the "Mahdi of
mass," the proponent of a bloodthirsty, amoral philosophy of offensive
warfare that prefigured or even caused the disasters of World War I. That
this view was without much foundation was indicated in our examination
of the British reception of Clausewitz before the war, yet it seems to have
been very widely accepted. Another view, which stressed Clausewitz's
emphasis on maintaining a rational relationship between war and policy
and which correctly understood him as a believer in the balance of power
and the state system, seems to have had far less currency. Nonetheless, the
latter view—descending in some measure from the work of Sir Julian

Corbett and greatly reinforced by the writings of German expatriates in America—preserved an appreciation of Clausewitz which would later come to predominate in the atmosphere of the Cold War.

The widespread rejection of Clausewitz was rooted in an understandable but in many cases unthinking antimilitarism, combined with Anglo-Saxon chauvinism, general Germanophobia, and, after 1933, anti-Nazism. To the extent that Clausewitz was discussed among military intellectuals, his reputation and message were severely distorted in the course of J. F. C. Fuller's and Basil Liddell Hart's attempts to reinvent military theory. Fuller's treatment of *On War* was ambivalent, usually favorable but dismissive and often very misleading. Only after 1945 did Fuller become a staunch advocate for the study of Clausewitz. Liddell Hart's public attitude toward Clausewitz, on the other hand, remained consistently hostile, ill considered, and tremendously influential. Representatives of the prewar generation of military thinkers (like Spenser Wilkinson) and newer writers (like Cyril Falls and F. B. Maurice) conducted a rearguard effort to preserve a British appreciation for the theoretical subtleties of *On War*, but this effort shed relatively little light into the shadows created by Liddell Hart, Fuller, and reaction to the Great War.

During the same period, serious studies of Clausewitz finally began to appear in the United States. This was in part a result of the study of *On War* by individual American soldiers and in part a natural outgrowth of the continuing study of German methods in American military schools. There is, however, little evidence that Clausewitz's works were a significant element in the American military educational system between the two world wars. In the army's schools, Clausewitz's name was used, but his key ideas were largely ignored, distorted, or rejected. In the navy, Clausewitz's ideas were spread more accurately through the works of Wilkinson and Corbett; his ideas on the relationship between war and policy were better accepted most likely because they were so compatible with Mahan's.

Clausewitz entered the military intellectual mainstream in America only in the mid-1940s, under the pressure of war and largely through the influence of Edward Mead Earle's seminal 1943 anthology, *Makers of Modern Strategy*.[1] The first "American" translation of *Vom Kriege* also appeared in 1943, produced by a German expatriate.[2] It was in some respects an improvement on the earlier Graham translation, but Graham's work remained the most widely used version and served as the basis for most subsequent treatments of Clausewitz.

The most sophisticated analyses of Clausewitz to be published in America were the work of German expatriates like Alfred Vagts, Hans Rothfels, and Herbert Rosinski. Rothfels's essay on Clausewitz in Earle's *Makers of Modern Strategy* was by far the most widely read positive treatment, but in the longer run the most important of these expatriates may have been Rosinski, who was actively involved in American military education. These German scholars, none of whom were military professionals, introduced into English-language discussion the new approach of

German scholars to the study of Clausewitz, that is, the attempt to get beyond a literal reading of his published works—principally *On War*—and to approach the ideas they contained by examining them in their original historical context and by relating them to a deeper understanding of their author as a human being. The attempts of Rosinski and Hans Delbrück to build on Clausewitz's work to create a more applicable—if more narrowly strategic—theory also found their ways into English in this period. It was the German expatriates who laid the basis for the post–World War II American interest in *On War*, an interest that would blossom after Korea and veritably explode following the Vietnam War.

Aside from some of the works by German émigrés, however, little of the American comment on Clausewitz between 1914 and 1945 exceeded the sophistication of that published in England between 1902 and 1914. A major exception was Captain (USN) George J. Meyers's work, but Meyers's highly Clausewitzian book *Strategy* seems to have had no noteworthy impact.

Overall, the predominating Anglo-American image of Clausewitz in this period was probably the distorted one painted dishonestly by propagandists, unintentionally by Fuller, and unreasonably by Liddell Hart.

13

Clausewitz During
World War I

During World War I, Clausewitz continued to be discussed, although many sophisticated military thinkers were soldiers who now had little time for theoretical meditation. General Colmar von der Goltz, for example, probably the most widely read commentator on Clausewitz, died in Baghdad in 1916 pursuing an "Eastern solution" to the struggle. There were some exceptions to this rule; Repington's and Wilkinson's wartime references to Clausewitz have already been mentioned. It is difficult, however, to detect any particular trends in the reception of Clausewitz during the war.

One thing that does seem clear is that the war brought about the virtual eclipse of Jomini. This was partly because the latter's maneuver orientation and rather regressive attitude toward popular national warfare had relatively little relevance to the problems at hand and partly because of the obvious dominance of the German military model.

Nonetheless, the urge to apply Clausewitz's writings in a prescriptive, Jominian fashion did not disappear; indeed, it lingers to the present day. Most representative of the efforts in this direction was Robert Matteson Johnston's *Clausewitz to Date* (1917), published in a handy, pocket-sized version designed for reading under trench conditions.[1] Johnston thus became the first American to publish a significant commentary on Clausewitz.

Robert M. Johnston

Robert M. Johnston (1867–1920) was the son of the *Ohio State Journal*'s foreign correspondent, an American of old family who arrived in Paris in

1852 and remained there until his death thirty-four years later.[2] Young Robert was educated in America, France, and Germany and received a master's degree from Cambridge in 1889. His first historical writing was on Roman politics and religion, but his travels in Italy excited an interest in Napoleon. He wrote a series of books on the French emperor that were well received in Europe, and then he turned to apply the military lessons learned to the study of the American Civil War. In 1902, he began lecturing in European history at Harvard, where he remained for the rest of his life except for his military service in World War I.

Johnston represented in large measure the new "scientific" spirit then sweeping the historical profession in America, and he was very active in the American Historical Association. His interest in military history was quite unusual among the new breed of professional historians, however. In the century between 1820 and 1920, approximately nine thousand Americans matriculated at German universities. Germany was particularly popular between 1870 and 1900: In 1895, there were two hundred American students in Berlin and only thirty at the Sorbonne in Paris. After 1870, the preponderance of these students were in the liberal arts and social sciences, including history. Despite their fascination with the scientific approach of German historians like Otto von Ranke, however, America's new professional historians appear to have specifically ignored military matters.[3] Since the focus of this book is on military commentators, it would be digressing to consider why this should be so, but the broad disinterest of American scholars in military affairs is nevertheless worth noting.

In 1911, Johnston began lecturing at the Naval War College in Newport, Rhode Island, and was lecturing at the Army War College by 1914. Although he was impressed by Arthur Conger's efforts at Fort Leavenworth, Kansas,[4] he grew to be very critical of the American military educational system: "We are grateful to Mr. Root for founding the Army War College, even if, as an institution of learning, it remains a joke; we are grateful to Mr. Root for founding the General Staff, even if, as the brains of the army, it remains a farce."[5]

In 1918, the overweight Johnston managed to overcome medical objections and obtained a commission as a major in the U.S. Army. He soon became chief of the historical section of the general staff in France, having been one of the major proponents for the creation of such a section.[6] In this capacity he worked himself sick. Posted back to the United States to organize the military archives in Washington, he worked himself to death, dying of a heart attack in January 1920.

Johnston was a strong believer in the interplay of tactics, strategy, and economics. Together, he and Arthur Conger founded a high-quality (if short-lived) journal at Harvard with the goal of stressing that interplay, *The Military Historian and Economist* (1916–18). Despite his strong interest in economics, which Clausewitz had ignored, Johnston's attitude toward military history and theory was distinctly compatible with the Prussian's: "We shall . . . view war in an evolutionary sense, with theories fitting the conditions of any given epoch and open to continuous modification."[7]

Johnston has not, however, been considered much of a Clausewitz enthusiast. Russell Weigley remarked that Johnston "remained in the American professionalist tradition where Clausewitz had yet to become a major prophet, and he was skeptical of Clausewitz's dicta. He was not convinced that moderation in war is absurd, especially when the abandonment of moderation meant the levying of mass and necessarily unskilled armies."[8]

Weigley's implied description of Clausewitz is itself a distortion, of course, and Johnston's opening statement in *Clausewitz to Date* is hardly consistent with Weigley's argument: He wrote that the "supremacy of Clausewitz in the domain of military theory remains unchallenged." He went on to say:

> To what . . . does he owe this supremacy? Wholly to the solidity of his foundation stones; it would be useless to search for their equivalents in any other military writer. These foundation stones were three: his emphasis on psychology; his philosophic breadth; his constant subordination of theory to the will to fight. . . . Could Napoleon have read Clausewitz, he might not have repeated what he said to Balatcheff of another author: "You all think you understand war because you have read Jomini's book! Is it likely that I should have permitted its publication if it could accomplish that?"[9]

Of course, editors of books and writers of forewords are customarily kind to the authors they introduce, and it is uncertain at what date Johnston first became personally familiar with the German writer's work. Still, Weigley's statement disassociating Johnston and Clausewitz appear to be rooted in Weigley's views of the philosopher, not in Johnston's. In his analysis of the battle of Bull Run, published in 1913, Johnston praised Clausewitz's understanding of the relationship of war and politics.[10] His assessment of that battle hinged on his views of the inherent relationship between the offense and defense, on which point he was both well aware of and in agreement with Clausewitz's argument. The World War only confirmed him in this attitude.[11] His brief essay on the study of Napoleon's generalship, published in 1914, seems to condone Clausewitz's criticisms of Jomini. His journal, *The Military Historian and Economist*, frequently carried references to Clausewitz.[12] Discussing Clausewitz's *Campaign of 1812 in Russia* in 1918, he said "We find Clausewitz in the field of criticism and theory rising to the same height of conception and boldness that was Napoleon's in the field of action."[13]

In 1919, Johnston's discussion of the peace settlement was based on one of Clausewitz's "best-known distinctions, that between limited and unlimited war." His only complaint was that *On War*'s discussion of this topic did not pursue the matter as far as it could have, certainly a legitimate gripe. Johnston's interpretation of Clausewitz's limited war ideas varied, sometimes based on a literal reading of *On War* and sometimes derived—like Caemmerer's—from Clausewitz's examination of the military situation in 1830.[14] In any case, Johnston's treatment of Clausewitz was both sophisticated and positive.

Weigley's conception of Johnston as anti-Clausewitzian may stem from Johnston's objections on a rather minor point, Clausewitz's comments on the dubious efficacy of surprise in war. Even there, however, Johnston's comments were hardly condemnatory: He merely noted that Clausewitz's remarks seemed "a little sweeping."[15]

The contrast between Johnston's belief in a professional army and Clausewitz's discussion of the nation in arms is more important, but raising this issue is a little like comparing apples and oranges.[16] Clausewitz was a professional officer and he certainly recognized the value of professional preparation for war. He saw mass armies as inevitable (and therefore necessary) under the historical circumstances brought about by the French Revolution. He suspected that those circumstances would be repeated, and he was right, although he acknowledged that a reversion to eighteenth century–style limited warfare was also a possibility.[17]

It is certainly true that Johnston preferred the professional to the amateur army. He may occasionally have wavered somewhat on the subject, since in 1920 he stated, "I have considerably modified my own views on this matter. I no longer believe in the advisability of improvising soldiers on short terms of training . . . and so forth." It is not clear when, if ever, he had held these other views.[18] Before World War I, he had argued that a large, disciplined, standing federal army would have made short work of the Confederacy and thus precluded the mass destruction of the Civil War. Recognizing that all of the armies in the Great War itself were formed from masses of minimally trained citizen soldiers, Johnston believed that "the German army in defeat was still the best army in the field [in late 1918] in everything except its psychology."[19] In 1920 he argued that a "force of 100,000 highly trained professional troops could have marched through many places in the Western front, and in either direction." His description of such troops was, however, somewhat utopian:

> By highly trained soldiers I have in mind enlisting men as boys, at sixteen, passing into the ranks three years later, thoroughly competent in another five years, and serving eight years thereafter. With such a soldiery every man would be capable of individual decisions and action, always harmonizing with the general plan and with the tactical situation.[20]

Johnston's stated opinion on this matter was largely wishful thinking. Insofar as it was a hard prescription, it was based on speculation—very similar to Clausewitz's—that another generation might see war in different terms. Despite his wishful thinking, Johnston's speculation on this matter did not constitute a fundamental challenge to the Prussian writer's theories, and he did not see it as such.

Johnston's disdain for amateur armies may, however, explain why his book was based largely on Clausewitz's "Instruction for the Crown Prince," an essay that had been written for the edification of a child with the object, as Clausewitz put it, of not "taxing the Prince's mind too much."[21] Johnston strove to apply even Clausewitz's observations on tactics (e.g., his discussion on night fighting). He acknowledged, however, that circumstances on the Western Front had forced him to abandon any attempt to use Clausewitz's offensive tactics.

Weigley, with a view of Clausewitz evidently influenced by the complaints of Liddell Hart, asserted that "Johnston did not accompany the disciples of Clausewitz in their devotion to battle as the overwhelmingly preeminent object of strategy. He recognized that battle is the military pay-off," he wrote, and quoted Johnston as saying that "whatever strategical advantage an army may obtain, there always comes the moment when the tactical decision must be fought for." Nonetheless, Weigley noted, Johnston understood that "strategic advantage could prejudge the tactical decision." Why this should be seen as a contrast with Clausewitz is somewhat mystifying, as it hardly contradicts Clausewitz's argument.

Like many other participants in the war, Johnston was shocked and disgusted by what he had seen. Unlike some British survivors, however, he did not blame Clausewitz. His comments in 1919 were no less complimentary than in 1913: "But to old Clausewitz, as usual, we can all, whether in Germany or not, still turn with profit."[22]

Thus it appears that Johnston's reception of Clausewitz was, in fact, a positive one, but whether he did in fact profit from his familiarity with the philosopher's works is another question. Despite his sharp intellect and historical sophistication, Johnston was at heart a military romantic. Although he was likely to cite Clausewitz with approval when dealing with war in the abstract, his practical suggestions seem always to have been a trifle unrealistic. Although he acknowledged that "war is the continuation of policy by other means," he had a profound contempt for civilian politicians. He always portrayed Lincoln as a military buffoon and argued that war could be waged effectively only by professionally trained military leaders. He saw military history as the story of generals and their battles, and he was quite uninterested in the motivations driving the common soldier and society at large.

One of the most curious aspects of Johnston's attitude toward Lincoln is its contrast with that of most other self-professed Clausewitzians. Although G. F. R. Henderson had similarly despised the American president, writers like John McAuley Palmer and F. N. Maude thought him a genius. Johnston's own close collaborator, Arthur Latham Conger, considered Lincoln's political–military handling of the war to be brilliant.[23]

Even though Russell Weigley's 1962 views of Clausewitz and on Johnston's attitude toward him were incorrect, he was certainly right in arguing that Johnston's concept of a small but highly professional American army was no answer to the problems that the nation faced in his time.

By failing to appreciate the "spirit of the age," Johnston failed in his application of theories he acknowledged to be supreme.

T.D. Pilcher

One Englishman who retained his faith in Clausewitz was Major-General Thomas David Pilcher (1858–1928). A veteran of numerous colonial wars and the conflict in South Africa, Pilcher became aide-de-camp to the king in 1901 and was promoted to major-general in 1907. He held various commands in India until 1914. He fought with the British Expeditionary Force in 1915 as a division commander (Seventeenth Division) and was wounded in 1916. In 1918 he undertook to publish a condensation of the first volume of *On War*,[24] based on a comparison of the Graham translation with the newer fourth German edition.

Pilcher's editorial comments on Clausewitz's work were unexceptionable, and it is noteworthy that despite the antagonisms of the war he remained an admirer of Clausewitz's generation of military reformers in Prussia. He also stressed the possibility of both limited and unlimited wars. His major concern, however, was the immediate problem of 1918 (i.e., the German offensives in the spring and the successful Allied counteroffensive), and his work was clearly aimed at the man in the street as well as at policymakers. Pilcher emphasized that the ongoing war was of the unlimited, life-or-death variety; the argument that the exploitation of victory requires a vigorous pursuit; the necessity of fighting to the end of one's resources; and the recognition that decisions in war are not necessarily final.[25]

Pilcher made this last point with an evident eye on the armistice negotiations: "Whilst on this subject the remark [by Clausewitz] that the object of a combatant may sometimes be to bring about an inconclusive peace with the object of again starting hostilities on a more favourable opportunity is very pregnant at the present moment."

Pilcher was criticized for the obvious haste of his work,[26] but he felt his hurry justified because at the time of publication "the matters dealt with are of special importance." Whether his hopes were realized in the harshness of the armistice terms or dashed in the Allied failure to pursue the German army to Berlin is uncertain.[27]

14

The Clouding of Clausewitz's Reputation

In some ways the experience of World War I served to confirm the Anglo-American enshrinement of Clausewitz as the preeminent theorist of war. By 1914, *On War* had been well ensconced as a military classic. It remained so, if for no other reason than that it was perceived—incorrectly, in all probability—as the key to German military behavior.[1] The Graham/Maude version of *On War* was reissued in 1918 and 1940, and a new translation of the "Instruction for the Crown Prince" appeared in the United States in 1942. The following year, a new translation of *On War* came out, also in the United States, along with a new condensation derived from the older Graham/Maude version.

There was, in any case, no revival in the popularity of Jomini. By 1947, U.S. Marine Corps Brigadier General J. D. Hittle could open his introduction to Jomini's *Art of War* with the observation that the "military world that today burns gunpowder at the altar of Clausewitzian doctrine has all but forgotten Antoine Henri Jomini." Lynn Montross made virtually the same point at about the same time: "The Prussian writer's theories have endured to shape the warfare of a day which has forgotten the *Précis*."[2]

Several considerations, however, led to changes in the British attitude toward Clausewitz, and Pilcher's condensation represented the last British effort until 1967 to popularize his work.[3] The general postwar disillusionment led to widespread anti-militarism and probably intensified the seemingly innate British skepticism toward military theory. Since Clausewitz's name was popularly associated with the military developments that had led to the immense bloodletting of the war, those military thinkers who did retain an interest in theory evidenced a desire—largely futile, it seems in retrospect—to find some new theoretical basis for military strategy. Also significant was a lingering anti-German sentiment, which came to be directed against Clausewitz himself.

This sentiment became apparent very early in the war; even Wilkinson showed a reluctance to quote Clausewitz while it was in progress. In his 1916 lecture on the theory of war, Clausewitz is conspicuous only by the near-total absence of his name.[4] French war propaganda translated into English described Clausewitz's theories as an underlying cause of the horrific German atrocities reported to have occurred in France and Belgium. The German soldiers' alleged habit of tossing Belgian babies from bayonet to bayonet was held to be a natural extension of Clausewitz's views on the absurdity of introducing a principle of moderation into the theory of war.[5] Similar war propaganda appeared in Britain during the war of 1939–45: "Coupled with this glorification of war and this excitement to plunder, there was an advocacy of ruthlessness in the conduct of war which marked the depth of barbarism whereto Germany had been sunk by the leaden heel of Prussia. Clausewitz had set the tone."[6]

This view of Clausewitz became a fixture in British military writing about German atrociousness. For example, J. H. Morgan's 1946 work on clandestine German rearmament noted that barbarity "is the traditional German doctrine—*cf.* Clausewitz in his *Vom Kriege*, I, Kap. 1 (2) and V, Kap. 14 (3), where he argues that 'ill-treatment' of the civil population, in order to break 'the spirit' of the enemy, should be 'without limit.'" This required a rather creative rewriting of *On War*. The relevant portions of *On War* actually give only a matter-of-fact description of the system of requisitions by which the Napoleonic armies maintained themselves in the field. The term "ill-treatment" appears, but only to say that the natural fear of such treatment is one factor that leads the subject population to comply with the invader's demands. The discussion of requisitions says nothing about "breaking the spirit" of that population or about "limits." In fact, Clausewitz noted that military officials

> naturally do all they can to equalize its [the army's] pressure as much as possible, and to alleviate the weight of the tax by purchases; at the same time, even an invader, when his stay is prolonged in his enemy's country, is not usually so barbarous and reckless as to lay upon that country the entire burden of his support.[7]

Morgan, like many other hostile interpreters of Clausewitz, willfully confused his abstract discussion of the nature of war with his descriptions of its actual conduct, in order to produce a barbarous prescription quite at variance with his actual expressed views.

> Clausewitz, a typical Prussian, indoctrinated the . . . German military thinkers with the "philosophy" of brutality, . . . warned his pupils against attempting to disarm an enemy without *the maximum* of "bloodshed,"

begged them to avoid a "benevolent" spirit towards a stricken foe, dismissed all humanitarian restrictions on the conduct of war as "hardly worth mentioning," and denounced "moderation" in an officer as an "absurdity."[8]

Morgan was a prominent international lawyer with a long résumé of government service in Britain, Australia, and India. Among many other things he was legal editor of the *Encyclopædia Britannica* and adviser to the American War Crimes Commission at Nuremberg (1947–49). One hopes that his legal briefs were written with more care and judgment than were his comments on Clausewitz. That the philosopher's manner of argumentation and expression lent itself to such distortion does not change the fact that it is a distortion, of a most grievous sort.[9]

British Clausewitzians like Spenser Wilkinson also came under attack. Caroline Playne, writing in 1928, devoted several pages to an attack on the "militarist" Wilkinson, who "holds the doctrine of Clausewitch (*sic*) that war is the continuation of policy, an end in itself." Whatever her ignorance of Clausewitz, Playne was evidently quite familiar with Wilkinson's works, acknowledging the strong ethical elements in his view of Britain's strategic policy but believing them to be negated by his belief in military preparedness.[10] Her comment on war and policy can only be characterized only as a willful misunderstanding, since war cannot be both a continuation of policy and an end in itself. Playne's denunciation is especially ironic given the emphatic rejection of Clausewitz by the man who had been Germany's virtual wartime dictator, General Erich Ludendorff, in which he did indeed portray war as an end in itself: "All theories of Clausewitz have to be thrown overboard. War and Politics serve the survival of the people, but war is the highest expression of the racial will to life."[11] The distinction between Ludendorff's and Clausewitz's views had in fact been clear to many Germans during the war. The peace faction in the Reichstag had cited Clausewitz in opposition to the militarists.[12] Delbrück had been outraged by the policies of the general staff. Military violations of Clausewitz's and Delbrück's guidance were also cited by parliamentarians in the postwar inquest.[13]

Playne also made the somewhat more sensible argument that "Clausewitch's" view of war was "just the opposite from [that of] the enlightened statesmen who regard it as the outcome of the *failure* of policy."[14] The problem with this view, of course, is that war is never the outcome of the policy of a single actor. One state's aggressive policy is not subject to the peaceable control of its victim, barring craven submission. "A conqueror," said Clausewitz, "is always a lover of peace (as Buonaparte always asserted of himself); he would like to make his entry into our State unopposed."[15] Perhaps craven submission was the solution that Playne would have recommended, since she blamed Wilkinson for stimulating Britons to "defiance" of Germany in the prewar years.

This peculiar equation of Clausewitz with his opposite appeared with increasing frequency as the German national image sank, especially after the rise of Nazism. As Paul Birdsall (an American professor of history at Williams College) put it in 1941 in his pro-Wilsonian attack on the Versailles settlement, the

> post-war association of Hitler and Ludendorff was no mere coincidence. . . . The ideological trappings of Hitler's book clothe a traditional German military logic which can be traced far back in the nineteenth century to the great Prussian philosopher of war, von Clausewitz. . . . It is a logic so rigid that it has no room for what Bismarck called the "imponderables." Its victims lose all flexibility of mind, all imagination about the attitudes of other people, of "public opinion" in general. . . . Hitler's treatment of his victims is the logical application of the Von Clausewitz philosophy of war and the extension of Ludendorff's specific plans for German hegemony in Europe.[16]

The comment about popular views is a particularly surprising point to make about Clausewitz, since "public opinion" is one of his "three principal objects in carrying on a war."[17] But the development of such an attitude was perhaps inevitable given the Nazis' adoption of Clausewitz as an honorary fascist.[18]

An unreasoningly hostile attitude also began to show itself in discussions by military writers. The article on Clausewitz and the Jena campaign that appeared in the *Army Quarterly* in 1941 was a startling contrast with the article on the same subject that had been published in the *Army Review* in 1914. Hostile to Clausewitz throughout, it characterized him as a Pole "not only in name but in blood"—thus depriving him of membership in the militarily most prestigious nation. (The characterization of Clausewitz as a Pole is common in hostile treatments, but despite the Polish origins of the name, the family had by the eighteenth century been thoroughly Prussianized.) The article stigmatized him as a "theoretical soldier" who "slur[red] over" practical matters. It also accused him of manipulating facts and figures in order to make personal attacks on rival Prussian officers and to excuse the Prussian defeat. It is true enough that Clausewitz had taken the opportunity to vent his wrath on certain individuals, but the second point is a truly astonishing interpretation of Clausewitz's assessment of his nation's failures in the war. This article seems, in fact, to have had no purpose but to sneer at Clausewitz.[19]

It is in fact possible that both articles on Jena were written by the same man, J. E. Edmonds (1861–1956). Edmonds was an accomplished linguist (especially fluent in German) and a military intellectual, a valued and versatile staff officer considered temperamentally unsuited to command. His 1914 piece on Clausewitz and the battle of Jena was balanced and respectful, speaking of the battle study by "so eminent an authority . . . written in the maturity of his judgement," although he was mildly critical of Clausewitz's "failure to appreciate Napoleon's methods."

Edmonds's 1951 article on Clausewitz and Jomini, on the other hand, contains all of the usual attacks on the former along with a tactically oriented praise of the Swiss theorist that is difficult to understand at such a late date.[20] Like the unsigned 1941 article, it refers sneeringly to Clausewitz as a Pole and as a man with little real soldiering experience, an argument contradicted by Edmonds's own 1914 summary of Clausewitz's military career. Written when Edmonds was a very cantankerous ninety years old, the 1951 piece is a bitter diatribe full of errors (Clausewitz's book is called *Zum Kriege*) and hatred for all things German. He vociferously denied that he—or any other patriotic Englishman—had ever actually read *On War*. Edmonds's own claim never to have read Clausewitz should not be taken too seriously, as he was given to such statements. As Cyril Falls put it in his entry on Edmonds in the *Dictionary of National Biography*, "His humour as chief [director of military history] was mordant, but when he denounced one man as a crook, another as a drunkard, and a third as utterly incompetent, he was nine-tenths of the time playing an elaborate game." In any case, Emdonds clearly had read Stewart Murray's condensation.

Perhaps the best example of this odd change in attitude is T. E. Lawrence's postwar expression of disillusionment with Clausewitz. Lawrence had been profoundly impressed by him before the war, but during it he found that the works of Marshal Saxe were more relevant to the problems he himself faced in the Arabian desert. "If we were patient and superhuman-skilled, we could follow the direction of Saxe and reach victory without battle, by pressing our advantages mathematical and psychological."[21] Still, Lawrence acknowledged that Clausewitz's theory had helped him appreciate the specific peculiarities of his situation: "To me it seemed only a variety of war: and I could then see other sorts, as Clausewitz had numbered them, personal wars for dynastic reasons, expulsive wars for party reasons, commercial wars for trading reasons."[22] Cyril Falls later pointed out some distinct parallels between Lawrence's guerrilla war theories and Clausewitz's discussion of "a peasants' war."[23]

After the war, however, in a letter to Liddell Hart, Lawrence expressed dismay about the philosopher's influence. "Clausewitz had no humanity, and so his War became a monstrous inanimate science; it lost its art. Saxe was flesh and blood, and so his creation of war came to breathing life."[24] "The logical system of Clausewitz is too complete. It leads astray his disciples."[25]

It is quite possible that Lawrence was simply telling Liddell Hart what he wanted to hear.[26] Liddell Hart was fond of quoting Saxe in support of his own approach and in contrast with Clausewitz's alleged bloody-mindedness. The comment on Clausewitz's "disciples" is also redolent of Liddell Hart and does not reflect directly on Clausewitz. In fact, Lawrence suggested that Liddell Hart's own fate might be similar:

> You, at present, are trying (with very little help from those whose business it is to think upon their profession) to put the balance straight

after the orgy of the last war. When you succeed (about 1945) your sheep will pass your bounds of discretion, and have to be chivvied back by some later strategist. Back and forward we go.

Lawrence and other British survivors of the war seem to have been reacting against the rather un-English fling with theory in the period after the South African War and returning with a new bitterness to a more characteristic skepticism: "[Clausewitz's] book [was] so logical and fascinating, that unconsciously I accepted his finality, until a comparison of Kuhne and Foch disgusted me with soldiers, wearied me of their officious glory, making me critical of all their light."[27] It is as if, for a brief moment in history, British soldiers had thought they held the key to war. Finding that the most profound understanding of war did not change its hideous nature or render it much more controllable, they flung away the key in disgust.

15

J. F. C. Fuller and Basil Liddell Hart

It is ironic that the war that so damaged Clausewitz's reputation also produced the first true military theorists in British history—since Henry Lloyd (c. 1720–83), at least. By far the most prominent British theorists who emerged after the war were Captain Basil Liddell Hart and General J. F. C. Fuller. Both men were controversial in their lifetimes (and have remained so); both left important memoirs; and both have been the subjects of major biographies. Their attitudes toward Clausewitz have been discussed in some detail, in both the biographies and in articles especially devoted to that topic.[1] In fact, it has been widely assumed that the discussions of Clausewitz by these two men mark the parameters of his British reception.

Liddell Hart

Captain Sir Basil Henry Liddell Hart (1895–1970), the junior of the two, probably had more readers, but his reputation has not weathered well. He was born in Paris, the son of an English Protestant minister. In 1913 he entered Corpus Christi College at Cambridge to read modern history; he joined the Officer Training Corps upon the outbreak of war. In 1915 he was commissioned in the King's Own Yorkshire Light Infantry and, after three relatively short tours in the front lines, was badly gassed on the Somme in July of the following year. A pamphlet on platoon tactics that he wrote during his convalescence was issued to the army in 1917. Later, he wrote the tactical half of the army's official infantry manual, a work "which was promptly de-written by anonymous hands in the War Office."[2] He remained in the army after the war but was invalided out in 1924 and placed on the retired list, as a captain, in 1927.

Unable to afford a return to academia, Liddell Hart gravitated into journalism. In 1925, he succeeded the Clausewitzian Colonel Repington in the prestigious post of *Times* military correspondent, where he remained for the next ten years.

Along with Fuller, Liddell Hart became known as one of the leading proponents of mechanization, although his actual influence, particularly in Germany, is a matter of some dispute. Somewhat paradoxically, but as a natural outgrowth of his experience on the Western Front in World War I, he also became a strong believer in the superiority of the defense. He was most closely associated with the doctrine of "limited liability," the purpose of which was to avoid or minimize Britain's commitment to combat on the continent. In practice, his policy proved untenable under the circumstances of coalition warfare.

"Limited liability" was a natural expression of Liddell Hart's broader strategic theory, which he characterized as the "indirect approach" or "the British way in war." His overarching goal was to find some indirect way to strike at an enemy's strategic vitals, bypassing his main strength and thus avoiding the head-to-head confrontation that had led to the bloodbaths of the Great War.

Liddell Hart enjoyed considerable influence in the later 1930s through his advice to Secretary of State for War Leslie Hore-Belisha. Unfortunately, his suggestions on policies and personnel alienated much of the army establishment, and his personality was ill suited for participation in practical government. As one French admirer observed, "It is odd that Liddell Hart never realized that in peace, as in war, it is usually necessary to employ the strategy of indirect approach."[3] Discredited by the events of 1940, Liddell Hart painfully rebuilt his reputation after the war. In this he was aided by the advent of nuclear weapons, which made his limited approach to war seem more applicable, and by a gift for shameless self-promotion. Acclaimed by such luminaries as John F. Kennedy, who called him "the Captain who teaches Generals," he was knighted in 1966.

A charming man who had many enemies but far more friends, Liddell Hart's reputation as a military thinker stood very high at his death in 1970. Postmortem assessments, however, have been more ambivalent. His long-term place in military history is not yet settled, but he was clearly a man of both great talents and perhaps greater limitations.[4]

Throughout his writing career, Liddell Hart was persistently and bitterly critical of Clausewitz, portraying him as the "evil genius of military thought," as the "apostle of total war," and as a relentless advocate of mass and the offensive.[5] In his view, Clausewitz and/or his "disciples" were responsible for the bloodbath on the Western Front, 1914–18. In his more temperate comments, he placed the blame for the disasters of the Great War not on Clausewitz himself but on disciples who had "mis-interpreted" the subtleties of *On War*. He may have gotten this idea from Maude, a writer also very selective in his appreciation of Clausewitz, who claimed before the war that "it is to the spread of Clausewitz's ideas that the present state of more or less immediate readiness for war of all European armies is due."[6]

Liddell Hart greatly overestimated, however, the extent to which Clausewitz's work had been read and accepted. He believed that Moltke's successes and praise of Clausewitz had "brought an immense extension of Clausewitz's influence. Henceforth his gospel was accepted everywhere as true—and wholly true. All soldiers were quick to swallow it, although few were capable of digesting it."[7]

Liddell Hart freely credited Clausewitz with keen perceptions on the moral and psychological elements in war and cited him in support of his own arguments whenever it seemed useful. In 1951, for example, he fell back on the authority of Clausewitz's views on the defensive form of war when trying to justify his pre-1939 predictions that the defense would triumph.[8] Ultimately, however, he held that "the responsibility [for World War I] lies heaviest on Clausewitz" because—and here Liddell Hart made the same complaints that Jomini did—his "metaphysical" approach and his "abstract generalizations" so readily led people into error.

> Not one reader in a hundred was likely to follow the subtlety of his logic, or to preserve a true balance amid such philosophical jugglery. But everyone could catch such ringing phrases as—"We have only one means in war—the battle." "The combat is the single activity in war." "We may reduce every military activity in the province of strategy to the unit of single combats." "The bloody solution of the crisis, the effort for the destruction of the enemy's forces, is the first-born son of war." "Only great and general battles can produce great results." "Let us not hear of generals who conquer without bloodshed."
> By the reiteration of such phrases Clausewitz blurred the outlines of his philosophy, already indistinct, and made it a mere marching re-frain—a Prussian "*Marseillaise*"—which inflamed the blood and intox-icated the mind. In transfusion it became a doctrine fit to form corporals, not generals. For, by making battle appear the only "real warlike activity," his gospel deprived strategy of its laurels, reduced the art of war to the mechanics of mass slaughter, and incited generals to seek battle at the first opportunity, instead of creating an *advantageous* opportunity.[9]

Apart from his stylistic objections, which were in fact his fundamental complaint, Liddell Hart's critique of Clausewitz's theories concentrated largely on five points. First, he objected to the theory of absolute warfare and the nation in arms. He ignored the facts that the term "absolute war" was a philosophical abstraction and that the "nation in arms" was a historical reality rather than a product of Clausewitz's fevered imagination. *On War* was, of course, inconsistent in determining whether Napoleonic warfare had in fact attained the form of "total war." Nonetheless, it is certain that Clausewitz's "absolute war" and Ludendorff's "total war" were unrelated concepts.[10] Clausewitz's use of the former term was not the source of the war that embittered Liddell Hart.

Second, Liddell Hart objected to Clausewitz's alleged dictum that the strategic objective must be the destruction of the enemy's armed forces. This was, in fact, the objective that Clausewitz had concentrated on most heavily, but his discussion of the "center of gravity" in *On War* made clear that the focal point could be elsewhere, depending on social, political, and historical circumstances. Indeed, the term makes no sense unless it can be used to distinguish among a variety of different possible objectives.

Third (and it is a connected point, since it too relates to the concept of the "center of gravity"), Liddell Hart objected to Clausewitz's concentration on the destruction of the main enemy. He believed that this prescription was responsible for the "Westerners'" fixation on the battle of attrition in France, as opposed to the more creative "Easterners'" attempts to get at the Central Powers' alleged weak points on other fronts.[11] The frustration of Eastern projects that were undertaken at Salonika and Gallipoli and in Syria, in which a third of all British casualties were suffered, did not dissuade Liddell Hart from this view, nor did the fact that Corbett, a dyed-in-the-wool Clausewitzian, was an Easterner.

Fourth, Liddell Hart argued that Clausewitz, whom he nicknamed the "Mahdi of Mass," had reduced strategy to the simplistic act of bludgeoning the enemy to death with overwhelming numbers. The question, however, is not whether Clausewitz believed in the advantages of numbers (for he clearly did) but, first, whether he was right and, second, whether his theory could account for contrary historical examples. Regardless of what Clausewitz had said concerning the specific example of European armies at the close of the Napoleonic wars, his theoretical discussion of numbers made it clear that numerical superiority was only one of many factors deciding any particular contest.

Fifth, Liddell Hart complained that Clausewitz had focused on war to the detriment of the subsequent peace. This was probably his most legitimate charge, although considerations of the peace would fall naturally under the heading of "policy," which Clausewitz had assumed— for the purposes of theoretical discussion—would be designed with the best interests of the nation in mind. This assumption was perhaps the weakest link in Clausewitz's theory, or at least the most easily misunderstood, but then, Clausewitz was writing a book about war, not about policy.

Although containing considerably more than a grain of truth, Liddell Hart's condemnations of Clausewitz must be rejected as fundamentally wrongheaded. First of all, no writer can be held responsible for his readers' allegedly sloppy reading of his work, a doctrine that would paralyze creative thought. That would be rather like holding Christ responsible for the Inquisition. Second, it is clear that Clausewitz's most prominent readers and popularizers did, in fact, understand him accurately. Those who went on to promulgate the philosophy of war that Liddell Hart condemned were quite conscious and open in rejecting key aspects of the philosopher's analysis. Liddell Hart's argument is both contemptuous of other readers and misleading in claiming that Clausewitz's "ringing phrases" were somehow set apart from his "qualifications," which, he said, "came on later pages, and were conveyed in a philosophical language that befogged the plain soldier, essentially concrete minded."[12] As Michael Howard has pointed out, "the 'qualifications' are very emphatically set out, as an intrinsic part of Clausewitz's argument, not 'on later pages,' but [in] the very first chapter."[13]

In failing to respect the fact that Clausewitz had sought to create a dynamic, descriptive theory applicable under changing historical circumstances, Liddell Hart often committed the very mistakes of which he accused the philosopher's disciples. Like most of the prewar writers he condemned, he tailored his own efforts to purely contemporary circumstances and to forecasting the nature of the next war.

More important, Liddell Hart's blurring of the distinctions between Clausewitz and his later "disciples" led him into some impossible contortions. For example, he characterized "the narrow concept that war was purely the province of the armed forces, and that once war began the statesmen ought to abdicate from its direction in favor of the generals" as "pseudo-Clausewitzian."[14] It was, in fact, a blatant rejection of Clausewitz. He also criticized Clausewitz's definition of strategy because it "intrudes on the sphere of policy, or the higher conduct of the war, which must necessarily be the responsibility of the Government and not of the military leaders it employs as its agents."[15] In his critique of Erich Ludendorff, Liddell Hart opened with an attack on Clausewitz and then blasted Ludendorff for failing to appreciate the wisdom of Clausewitz's views.[16]

The Liddell Hart view of Clausewitz had a great influence on the views of many of his readers. In 1946, for instance, the U.S. Marine Corps historian Lynn Montross wrote that

> In the long run a military theorist must be judged not only by his writings but also by the interpretation of them on future battlefields. . . . [I]f Clausewitz fathered the most bloody and wasteful era of warfare in modern times, it is because lesser minds accepted his philosophy rather than his tactics [?], his flashing phrases rather than his sober modifications.

Montross's book remains on the reading list for the Marine Corps's Command and Staff course, which is somewhat amusing, since the newest Marine Corps doctrinal works draw so heavily on Clausewitz.[17] As another example, Russell Weigley's 1962 assessment of Robert M. Johnston (discussed earlier) appears to bear the Liddell Hart stamp. Barbara Tuchman's popular 1962 book on the outbreak of World War I, *The Guns of August*, relied on Liddell Hart's description.[18] Liddell Hart himself persisted in his criticisms of Clausewitz to the very end: His foreword to Samuel Griffith's 1963 translation of Sun Tzu's *Art of War* repeats the charges.[19]

Bernard Montgomery was very enthusiastic about Liddell Hart, a personal acquaintance of forty years. (He also read a lot of Henderson's work.) In 1968, Montgomery stated: "I did make attempts to read the writings of Clausewitz, a Prussian, and Jomini, a Swiss . . . but I couldn't take them in, and I turned to historians of my own nation and language." Montgomery was not, however, hostile to Clausewitz. Indeed, he considered the Prussian's insights into the moral, psychological, and political elements of war to be profound, especially in contrast with Jomini's. Although he found Clausewitz's language to be "exceedingly difficult to understand," he perceived that Liddell Hart's criticisms had been aimed at the philosopher's misinterpreters rather than at his concepts. In any case, he was satisfied with Liddell Hart because "whereas [Clausewitz and Jomini] were often wrong, Liddell Hart has proved to be generally right."[20]

Liddell Hart's success in distorting Clausewitz's legacy and reputation was unfortunate, and it raises some disturbing questions. That he was himself very interested in his Prussian predecessor is clear. He even acquired an original German edition of *Vom Kriege* and some writings in Clausewitz's own hand.[21] Indeed, in his own decision to make his name as a writer, Liddell Hart saw Clausewitz as something of a model: In a note to himself, he said

> To influence man's thought is far more important and more lasting in effect than to control their bodies or regulate their actions. . . . The men who have influenced thought by their words, especially their written words, are engraved more deeply in history . . . than the host of conquerors and kings, of statesmen and commercial magnates. . . . Even in the realm of war, which has covered so great a part of human activity, and affected so greatly human life and history, the name of Clausewitz stands out more and is better known to soldiers, who as a class are of limited education, than any of the generals of the 19th century, save perhaps Lee and Moltke.[22]

That he had read and in many respects understood the philosopher very well indeed is apparent in many of his references to *On War*, which are often quite perceptive.[23] Many writers have made the point that much of what Liddell Hart had to say was simply a restatement of Clausewitz. Much was also suspiciously similar to Corbett. (Wilkinson's views on this matter are discussed later.)

Further, Liddell Hart's criticism of Clausewitz's "disciples" is, in fact, a form of praise for their master, and Liddell Hart himself believed that he had clearly distinguished between the two. Responding privately to a review of his book *Strategy*, a review that strongly criticized his attacks on Clausewitz, Liddell Hart noted that the reviewer had "evidently read my analysis of Clausewitz rather superficially, for he fails to see that what I am attacking is the normal interpretation of Clausewitz, in contrast to the later trend of Clausewitz's own thought."[24]

Perhaps the reason that readers did not get this point was because Liddell Hart's idea of the "normal interpretation" was so wrong and because the positive aspects of his outlook on Clausewitz never came through clearly in his published writings. Extending the interpretation of John Mearsheimer, we might almost be tempted to describe his attacks on the philosopher as a symptom of careerism, of consciously distorting Clausewitz's message in order to make his own seem fresh.[25]

This is probably too Machiavellian a view. If Liddell Hart was deceiving anyone it was most likely himself. He was contemptuous of the mental faculties of the British military leadership, sometimes absurdly so. He and Fuller were among the principal architects of the "Colonel Blimp" image that has so distorted our conception of British military behavior in World War I and the interwar period. On the other hand, he was himself touched by the anti-intellectual traditions of the British army. His most virulent attacks on Clausewitz reflected resentment of the mental effort that the philosopher demanded from his readers, and it was the alleged complexity of the ideas expressed, not their content, that really incensed him. Further, as even his friendliest biographers have acknowledged, he tended to get tangled in his own prejudices and was never receptive to criticism.[26] Liddell Hart's attacks on Clausewitz are symptomatic of the curious blind spots in his often brilliant intellect that his biographers have often noted.

Liddell Hart's biggest blind spot was probably caused by his conception of himself as an original thinker. If that self-image was to be maintained, the power of Clausewitz's vision would have to be denied. If one were to delve into the murky waters of "psychohistory," one might speculate that Liddell Hart's subconscious mind accomplished this by blurring the distinction between Clausewitz and his "misinterpreters."

Toward the conclusion of his career, Liddell Hart's stated views did soften somewhat. He began to stress the idea that Clausewitz had, at the very end of his life, begun to develop a wiser attitude toward war. He nonetheless took a rather extreme position in the debate over how nearly finished a book *On War* is, lamenting that the German philosopher-soldier had been able to put down so very little of his newfound wisdom before his untimely death in 1831. The most balanced treatment that Liddell Hart ever gave Clausewitz appeared in his 1960 chapter on warfare in the *New Cambridge Modern History*. In it, he had much to say that was positive, but he also repeated *in toto* his customary attack.[27]

Curiously, Clausewitz's modern German editor, Werner Hahlweg (1912–89), wrote Liddell Hart and praised a draft version of this chapter, saying:

> I was especially interested in your thoughts on Clausewitz. After having carefully read all what you have written in your chapter here about the German philosopher of war, I must say, that I agree with you; and I

think, it will be valuable that your chapter will appear in the Cambridge modern history. Especially I agree with your pointing out the *misinterpretation* of Clausewitz, and people should be indebted to you, that you have given such instructive description of Clausewitz's main ideas and made clear the tension between idea and reality.[28]

Of course, Hahlweg was writing to Liddell Hart as a personal friend and at a time when the British writer was at the height of his prestige.[29] Perhaps Hahlweg simply realized that Liddell Hart could not be moved by a frontal attack and sought to move him by degrees to a more reasonable attitude. Also, his positive treatment of Liddell Hart in his discussion of "Clausewitz in the Anglo-Saxon World" cleverly served the double purpose of pacifying Liddell Hart and enlisting his support for the greatness of the Prussian philosopher.[30] That Liddell Hart went along with this is further evidence of his own belief that he had indeed given Clausewitz his due.

Hahlweg's approach may have had some effect, for ironically, Liddell Hart later participated at least nominally with him in the "Clausewitz Project" at Princeton. Organized in the early 1960s and involving such scholars as Gordon A. Craig, Bernard Brodie, John Shy, Peter Paret, Michael Howard, and Klaus Knorr, the project eventually resulted in the 1976 Howard/Paret translation of *Vom Kriege*.

This involvement came too late in Liddell Hart's career to have any impact on his legacy, however, and he remained opposed to giving Clausewitz a position in military studies that might rival his own. Peter Paret asked him in 1962 to write a letter in support of Paret's grant application for research and writing on Clausewitz. Liddell Hart graciously complied, but privately he wrote Paret that

> I am inclined to question a sentence in your descriptive note which suggests that "Clausewitz was one of the intellectual ancestors of the whole family of present-day doctrines of unconventional war." I shall be very interested to see how you fit him into the family tree in such a top position.[31]

Fuller

Major-General J. F. C. (John Frederick Charles) Fuller (1878–1966) is often associated with Liddell Hart, but the men were in many ways quite different. Fuller belonged to an older generation; his practical military experience was much greater; his interests were until a rather late date more narrowly tactical and technological; and his view of Clausewitz was much less static, undergoing considerable evolution.

On the other hand, they shared a tendency toward contempt for the intelligence of others and for that of the British officer corps in particular. Fuller once remarked that "putting over the truth is rather like giving a puppy a bolus, it has got to be wrapped in something the little creature likes, [and] I am afraid I am not very good at sugaring pills."[32] The title page of his memoirs quotes Herakleitos: "Asses would rather have refuse than gold." Fuller made it quite clear that this line was directed at the British military leadership. Someone skeptical of Fuller's approach might observe that the asses in this case were simply being sensible, preferring the digestible to the merely ornamental.

Both men were also profoundly shaken by the experience of World War I; both made their reputations as advocates of mechanization; and both suffered an eclipse in reputation during World War II (Fuller for his prewar connections with British fascism and for his alleged advocacy of an all-armored, tank-heavy force, universally rejected by 1943). Once out of uniform, each made his living through journalism, a profession that greatly affected the style, if not necessarily the content, of their writings. Both ended their days as rehabilitated military prophets, with considerable honor in their own countries as well as abroad.

Fuller came from a solidly middle class background. Like Liddell Hart, he was the son of a churchman. His mother was French, although she had been raised in Germany. Her son was known as Fritz until the Great War made it advisable to seek a new nickname, and his wife Sonia was German. His new sobriquet was Boney, descriptive of both his physical appearance and his Napoleonic stature, knowledge, and behavior. His biographers have made much of his small size and its impact on his sometimes bellicose personality.

Intelligent and highly literate, Fuller entered Sandhurst in 1897, was commissioned in 1898, and was immediately posted to Ireland. In late 1899 his regiment left for South Africa and arrived at Capetown at the hour of one of Britain's major military embarrassments. Fuller had been in the country long enough to determine that the British army had no idea what it was doing when he was struck down by appendicitis. He was evacuated to England but returned in time to participate in the last phases of the war. After some desultory regimental combat duty, he wangled a more exciting assignment as chief of a largely native reconnaissance company. This was an exciting, educational, and dangerous job (since the Boers put a death sentence on white officers leading black troops). The independence and intensity of this position made it a formative experience for young Fuller.

His next formative experience soon followed. He was posted to India, where his combat experience was slight but he took the opportunity to delve into Hindu mysticism. Fuller also became acquainted with the English mystic Aleister Crowley, who—aside from his frankly bizarre influence on Fuller's private life—introduced Fuller to Maude and thence to Clausewitz. Although the latter connection proved fruitful, Fuller's mystical interests became a source of embarrassment for both Fuller and his acolytes: J. E. Edmonds (as bitter a critic of Fuller as of Clausewitz) was brutally sarcastic in his reviews of Fuller's work, assailing him not only for the shallowness of his attempts at universal military theory but also for his unfortunate essays into mysticism. In particular, Fuller's obsession with the number 3 brought down a devastating barrage. To Fuller's trinities of "earth, water, and air" and "men, women, and children," Edmonds suggested adding "coat, trousers, and boots" and "knife, fork, and spoon."[33] (Curiously, Fuller seems never to have picked up on the mystical significance of a number of three-part arguments and trinities in *On War.*)

Posted back to England in 1906, Fuller served as the adjutant (and only regular officer) of a volunteer regiment. This assignment was important in a couple of ways: first because it gave him experience with the sort of citizen soldiers who would fight the coming world wars and second because it gave him time to do—for the first time in his military career—some serious military reading. He entered Camberley in January 1914 and was saved from the initial slaughter of junior BEF officers by his subsequent assignment to the general staff.

During this same period, Fuller began to write seriously on military topics. (He had already published some works on mysticism.) These articles generally concerned troop training and tactics. He also began developing his ideas on the "Principles of War," that is, the objective, mass, offensive, and so forth (the list went through several evolutions). As familiar as that sort of list may seem to soldiers today, it originated (insofar as any such idea "originates") with Fuller.

As a corps staff officer in France by 1915, Fuller soon became involved in setting up and running a series of highly successful rear-area courses for frontline officers, many of them quite senior to Fuller. Thus began his habit of lecturing to his superiors.

In mid-1916, Fuller was introduced to the weapon with which his name is usually linked, the tank, the development of which was entirely out of his hands. Its tactical employment, however, bore his stamp. By December he was a member of what became the Tank Corps. He was involved in planning most of the major tank attacks, particularly those on Cambrai in November 1917 and on Amiens in 1918. Functioning always as a staff officer rather than a commander, Fuller was known as the "brain of the Tank Corps," a job that made his reputation.

Fuller's most famous scheme was one that was never executed, "Plan 1919." Developed in May 1918, this plan has been hailed as the precursor of the blitzkrieg. It was based on the ideas of massive armored attacks, tactical air support, and the aim not of physically destroying the enemy but of paralyzing his command system.

After the war, Fuller (a colonel in 1919) held a series of interesting and important jobs. He was chief instructor at Camberley from 1923 to 1926, then military assistant to the chief of the Imperial General Staff, and then commander of the Experimental Mechanized Force. Unfortunately, he quit the last job in a huff, proceeded to antagonize the army's leadership on a number of often peripheral issues, published several con-

troversial books, and was retired in 1933 as a major-general. Thereafter
he made his way primarily as a military journalist. He also fell in with Sir
Oswald Mosley, the leader of British fascism, a serious error that damaged
his relationship with Liddell Hart and probably precluded (if his feud with
the military leadership had not already) his active employment in the war
of 1939–45.

It would be impossible to summarize Fuller's military thinking here,
and the interested reader should consult A. J. Trythall's and Brian Holden
Reid's capable biographies.[34] In regard to his views on Clausewitz, Fuller
appreciated the philosophy of *On War*, albeit in a creative, erratic, and
typically idiosyncratic manner. It is questionable whether Fuller's early
outlook on war was directly shaped by it, although he was a member of
the prewar generation of thinkers and he undoubtedly absorbed a great
deal indirectly through other reading or through the influence of F. N.
Maude, who introduced him to *On War* around 1906. For all his enthusiasm for Clausewitz, however, Maude was one of those who rejected key
aspects of his argument.

In contrast with Liddell Hart's, Fuller's attitude toward Clausewitz
shows a steady evolution. In the 1920s and 1930s, he was likely to use
Clausewitz to make or support a point, but he ignored him on the most
basic issues. In 1926, he dismissed *On War* as "little more than a mass of
notes, a cloud of flame and smoke." Fuller's attempt to create a "scientific"
theory of war was fundamentally alien to the message of *On War*; he called
Clausewitz's comment on the absurdity of the term "science of war" a
"preposterous assertion."[35] In *The Dragon's Teeth* (1932), although he
gave the philosopher credit for his insight into the political nature of war,
he portrayed Clausewitz as obsolete, a "general of the agricultural period
of war." Clausewitz's experience and mode of thought described a system
of absolute war that "was waged not to create a better peace but utterly to
destroy the enemy." "In spite of these defects," his book *On War* had gone
on to become "the military bible of Europe." "We must dethrone Napoleon the prophet and his high-priest Clausewitz, and must breathe into war
the spirit and energy of science, and so militarily try and catch up, by a
process of rapid transformation, with the position industry has arrived at
today." Fuller quoted Liddell Hart's assault on Clausewitz approvingly.[36]

Shortly afterward, in *War and Western Civilization*, Fuller quoted
at length from *On War*, but his purpose was to accuse Clausewitz of
"democratizing" war, part of the larger condemnation of democracy that
accompanied his movement into authoritarian ideologies and the British
fascist movement. The connection is understandable, but the accusation
is not. As Michael Howard has put it, "The transition to democracy, as
Clausewitz was the first thinker to recognize, so far from abolishing war,
brought into it an entirely new dimension of violent passion to which
advances in technology could, unfortunately, give free rein."[37] Fuller's
attitude toward the Prussian's contribution was now rather schizophrenic;
he was sweepingly critical in places yet spoke elsewhere of "the solid rock

of Clausewitz." (Liddell Hart, in contrast, called Clausewitz's theories "a house built on sand.")[38]

In his *Memoirs* (1936), all of Fuller's few references to Clausewitz are positive, although often used in humorous reference to his own frustration with the British army: "Though Clausewitz said that 'in war the simple is difficult,' he should have added 'in peace it is generally impossible.'"[39]

By 1943, in *Machine Warfare*, Fuller took a much more positive attitude, seeking now to condense *On War* for the enlightenment of his readers. His summary, however, which was very similar to that given in *War and Western Civilization*, still presented only the extremes in Clausewitz's theories. Fuller thus—unintentionally at this point—lent support to Liddell Hart's caricature.[40]

In 1945, Fuller wrote a brief introduction to the British edition of the American colonel Joseph I. Greene's condensation of *On War*. Although his stated purpose was to spread a better understanding of the German military mentality, he noted unequivocally that "as a philosophy of war it still remains unrivalled." Considering Fuller's own attempts to produce a coherent "science" of war, this is a remarkable admission, although his endorsement of Clausewitz's view that war belongs to the province of social life rather than art or science was carefully hedged.[41]

After 1945 and Hiroshima, Fuller's attitude toward Clausewitz became still more enthusiastic. This change accompanied his personal evolution from a mere contemporary-oriented military critic to a genuine military historian with considerable claim to academic status. The references in his 1949 *The Second World War*, a book that played an important role in the reestablishment of his reputation, are penetrating and entirely positive, save for a justifiable lamentation on the briefness of Clausewitz's discussion of limited war. (He also discussed, briefly, Delbrück's extrapolations from Clausewitz's theories.)[42] In his last major book, *The Conduct of War* (1961), Fuller noted that "had the statesmen and generals of the two world wars heeded [Clausewitz's] words, they could not have blundered as they did." He repeated the Liddell Hart's criticisms, saying that Clausewitz "indirectly was responsible for the vast extension of unlimited warfare in the twentieth century," but he added:

> On the other hand, his penetrating analysis of the relationship of war and policy has never been excelled, and is even more important today than when first expounded. Strange to relate, its lack of appreciation was an even more potent factor in the extension of unlimited warfare than his absolute concept.

He devoted a whole chapter to Clausewitz's theories, producing a much more balanced treatment than ever before. This included intelligent if sometimes cranky understandings of the discussion of "real" as opposed to "absolute" war, the dynamic relationship of attack and defense, and the "center of gravity." Most remarkable, perhaps, was Fuller's final surrender on the issue of war as art or science: Clausewitz "was the first, and remains one of the few, who grasped that war 'belongs to the province of social life.'"[43]

In sharp contrast with Liddell Hart, Fuller embraced Clausewitz's conception of the decisive battle, which is perhaps not too surprising in the case of the author of "Plan 1919." Following his original mentor on the subject, Maude, Fuller insisted vehemently (despite his earlier reference to Clausewitz as Napoleon's "high-priest") that Clausewitz did not grasp Napoleonic warfare. His own final criticism remained:

> But of all Clausewitz's blind spots, the blindest was that he never grasped that the true aim of war is peace and not victory; therefore that peace should be the ruling idea of policy, and victory only the means to its achievement. Nowhere does he consider the influence of violence on eventual peace; actually, the word "peace" barely occurs half a dozen times in *On War*. In Napoleon he found the past-master of his theory of absolute war; yet to where did absolute war with its maximum of violence lead him? Not to the peace he aspired, but to St. Helena. Violence pushed to its utmost bounds ended in absolute failure. Better the advice of Montesquieu: "That nations should do each other the most good during peacetime and the least harm during wartime without harming their true interests," if peace is to be anything more than a temporary suspension of arms.

Fuller's criticism is based on the impact of the Versailles settlement after 1918 rather than the experience in Europe after Vienna in 1815 or in Germany and Japan after World War II. Both of the last experiences indicate that ruthless violence in war is much more easily forgiven than is inequity in peace. In actuality, the word *peace* appears in *On War* at least one hundred times. It shows up twenty-seven times in Book 1, five times in Chapter 1 alone. Clausewitz also said of ends and means in war that "the original means of strategy is victory—that is, tactical success; its ends, in the final analysis, are those objects which will lead directly to peace."[44] Fuller's criticism of Clausewitz's alleged adoration of Napoleon also misses a crucial point: Clausewitz, of course, regarded Napoleon's failure as a virtual inevitability, given the workings of the balance of power.

It would be easy to arrive at the conclusion that Fuller sought by extending Clausewitz's view of war as a rational extension of a state's legitimate policy and his assumption that the balance of power would always work to counteract a would-be conqueror. It is interesting to note in this regard that in one of his earliest essays on Clausewitz, Michael Howard concluded by noting precisely the message that Fuller and Liddell Hart had found missing: "It is salutary to re-read Clausewitz and to learn again that though victory may be the proper object of a battle, the proper object of a war can only be a better peace."[45]

In a 1961 exchange with his editors at Rutgers, one of them suggested to Fuller that his *Conduct of War* had

given the impression that your intention is nothing less than to outmode Clausewitz. . . . Having made extensive use of Clausewitz myself
during the Second World War when I was on tap as a speaker about
the relationship between books and the conduct of war, I take this
intention of yours with perhaps undue seriousness. Neither of us will
be around forever but I should very much like that your book should
be.

Fuller replied:

As regards Clausewitz, my intention is not to outmode him, but—were
there such a word—to in-mode him; to bring him into fashion [and]
get people to read him instead of quoting him. The unfortunate thing
about "On War" is that about nine-tenths of it is now obsolete, and
the one-tenth, which is pure gold, gets lost in the rubble. In Chapter
IV I have panned out the latter in some five or six thousand words. If
statesmen [and] generals cannot digest that much, then they had better
pack up.

In my opinion, Clausewitz's level is on that of Copernicus, Newton,
[and] Darwin—all were cosmic geniuses who upset the world. They
could not help doing so, and the same may be said of Gautama, Christ
[and] Mahomet. If my [*Conduct of War*] follows suit, it will not be
because of what I have written, but because my study of Clausewitz
has compelled me to write it.[46]

Fuller's obeisance to Clausewitz did not, however, come across very
clearly in his published work. His impact on Clausewitz's image and
reputation is hard to trace or to judge, but his attempts to summarize
Clausewitz for those who were in his view too boneheaded to read or
understand *On War* for themselves often backfired. In "panning out"
Clausewitz's essence, Fuller reduced *On War*'s philosophy to its extremes, tending unintentionally to support the image projected by Liddell
Hart.[47] Fuller's American disciple Hoffman Nickerson certainly picked up
much of his early ambivalence toward Clausewitz and, along with Fuller,
grew more respectful during World War II. That Fuller was unable to take
a more consistent position and to be more critical of his own work in
light of Clausewitz's example was a function of Fuller's eccentric personality and constant drive to assert his own individuality. Nonetheless, his
assessment was clearly more positive and sophisticated than Liddell Hart's.

Wilkinson on Liddell Hart and Clausewitz

Ironically, Fuller's own attempts to create a "scientific" military theory
were fundamentally incompatible with Clausewitz's, whereas the ideas of
Liddell Hart could, with relatively little effort, have been restated in
Clausewitzian terms. Such at least was the argument made by Spenser
Wilkinson in 1927.[48] Wilkinson was personally fond of Liddell Hart but
skeptical of him as an original theorist: "Liddell Hart is a keen fellow

whom I am disposed to like," but "a little too much the slave of his own theories, which he makes into dogmas."[49]

The title of Wilkinson's critique, "Killing No Murder," was a clever double entendre based on Liddell Hart's advocacy of gas warfare and indiscriminate bombing against defenseless enemy cities. According to Liddell Hart, obviously influenced by the ideas of the Italian air theorist Giulio Douhet, such a policy could hardly be a crime if it led to the speedy conclusion of the war and a consequent minimization of overall casualties. Wilkinson's counterargument, based on his own views on the strategic value of the moral high ground, was that killing off a harebrained proposal of this nature was no crime either.

Wilkinson's article was basically a rebuttal of Liddell Hart's *The Re-making of Modern Armies*, which contained the usual attacks on Clausewitz.[50] In his chapter "The Napoleonic Fallacy," Liddell Hart had denounced the "orthodox schools" of military thought. Wilkinson, although attracted to aspects of his approach, rejected Liddell Hart's claims to theoretical originality.

> I should like to persuade Captain Liddell Hart that he is himself a disciple, in my sense, of the orthodox school, and that in this chapter he is propounding a paradox. . . . The doctrine which Captain Liddell Hart denounces as erroneous and mischievous, and which he calls Napoleonic, is attributed by him not to Napoleon but to "his great German expositor, Carl von Clausewitz." The classical interpreter of Napoleon's methods was not Clausewitz, but one of Napoleon's generals, Jomini. Clausewitz is the representative of the ideas not of Napoleon, but of his chief German adversaries, Scharnhorst and Gneisenau. . . . This being the theory of Clausewitz, what is according to Captain Liddell Hart the true doctrine to be contrasted with it? I give it in his own words: "The aim of a nation in war is to subdue the enemy's will to resist, with the least possible human and economic loss itself. . . . [O]ur goal in war can only be attained by the subjugation of the opposing will. . . . [A]ll such acts as defeat in the field, propaganda, blockade, diplomacy, or attack on the centres of government and population are seen to be but means to that end; we are free to weigh the respective merits of each, and to choose whichever is most suitable and most economic, *i.e.*, that which will gain the goal with the minimum disruption of our national life during and *after* the war. . . . The destruction of the enemy's armed forces is but a means—and not necessarily an inevitable or infallible one—to the attainment of the real objective."
>
> With the best will in the world I fail to see that this is anything more than a repetition of Clausewitz.

In arguing that Liddell Hart's arguments bore more than a passing resemblance to Clausewitz's, Wilkinson was by no means alone.[51]

Wilkinson also took Liddell Hart to task for his contradictory attitude toward violence in war. Despite his evident willingness to bomb defenseless civilians, "it turns out that he is after that old will o' the wisp, victory without battles or bloodshed." Wilkinson brought up Liddell Hart's selective quotation from Maurice de Saxe (T. E. Lawrence's alleged mentor): "I am not in favor of giving battle. . . . I am even convinced that a clever general can wage war *his whole life* without being compelled to do so."[52] Liddell Hart contrasted this sensible attitude with Clausewitz's and Foch's bloody-mindedness. Unfortunately, as Wilkinson pointed out, Saxe had gone on to say "but for all that I do not pretend to say that when you find the chance of crushing the enemy you ought not to attack him . . . and, above all, [you] must not be satisfied with merely remaining master of the field." That is, one must pursue, à la Clausewitz. Such pursuits are bloody by definition. Saxe had, after all, built his own reputation on three victorious battles.

Wilkinson's defense of Clausewitz has something of the quality of a rearguard action. Liddell Hart certainly read it but, to judge by his reply and subsequent writings, failed to heed most of it. Citing Wilkinson, Liddell Hart subsequently provided a more balanced assessment of Saxe in *The British Way of Warfare* (1932) and also one of his most subtle appreciations of Clausewitz's own (as opposed to his "misinterpreters'") argument.[53] He soon returned, however, to his customary broadside attack.

Nonetheless, it is clear that both Liddell Hart and Fuller found a great deal of inspiration in *On War*.

16

Clausewitz's British Proponents

Liddell Hart's attacks on Clausewitz may not have convinced all of the military intellectuals, but they provided the conventional wisdom among nonintellectual soldiers and many nonmilitary writers. Apart from Wilkinson's critique of Liddell Hart, there were few voices raised against him in direct defense of Clausewitz. George Orwell found the description of Clausewitz given in Liddell Hart's *The British Way in Warfare* to be unconvincing, but whether Orwell himself had read Clausewitz is uncertain. He did note, however, that "a theory does not gain ground unless material conditions favor it," a comment that reflects a historicist view very similar to Clausewitz's.[1] The American writer Hoffman Nickerson lambasted Liddell Hart for "criticizing the great Clausewitz" but did so near the end of the war when the British theorist's prestige was at its lowest ebb.[2]

Fuller's critics included Major-General H. Rowan-Robinson, who questioned both Fuller and Liddell Hart for making excessive claims for mechanization.[3] Like Fuller, Rowan-Robinson drew freely and selectively on Clausewitzian arguments, but he made no specific defense of or attack on Clausewitz himself. Rowan-Robinson's use of Einsteinian space–time imagery, like Fuller's "science of war," marked an attempt to recast military theory in the image of the most modern physical sciences, an attempt fundamentally at odds with Clausewitz's view of war as a social phenomenon.[4] He accepted that war was essentially social in nature but held that this was irrelevant to its conduct, which depended on a mastery of scientific techniques—logistics, engineering, gunnery, and the like. Leadership was indeed an art, but the practical business of war was rooted in science: "Napoleon was a consummate artist. Berthier, his chief of staff, was a scientist."[5] The difficulty with this partial acceptance of Clausewitz's definition is that it essentially equates the war leader's problem with the engineer's: War remains a passive thing to be manipulated (whether through "science" or "art"), rather than a conflict between active and sentient wills, with a dynamic of its own.

One of the more solid British treatments of Clausewitz in the early 1940s came from Cyril Falls (1888–1971). An army captain (Royal Inniskilling Fusiliers) and a general staff officer in the Great War, Falls was an official historian of the war from 1923 to 1939. In 1939 he became military correspondent for the *Times*, as had Repington and Liddell Hart before him. Following in Wilkinson's footsteps, he served as Chichele Professor of Military History at Oxford from 1946 to 1953, a post that Liddell Hart craved but failed to win. Falls wrote at least one novel and dabbled in literary criticism, but he was primarily a nuts-and-bolts military historian, writing unit histories, broader histories of the world wars, and general treatments of the art of war.

Falls's two most interesting books from our point of view were discussions of the contemporary problems of World War II: *The Nature of Modern Warfare* (a collection of his Lees Knowles lectures at Cambridge in 1941) and *Ordeal by Battle* (1943).[6] Falls's anguish over the barbarization of war led him into some moral arguments similar to Wilkinson's, and his wartime books were to some extent attempts to explain that barbarization, to estimate to what extent Britain must adjust to it, and to determine to what degree she could safely resist it. It is uncertain when Falls first read Clausewitz, but it was probably in the very late 1930s and certainly before he wrote these two books.

In *The Nature of Modern Warfare*, Falls drew heavily on Clausewitz. Given Falls's frequent lamentations about the barbarity of war, it is surprising that he was so comfortable with a military philosopher so coldly logical on the subject. Nonetheless, his attitude was entirely positive: "If I frequently cite Clausewitz, it is because his is the only great mind that I know of which has ever made a study of warfare wherein profound philosophical conceptions are allied with wide practical experience." (Falls suggested that only Sun Tzu might be placed in the same league.)[7] In order to distinguish the "general elements of war" from the shifting impressions wrought by current events, he attempted to approach Clausewitz's philosophical goals. He did connect Clausewitz ("honourable and high-minded man though he was") to the steady deterioration in German military behavior but did not hold him responsible for it. He distinguished clearly between Clausewitz's "absolute war," which is never attained in reality, and Ludendorff's "total war." Falls went to considerable lengths to explain the theoretical superiority of the defense despite the events of 1940. Rather oddly, although he raised the old idea of pursuing a strategical offensive while relying on the tactical defensive (as J. F. Maurice did), he rejected the concept of a strategic defensive carried out through offensive tactics (which is much closer to Clausewitz's original discussion). Falls's discussion of mountain warfare made much the same argument as had *On War*, but his discussion was based on the work of Pierre de Bourcet (1700–80), one of Clausewitz's French predecessors and a favorite of Spenser Wilkinson.[8]

Although he was a solid and earnest writer, Falls lacked the penetrating brilliance of Wilkinson. He was, of course, immensely pleased by the praise that Herbert Rosinski bestowed on his book in a review focused almost entirely on its Clausewitzian elements. A close reading of Rosinski's review nonetheless shows that despite his free use of adjectives like *brilliant*, *vivid*, and *striking*, he took a rather condescending view of Falls's work.[9] (In fact, nearly all of Rosinski's reviews tended to gush a bit, probably because of his rather desperate personal situation, which mandated caution and an energetic search for allies. The condescension was also typical.) He concluded, however, by saying: "It is high praise for Captain Falls that his work can be discussed in the light of the thought of that master of military thinking."

Falls responded to Rosinski's compliments with another heavily Clausewitzian book, *Ordeal by Fire*. A more ambitious work than its predecessor, it did not differ materially in its treatment of Clausewitz. With this work he clearly sought, as he put it, to be placed at least on the same shelf with Clausewitz, and at least one of his reviewers put it there. This was not necessarily a compliment. Though impressed by Falls, the reviewer was not particularly fond of the Prussian philosopher, identifying him as a Pole and complaining of his "ponderous, tiresome" book.[10]

Falls's inaugural lecture as Chichele professor in 1946 made positive references to Clausewitz, and its key theme was the human factor in war, but he also stressed the economic component that Clausewitz had generally ignored. Falls argued that economics is just as important to war as policy is but seemed to think that the two were somehow completely distinct from each other. By this point, Falls had ceased to quote Clausewitz so frequently. Not, it appears, because he had begun to doubt but because he thought he had pretty well absorbed *On War* and it was time to push on.[11] Falls's book, *The Art of War: From the Age of Napoleon to the Present Day* (1961), makes several references to Clausewitz.[12] The treatment is basically very positive, but there are some caustic phrases; for example, "The cloudy, diffuse, and repetitive Clausewitz, master of the obvious, yet ever and anon giving out sparks of genius, is never likely to be deposed from the office of high priest in the temple of Mars." I would speculate that this was a defensive reflex in reaction to Liddell Hart, then in his ascendancy. More curious is Falls's criticism of Corbett's "belittlement of the doctrine of 'seeking out and destroying the enemy,'" especially given Falls's strong support of Clausewitz's position on the strength of the defense.[13]

Another positive treatment of Clausewitz came from old Frederick

Maurice's son, Major-General Sir Frederick Barton Maurice (1871-1951). Maurice had an interesting military career, including service in the Boer War, a stint as instructor at the Staff College under "Wully" Robertson (1913), service in France (1914/15), and a long assignment as director of military operations at the War Office (1915–18), again under Robertson. This career was terminated rather abruptly when he resigned and went to the newspapers with accusations that Lloyd George was deceiving Parliament about the strength of the British army in France. Lloyd George prevailed (evidently by lying), and Maurice was retired without inquiry by the Army Council. Later, he became one of the most thoughtful critics of the theories of Fuller and Liddell Hart.[14]

In his frequently cited 1929 book, *British Strategy*, Maurice said of Clausewitz that his "three volumes *On War* . . . are still today the best general study of its art."[15] Maurice drew heavily on Clausewitz, Henderson, and Foch, comparing their differing interpretations of the "principles of war" with Fuller's.[16] On the principle of "economy of force," he correctly understood Clausewitz's use of the term, "which may be put in colloquial language as taking care that all parts of an army are pulling their weight."[17] His overall analysis, however, emphasized Clausewitz's view that war was a development of social life, stressing the role of public opinion.

Maurice also addressed the problem of interpreting Clausewitz's famous statement that "war is a continuation of policy." To him it meant that "the function of the state was to decide on the policy which was in its best interest, to be strong enough to enforce that policy, and in the last resort to use war to carry it through." This view, said Maurice, had gained general acceptance in Europe before 1914. He criticized the Germans, however, citing Freiherr von Maltzalm (*sic*) in particular, for getting carried away with the idea: "War has for its aim [said Maltzahn] to compel peace on our conditions. Armed peace aims at preparing the means for war in such strength and in such a state of readiness that the enemy, the State with whose interests our interests conflict, will remain at peace under our conditions." Like Clausewitz and Moltke, Maurice had great faith in the workings of the balance of power, and he observed that that system could not tolerate such a policy. The Great War was the result, but the war proved that in a contest between the Great Powers even the victors would suffer material losses. "There has, therefore, been a revulsion against the doctrine that war is the continuation of policy." Perhaps overly optimistic about the power of world opinion, Maurice argued that "no great Power, no General Staff, will henceforth openly assert that war is a continuation of policy in the sense in which that phrase was interpreted in Germany. Therefore, as a principle of war it is dead."

Still a realist, he added, "None of which alters the fact that war is a political act." The pursuit of inimical policies by competing states would again, inevitably, lead to war. Maurice felt that the change in public attitudes in Europe as a whole would, however, have the advantage for

Britain that the next war, when it did come, would likely find all of the belligerents as ill prepared for it as Britain habitually was.[18] This was a view which might have had some validity had it not been for the rebirth of militarism in the virulent form of fascism.

While Maurice was critical of Corbett for his speculations on the possibility of limited wars between the Great Powers, he was hopeful that the League of Nations, using the weapon of blockade, could enforce a version of collective security "without employing any other form of military action."[19] This faith in the League of Nations was unusual among military theorists (those in uniform, at least) and was probably transitory; *British Strategy* was written in the unrealistic international atmosphere that surrounded the signing of the Kellogg–Briand Pact in 1928. The pact specifically called for the renunciation of "war as an instrument of policy," the use of this term being perhaps its only concession to Clausewitzian theory.

Rowan-Robinson, however, viewed the creation of the League in a somewhat similar manner and described it in explicitly Clausewitzian terms:

> [Clausewitz] intended to convey to the mind of his readers that a government in pursuit of a policy, if unable to overcome opposition by other means, such as friendly consultation, diplomatic and economic pressure, would eventually turn to war for the achievement of their purpose. . . . There is a prospect that the pressure of states, whose interests are not immediately engaged, will deflect the continuation of policy from the direction of war to that of conciliation and arbitration. To this end, the nations, harrowed by the ghastly tragedy of the Great War and desperately anxious to avoid the possibility of another such catastrophe, created the League of Nations. . . . [T]he experiment has not proved an unqualified success; but the lessons learnt from its failures may enable the League to be rebuilt on firmer foundations and thus eventually achieve its noble aims. At the moment, however, war—not arbitration—remains the continuation of policy.[20]

In this case, Maurice's and Rowan-Robinson's analyses seem to have taken them close to Clausewitz's essentially conservative views on the workings of the balance of power.

On War was thus by no means unread in the British Empire in this period. Beyond Falls's and Maurice's positive treatments in dealing with contemporary issues, classicists like F. E. Adcock and the Australian W. J. Woodhouse made extensive use of Clausewitz's historical philosophy in their investigations of ancient campaigns.[21] F. N. Maude corresponded with various other writers, British and American, concerning Clausewitz's putative influence on Lincoln during the American Civil War.[22] Clausewitz continued to exert an influence through prewar British writings, through translated German military writings, and through his impact—denied, disguised, or distorted though it was—on the thinking of Fuller and Liddell Hart. Many British officers important in World War II but quite junior during the pre–World War I craze for Clausewitz had read his major work. For example, Field Marshal Sir Claude Auchinleck (1884–1981), victor in the first battle of Alamein, told Liddell Hart of a youthful infatuation with *On War*.[23] Auchinleck's letter indicated that he had gotten over this infatuation, but such comments made to Liddell Hart are always suspect. Nonetheless, the image connected with Clausewitz's name drifted away from the reality and is probably best summed up by Liddell Hart's nickname for him: "the Mahdi of Mass and mutual massacre." One seeks in vain for any meaningful reference to Clausewitz in writings by or about such significant British figures as Churchill (despite Churchill's reported interest in Corbett) or the air power theorists (discussed next).

17

The Air Power Theorists

In his 1966 book, *The Military Intellectuals in Britain, 1918–1939*, Robin Higham states that "Like the *philosophes*, the airpower theorists in a perfectly logical way had created another heavenly city built, this time, upon a solid nineteenth-century Clausewitzian base."[1] It is rather difficult to determine what Higham meant by this, since his long discussion of the air power thinkers contains few meaningful references to Clausewitz. British airman E. J. Kingston-McCloughry—who, Higham says, "took the Clausewitzian assumption that the only way to defeat the enemy was in battle"—later derided Clausewitz's work as a "dead schema" and discussed his ideas only in the past tense.[2] Higham's definition of "Clausewitzian" appears to derive from Liddell Hart's, but Liddell Hart thought that his own "Argument for Airpower" was a decisive refutation of Clausewitzian thought.[3]

It is in fact difficult to find any positive reference—or, for that matter, any reference at all—to Clausewitz in the works of any of the major interwar air power writers in either Britain or the United States. As far as I can determine, Billy Mitchell (1876–1936) never mentioned Clausewitz. Neither did the influential Italian theorist Giulio Douhet (1869–1930), whose book contains no direct reference to Clausewitz although it clearly is influenced by the quasi-Clausewitzian currents of pre–World War I continental military writing.[4] In his post–World War II book, *Air Power,* the Russian-born American Alexander de Seversky remarked that the air power theorists "might not always find a common language with Clausewitz, but they speak the same strategic idiom as Mahan. The military problems and laws of action of air and seapower are almost identical—merely transposed to the third dimension." In his single direct reference to Clausewitz, he quoted him to the effect that "the destruction of enemy military forces is the chief objective of the whole act of war."[5]

This absence of interest is not too surprising, given that Mitchell and Douhet, like most of the air power enthusiasts, felt that the coming of the air age represented a new era in human history and that the determinants of the form of war in any epoch were essentially technological. Dated historical theories were of little relevance.[6] Still, it is a bit curious that the early proponents of strategic bombing did not attempt to use Clausewitz's discussion of "absolute war" for theoretical justification.

Although Clausewitz made no appearance in the works of the major air theorists, he received at least some attention from the U.S. Army Air Corps at the doctrinal level. Lieutenant (later Major General) Haywood S. Hansell was an instructor at the Air Corps Tactical School (ACTS) at Maxwell Field, Alabama, from 1935 to 1938. Later, he was a member of Hap Arnold's staff and helped develop *AWPD-1*, the Air Corps basic doctrinal manual for strategic air warfare during World War II. His lectures at ACTS make some reference to Clausewitz, and Clausewitzian terms like "center of gravity" appear in Air Corps doctrine. In fact, the key difference between Army and Air Corps doctrine lay in the location of that center; the soldiers saw it in the enemy's army, the airmen in the enemy's industrial war-making capacity. ACTS training materials, however, contain very little overtly theoretical discussion, and there does not appear to be any reason to consider Clausewitz to have been a significant influence on either Hansell or *AWPD-1*.[7]

On the other hand, historian Martin Kitchen recounts an interesting incident in the air war that might lead somewhere for a diligent researcher. "In the summer of 1943," he reports, "the allies dropped leaflets on Germany saying that Hitler should have read his Clausewitz more carefully."[8]

18

Clausewitz and the Americans

The post–Vietnam War American passion for Clausewitz has led many recent writers to project an appreciation for his work back onto the American soldiers of the interwar period, often with an eye toward explaining U.S. successes in World War II. For example, Colonel (USA) Charles F. Brower IV argued in his 1987 Ph.D. dissertation, "The Joint Chiefs of Staff and National Policy: American Strategy and the War with Japan, 1943–1945," that "well-schooled in their study of Mahan and Clausewitz, the Joint Chiefs of Staff understood clearly the political relationship of war and national policy and the pervasive and continuous influence of policy upon strategy."[1]

Unfortunately, Brower never demonstrated how they came to be "well-schooled" on Clausewitz, nor did he ever cite any Clausewitzian argument other than the overworked and underanalyzed line that "war is the continuation of policy by other means." Although that particular phrasing is Clausewitz's, the idea in its most widely understood meaning could have come just as easily from Mahan, Jomini, or even Machiavelli. Also uncited are the most significant British and American transmitters of Clausewitz's ideas, Corbett, Meyers, and Wilkinson. Since all of Brower's quotations from Clausewitz come from a 1976 translation that differs in some noteworthy respects from any version that the 1943 Joint Chiefs of Staff might have perused, this particular part of his thesis remains to be substantiated.

Similarly, a paper recently written by a student at the U.S. Army's School for Advanced Military Studies states that at the end of the interwar period, "the officer education system had ingested Clausewitz."[2] The paper's many references to a Clausewitzian influence on American doctrine fail, however, to demonstrate that he had been *di*gested. Particularly puzzling is the remark that the U.S. Army doctrinal publication *Principles of Strategy for an Independent Corps or Army in a Theater of Operations* "was remarkable for its synthesis of modern thought combining Clausewitz, the indirect approach, and modern technology."[3]

In actuality, this 1936 manual shows the influence of Liddell Hart (the "indirect approach"), Fuller (the list of "principles of war"), and Jomini via Hamley ("strategic bases and lines"), but there is little evidence of Clausewitz. The definitions of strategy, tactics, and economy of force are not his; neither is the emphasis on taking the offensive under all circumstances. The discussion of "The Relationship of Politics to the Conduct of War" appears to be based on Jomini, Mahan, and Moltke and includes the lines "Politics and strategy are radically and fundamentally things apart. Strategy begins where politics end. All that soldiers ask is that once the policy is settled, strategy and command shall be regarded as being in a sphere apart from politics."[4] Such "Clausewitzian" elements as are present are unattributed and appear to be derived from Goltz. Clausewitz himself is not mentioned at all, although Napoleon and Mahan are cited by name as influences.

It certainly can be demonstrated that Clausewitz was discussed by American military educators, journalists, and historians during the interwar period and World War II, but it would be difficult to claim that his work had any great direct impact on military doctrine, organization, or the writing of military history. Clausewitz did receive mention in the writings of several important American generals of this period. In most cases, these references are not substantial enough to determine the philosopher's impact or even to suggest any particular interpretation. Still, they are worth mentioning as evidence that Clausewitz was actually a factor in shaping the views of some significant American military leaders.

George S. Patton (1885–1945) discovered and read *On War* in 1910, although he did not acquire a decent translation until 1926 (see Chapter 8). Aside from a complaint about *On War*'s "abstruceness," there do not appear to be any direct references to Clausewitz in Patton's papers or writings, so any discussion of Clausewitz's influence on Patton would be inferential.[5]

A somewhat similar case is that of General Albert Coady Wedemeyer (1896–1990). Wedemeyer was that rare commodity, an intellectual in American uniform during the interwar years. Among other points of interest, Wedemeyer actually attended the German Kriegsakademie in Berlin from 1936 to 1938. He was involved in war planning in Washington in 1941, and his staff paper "Ultimate Requirements Study: Estimate of Army Ground Forces," has been called the "Victory Plan" by which the United States won the war.[6] He is generally associated with America's China policy; he was a great admirer of Chiang Kai-shek and succeeded

Joseph Stilwell as Chiang's chief of staff and American commander of the China theater. He certainly was aware of Clausewitz and occasionally cited him.[7] Wedemeyer's writings are full of references to war, policy, and politics, and it is easy to infer that he drew a lot from *On War*. As with Patton, the sources do not permit any solidly grounded discussion of his views on the Prussian military philosopher. Wedemeyer has, however, been cited as evidence that the Germans were paying no more attention to Clausewitz than the Americans were, as his voluminous notes on his experiences in the German war college made virtually no reference to Clausewitz.[8]

Of greater interest are the comments of Generals John McAuley Palmer and Dwight Eisenhower. Palmer was a professional army officer who was suspicious of the officer corps as a class and a great believer in the concept of a "citizen army." He played a direct role in shaping Congress's attitude toward the army after World War I, and his arguments in favor of "universal military training" formed the basis for a major domestic debate on the subject at the end of World War II. Palmer's understanding of Clausewitz was important to helping him understand and organize his own views on national military organization.

Although Eisenhower read Clausewitz in the 1920s and subsequently rose to become supreme allied commander in Europe, it is difficult to identify a specifically "Clausewitzian" influence on his behavior as a general. Eisenhower was not, of course, a military theorist in any academic sense; a cynic might be tempted to speculate that this was why he was so successful. A strong case can be made, however, for a clear connection between his knowledge of *On War* and his behavior as president of the United States from 1953 to 1961.

The U.S. Army's Schools

It is true that immediately after World War I, Clausewitz's name did begin to show up with some frequency in the curricula of the U.S. Army's advanced schools. This was not an entirely new development, since Clausewitz had figured prominently in the translated German texts of writers like Goltz and Balck which had formed the basis of prewar teaching at Fort Leavenworth and at the Army War College.[9]

There had been a long-standing demand by American officers for an American textbook, albeit one containing the lessons that Germany had to offer. In some of the homegrown texts produced after 1919, *On War* came to be quoted directly, and some minor aspects of Clausewitz's approach assumed a central place in the teaching of military history and doctrine. For example, the school year at the Army War College was divided into two parts based on a distinction made by Clausewitz, "Preparation for War" (September to February) and "Conduct of War" (February to June). The War College history attributes this to the direct influence of Clausewitz's book, but Clausewitz devoted little discussion to the preparation phase; he was interested in the art of the fencer, not that of the swordsmith.[10] Clausewitzian-sounding terms abound in doctrinal writing (especially in discussions of "breaking the enemy's will"), but these were by then the common currency of military discussion and denote no direct influence by Clausewitz's own writings.

On War itself was not used as a textbook either at the War College or at Fort Leavenworth, possibly because of the short length of courses and the consequent need to stress practice over theory. More likely, however, its nonuse stemmed from a massive lack of interest. Clausewitz himself seems to have remained a rather shadowy character: One writer in the Command and General Staff School's quarterly *Review of Military Literature* apparently believed him to be a contemporary figure, noting in a book review that "Clausewitz illustrates his statements [on mountain warfare] by the historical experiences of Italians in the Alps in 1917."[11]

One of the first American military textbooks to appear after the war was *Principles of Strategy* (1921), written by Colonel William Naylor, director of the General Staff School at Leavenworth. It is a supremely eclectic work that is not footnoted, so it is difficult to judge the source of any particular idea. Clausewitz was quoted several times, usually indirectly (apparently via Goltz or Bernhardi), but his terminology was conspicuously absent even though many of his concepts were undeniably present (e.g., the "culminating point of the offensive"). Much of this apparent influence seems to come via later writers' discussions of the American Civil War and South Africa.

Most of Naylor's book revolved around issues of attack and defense, and it made a balanced presentation of the advantages of each. Evidently, however, Naylor saw Clausewitz as a proponent of the defensive; at least, he failed to grasp the Prussian's subtle understanding of the dynamic relationship between the two forms: "Notwithstanding Clausewitz, we must contend that of the two, offensive or defensive, the former is to be preferred."[12] On the matter of war and politics, Naylor largely avoided the issue but indicated support for Moltke's view that the political leadership had no role in the conduct of operations.[13] Like most doctrinal works, Naylor's book has the flavor of a committee product, but it is difficult to believe that Naylor had read *On War* for himself.

On War was "specially recommended" as the top priority reading on strategy at the Command and General Staff School by 1923; Jomini came sixth, listed after two books each by Foch and Goltz and just before Corbett.[14] The reading list was compiled by Colonel Conrad H. Lanza, who in 1922 had put together a sourcebook on the Jena campaign including a lengthy (ninety-six-page) extract he had translated from Clausewitz's "Notes on Prussia During the Catastrophe of 1806" and the tale of "Prince August's Battalion in the Battle of Prenzlau."[15] Lanza's interest in Clausewitz is thus self-evident, but there is no reason to believe that his recommendation was widely followed.

Of the 785 officers who wrote Leavenworth papers in the seven year history of the two year course [1928–35], not a single one selected option #388, "Clausewitz—His influence on principles and doctrines of modern warfare." In fact, in the entire two year curriculum, Clausewitz was cited but once, with the admonition that his classic work, *On War* was "not required to be studied."[16]

The first military textbook written by an American soldier that drew heavily and directly on Clausewitz's work was Lieutenant Colonel Oliver Prescott Robinson's 1928 *Fundamentals of Military Strategy*.[17] Robinson, who had been chief of staff for the American Expeditionary Forces in Siberia, 1918/19, based his book on lectures he had given at the Command and General Staff School while stationed at Leavenworth from 1923 to 1927. Robinson was much less eclectic than Naylor. It is clear that he considered Clausewitz to be his guiding light, observing that

> a little research, a little study and reflection brings out the fact that Clausewitz's book on war . . . occupies about the same relation to the study of the military profession as does the Bible to all religious studies. Most books on strategy for the past one hundred years are in great part a compilation or an attempt to reduce to simpler form and to explain Clausewitz. . . . As far as known, there is not a single proposition relating to strategy which Clausewitz did not cover in a broad general way. This remarkable man treated his subject in such a way as to make his propositions as applicable today as they were one hundred years ago.[18]

Robinson acknowledged accusations that Clausewitz did not properly understand Napoleon, but offered the somewhat half-baked excuse that no "methodically thinking German of that day [could] appreciate the boldness and rapidity with which Napoleon perfected his combinations, seemingly in violation of the fundamental ideas as to war."[19] Still, his understanding of *On War* was not unsophisticated. Although he organized his book around the theme of "principles of war" (i.e., security, the objective, surprise, and so forth), he was skeptical of the term *principles* and challenged the cook-book approach to doctrine, arguing that every military decision required consideration of unique and specific factors. His discussion of the offense and defense was balanced and lacked the usual snickers at the latter, quoting Clausewitz on the superiority of the defense in pursuit of the negative goal without painting him as an "apostle" of either.[20]

Responding to Clausewitz's ideas on moral forces in war, Robinson got a bit carried away with the role of public opinion and the balance of power, arguing (parallel to Wilkinson) that

> no nation will use its air forces to bomb cities, just for the purpose of destroying the morale of the people by instilling them with fear, any more than it will gas women and children. Why? Because *strategy* knows

that such action could only bring on that nation the active resentment of the rest of the civilized world, a thing that no nation can afford.[21]

This view was rooted in the idea of maintaining a rational relationship between policy and strategy and in a perception of the balance of power system similar to that of Clausewitz. Events shortly thereafter in Europe would demonstrate that it was good advice but poor prophecy.

Perhaps the most interesting aspect of Robinson's treatment involved the role of battle in strategy. He based his definition of strategy on Clausewitz's but substituted "operations of war" for "battle," so that "Strategy is the use of the operations of war to gain the end of the war."[22] Robinson's purpose was not to deemphasize battle but rather to stress Clausewitz's point that it is the possibility of battle rather than its actuality that drives military operations. This subtle perception of Clausewitz's meaning, frequently repeated in Robinson's book, is quite uncommon.

Robinson's discussion of the relationship of political and military leaders was confused, however, and ultimately he argued that "the soldier condemns, and resents as unwarranted and likely to lead to disastrous results, any attempt on the part of statesmen to interfere in the conduct of military operations." This is essentially the same view that appeared in Naylor's 1921 *Principles of Strategy* and in the 1936 *Principles of Strategy for an Independent Corps or Army in a Theater of Operations;* it may represent the orthodoxy of Fort Leavenworth rather than Robinson's own considered opinion. The consistency with which this argument showed up in interwar American doctrinal writing is somewhat surprising, especially considering its relative rarity in British thinking. Frequently justified by reference to Lincoln's interference with McClellan and the free hand he later gave to Grant, these doctrinal statements presage the Truman–MacArthur contretemps in Korea.

It would be wrong to minimize the accomplishments of the U.S. Army school system during the interwar years. Although the army's performance in World War II was not without its serious flaws, its officer corps performed remarkable feats of staff work and logistics at echelons that had never even existed before in American armies. It would simply be wrong to credit the institution's achievements (as opposed, perhaps, to those of individuals like Eisenhower) to an understanding of Clausewitz.

Dwight D. Eisenhower

Dwight D. Eisenhower (1890–1969) was born to a poor Kansas family of German (Mennonite) descent. He graduated from West Point as an infantry lieutenant in 1915 (ranked 61 of 164) but was deprived of war service in Europe by troop-training assignments in the continental United States. He was promoted to major in 1920, but his career was nearly blighted by a positive article on tanks that he published that same year, deeply angering his Infantry Branch superiors.[23] From 1919 to 1930 he had a number of assignments, the most important of which was a three-year tour under General Fox Conner in Panama. Eisenhower noted that "in sheer ability and character, [Conner] was the outstanding soldier of my time. . . . Outside of my own parents he had more influence on me than any other individual, especially in regard to the military profession."[24] Through a clever bureaucratic subterfuge by Conner, Eisenhower got around Infantry Branch objections and entered the Command and General Staff School in August 1925.[25] After some staff duty in Washington, he entered the Army War College (at that time located at Fort McNair), from which he graduated first of 275 in 1928.[26]

Between 1930 and 1942, Eisenhower spent eleven years working as a staff officer directly for either Douglas MacArthur (either in Washington or in the Philippines) or George Marshall. Although his relationship with MacArthur was rather tempestuous, it was these contacts that led to his rapid rise during the next war. Had it not been for that war, however, he might well have finished his career as a lieutenant colonel and regimental executive officer, the position he held in 1940 after twenty-nine years in the army.

Marshall's sponsorship led to Eisenhower's assignment as U.S. commander, European Theater of Operations, in June 1942. He became supreme allied commander in December 1943. In this job he was, of course, a tremendous success. Controversy nevertheless remains over some of his decisions, particularly the decision not to try to beat the Russians to Berlin, often held to be a sign of Eisenhower's political naiveté. He finished the war as a five-star general.

Eisenhower then spent two years as Army Chief of Staff. He left in 1948 to become president of Columbia University but was called upon by President Truman to become the top NATO commander in 1951. As the presidential election of 1952 neared, Eisenhower decided that he was a Republican, won that party's nomination, and was easily elected. Domestically, his administration was noted for its fiscal conservatism and its moderate expansion of welfare policies.

In terms of military policy, President Eisenhower had to deal with the Korean War, which he had promised to end, and with the Cold War's arms race against the Soviets. As a fiscal conservative very suspicious of the "military–industrial complex" (a term he coined), he presided over substantial military cutbacks and changes in national strategy generally described as the "New Look." These policies, which stressed air power, threatened to reduce to irrelevance the army in which he had so long served. One of the most controversial features of the Eisenhower administration was its reliance on nuclear weapons to deter communist aggression. At the strategic level this was known as the policy of "massive retaliation." At the tactical level, the emphasis was on battlefield nuclear weapons. These provided, in Eisenhower's words, "more bang for the buck."

The historiography on Eisenhower has undergone a rather sharp turn in the last decade or two.[27] For a long time, Eisenhower was viewed as a rather limited character who happened to be in the right places at the right times, a man who could hardly put together a coherent English sentence. This view of Eisenhower acknowledged the interpersonal skills that had made him so successful as manager of the complex alliance of World War II in Europe. His success, however, was said to be based more on the skills of a football coach (which Eisenhower had been) than on any deep military understanding. The attribution of any significant intellectual dimension to his leadership would have been dismissed as absurd. My own father (a liberal Democrat, to be sure) always characterized Ike as an "amiable dunce."

There were exceptions to this rule, of course, especially among those who knew Eisenhower well. Richard Nixon noted in 1962 that Ike "was a far more complex and devious man than most people realized." (Nixon went on to say "and in the best sense of these words.")[28] Other careful observers noted that the dominant interpretation was inconsistent with the immense success of Eisenhower's presidency, a success that grew more conspicuous with the comparative failures of each of his successors before Ronald Reagan. It was easy to dismiss these more positive assessments, given the impact of Ike's rather vague and unsophisticated (if homey and avuncular) public persona, his seeming lassitude and distance from events. That persona made it easy to assume that Eisenhower had been "managed" by his handlers, particularly his chief of staff, Sherman Adams, and his secretary of state, John Foster Dulles.

The unveiling of Eisenhower's personal papers in the mid-1970s shattered this impression.[29] It is now clear that Ike had a far stronger personality and intellect—and that he controlled his administration and its policies to a far greater degree—than outsiders had realized. The explanation for this sharp contrast between appearances and reality lies in Eisenhower's leadership style. Eisenhower pursued a most unusual personal strategy, that recommended by Moltke to staff officers: "Always be more than you seem."

An example is the way Eisenhower handled questions about how, in 1955, the United States intended to defend the Nationalist Chinese-held islands of Quemoy and Matsu in the event of a Red Chinese attack. The problem was a fundamental flaw in the strategy of "massive retaliation," that is, how the United States could reconcile its threat to use nuclear weapons, with all the consequences thereof, with the limited nature of such an attack. In March 1955, the State Department was so concerned about the implications of this question that it asked Eisenhower to refuse to discuss it with the press. Eisenhower's response: "Don't worry, . . . if that question comes up, I'll just confuse them."[30]

In regard to Ike's "managers," Fred Greenstein characterized Ike's style as one of "pseudo-delegation." Pretending to be shuffled around by his staff, he allowed them to take the heat for unpopular decisions while he posed as "a benevolent national and international leader." In itself, that is hardly unusual, but he was also willing to provide a heat shield for his subordinates by allowing the blame for awkward but necessary moves to fall on his own "political inexperience." He regularly let credit for his own successes go to his subordinates in order to maintain his cover. Based as it was on the immense prestige and personal popularity with which Eisenhower entered office, it was a stupendously successful approach.

Concerning Eisenhower and Clausewitz, there can be no question that Eisenhower was familiar with *On War*. The young Ike had had some interest in military history, but this was nearly extinguished by the pedanticism with which the subject was taught at West Point: "If this was military history, I wanted no part of it."[31] When he expressed his resulting ignorance to Fox Conner in 1922, Conner began gently to reintroduce him to the subject. He started by lending Eisenhower a few historical novels, soon upped the ante to actual campaign studies, and then made him read *On War* "at least three times."[32] It is uncertain which version he read.[33] Eisenhower did not read German, and it is hard to imagine anyone going through the complete Graham version three times, even given the rather leisurely life-style of the interwar U.S. Army officer corps. Eisenhower, Patton, and Conner were close, and it is possible that he had the same version Patton did: T. M. Maguire's. The Maguire condensation does have the saving grace of discussing the American Civil War, in which Ike had a great interest. In any case, Conner questioned Eisenhower relentlessly on the meaning and implications of what he had read.

In 1928, Eisenhower's group at the War College included the Clausewitz enthusiast Lieutenant Colonel Oliver Prescott Robinson. Major Eisenhower's own input is impossible to distinguish, but the group's report, "War and Its Principles, Methods and Doctrines," drew directly and heavily on Clausewitz.[34] It included prominent discussions of the philosopher's views on attack and defense and the diminishing power of the offensive. Its summary of military history also appears to have been drawn from *On War*. The very first line in the report is a Clausewitzian definition of war: "War is an act of violence intended to compel our opponent to fulfill our will." Interestingly, however, this definition left out the political aspect of war, and the report as a whole made almost no mention of political factors. This was consistent with the usual reception of Clausewitz by the U.S. Army as an institution.

Ike did not go on at any length about Clausewitz in his memoirs, but he noted in 1955 that the German writer "was often quoted in military staff colleges and classes and some few officers studied his books thoroughly." Eisenhower stated that he himself had been "one of the latter."[35] When asked in 1966 what book other than the Bible had had the greatest effect on his life, he answered

> My immediate reaction is that I have had two definitely different lives, one military, the other political. From the military side, if I had to select

one book, I think it would be ON WAR by Clausewitz. On the Civil
government side, I think the most significant publication would be THE
HISTORY OF THE UNITED STATES by George Bancroft.[36]

His presidential warnings to American warmongers are very reminiscent of
Clausewitz's discussion of the nature of war: "Remember this: when you
resort to force as the arbiter of human difficulty, you don't know where you
are going; but generally speaking, if you get deeper and deeper, there is just
no limit except what is imposed by the limitations of force itself."[37]

Unfortunately, there is little in the record to show how Eisenhower the
general interpreted Clausewitz or what relationship, if any, the philosopher's
teachings had to his conduct of the war in Europe. Although a number
of his biographers have mentioned Clausewitz in connection with this or
that operation, there is no evidence that these references are anything
more than interjections or inferences.[38]

On the other hand, the prominent American diplomatic historian
John Lewis Gaddis has offered an intriguing argument concerning Clausewitz's influence on Eisenhower's policies as president, particularly regarding the "New Look."[39] Gaddis's 1982 *Strategies of Containment* is an
authoritative critique of American national security policy from the begin-
nings of the Russo-American alliance in World War II through the era of
Henry Kissinger. His entire analysis is based on the ways in which the
various administrations adjusted means to ends and vice versa, an approach
Gaddis himself regards as Clausewitzian.[40] Gaddis sees the permutations
in American Cold War strategy from one administration to another as a
cyclical variation between "symmetrical" and "asymmetrical" approaches
to containment.

Gaddis defines an asymmetrical strategy as applying one's own strengths
against an adversary's weaknesses, of adjusting one's ends to suit one's
means.[41] The Eisenhower administration's reliance on its nuclear superiority to deter Soviet expansionism clearly fits this definition. It economized
on defense expenditures (thus preserving America's greatest strength, its
economic superiority and stability), while hoping to deter aggression by
threatening a terrible retribution that the Soviet Union could not—at
first—match. This strategy gambled that the Soviets would refrain from
doing what we did not want them to do out of a fear that we might do
something that we did not want to do either.

A symmetrical strategy, conversely, requires that one match the enemy
strength for strength; it requires adjusting one's means to fit one's ends.
The Kennedy administration's policy of "flexible response" was such a
strategy. It gambled that we could meet and contain Soviet aggression at
a level that did not require us to draw the nuclear sword, at the risk of
destroying the economic system that was both the source of our strength
and a key reason for resisting in the first place.

> Fundamental to [his strong convictions ... on the proper relationship
> of ends and means] was Eisenhower's understanding of Clausewitz. . . .

The major premise Eisenhower retained from reading the Prussian
strategist was that in politics as well as in war, means had to be
subordinated to ends; effort expended without purpose served no
purpose, other than its own perpetuation. . . . [His strategy was] based
not just on fiscal conservatism or secret intelligence, but as well on the
proposition, derived ultimately from Clausewitz, that one must have
ends for all means. To maintain weapons irrelevant to the threat at
hand—and Eisenhower put excess missile capacity in this category . . .
was to expend limited resources carelessly, with the result that the
nation in the end would be unable to afford what really was necessary.
. . . "The important thing . . . was to remain true to our own beliefs
and convictions." This Eisenhower largely did, in the face of much
opposition—and there is little evidence that national security suffered
as a result.[42]

Aside from issues of means and ends, the line about remaining true
to convictions might well have come straight from Clausewitz's discussion
on the nature of military genius and his definition of "strength of character." The idea was most succinctly articulated in the "Instruction for
the Crown Prince": "The great difficulty is to adhere steadfastly in execution to the principles which we have adopted."[43]

A major determinant underlying the choice of strategies may be
economic philosophy. Certainly Eisenhower's fiscal conservatism reflected
a very different attitude toward means than did Kennedy's Keynesianism.
Ike saw no point in buying security at the price of bankrupting the nation;
Kennedy saw no purpose in keeping expenditures down if the upshot was
a nuclear holocaust. At a more basic level, the choice also reflects an
attitude toward rationality in human affairs: Eisenhower's strategy was
to make the irrational seem credible. Kennedy's approach was self-consciously logical and rational but, if consistently followed, predictable.
One's intellectual tastes, rather than the relative success of Ike's policies,
are likely to determine one's judgment on the merits of these two approaches. It is doubtful that Eisenhower's fiscal conservatism and his views
on the nature of American society, which were fundamental to his approach to national security policy, were derived from Clausewitz. It was,
of course, his own experience and predispositions that led him into this
approach. Nonetheless, the case clearly can be made that the intellectual
components of Ike's approach to policymaking were significantly shaped
by the arguments of *On War*.

The U.S. Navy

The Naval War College at Newport was not the thriving source of military
intellectual activity during the interwar period that it had been before
World War I. Nonetheless, Clausewitz continued to receive some attention
there, and a better case can be made for a Clausewitzian influence on the
navy than on the army. For the most part this influence was indirect,

coming via Wilkinson, Corbett, and—less distinctly—other British writers like G. F. R. Henderson and F. B. Maurice. Except for the work of Captain (USN) George J. Meyers (discussed later), there does not seem to have been much original writing on Clausewitz by U.S. naval personnel.[44] On the other hand, one does not find in the navy the same resistance to the political direction of war that was so prominent in the army; on this point, Mahan's and Clausewitz's teachings were in fundamental harmony.

The works of Wilkinson were used extensively at Newport, especially in the 1920s, under the influence of commandant Admiral William S. Sims (1858–1936). Sims and Wilkinson shared a tendency toward reformism. Naval historian Ronald Spector calls Sims a "decidedly odd duck. . . . While at Newport he had been observed at Women's Suffrage meetings and it was rumored that he had even made a speech at one." While commanding U.S. naval forces operating in European waters, Sims had met Wilkinson in England during the war, discussed naval education with him at some length, attended his lectures (taking along his staff), and corresponded with him afterward. Sims wrote Wilkinson several times in order to procure thirty, then one hundred copies of Wilkinson's *Brain of the Navy*.[45]

Julian Corbett's book *Some Principles of Maritime Strategy* also appears to have been encouraged reading at the Naval War College, along with his earlier historical works. It was required reading through much of the 1930s, and sufficient time was allowed in the course syllabi actually to digest it.[46]

Aside from an occasional lecture by visiting scholars like Herbert Rosinski, however, *On War* itself does not appear to have received much attention at Newport. Although it was included on various reading lists, only relatively small excerpts were required reading.[47] In 1894, in contrast, it had been the first book on the reading list.[48] As with the army schools, one reason may have been the short time allotted to courses, and Stewart Murray's excellent condensation *The Reality of War* was occasionally included in reading lists. Still, there is little indication that time limitations were the deciding factor. Neither Clausewitz nor Corbett is mentioned with any frequency or in any meaningful manner in the American naval literature of the interwar period.[49]

One rather startling exception to that observation was Captain (USN) George J. Meyers's 1928 *Strategy*.[50] Meyers (1881–1939) was the son of a German immigrant who had served with the Union during the Civil War. He graduated from the Naval Academy in 1901 with a strong background in engineering and was promoted to captain in 1924 and rear admiral in 1935. He was sent to the Naval War College in 1921 and the Army War College in 1922 and then taught at the latter institution in 1923/24. He was assigned to the Army War College again from 1926 to 1929, not as an instructor but as naval liaison. Thus he was there while Eisenhower and Robinson were students, although there is no evidence of any cross-fertilization. He died suddenly at age fifty-eight aboard his own flagship in December 1939, ironically poor timing for such an ambitious strategist.

Meyers's book on strategy was evidently written during his stint as naval liaison at the Army War College. It is rather dry reading, containing no historical illustrations of its argument. But it is also quite sophisticated and full of Clausewitz, and it may well have influenced (or been influenced by) army thinkers like Oliver Prescott Robinson. Meyers's approach was in essence to merge Mahan and Clausewitz, with an emphasis on the latter. He drew his understanding of Clausewitz's "economy of force" from R. M. Johnston.[51] Meyers also referred frequently to Corbett's naval histories, but he seems to have rejected Corbett's theoretical works, particularly *Some Principles of Maritime Strategy*, perhaps because of Wilkinson's obvious influence.[52]

As with Corbett's theoretical work, Meyers's incorporation of Clausewitz is too broad, deep, and thorough to be summarized here. His major concerns were the integration of land and sea operations, the need to pursue strategic designs in peace as well as in war ("strategy is continuous"), and the need to educate both military personnel and statesmen on each other's problems and functions. Meyers's definition of strategy was not an operational one like Clausewitz's but rather one based on overall state policy in peace and in war—in other words, "grand" or "national" strategy. He was in fact very critical of Clausewitz's definition, arguing that it applied only in wartime and excluded diplomacy as a weapon.[53]

Meyers produced a very detailed "reading course" clearly designed for use at both the Naval War College and Fort Leavenworth. Sophisticated as his book was, however, it seems to have been a dead end in American Clausewitz studies. Its publication appears to have been a private venture by Meyers. Although it was listed as supplementary reading for the Naval War College senior class of 1931 (where it is given as the alternative to *On War*), it was gone from the list by 1934. Aside from a couple of contemporary reviews, it has very seldom been cited.[54] One reviewer noted that "the recent multilateral renunciation of war as an instrument of policy [the Kellogg–Briand Pact] may necessitate reformulation of [Meyers's] definition of war." This concern may have been one reason that Meyers's book was not adopted as a text, but that is speculation.[55]

Hoffman Nickerson

Another noteworthy American writer on military affairs was Hoffman Nickerson (1888–1965), the independently wealthy scion of a venerable American family.[56] His ancestor William Nickerson had bought Cape Cod from the Indians in 1637. Hoffman Nickerson did his best to uphold his inherited aristocratic ideals: One of his domestic goals was the creation of an American "landed gentry" to offset the noxious influence of the nation's philistine business class and its "servant or parasite—the lawyer politician." He was nonetheless active in the Republican party. A student of R. M.

Johnston, he became a disciple of Fuller (Nickerson's *The Armed Horde* was dedicated to Fuller, "Master-analyst of War"), but he grew increasingly critical of Liddell Hart, particularly over the issue of the latter's treatment of Clausewitz. He shared Fuller's suspicions of mass democracy:

> We must conflict with those who use Democracy as a slogan or substitute for religion. . . . Less hasty readers, let us hope, will remember that Democracy and Despotism have not always been divorced. What tyrant is so despotic as a tyrannous majority? . . . No dictator, aristocracy, or admitted oligarchy, but the United States, recently tried throughout fourteen years of peace to control the diet of its citizens through the Prohibition Amendment.[57]

In his contempt for mass politics, Nickerson was especially opposed to mass armies. His primary military goal was, as the titles of his books suggest, to limit war, principally by professionalizing it.

He earned a bachelor's degree in 1911 and a master's in 1913, both at Harvard (where Johnston was then a professor). Excited by the prospect of American participation in the war in Europe, he obtained a commission in the New York National Guard in 1916. He served under Pershing during the pursuit of Pancho Villa and, after the American declaration of war on Germany, with the general staff of the American Expeditionary Force as an intelligence officer. Nickerson stayed on in Europe after the war as a staffer with the Interallied Armistice Commission. Afterward, he made his way primarily as a writer on history and on military affairs, although he returned to the army as a major during World War II.

Nickerson evidently drew his very positive views on Clausewitz from Johnston, although it was apparently his contrasting of the two writers' views on mass armies and on the efficacy of tactical surprise that led Russell Weigley and Hans Rothfels to see Johnston as anti-Clausewitzian.[58] In the 1930s, Nickerson was very interested in both Fuller and Liddell Hart, largely because their theories tended toward the professionalization of war and the elimination of the mass armies he detested. Even in 1942, Nickerson was arguing that mass armies and popular warfare were on the decline, although he acknowledged that contemporary events "might tend superficially" to contradict that thesis. He had a point—popular participation in these wars had lost the exuberance of 1914—but the relevance of his theory to practical policymaking was dubious at best.

Despite certain similarities in their approaches, Nickerson grew increasingly unhappy with Liddell Hart, especially his "Douhetism," that is, his advocacy of war from the air against defenseless populations. When Liddell Hart's prestige plunged dramatically after May 1940, Nickerson was positively gleeful about it.

> Few military writers have wielded more influence than he in the years just before '39, or have theorized more boldly, and few have seen their theories so promptly demolished. He might indeed point to certain qualifications and saving clauses in his writings, but he himself, when

sharply criticizing the great Clausewitz . . . has insisted that writers should be judged not on qualifying clauses but on the general drift of their work and the chief impressions of that work upon their readers.[59]

It is curious (and instructive) that Nickerson, with his opposition to mass armies, should have been so positive in his treatment of Clausewitz. He took the long view and generally saw Clausewitz's theories as applicable in all periods; the mass participation in the wars in which Clausewitz himself had fought and from which he had drawn most of his examples was merely a transitory phenomenon. Nickerson nonetheless thought at times that *On War* could use some updating. His 1940 article on Clausewitz (published in July but obviously written before the collapse of France in May and June) attempted to update Clausewitz's discussion of three key military objectives: (1) to conquer and destroy the enemy's armed force, (2) to seize his material resources and, (3) to gain public opinion.[60] He felt that Clausewitz's ideas were wholly inapplicable to naval warfare, but then, Nickerson's grasp of sea power was weak: He rarely mentioned Mahan and appears to have been unaware of Corbett. He further argued that even on land his priorities would have to be reversed: It was the propaganda war that was now most important, and the actual destruction of the enemy's forces was to a large extent a mere adjunct to the effort to gain public opinion. As evidence that decisive battle was on its way out, partially as a result of the immense superiority of the defense, Nickerson pointed out that "neither Germany nor the Anglo-French Alliance has even attempted to gain a decision by battle during the first phase of the present war."[61] He also argued that Clausewitz had undervalued the effects of blockade, although he noted that those effects could be subsumed under the heading "seizure of material resources."[62]

Perhaps it was the events that intervened between the writing of this article and its publication that led Nickerson to stop trying to update Clausewitz. Although he later reprinted sections of this article, his appraisals of the relevance of *On War* to modern warfare (like Fuller's) grew steadily more enthusiastic.

Nickerson was never entirely uncritical. He occasionally threw out a phrase from Fuller's critique and referred to Clausewitz as Napoleon's "high priest."[63] He failed to recognize the balance-of-power elements in Clausewitz's thought, arguing that the Prussian writer had "indulge[d] in romantic hero-worship, calling Bonaparte the 'God of War,'" and had failed to learn the lesson of Napoleon's fall.[64] He also complained about some ambiguities in Clausewitz's use of the term *destruction*, and argued that this had led to a lack of subtlety in his approach to strategy. "He did not see that the Eighteenth Century idea of skillfully minimizing losses, weighing carefully in Jomini's fashion the chances of the profit from an offensive against the probable loss to be endured, might be more than mere humanitarianism, might indeed be mere self-interest enlightened by common sense."[65] This is nonsense, of course. The conservation of one's own forces is an important aspect of Clausewitz's discussion of the defense: "We have now to consider the opposite of the destruction of the enemy's armed force, that is to say, the preservation of our own."[66] This criticism by Nickerson appears to be Fuller's influence at work, but Nickerson stopped well short of endorsing the Liddell Hart position.

> Only when we turn from his admirable definition of war and his equally admirable classification of its different forms to his analysis of military objectives and methods does controversy become possible. Even here his thought is so powerful, lucid, and orderly that those who differ with him can hardly do so more effectively than by commenting on his work. Even those who deplore his influence must study him because of his enormous effect upon warfare of this day.[67]

Although Nickerson's works were cited by many later writers on military affairs, his practical influence is—even more than that of most writers—hard to judge.[68] His patrician attitudes and prejudices removed him from the American mainstream, and some of his reviewers dismissed him as a harmless crank.

John McAuley Palmer

In many ways the opposite of Nickerson was John McAuley Palmer (1870–1955). Palmer was the grandson of a volunteer Union general (and professional politician) of the same name. He graduated from West Point in 1892, in his own words "trained but scarcely educated."[69] He served briefly with the occupation forces in Cuba and soon after went to China as part of the international expedition against the Boxers. Palmer saw no combat, however. He was a chemistry instructor at West Point from 1901 to 1906, served as governor of Lanao in the Philippines in 1906 and 1907, and graduated from the General Staff College in 1910.

In 1911, Palmer served Secretary of War Henry L. Stimson on a commission assigned to figure out how to integrate the militia system into the regular army. This was a question on which Palmer had been cogitating since his first assignment in the regular army. He told Stimson that the problem was not merely a technical one: "What we needed was nothing less than a comprehensive military policy for the United States."

Palmer's attitude toward this matter was, to say the least, unusual for a professional officer. It was based on his observation that historically, the United States had relied on a small professional army in peacetime and on large citizen armies for war. In his initial ruminations on the problem, he had accepted the "expansible army" ideas of John C. Calhoun and Emory Upton. When he sat down to work out a detailed plan, however, he ran into a problem. He came from a political family, and it was clear to him that the Congress would never authorize a professional army cadre large enough to provide a genuine foundation for the kind of army the nation would field in a great war. If instead he tried to work out how a more realistically scaled professional army might be expanded for war, he found that either the resulting force would be much too small or the professional soldiers would simply be overwhelmed by masses of raw recruits. He settled instead on a scheme for fielding a small but fully ready professional army in peacetime, to provide garrisons and expeditionary forces, while training masses of civilians as soldiers and officers for use in large-scale wars. His model was the Swiss army.[70]

Palmer's ideas formed the basis for a military reorganization scheme actually put forward by Stimson in 1912. Unfortunately, and much to Palmer's regret, the proposal went nowhere with either Congress or Woodrow Wilson's new Democratic administration.

> Had the reorganization . . . gone into effect, we should have had at least four Regular Army divisions and at least twelve National Guard divisions fully organized when we entered the war in 1917. In addition to this, we should have had approved plans all ready for the prompt formation of a first wave of at least twelve National Army divisions of citizen soldiers. In the event . . . the nation blundered toward war woefully unready.

In 1912, Palmer was an observer at the French and German armies' autumn maneuvers and then spent the next several years in garrison duties in China and the Philippines. In 1916, he returned to Washington to head a committee on the problems of sending an army to Europe. The committee proposed a plan for universal military training. Once the nation had entered the war, Palmer went to France as a lieutenant colonel, assistant chief of staff for the AEF. There he established a reputation that might have carried him to a high position in the army but, like R. M. Johnston, he nearly worked himself to death. His health broke, and he was sent home for a long convalescence. He recovered in time to return to France in 1918 as a frontline brigade commander (Fifty-eighth Brigade, Twenty-ninth National Guard Infantry Division), with which he participated in the Meuse–Argonne offensive.

In October 1919, Palmer was called to testify before the Senate Military Affairs Committee concerning postwar military organization. Despite his assignment to the War Department, Palmer electrified the committee by his statement that the army's official proposals were "not in harmony with the genius of American institutions."[71] Although the army hierarchy was highly displeased, the Senate committee requested that Palmer be assigned to it as military adviser. His ideas were incorporated into the National Defense Act of 1920. Palmer's insistence on peacetime conscription was rejected, but he proved flexible enough to argue for the next twenty years that volunteer forces would be sufficient. A regular army of 280,000 would garrison vulnerable territories and act as an expeditionary force. The real war-fighting force, however, would be based on the National Guard and the "organized reserves." This was Palmer's "citizen army," which would be trained by professionals but would provide its own officers upon mobilization.

The 1920 act's practical impact was greatly reduced by the Congress's failure to fund the forces it had designed. Unable to recruit more than half the troops originally authorized, the army insisted on retaining all of the original divisions, thus creating a hollow, "expansible" army in spite of Palmer's success in putting across his contrary ideas to civilian leaders. The professional officers needed to train Palmer's citizen army were withdrawn to serve the regular formations. The 1920 scheme quickly collapsed.[72] Palmer himself retired in 1926 as a brigadier general.

Always a prolific writer, Palmer continued to popularize his organizational ideas in books and magazine articles. In 1941, he was recalled to active duty in the War Department's Special Planning Division to work on plans for postwar military organization. His was the mind behind George Marshall's campaign for universal military training after World War II.[73] Palmer himself retired (again) in 1946 and died in 1955.

The process by which Palmer arrived at his organizational ideas is interesting in the context of this book. As a new second lieutenant assigned to an infantry unit at Fort Sheridan, Illinois, he had decided on his own to design a new scheme for organizing the army.

> How it would have affected the cavalry I do not recall, but it would have promoted every second lieutenant of infantry to the grade of captain. When I submitted my plan to Captain Cornish [Palmer's commander] he was most enthusiastic. It would have made him a lieutenant-colonel at once. He advised me to polish it up and show it to my grandfather Palmer who was then a member of the Senate Military Affairs Committee.

While working on this organizational plan, a project that would evolve into his lifework, Palmer made his great discovery. In his memoirs, Palmer recalled his introduction to *On War*.

> While polishing up my plan, I found an unanswerable argument for national military organization in one of Cornish's books. This was an English translation of Karl von Clausewitz's famous treatise on war. In browsing through it I found the striking statement that "war is not a separate thing in itself but is merely a special violent phase of human politics." This truth was so startlingly simple that I could not grasp it at first. But it gradually dawned upon me that here was a fundamental military concept which I had never heard about in my four years at West Point. I had read and studied about war, but none of my professors or textbooks had ever told me what war really is. There had been no trace of this fundamental thought in the whole curriculum. We had thought of peaceful international intercourse as one separate entity and of war as another separate entity. We had never been told that they are simply transitory aspects of the same thing, international politics—both governed by the same fundamental laws and neither of them understandable without an understanding of the other.

Here was indeed new food for thought. If war is a phase of politics, then every *complete* political system should include machinery for dealing with this specific phase of political action. My grandfather would grasp this at once and would agree with me that the American political system had been incomplete in this essential respect since the founding of our government. I would submit this to him at our next meeting. It would prepare him to welcome my plan. I would thus enable him to round out his long career with constructive legislation of the highest national importance. He would be very grateful to his grandson.[74]

It did not, of course, work out that way, and Palmer remained a second lieutenant for quite some time.

Palmer's subsequent interest in Clausewitz usually centered on the phrase "War is merely a continuation of politics with the admixture of other means," an idea he called the "tap-root of war." It sparked virtually every explicit discussion of Clausewitz that he ever published.[75] He sometimes used the phrase in discussions of international policy, as in his 1921 report on the Far Eastern question (a staff study done in preparation for the Washington Conference of 1921/22). After citing Clausewitz, he observed:

In an intelligent nation like Japan, national policies and the wars necessary to maintain them are studied and planned together. She plans wars merely to carry out policies and she does not adopt policies that she does not believe she can maintain in war. It is practically certain that the statesmen who represent Japan in the [upcoming Washington naval] conference will each of them thoroughly understand the interrelation of national policies and the military preparations necessary to enforce them. They will each be experts upon policy and upon the military and naval consequences of that policy. With us, there is the possibility at least that our representatives will continue to regard policy and war as entirely distinct and separate things.[76]

Palmer did occasionally draw on some other aspect of *On War*. For example, in his 1919 testimony to the Senate he noted that the "very first requirement of strategy is superior numbers," a misrepresentation of Clausewitz's argument but quite likely derived directly from *On War*.[77] Most often, however, Palmer's discussions of Clausewitz, war, and politics were oriented toward domestic affairs, and more specifically toward the domestic political implications of the various possible forms of national military organization.[78] His literary *raison d'être* was to argue for his concept of a citizen army on the Swiss model. Except insofar as he regarded preparation for war as an integral part of war strategy, Palmer was largely unconcerned with operational military problems. He might well have paraphrased Clausewitz to say that "organization for war is a continuation of organization for politics." (This is my formulation, however, not Palmer's.) He argued that "the American genius" demanded a native model for military organization and that the Prussian model, beloved of professional American officers, was the product of an alien feudal tradition and a recipe for the domination of society by a narrow military caste bent on aggressive war in pursuit of its own class interests.[79]

Although he called expansible army thinkers (including himself as a young officer) "cryptomilitarists," Palmer did not fear the development of such a situation in America. Much of Palmer's suspicion of the professional army derived from his grandfather's Civil War experience and bitterness over what he had seen as the favoritism of West Point graduates to one another over volunteer officers like himself. He did argue, however, that the disjunction between "the American genius" and its alien military system was a source of great military weakness and inefficiency.

Palmer's ideas on military organization were, of course, in direct opposition to those of certain other American Clausewitz enthusiasts, most notably R. M. Johnston and Hoffman Nickerson. In 1941 when Palmer published a new book setting forth his citizen army ideas, Nickerson "was so anxious to attack Palmer's thesis that he wrote to several editors begging for an opportunity to review it."[80] (Curiously, Palmer made none of his usual references to Clausewitz in this book. Quoting German generals in a positive manner was probably not good politics in 1941.) It was not these writers' understanding of Clausewitz himself but rather their views of the "spirit of the age" and of the nature of American society that were in conflict.

From the professional historian's point of view, Palmer had an unfortunate habit of ascribing an understanding of "Clausewitz's dicta" to other people—for example, Bismarck and Lincoln—on the basis of their actions, even to people he knew quite well had never heard of him, such as George Washington and Frederick the Great. Such anachronisms grate on the ears, but Palmer certainly recognized them as anachronisms. His point was that great military and political leaders are naturally aware of the relationship between war and politics, regardless of whether they had actually read Clausewitz. In Lincoln's case, however, Palmer went to great lengths in arguing that the Union president actually was aware of Clausewitz's ideas (an argument discussed in Chapter 4). But he was honest enough to acknowledge that the evidence, however strong in his own view, was circumstantial at best.[81]

Palmer was thus the first native-born American soldier who is known to have actually examined *On War*. His personal interpretation of the meaning of Clausewitz's discussion of war and politics played an important role in his development and advocacy of plans for an American "citizen army." These plans did gain considerable influence even if, in the end, they were never truly adopted. Whether his insight into the relationship of the American "national genius" to military organization really was sparked by Clausewitz or stemmed from his own family's practical politics is, of course, unknowable, but he certainly used Clausewitz in his attempts to promulgate his own ideas.

Other American Writers

During the later part of the interwar period, Clausewitz's name appeared with some frequency in U.S. Army branch publications like the *Infantry Journal* (now *ARMY*). Its editors, Major John H. Burns (editor, 1936–40) and Colonel Joseph Ingham Greene (editor, 1940–53), were strong proponents of the study of *On War*. Joe Greene (1898–1953) was the more significant figure.[82] He had enlisted in the army in May 1918, entered West Point a year later, and graduated with the class of 1923. He later graduated from the Infantry School and the General Staff College. Although Greene saw no war service, he did serve overseas in China and the Philippines. He joined the editorial staff of the *Infantry Journal* in 1938, assuming the editorship upon Burns's sudden death. He served as president of the American Military Institute for several years and was instrumental in founding the Association of the U.S. Army (AUSA), a project he undertook in hopes of breaking down the army's crippling branch parochialism.

Medically disqualified from war service, Greene threw himself into military journalism. Under the pseudonym "G. V." ("Guiseppe Verdi"), he wrote literally hundreds of pieces, a great many of them quickie book reviews, but he also found time to dabble in poetry and wrote at least one short story. His articles often appeared outside the military press; it was not unusual to find his byline on pieces in the *Saturday Review of Literature* or the *New York Times*. He was interested in psychology, which may have been one source of his interest in Clausewitz.[83] His self-defined primary mission as editor of the *Infantry Journal*, however, was to stimulate officers to read and write about their profession.

Greene did much to bring the ideas of Clausewitz to the attention of soldiers in the United States. He published a number of important articles and reviews by his friend Herbert Rosinski.[84] The Jolles translation of *On War* (originally published by Random House in 1943) was reprinted by Greene's Infantry Journal Press in 1950. He wrote the foreword—greatly influenced by Rosinski—which heavily stressed the idea of specificity that characterizes Clausewitz's approach to war and strategy. During the war, Greene's Infantry Association made it available to soldiers for the princely sum of $1.45.

He also contributed a longer and very thoughtful introduction to a condensation of *On War* (based, oddly enough, on the old Graham translation) which was published in both the United States and Great Britain as *The Living Thoughts of Clausewitz*. Greene's sixteen-page introduction was clearly influenced by Rosinski and possibly by Rothfels. It stressed Clausewitz's personal qualities and the historical circumstances in which he had developed his theories and sought to overcome propaganda images of the philosopher as a "proto-Nazi" and the "father of total war and the *Blitzkrieg*." Greene also greatly exaggerated

Clausewitz's influence, indicating that he had been praised in books by, among others, Stonewall Jackson (probably referring to G. F. R. Henderson's *Stonewall Jackson*) and Emory Upton.[85] A paper-bound edition of *The Living Thoughts* was distributed for twenty-five cents a copy.

Dallas D. Irvine (1904–), an archivist for the National Archives and for the most part a Civil War historian, for some reason produced an interesting piece on Clausewitz and the French.[86] His point was that the French had ignored the German Clausewitz and had also lost track of the essence of their own hero Napoleon until the disasters of the Franco-Prussian War awoke them to their own military backwardness.

Although what Irvine had to say about the French is interesting, his stated view of Clausewitz leads one to believe that he had read the "Instruction for the Crown Prince" but not *On War.*

> One need merely say that [Clausewitz] inducted his theories from peculiar conditions of war existing in his own time. . . . For the most part, his work was based upon an intensive study of the campaigns of Napoleon. In selecting so narrow a field on which to base his theories, he fell into the egregious error of neglecting the effect of the evolution of the conditions of war as set by changes in civilization.

Irvine stressed Clausewitz's "doctrine that absolute war is the form to be approximated as closely as possible." Nonetheless, he added, "The work was far sounder than the use made of it," especially by French thinkers. He felt that Clausewitz's greatest positive contribution had been his condemnation of formal systematization, but this attitude was "absolutely counter to the French mentality."

The American who probably did the most to stimulate an American interest in Clausewitz never wrote anything significant on the subject. Edward Mead Earle (1894–1954) graduated from Columbia University in 1917, receiving a master's degree there in 1918 and a doctorate in 1923. Somehow in the course of that academic effort he managed to enlist as a private, attend Officer Training School, obtain a commission as a second lieutenant in the field artillery, transfer to the Air Service, and emerge as a first lieutenant by 1919. He then left the army to work in banking but was soon back at Columbia as a lecturer and, after 1923, as a professor of history. He also managed to travel widely in Europe and the Middle East, soon becoming known as an expert in international affairs and American diplomatic history. His 1923 *Turkey, the Great Powers, and the Bagdad Railway* was particularly well received. From 1934 on he was associated with the Institute for Advanced Study at Princeton, as a professor in both the School of Economics and Politics and the School of Historical Studies. He maintained a close relationship with the army, however, lecturing at the War College between 1924 and 1927 and again in 1939/40. During World War II Earle had numerous military connections as a lecturer, analyst, and consultant. After the war he spent considerable time in England, teaching at the Joint Service Staff College from 1948 to 1950. In the latter year he taught at the Royal Naval War College and also served as Chichele lecturer at Oxford.

Earle's own work makes no significant reference to Clausewitz, and he probably never made any particular study of him.[87] Rather, his contribution to Clausewitz studies lies in the seminar on military strategy at the Institute for Advanced Study that he organized in 1940, motivated by his concern about the abysmal American ignorance of things military. This seminar laid much of the groundwork for the later dissemination of Clausewitz's thought among American military intellectuals. Other participants included Harvey DeWeerd,[88] Harold Sprout, Bernard Brodie, Stefan T. Possony,[89] Felix Gilbert, Herbert Rosinski, and Alfred Vagts. This wartime meeting of American and German historians and military intellectuals on American soil was almost bound to focus on *Vom Kriege*; as Felix Gilbert (another expatriate) points out, "It was quite impossible to study modern history in Germany without becoming familiar with Clausewitz."[90] There was some tension between the expatriates and the Americans, however, based on the perception of some of the former that some of the latter were not terribly sophisticated. One source who prefers to remain anonymous recalls hearing that one of the German refugee scholars had referred to Bernard Brodie as "*dieser Auswurf des Chicagoer gettos*" (this scum of the Chicago ghetto).

One of the most important results of the seminar (or at least of the informal relationships it spawned) was the publication of the original *Makers of Modern Strategy*, which Earle edited in 1943. The idea originated with Vagts and Earle's assistant Gilbert, who agreed that "it might be a good idea to have a collection of essays which showed the development of the ideas of modern strategy from the beginning of modern times on."[91] Earle jumped at the idea. Hans Rothfels's chapter on Clausewitz and Gordon Craig's on Delbrück are discussed later; both have been heavily cited in later military studies. For Craig, working on *Makers of Modern Strategy* provided his introduction to Clausewitz, and the same was no doubt true of other American participants.[92] Rosinski also participated in shaping this book, although his own contribution was rejected.[93]

In all, ten of the twenty-one chapters in the 1943 version of *Makers of Modern Strategy* made some reference to Clausewitz (as compared with seventeen out of twenty-eight chapters in the 1986 version). Virtually all of the comment was positive.[94] The publication of Earle's book was an epochal event in the development of American military studies as an academic field and surely significant in the more narrow terms of Clausewitz's reception in America. It could have had little impact on the conduct of the war, however.[95] As John McAuley Palmer wrote to Rosinski concerning the latter's search for government funding for his highly Clausewitzian theoretical writings,

While I am sure that you have a highly important contribution to strategic science . . . I do not see how it can be given immediate practical application in the conduct of the war. Our military and Naval leaders are already engaged in a war and they must wage it with such doctrine as they have. If there is any defect in their education, it is too late to educate them now.[96]

Observations

Although it is clear that *On War* was known and occasionally read within the U.S. Army's educational system during the interwar years and that bits and pieces of its author's thought were adapted into class lectures and textbooks, many of Clausewitz's basic concepts that did surface were rejected, distorted, or altered almost beyond recognition. On the relationship of the offense and defense, the dynamic relationship that Clausewitz described was usually either misunderstood or not ascribed to him; abstract discussions of the offensive usually described it as inherently superior regardless of circumstances. On the critical issue of the relationship between the military and the political leadership during wartime, it was Moltke's rather than Clausewitz's view that prevailed. Although the German model was clearly dominant, and Robinson appears to have drawn a lot directly from *On War*, Clausewitz cannot be said to have achieved a significant role in the army's school system.

In the navy, a Clausewitzian influence on education is easier to substantiate. Many of Clausewitz's concepts were transmitted quite faithfully by Wilkinson and Corbett, although both of those authors were creative and had agendas of their own. The navy seems to have accepted more easily than the army the subordination of strategy to politics, most likely because that element of Clausewitz's teaching was so compatible with Mahan's. Meyers's sophisticated study, however, appears to have had few readers. *On War* itself (except for tiny pieces) was never assigned reading at Newport, nor was it frequently cited in U.S. naval literature.

Clausewitz does not, therefore, appear to have had a significant direct influence on formal military education or doctrine in the United States before World War II, and indirect influences—particularly in the army—were often distorted and incoherent. Further suggestions that Clausewitz was in fact a major factor in American institutional military thinking will have to be better substantiated than heretofore.

Aside from professional military educators and journalists like Oliver Prescott Robinson, John Burns, Joe Greene, and George Meyers, there were very few American-born commentators on Clausewitz, and almost all of them spent some considerable time in uniform. Clausewitz remained almost exclusively the property of soldiers like Eisenhower, of military historians like Robert M. Johnston, and of would-be shapers of military policy like Hoffman Nickerson and John McAuley Palmer. Despite the importance of his book in the promulgation of a more positive view of *On War* in America, the editor of the original *Makers of Modern Strategy*, Edward Mead Earle, made no comment of his own on its author. The political scientist Quincy Wright, perhaps the most prominent civilian student of war in the interwar United States, gave no sign of ever having read *On War* for himself.

19

New German Influences: Delbrück and the German Expatriates

The influence on the English-speaking world of German military books continued into the interwar period, with some new additions—most of which had nothing particularly new to say on the subject of Clausewitz.[1] Arguably the most important German military historian and military critic of the first quarter of the twentieth century, and one with an important new interpretation of Clausewitz's theories, was Hans Delbrück. During World War II, his work drew serious American attention for the first time. Another source of new German influences on American military thought came from German military intellectuals who fled to the New World after fleeing Hitler's New Order.

Delbrück

Hans Delbrück (1848–1929) was born into a family with both scholarly and administrative pedigrees. He was educated at Heidelberg, Greifswald, and Bonn, receiving a doctorate in history in 1873. He took time out from his studies to serve in the Franco-Prussian War, in which he was felled by typhus. After the war he continued to serve as a reserve officer.

In 1874, Delbrück was appointed as tutor to the son of the Prussian crown prince, Prince Waldemar, and began to study military history seriously. Service in the royal household naturally sensitized him to the interplay between politics and military affairs. He returned to the university in 1879 (when young Waldemar died) and was a professor of history at the University of Berlin from 1896 to 1921. From 1882 to 1885 he was a deputy in the Prussian Landtag and from 1884 to 1890 a member of the Reichstag. He also joined the staff of the prestigious *Preussische Jahrbücher* in 1883 and was its editor from 1890 to 1919. He served as a member of the German delegation to the Paris Peace Conference after World War I.

Delbrück's chosen specialty as a military historian did not win him any great prestige in German academia. His writings reflect a great bitterness at the superciliousness of colleagues who felt that this was not a proper topic for a serious scholar. When he presented to Theodor Mommsen a copy of the first volume of his *History of the Art of War Within the Framework of Political History*, Mommsen thanked him but indicated that he really would not have time to read it.[2] His radical reinterpretation of military history, and especially of Frederick the Great, did not win him many friends with the German general staff. Neither did his increasingly frantic critiques of German strategy during the war, which centered on Germany's failure to make the political moves that might have permitted her enemies to accept a limited German victory in the West. After the war Delbrück was bitterly critical of Ludendorff.

Delbrück was by no means ignored by Germany's soldiers; in fact, his historical methods were put to use by the general staff. His dissection of the battle of Cannae had an important influence on Field Marshal Count Alfred von Schlieffen,[3] and thus on subsequent German thinking on envelopment.

Although Wilkinson was aware of his works,[4] Delbrück remained largely unknown in English until Gordon A. Craig published an important essay on him in Edward Mead Earle's 1943 *Makers of Modern Strategy*.[5] None of his major military historical works appeared in English before the 1970s.[6]

Craig (1913–) was born in Scotland and emigrated to the United States with his parents in 1925. Craig graduated from Princeton in 1936, received a master's degree in 1939, and a doctorate in 1941. He taught first at Yale and then at Princeton from 1941 to 1961. At Princeton he worked closely with Earle; he is listed, along with Felix Gilbert, as a collaborator on *Makers of Modern Strategy*. He also joined the Marine Corps Reserve in 1944, eventually retiring as a captain. In 1961 he moved to Stanford, where he remains. He made his first visit to Germany in 1935 and has since become one of the most important American historians of that country. His work best known in military circles is probably *The Politics of the Prussian Army* (1955), although his *Germany, 1866–1945* (1978) and *The Germans* (1982) also won a number of awards.[7]

Craig had never heard of Delbrück before being assigned to write on him for *Makers of Modern Strategy*.[8] From the standpoint of the Anglo-American understanding of Clausewitz, his discussion of Delbrück has three major points of interest. The first, of course, is Delbrück's dualistic theory of strategic analysis, which was built on

Clausewitz's theories. The second is Craig's own evident uncertainty concerning Clausewitz's message. The third is Delbrück's application of Clausewitz's advice on the writing of military history.

Like Herbert Rosinski (discussed later), Delbrück sought to push Clausewitz's theories further along the line that, he presumed, the philosopher had been following just before his untimely demise. Unlike Rosinski's, Delbrück's quest bore tangible fruit in the form of a new, clear, and understandable—if often disputed—basis for strategic analysis. This theory was essentially an extrapolation from Clausewitz's unfinished musings on the difference between Napoleonic and eighteenth century warfare.

Delbrück's idea was based on the concepts of *Niederwerfungsstrategie* (the "strategy of annihilation") and *Ermattungsstrategie* (the "strategy of exhaustion or attrition"), which revolved around the two "poles" of military strategy, battle and maneuver. Annihilation strategies rely almost exclusively on the former, whereas attrition strategies are always subject to a tension between the two poles. The analytical usefulness of those concepts was well demonstrated in Craig's explanation of Delbrück's critique of German strategy in the war of 1914–18.[9]

Delbrück's analysis was controversial in part because he considered Frederick the Great to be a practitioner of an attrition-style warfare while upholding Napoleon as the model annihilation strategist. Just as British proponents of the offensive found Corbett's analyses subversive to the legacy of Nelson, German soldiers found Delbrück's analyses demeaning to the great Fritz.

Although the 1943 and 1986 versions of Craig's essay on Delbrück are largely identical, there are some noteworthy differences in Craig's discussion of Clausewitz. These reflect uncertainties in Craig's initial understanding of the Prussian philosopher and evidently the influence of the Liddell Hart's presentation. For example, in 1943 Craig wrote that Delbrück's

> study of the military institutions of the past had shown him, in every age, the intimate relationship of war and politics, and had taught him that military and political strategy must go hand in hand. Clausewitz had already asserted that truth in his statement that "war admittedly has its own grammar but not its own logic" and in his insistence that war is "the continuation of state policy by other means." *But the Clausewitz dictum was too often forgotten by men who remembered that Clausewitz had also argued for the freedom of military leadership from political restrictions.*[10]

In the 1986 version, the line italicized here was changed to "But Clausewitz's dictum was too often forgotten by men who misinterpreted Clausewitz as having argued for the freedom of military leadership from political restrictions."[11] This change reflects a closer understanding of Clausewitz's own argument, but it is still a variation on the Liddell Hart view. Similarly, in 1943 Craig wrote that "under the influence of

Clausewitz's book *On War*, the great majority of military thinkers in Delbrück's day believed that the aim of war is the complete destruction of the enemy's forces and that, consequently, the battle which accomplishes this is the end of all strategy."[12] In 1986, this section read: "The great majority of military thinkers in Delbrück's day believed the aim of war to be the annihilation of the enemy's forces and that, consequently, the battle that accomplishes this is the end of all strategy. Often they selectively cited Clausewitz to support their claim."[13]

As for the writing of history, Craig explained Delbrück's approach to research and the writing of military history as the execution of Clausewitz's "critical analysis" and Leopold von Ranke's historiographical ideals. Delbrück called his method for reconstructing battles (and thus understanding tactical systems, their social bases and implications, and their interplay), "*sachkritic.*" This essentially involved a severely critical evaluation of the written sources in the light gained through an examination of the actual terain; a consideration of the actual capabilities of weapons, equipment, and logistical means; and a comparison of suspicious accounts with more reliable records from similar battles.

It is Delbrück's scientific approach to military history within the framework of political history that marks his greatness as a military historian. Craig used Delbrück's examination of the battle of Marathon as a model.[14] Delbrück's ideas, especially those of *sachkritic,* are directly reflected in the approaches of such later historians as Lieutenant-Colonel Alfred H. Burne and John Keegan. Burne developed what he called the principle of "inherent military probability," meaning that many obscurities could be solved by estimating what a trained soldier would have done given the circumstances.[15] Keegan, whose book *The Face of Battle* ranks among the finest works of modern military historical scholarship, called Delbrück "the figure who bestrides the military historian's landscape."[16]

Judging by the frequency with which Craig's discussion of Delbrück has been cited by subsequent writers, his essay has had a significant impact on the writing of military history in the United States since World War II, either in and of itself or by stimulating an interest in Delbrück and clarifying his debt to Clausewitz. Delbrück's particular approach to strategic analysis, however, is not often used by modern American military commentators.

The German Expatriates

Delbrück remained at home in Germany where, despite the controversies over his views, he enjoyed considerable prestige and security. Exercising a much more direct influence on the Anglo-American view of Clausewitz were a number of important German expatriate writers on military affairs who published in English during the later interwar years and World War II. The most important of these from our point of view were Hans Gatzke, Alfred Vagts, Hans Rothfels, and Herbert Rosinski. The latter two had done significant research and writing on Clausewitz in Germany before being driven out by National Socialism. Another expatriate German who figures significantly in Clausewitz studies in this period was O. J. Matthijs Jolles, who provided the translation for the 1943 "American" edition of *On War*. None of these writers had been German military professionals, and their approach to Clausewitz was that of scholars, not soldiers.

Hans Wilhelm Gatzke (1915–87) was born of Protestant parents in Germany. He first came to the United States when he was eighteen, attending Williams College as an exchange student. He then returned to Germany but emigrated to America in 1937. He graduated from Williams College in 1938 and got his master's degree from Harvard the following year. He then taught at Harvard, ultimately receiving his doctorate there in 1947. From 1944 to 1946, however, he was a second lieutenant in the U.S. Army, serving with Supreme Headquarters Allied Expeditionary Force (SHAEF). He taught at Johns Hopkins from 1947 to 1964 and then moved to Yale.

Gatzke was essentially a historian of Germany and of European diplomacy. His translation of Clausewitz's *Principles of War* appears to have been his only contribution to Clausewitz studies;[17] his other works make no mention of him. His brief introduction to *Principles* raises some doubt that Gatzke was really familiar with Clausewitz's more mature conceptions as expressed in *On War*, although he discussed the latter work at some length, primarily in terms of its emphasis on "moral forces." Gatzke's introduction stressed "Clausewitz' unlimited war of annihilation, his absolute war," without mentioning the other possibilities. He called Moltke and Schlieffen "great admirer[s] and disciple[s]" of Clausewitz, who had "recognized that certain adjustments had to be made in the application" of his theories. The dustjacket was even more misleading: it showed an armor-clad hand wielding geometric instruments to produce military blueprints. Gatzke's translation was not nearly so complete as the Graham version, the existence of which Gatzke does not appear to have been aware. Like the 1936 German edition from which it was derived, Gatke's version put into italics large sections of the work held to be obsolete. Nonetheless, Gatzke praised the book of *Principles*, saying "Like nothing else, . . . it may serve as an introduction to his theories on the nature and conduct of war."

In any case, this particular work has rarely aroused any enthusiasm among Clausewitz's more theoretically oriented students, since it too fails to reflect many of the most important of its author's later and deeper insights. This may account for the distinctly restrained reception accorded the new translation in Alfred Vagts's review,[18] but most of the American-born reviewers were enthusiastic and saw *Principles of War* as simply a shorter, more readable version of *On War*. It was particularly well received by uniformed American writers, one of whom observed that "Clausewitz wrote it . . . condensing *all* of the principles and maxims that he subsequently expanded in . . . *On War*." The same reviewer called it "the blueprint from which Nazi Germany has developed the present total war."[19] On the other hand, another reviewer noted that Clausewitz's *Principles*, along with those of Saxe, Frederick II, and Napoleon,[20] were of academic interest only: "Everything of value can be reduced to half-a-dozen principles which will be found set forth, albeit somewhat clumsily, in our training manuals." Nevertheless, he continued, "The Clausewitz pamphlet, of which . . . *Vom Kriege* was an expansion, . . . is the most valuable section."[21]

Alfred Hermann Friedrich Vagts (1892–1986) left the University of Munich in 1914 to serve—despite being a committed socialist—as a company commander in the German army from 1914 to 1918. He earned the Iron Cross first and second classes. Evidently not greatly impressed with the German military leadership, he said of Clausewitz (noting the questionable noble status and distant Polish origins of his family) that "only a Prussian officer who was not fully a Prussian could have been as great a thinker as Clausewitz was."[22] Vagts was active in the Social Democratic party after the war, serving in the military wing.[23] He visited the United States in 1924 as an exchange student from Hamburg University to Yale and married a daughter of the American historian Charles Beard in 1927. In 1932, alarmed by the rising power of the National Socialists, he emigrated to Britain. He had no trouble obtaining an immigrant's visa to the United States in 1933 and almost immediately became a citizen. He was a visiting professor at Harvard, 1938/39, and a member of the Institute for Advanced Study at Princeton, from 1939 to 1942.

Vagts is best known for his 1938 *A History of Militarism, Civilian and Military*, which drew an important distinction between "the military way" and "militarism." The former term described a reasonable, rational approach to waging war with the purpose of accomplishing the objectives of state policy, a manner "limited in scope, confined to one function, and scientific in its essential qualities." The latter involved a "vast array of customs, interests, prestige, actions and thought . . . transcending true military purposes . . . so constituted that it may hamper and defeat the purposes of the military way. . . . Militarism displays the qualities of caste and cult, authority and belief." Vagts also distinguished between militarism as practiced by professional soldiers and by civilians, often regarding the latter as the worst offenders.[24]

Vagts was not a major commentator on Clausewitz, although he frequently referred to him and had a sophisticated grasp of his theories. Vagts was unusual among the expatriate German military writers, however, in being essentially critical of the philosopher.[25] In large part, Vagts's critique was similar to Liddell Hart's in that he saw much of the negative impact of *On War* as being due to his disciples' misapprehension of the concept of "absolute war." Vagts argued that this was a misapprehension for which Clausewitz's method of expression was only partly to blame; the laziness and stupidity of his readers played as great a role. More fundamentally, Vagts argued that Clausewitz himself had not properly conceived the relationship between the army and the state:

That Clausewitz wrote as he did and was read as he was read was largely the outcome of the completed process of bureaucratization in the armies. His teachings, as they were apprehended, were embraced where and when this process was completed. The dates of the translation of his work into French, 1849, and English, 1873, are indicative of this fact.[26] One feature of that bureaucratization was the separation of armies from the generality of interests in their states. Home politics to Clausewitz, when measured by considerations of foreign policy and outside defense, constituted merely *faux frais*.[27] He ranks the military profession supreme over all; among the intellectually determined activities of man, the "warlike genius" takes the highest rank. . . . Clausewitz becomes the apparent promoter of that militarism which thinks solely of war and does not, as the Prince de Ligne recommended to soldiers, think of peace on the first days of war and of war on the first days of peace, but dreams only of war and disregards its economy. In that case, with "violence pushed to its utmost bounds" and after the maximum of exertion, war may not leave much that is worthwhile even to the victorious nation. At all events it was for the unconditioned and absolute war that the military in France and Germany finally prepared in the light of Clausewitz's teaching.[28]

On the other hand, Vagts dismissed the notion that the German army's approach to war was rooted in Clausewitz's work. The contemporary generation of German military leaders was too thoroughly dominated by "non-philosophical nihilists and military technicians."[29]

Like Vagts, Otto Jolle Matthijs Jolles (1911–68) was not a major commentator on Clausewitz, but he performed a major service to Clausewitz studies in the United States by providing the first American translation of *On War*. Jolles's translation is generally considered to convey more of Clausewitz's subtleties than Graham's does and is certainly clearer on some points, although it is not always a great deal more readable. It was based on an 1880 German edition, and thus reflects, as does Graham's, the textual corruptions introduced by Clausewitz's German editors.

Oddly, Jolles's translation did not catch on, and the Graham translation continued to serve as the basis for most subsequent condensations. This development was most likely a result of financial considerations rather than of the qualities of the respective versions, since the Jolles translation remained under copyright, whereas the Graham copyright had lapsed.

Jolles himself is a bit obscure to students of military affairs, largely because his translation of *On War* was his only published effort in that field. Even his nationality has been misidentified.[30] In the field of German literature, however, he is quite well known, especially for his work on Friedrich Schiller. Most of his published work is in German.

Born in Berlin of a Dutch father and German mother, Jolles was brought up as a German and educated at the Universities of Leipzig, Hamburg, and Heidelberg. He received his doctorate in the philosophy of literature from Heidelberg in 1933. He then served one year as a volunteer in the horse artillery. Although he was not Jewish, his anti-Nazi politics got him into trouble. In 1934 he emigrated to France, where he studied at the Sorbonne. The following year he emigrated to Wales, where he taught German. Offered a teaching position at the University of Chicago, he entered the United States with his new British wife in 1938. He became a professor of German language and literature, obtaining American citizenship in 1945. Leaving Chicago in 1962, he spent the remainder of his life at Cornell.

Even before the United States entered the war, the University of Chicago had begun casting about for ways to assist the war effort. These efforts grew out of both patriotism and self-interest: The university's leaders were concerned that unless they established Chicago as a center of military learning and research, the university's considerable assets (particularly in cartography and linguistics) might be hauled off in army trucks, "to be returned torn and soiled, if at all."[31] Courses in preinduction military training began as early as September 1940. A formal Institute of Military Studies was created in April 1941.

On War was high on university president Robert Hutchins's list of priorities. Having examined the texts available for basic instruction, including those used by the armed forces, he had found most of them useless and none satisfactory.[32] By February 1941 the institute's volunteer instructors had already found it necessary to "retranslate and mimeograph those sections of [Clausewitz's work] which we regard as indispensable reading." In June 1942, Hutchins cited the ongoing translation of *Vom Kriege* as a prominent reason that the university should be regarded as a "key defense industry," exempt from conscription.[33] The army and navy, however, had little use for university-based, unofficial military training programs.

The 1943 translation of *Vom Kriege* thus grew out of the local efforts of the military institute. There seems to have been no connection between Jolles and Earle's circle at Princeton. Since Jolles taught military German and German military organization, and *On War* was considered to be a key to German military behavior, he seemed to be the natural man for the job, even though he was not familiar with Clausewitz when he set out. His British father-in-law (a retired professor of classics) provided assistance with the English, although he too had little military background and was new to Clausewitz.

Jolles quickly developed a good appreciation of *On War*'s significance. His short but penetrating introduction stressed Clausewitz's fundamentally conservative, balance-of-power view of international affairs, finding its most important expression in Clausewitz's argument concerning the power of the defense.

> Clausewitz's aim was not merely to prove the strategic superiority of Napoleon's lightning attacks as so many writers and strategists—British and American, unfortunately, as well as German—seem to believe. This is but one part of his theory and not the most important one, for he goes on to show why Napoleon, greatest of all aggressors up to that

time, was necessarily in the end completely defeated. More than one third of his work *On War* is devoted to Book VI, on "Defense."[34]

Jolles's purpose was to argue that what Clausewitz had to say was much more relevant to the Western Allies than to Germany, and that the Germans' one-sidedly offensive interpretation of *On War* would prove to be, for them, a fatal error.

Yet another German expatriate was Hans Rothfels (1891–1976). Rothfels was born of Jewish parents in Kassel, but he himself converted from Judaism in 1910. On the eve of World War I he was studying history and philosophy at Heidelberg. He served in the German army as a junior officer in 1914, losing a leg on the Marne. He received the Iron Cross second class and remained in a military hospital until 1917. Returning to academics at Heidelberg, he received his doctorate in 1918 for the dissertation "Carl von Clausewitz: Politik und Krieg." This work was published in 1920 by Dümmlers Verlag, Berlin, Clausewitz's own publisher. Two years later, Rothfels edited and published a collection of Clausewitz's letters.[35]

From 1926 to 1934, Rothfels was a professor of modern history at Königsberg, but he lost this position because of his Jewish descent. Denied access to libraries and archives, he felt forced to emigrate in 1939. After a short stay in England (teaching at St. John's College, Oxford) and a short internment, he moved to the United States. During the war, he taught at Brown University, and afterward at Chicago. In 1951, he returned to Germany to a professorship at Tübingen.

The greater part of Rothfels's published work concerned Otto von Bismarck, whose letters he edited. He is also remembered for his work on the German opposition to Hitler, which made a significant contribution to postwar West German nationalism. For our purposes, of course, his most important works were those on Clausewitz.

Rothfels's two books on Clausewitz were written in German and have never been translated. He published only one notable piece on Clausewitz in English, but that essay appeared—along with Craig's essay on Delbrück—in a very prominent forum, Edward Mead Earle's 1943 *Makers of Modern Strategy*.[36] As Michael Howard later recalled, that essay was "the first serious study of Clausewitz that many of us ever saw." In it, Rothfels criticized Liddell Hart, Hoffman Nickerson (Fuller's American disciple), and, by implication, Fuller, for their "Mahdi of Mass" approach to the military philosopher.[37] He argued that even though the tactical portions of *On War* were obsolete, "it is nevertheless the first study of war that truly grapples with the fundamentals of its subject, and the first to evolve a pattern of thought adaptable to every stage of military history and practice."

Rothfels's greatest contributions to Clausewitz studies in English were historical in nature. He sought to place Clausewitz securely in the context of his times and to direct attention to the man himself, his personality, education, and experiences, and the manner in which these contributed to his theories. His work is still heavily cited, particularly by Peter Paret, who has carried on in that tradition. Paret—despite a number of differences in interpretation—has acknowledged a great debt to him.[38] These differences usually involve matters of Clausewitz's personality, philosophy, and general outlook rather than specifics of the theory contained in *On War*.

In particular, Paret has questioned Rothfels's view of Clausewitz as a tortured soul, a psychological "outsider" whose personal and career difficulties stemmed from the non-noble origins of his family. Rothfels's interpretation is flawed, in Paret's view, by a romantic nationalism and, perhaps more serious in an academic historian, a tendency to rely on a "mystical causality." Certainly, it is difficult to understand how Clausewitz's social status could have "caused his assignment to that part of the Prussian army in 1815 that was not present at the battle of Waterloo."[39] Such disputes over Clausewitz's personality and psychology would continue, with Paret and Bernard Brodie later discussing the issue at great length both in print and in their personal correspondence.[40]

Based on his role in stimulating American scholars to study Clausewitz, one of the most important of all the German expatriates active in this period may have been Herbert Rosinski (1903–62). Although Rosinski published relatively little, he was an energetic proselytizer of the gospel of Clausewitzian theory. While he recognized the unfinished nature of *On War*, he was worshipful in his praise of it. It was his ambition to carry on where Clausewitz had left off, but although his understanding of the philosopher's work was sophisticated and his explications often enlightening, it would be hard to argue that Rosinski made any great original contribution of his own to military theory.

Rosinski was born of well-to-do Protestant parents in Königsberg (now Kaliningrad).[41] Too young to serve in World War I, he became something of a professional student, spending the years from 1921 to 1930 in diverse studies at the Universities of Tübingen, Königsberg, Halle, and Berlin. He received his doctorate from Berlin in 1930. Forced by a change in his family's economic situation to seek work, Rosinski served as a civilian lecturer on military and naval theory at the German Naval Academy in Kiel, where he was evidently privy to a great deal of German war planning.

In 1936, however, the Nazis forced his dismissal because of a single Jewish grandparent. Bewildered, he emigrated that same year to England and became a lecturer on military history at Oxford. After a brief internment, he emigrated to the United States in 1940. There, Rosinski struggled unsuccessfully to find a secure academic or national security–related position and never achieved anything approaching financial security. At first he also had great difficulties in securing his wife's entry; later he found it difficult to support her. Eventually she divorced him and married his best friend. He remained a member of the household, however.

A sometimes brilliant but very erratic intellectual, Rosinski grew increasingly unable to complete a project, frequently pursuing the implications of an idea until the project expanded beyond a human capacity to cope and ultimately losing the thread of his argument. He died a thwarted and unhappy man in 1962.

Rosinski's 1935 article on the philosopher, which appeared in Germany and the Netherlands, has frequently been cited by Clausewitz scholars.[42] It aimed at reconstructing the various stages in the development of the philosopher's theory, based on the notes of 1816, 1818, 1827, and 1830.[43] (The dating of this last note is a matter of controversy.)[44] In fact, Rosinski's attempt to determine the steps by which Clausewitz arrived at his mature theories is probably his greatest contribution to Clausewitz studies.

Rosinski is best remembered for his book *The German Army*. First published in England in 1939, in the United States in 1940, revised in 1944 and again in 1966 (with a laudatory introduction by Gordon Craig), and translated into German in 1970, it is still considered a classic. The book is, of course, written from a "Clausewitzian" point of view, although Rosinski was characteristically scathing in his conclusion that the German general staff had never understood *On War*. He also commented on Delbrück, evidently accepting his ideas on Frederick the Great and Napoleon, and thus his theory of the "poles" of annihilation and attrition in strategy. Typically, he went on to make the rather remarkable statement that "unfortunately Delbrück's own interpretation of Clausewitz was so unsystematic and inaccurate that he completely failed to grasp the real importance of his discovery and did almost as much to confuse the issue again as he had helped to clarify it."[45] Of Bernard Brodie and Corbett, Rosinski observed, "Brodie is inclined to follow [Corbett] too closely because his scheme of naval strategy is the most convenient we possess to this day. Unfortunately, however, its distinctions are often more academic than practical."[46]

Later, in his review of Cyril Falls's *The Nature of Modern Warfare*, Rosinski was also very skeptical, though more polite, in stating his views on the reception of Clausewitz and military theory in general in the Anglo-Saxon world. He agreed with Falls that British strategic thought fell halfway between the French and the German:

> Its common sense has always kept it from falling victim to the extremes of French rationalism and has made the principles of warfare in England something markedly more tough and concrete than in France. Yet its instinctive aversion to systematic thought has prevented it from deriving as much benefit from the German side as it might otherwise have done.[47]

Rosinski and Rothfels drew on similar sources and made similar arguments concerning Clausewitz and his writings. Whereas Rothfels was interested in the historical context and personality of Clausewitz himself, Rosinski concentrated on the actual military theoretical aspects and implications of Clausewitz's work. His works on naval strategy derive largely from Clausewitz, Corbett, and the French naval thinker Admiral Raoul Castex, and he gave considerable lip service to Mahan. It was his ambition to develop those theories further into a more comprehensive understanding of war.

At one point during the war, Rosinski actually contracted with Oxford University Press to put together a collection of Clausewitz's translated writings. This work would total "about 175,000 words, consisting of some 350 typewritten pages of text and 250 pages of editorial matter."[48] But like many of Rosinski's grander projects, this fell through. Indeed, a great deal of the work published under his name was actually the product of extensive posthumous editing of his papers by other writers.[49]

Rosinski hinted constantly in his writings and lectures that he had discovered the "real" key to military theory, but he never said just what it was. In his later years, Rosinski grew increasingly paranoid and delusional about his great insight:

> What I have accomplished can be fairly ranked with the achievements of people like Kierkegaard, Marx, and Nietzsche. . . . Of course, I am not so penetrating as they were, but I have a really astounding ability to hit upon the right answers intuitively, long before their correctness has been demonstrated. Very systematic, too. . . . The truth must be told, because if it is not openly proclaimed—and acted upon—then the world will irretrievably go to the devil. . . . You see, it's a really frightful dilemma. If I say what I know, I make myself impossible in every camp. If I don't say it, I would have to reproach myself with being a coward and, for the sake of my own security, of having endangered the existence of the world. And, if one has once been granted such profound insights, one has the corresponding sense of responsibility.[50]

Rosinski's limited publication record prevented him from reaching a wide audience with his deeper thought on Clausewitz, although *The German Army* had much that was positive to say about the military philosopher. Moreover, Rosinski's talents as a teacher are open to some doubt. He was skeptical of the intellectual capacities of soldiers, and his attitude could be patronizing.[51] His great faith in military theory is in fact rather odd, given his conviction that soldiers could never understand it. As in his writing, he had great difficulty imposing realistic limits on his lectures. In a 1953 lecture at the Naval War College, Rosinski observed that "it is an extremely difficult task . . . to try to go into the whole of [Clausewitz's] thoughts and then to link them up in the very narrow span of about a single hour." Nonetheless, he proceeded to make just such an attempt, with the help of a set of graphs, charts, and slides that must have left his audience absolutely baffled.[52]

Despite the energetic support of his friend Admiral Henry Eccles, Rosinski's lectures at Newport were discontinued in 1957. The same year saw his last lectures at the Army War College. In 1959, a new general at Carlisle wrote to Eccles:

It is true that he was not well received by the students, and probably just as true that the students were not then prepared to discuss the problems at his level. However, this is beginning to be one of the great obligations of the advanced thinkers of our day—that they must learn to communicate with more than just the specialized members of their own backgrounds and disciplines."[53]

On the other hand, Rosinski was extremely gregarious and he traveled extensively, frequently lecturing on Clausewitz. It was through these lectures and even more through his personal contacts that he most effectively spread the gospel of Clausewitz studies. In Germany, in the early 1930s, he introduced Raymond Aron to the German military philosopher.[54] In England from 1936 to 1940, he lectured on *Vom Kriege* at Oxford.[55] In the United States after 1940, Roskinski discussed Clausewitz before both the American Military Institute and the American Historical Association. In Edward Mead Earle's seminars at the Institute for Advanced Study in 1940, he had a great deal to do with stimulating the discussion of Clausewitz.[56]

Rosinski was also close to Joe Greene and played an important role in feeding his interest in *On War*. He wrote regularly for Greene's *Infantry Journal*, almost invariably mentioning Clausewitz. He had a profound influence on Henry Eccles, who attempted to carry forward Rosinski's quest for a grand military theory.[57] He corresponded with J. M. Palmer from 1941 to 1946, and his praise of Cyril Falls's work encouraged that British author to press on with his attempts to apply Clausewitz's ideas to practical military problems.

Despite his many contacts and undeniable influence, Rosinski has a decidedly mixed reputation. His disorganization and preoccupation with his own problems tended to alienate potentially valuable contacts like Earle. His self-conscious sophistication and sometimes messianic behavior irritated Bernard Brodie, whose references to Rosinski are generally sarcastic.[58] (Rosinski reciprocated.)[59] Except for *The German Army* and his 1935 article on the development of Clausewitz's theories, Rosinski's work is not as widely cited as one might expect given his many connections to other writers.[60] In sum, he represents at once the best and the worst of the German expatriate influence on the Anglo-American understanding of Clausewitz.

Observations

The influence of the German expatriates on the Anglo-American understanding of military theory was in most respects positive. They unquestionably contributed to its sophistication. On the other hand, they have tended to dominate the field of Clausewitz studies to such an extent that the thread of a genuine Anglo-Saxon appreciation of Clausewitz—as represented by sophisticated writers like Wilkinson, Corbett, and Meyers—has been lost. The tendency of European expatriate writers has been to take a rather condescending tone toward British and American military attitudes and institutions and to what Rosinski called the Anglo-Saxons' "instinctive aversion to systematic thought." Such biases, though hardly groundless, have led to a fixation on the continental military model at the expense of the very different British and American military situations and experience. After all, Anglo-Saxon strategic successes are not grounded entirely in accidental factors like demographics and geography, and the Anglo-Saxon powers won their wars against Clausewitz's countrymen.

To be fair, of course, such distortions have a native origin as well, as is demonstrated in the writings of Fuller and Liddell Hart. A tendency to sneer at their own achievements and to turn defeated enemies (the southern Confederacy, the Wehrmacht) into models seems to be another Anglo-Saxon peculiarity.

German expatriates would continue to dominate this field. Henry Kissinger would be among the most prominent "Clausewitzians" to wield power or influence in postwar American military policy, although whether he deserves that sobriquet is unclear. Peter Paret, born in Berlin in 1924, remains unquestionably the dean of American Clausewitz scholars.

20

Assessment, 1914–1945

By 1914, and certainly by 1945, many concepts generally considered "Clausewitzian" had already been absorbed into mainstream English-language military thought, although they did not necessarily get there via Clausewitz. The phrase that "war is a continuation of policy" was common currency even among people whose military understanding was minimal (as is evidenced by its specific negation in the Kellogg–Briand Pact). The importance of moral and psychological factors in war had been common currency long before 1914. The role of "friction" was also widely recognized in theory, although not always under that name. Its organizational implications, however, primarily what we now call *Auftragstaktik*, do not seem to have been widely recognized or implemented.

The widespread acceptance of these aspects of Clausewitz's approach did not necessarily contribute to a wider or deeper appreciation of their author. Outside the limited sphere of military studies, the dominating elements in mainstream British commentary on Clausewitz were ignorance and hostility deriving from the emotional shock of World War I and from continuing hostility toward Germany and German militarism. The dominating fact about American commentary is that there was very little of it, until World War II focused the nation's attention on military concerns. There is little evidence that Clausewitz's work was known (except by his often-distorted reputation) to American political leaders or even to political scientists like Quincy Wright.

In the field of military studies, which was dominated by serving soldiers, military journalists, military historians, and—after 1933—refugees from German National Socialism, the picture is more mixed. In Britain, the two most important Anglo-Saxon military theorists of this period, Fuller and Liddell Hart, reflected in varying degrees the hostility that was common in society at large. Fuller eventually got over it, but Liddell Hart did not. Still, both men were intensely aware of the philosopher's work. Cyril Falls, journalist and eventually Chichele professor at Oxford, carried on in the much more positive tradition of his predecessor Spenser Wilkinson, but he lacked Wilkinson's brilliance. F. B. Maurice carried on the positive view of his father, J. F. Maurice.

Whatever the attitude toward him, Clausewitz was clearly an influence in Britain. It is therefore conceivable that Clausewitz's theories did have some fairly direct impact on British military behavior. Many senior British leaders in World War II had been impressionable junior officers affected by the burst of interest in Clausewitz that had followed the South African War of 1899–1902. A more immediate impact would have come via the influence of Maurice and Falls, whose derivations from Clausewitz were direct, acknowledged, and frequently operational in nature, and via Liddell Hart and Fuller, for whom Clausewitz's contributions were more thoroughly disguised. Churchill's knowledge of Corbett constitutes an important but undocumentable route for Clausewitz's influence. There is, however, no evidence of any direct interest in Clausewitz among such key figures as Montgomery or the air power theorists.

Among native-born Americans, Clausewitz was the almost exclusive property of a small band of uniformed military intellectuals like Robinson, Burns, Palmer, Joe Greene, and, in the navy, George Meyers. His influence on individual military leaders like Patton and Wedemeyer—though almost certainly real—is impossible to assess. A better assessment can be made in the case of Eisenhower, although the sources available make it more applicable to his role as president (1953–61) than to his operations as a soldier before 1945. Even those writers on Clausewitz who were not professional soldiers—Robert M. Johnston and Hoffman Nickerson— spent time in uniform and identified with the army. Although these American writers had a respectable understanding of *On War*, their work was not as influential as that of the British writers or as well known outside narrowly military circles.

The indirect transmission of Clausewitz's ideas via his interpreters was unreliable, especially for the American army, which depended largely on German authors like Goltz. The army as an institution was disinclined to accept Clausewitzian ideas on the interrelationship of politics and strategy. The navy benefited from the clearer transmissions of Wilkinson and Corbett and from the fact that on the crucial issue of political control, Clausewitz's views were compatible with Mahan's teachings. It would be difficult, however, to argue that the works of Clausewitz exercised any great practical influence on American military institutions, aside from whatever role Clausewitz had played in creating the broader German military model.

Much of the serious, sophisticated, and positive comment on Clausewitz in English was made by German émigrés, most of whom made their way to the United States. It was these émigrés—Rothfels, Rosinski, Jolles—who laid the basis for the post–World War II revival of Clausewitz studies. Dominance of American Clausewitz studies by foreigners writing in English would remain the case to a significant degree right up to the present day, although today such foreigners are less likely to be German than Israeli, like Azar Gat and Martin van Creveld.

Given the disparate origins, attitudes, and motivations of the various writers who discussed Clausewitz in English during this period, it is difficult to give any broad characterization to their interpretations. At best it can be called a period of quiet ferment, at worst an era of stagnation in the Anglo-Saxon understanding of the Prussian military philosopher. Nonetheless, by 1945 the stage had been set for a significant renewal in the study of Clausewitz's thought.

IV

Conclusions

21

Since 1945

By the early 1990s, Clausewitz's theories and concepts had come to permeate Anglo-American writing on military and national security topics. Clausewitz's reception after 1945 is so large and complex a story that continuing the detailed and chronological approach of the main treatment would be impracticable. It nonetheless seems useful here to identify the various kinds of considerations—political, military, intellectual, and organizational—that have made Clausewitz so influential, in order to put the earlier story into proper perspective.

Continuing Hostility to Clausewitz

It is true enough to say that by 1945 the stage had been set for a significant renewal in the study of Clausewitz's thought, but that renewal would be slow getting under way and would take place under circumstances that were radically different from those of the earlier period. Considerable hostility to Clausewitz lingered on, well into the 1960s.

Liddell Hart's and J. E. Edmonds's post-1945 attacks on Clausewitz have already been discussed. In 1957, one of the most vituperative attacks ever made on the philosopher appeared in Fort Leavenworth's *Military Review*.[1] It called Clausewitz the "pied piper of modern military thought" and attacked him for the utter immorality of his theory of war. It held up Sun Tzu as an example of the ethical soldier, which seems rather odd. Despite his emphasis on the "bloodless battle," parts of Sun Tzu's *Art of War* are distinctly fiendish.[2] The purpose of the article was to blame

Clausewitz for the thinking behind total war strategies and the Eisenhower administration's insane "massive retaliation" policy, and it was, of course, probably right in making some connection. Other than that, the article is a tissue of shallow perceptions, misinformation, and venom. It concluded with a great deal of satisfaction—and medical inaccuracy—over Clausewitz's death in 1831 "of a ratborne disease." The writer (U.S. Army master sergeant Forrest K. Kleinman) evidently based his assault on a partial reading of the first chapter of *On War* and on the guidance of Liddell Hart. It is strange that Kleinman was able to get so worked up about something he obviously knew so little about and even stranger that *Military Review* saw fit to publish it.

A more serious and intelligent attack on the Clausewitzian legacy appeared in 1968 in an American abridgment of the Graham translation of *On War* edited by Anatol Rapoport.[3] Born in Russia in 1911, Rapoport was a professor of mathematical biology at the Mental Health Research Center at the University of Michigan, something of a Renaissance man, with varied interests and noteworthy musical accomplishments.

Rapoport approached *On War* with considerable philosophical sophistication. He also had a set of political biases, particularly against the nation-state system, which he considered obsolete. These rendered his analysis rather unrealistic.[4] He rejected war as a legitimate tool of state policy, arguing that Clausewitz's definition of war as an extension of politics meant that "peace is the continuation of struggle by other means." Rapoport argued that this unfortunate and unnecessary struggle needed no justification in Clausewitz's view, not only because the Prussian writer had seen it as fundamental to the human condition, but also because his own professional advancement had depended on it. Rapoport appreciated Clausewitz in terms of his historical contribution, but he sought to discredit what he called the "neo-Clausewitzian" school of modern strategists.[5]

These neo-Clausewitzians were nuclear strategists like Herman Kahn and Henry Kissinger. The basis for the characterization was that they seemed to regard nuclear war as a rational tool of state policy. Rapoport rejected this notion even more energetically than he rejected war in general and the legitimacy of the state. The accuracy of the term, however, is dubious. Although the title of Kahn's book *On Thermonuclear War* sounded, as Rapoport noted, like "an obvious bid for the mantle of Clausewitz," there is in fact no indication that Kahn had ever consulted Clausewitz's own work on the subject. There was one reference to "the classical notion of 'strategy' as an attempt to force one's will on the enemy," but no indication that Kahn knew or cared about either the origins of the phrase or its inaccuracy as a quotation from Clausewitz—this is a definition of war, not of strategy.[6] The only reference to Clausewitz in Kahn's famous (or infamous) *Thinking About the Unthinkable* was in Raymond Aron's introduction.[7] As Michael Howard put it, "Kahn and his colleagues . . . ignor[ed] all three elements in the Clausewitzian trinity: popular passion, the risks and uncertainties of the military environment, and the political purpose for which the war was fought. Their calculations bore no relation to war as mankind has known it throughout history."[8]

Kissinger also does not appear to have been driven by any particular fixation on Clausewitzian theory. Few of his biographers mention Clausewitz except in passing, and Kissinger's own references are few and far between.[9] Some similarities between Kissinger's and Clausewitz's views may derive from a common influence by Kant (Kissinger's senior thesis at Harvard was entitled "The Meaning of History: Reflections on Spengler, Toynbee, and Kant"). The French Revolution and the Napoleonic wars were another set of common influences: Kissinger's doctoral dissertation concerned the Vienna settlement of 1815.[10] As both diplomat and historian, Kissinger took a conservative approach to the balance of power. Although his approach coincides with Clausewitz's, there is no evidence that Clausewitz was his inspiration.

Nonetheless, working on the issue of how nuclear weapons would affect practical warfighting, Kissinger did recognize the contradictions between the philosophy of *On War* and the approach taken by many of the nuclear strategists. He eventually concluded that the latter were in error because their proposed strategies bore no relationship to rational state policy. The extended discussion of *On War* in his 1957 *Nuclear Weapons and Foreign Policy* (Kissinger's only detailed published discussion of the philosopher) shows that he had a deep and subtle understanding of Clausewitz's concepts.[11]

Kissinger's interpretation of Clausewitz was shaped in important ways by Lenin's, but this was not particularly evident in his sophisticated 1957 treatment.[12] Unfortunately, it was Lenin's interpretation that stuck with him over the years. In his 1982 memoirs, Kissinger mentioned Clausewitz twice, referring to his (alleged) idea that diplomacy was just another form of warfare, turning the philosopher's famous line on its head in Lenin's manner. In itself that concept may have been accurate enough when discussing the Cold War, but it was debatable at best as a representation of Clausewitz's own views. Hans Morgenthau made the same point in his classic textbook on international relations, but he correctly distinguished Clausewitz's original formulation from Lenin's.[13]

The treatment of Clausewitz at the U.S. Military Academy also long reflected a distorted view. West Point's 1951 training pamphlet *Jomini, Clausewitz, and Schlieffen* stressed the concept of absolute war and claimed that the German war machine had been based on a faithful following of *On War*'s violent philosophy. "Clausewitz's philosophy is not dead. The philosophy of *On War* is the philosophy of Bismark's (*sic*) *Blood and Iron* and the Philosophy of *Mein Kampf*." (The 1964 revision, however, was a considerable improvement, picturing Clausewitz as "a practical believer in the strength of the defense, the man who urged a greater democracy for Prussia's citizens, the thoughtful soldier-statesman who thought that war was a serious and hazardous business.")[14] The projection of Clausewitz as an unremitting proponent of the offensive continued to appear as late as 1976, when the ubiquitous American military analyst Edward Luttwak referred to the ancient Romans' "seemingly ineradicable Clausewitzian prejudice against defensive strategies."[15] "Just-war" theorist Michael Walzer attacked Clausewitz in 1977 for his alleged failure to put any limits on violence in war.[16]

Indeed, hostility to Clausewitz is born anew whenever the militarily unsophisticated hear a few choice quotations from his work.

> A dead Prussian haunts the Pentagon, the White House and Capitol Hill. Lately he's been in those Senate hearings on the Persian Gulf crisis, swaggering among the experts, whispering in their ears, seizing their tongues, making them parrot the ideas of a book from another century—*his* book.[17]

The author of this piece, *Washington Post* staff writer Joel Achenbach, is obviously a neophyte in military terms: He thinks that "objectives" is "a Clausewitz word," expresses surprise on hearing that military officers go to graduate school, and calls the phrase "war college" a "virtual oxymoron." On the other hand, he has clearly done some research on contemporary military analysts (Summers, Luttwak, and others) and has been forcibly struck, despite his lack of preparation in the field, by the dominance of Clausewitz's influence in present-day American military thinking.

Overt hostility was not the only barrier that Clausewitz faced. Many people (particularly political scientists) continued to regard Clausewitz as a quaint relic of the past. In 1975, Manus Midlarsky had the temerity to title his own book *On War*. There was of course no need to consult any ancient tomes on the subject. Midlarsky's single reference to Clausewitz cited not the philosopher's books but Bartlett's *Familiar Quotations*.[18]

New Sources of Interest

Generally, however, this negative view of Clausewitz has faded away under the pressure of events. There were three factors above all that would lead, via several avenues, to a new urgency in the Anglo-American study of *On War*: the atomic destruction of Hiroshima and Nagasaki, the Cold War between communism and liberal democracy, and the American defeat in Vietnam. The prospect of nuclear war was itself a new problem, one that turned Clausewitz's concept of "absolute war" from an abstract concept into a potential reality. That reality also perforce brought to the fore another and contrary Clausewitzian concept, that of limited war, which had seemed to most so inapplicable to warfare in the first half of the twentieth century. As for the Cold War, the widespread perception that Clausewitz's ideas underlay much of Marxist–Leninist[19] and possibly Maoist[20] military theory was also a major impetus to the study of *On War*. These factors sufficed to bring Clausewitz into the intellectual mainstream, but it was only the disaster in Vietnam that led American military institutions to turn to his guidance.

Some of the nuclear strategists have already been discussed. Quite a few of them mentioned Clausewitz in their works, and some were quite sophisticated—Thomas Schelling, for example. Bernard Brodie, originally a naval theorist, also had a strong interest in *On War*. Curiously, the nuclear theorists seem never to have used the concept of absolute war as a model or a justication for nuclear war. As was the case with Kissinger and Brodie, Clausewitz's demand for political relevance was nettlesome and always acted as a brake upon their ambitions rather than a prod.[21]

As for the countervailing concept of limited war, it was the Korean War that served, after some delay, to bring Clausewitz's ideas to the forefront of military theoretical discussion. In combination with development of the hydrogen bomb, which eliminated any lingering idea that the nuclear warhead was "just another weapon," Korea made it clear to many that total war now occupied the same position of impracticality that limited war had held in the first half of the twentieth century. The term was quickly drafted into the ongoing strategic debate, but its origins with Clausewitz were only very slowly explored. As early as 1946, Liddell Hart had published an important article entitled "War, Limited." In it he made all the usual attacks on Clausewitz and his "misinterpreters" but naturally gave no credit to the German philosopher for having anything useful to say on the subject.[22] Even after Korea gave impetus to this line of thought, the impact on Clausewitz studies was delayed and inconsistent. Although discussions of Clausewitz figure prominently in some of the literature on the Korean War, many writers on Korea and on the topic of limited war itself fail to mention him at all.[23] Many of those who do seem to be making mere genuflections without much comprehension.

Perhaps the breakthrough year in terms of gaining a large audience for Clausewitz's ideas, particularly on limited war, was 1957. In that year, Henry Kissinger's *Nuclear Weapons and Foreign Policy* discussed Clausewitz in a positive manner, as did Samuel Huntington's *The Soldier and the State* (discussed later). But it was Robert E. Osgood's widely read book, *Limited War*, that provided the first truly important, historically grounded, and theoretical discussion of the concept that enlisted Clausewitz's authority.[24]

Osgood (1921–86) was a political scientist associated with the University of Chicago's Center for the Study of American Foreign Policy and later with Johns Hopkins University's School of Advanced International Studies. Although he linked Clausewitz with the Leninist and Maoist approach to war, he heavily stressed *On War*'s emphasis on a rational relationship between military and political policy. By 1979, Osgood was calling Clausewitz "the preeminent military and political strategist of limited war in modern times," a new image for the military philosopher radically different—if almost equally disputable—from the image that had previously held sway.[25]

Osgood's portrayal has caught on, especially among political scientists. One of the most thoroughgoing revisionist treatments of Clausewitz came in 1988 from the political scientist Ned Lebow, who asserted:

> Clausewitz's argument seems to stand in direct opposition to his frequently quoted assertion that "war is a continuation of political activity by other means." Like many contemporary strategists he was contending that war had become increasingly impractical. The cost of general war was so great, he warned, that there were few, if any, political goals commensurate with it. Limited war, which he still thought feasible, nevertheless threatened to escalate into general war because of the difficulty of controlling it. Caution and restraint were the order of the day.[26]

Lebow was clearly overemphasizing the degree to which Clausewitz himself had been attached to the limited war aspects of his theory.

The nuclear problem aside, the Cold War posed many problems for American political thinkers, not least of which was the problem of how military institutions—to which Cold War tensions gave a much more prominent peacetime role—fit into a democratic society. Clausewitz made a major entry into American civil-military theory (also in 1957) when Samuel P. Huntington published his first book, *The Soldier and the State*. Huntington pointedly disagreed with Liddell Hart's caricature of Clausewitz. He referred to "Clausewitz's concept of the dual nature of war" (i.e., that war in the idealized concept of "absolute war" was autonomous, whereas real war was in practice subordinate to policy) as a key to the formulation of a truly professional military ethic.

> This concept of war is a true professional one, embodying as it does the essentials of any profession: the delimitation of a unique subject matter independent of other human thought and activity and the recognition of the limits of this subject matter within the total framework of human activity and purpose. Clausewitz expresses many other elements of the professional military ethic. But these are secondary. His seminal contribution is his concept of the dual nature of war and the role of the soldier. Given this, virtually all the other aspects of professionalism must necessarily follow.[27]

There were other factors driving Clausewitz's new respectability in the American national security community. The very newness of the postwar strategic environment sent the traditional military services scrambling to justify their roles and very existence. Just as an imminent hanging tends to concentrate the mind, so the threat posed by the new strategic nuclear forces to the traditional military services led to a more serious consideration of military theory. In the process, Clausewitz caught the attention of "in-house" military thinkers like Admiral Henry Eccles. Military-sponsored think tanks like the U.S. Air Force's RAND Corporation hosted the work of thinkers who, like Bernard Brodie, found the ideas of *On War* particularly suited to the new international security environment.[28] In the later 1960s there was even an attempt to computerize Clausewitz.[29] (This was a "conceptual index" of *On War* based on twenty-seven conceptual categories. The printed result, however, was as long as the original and a good deal less comprehensible.)

Perhaps most striking was the post–Vietnam War enthusiasm for Clausewitz in America, so very similar to the fashion for Clausewitz in England seventy-five years earlier following the embarrassments of the South African War. The sudden acceptability of Clausewitz is not difficult to understand, for among the major military theorists, only Clausewitz had seriously struggled with the dilemma that American military leaders now faced. Clearly, in what had come to be called in scathing terms a "political war," the political and military components of the American war effort had come unstuck. It ran against the grain of military men to criticize elected civilian leaders, but it was just as difficult to take the blame on themselves. Clausewitz's analysis could not have been more relevant:

> The more powerful and inspiring the motives for war, . . . the more closely will the military aims and the political objects of war coincide, and the more military and less political will war appear to be. On the other hand, the less intense the motives, the less will the military element's natural tendency to violence coincide with political directives. As a result, war will be driven further from its natural course, the political object will be more and more at variance with the aim of ideal war, and the conflict will seem increasingly political in character.[30]

> . . . when people talk, as they often do, about harmful political influence on the management of war, they are not really saying what they mean. Their quarrel should be with the policy itself, not with its influence. If the policy is right—that is, successful—any intentional effect it has on the conduct of the war can only be to the good. If it has the opposite effect the policy itself is wrong.[31]

By clarifying the interplay among the trinity of army, government, and people and clearly describing the two sides of the civil–military relationship, Clausewitz offered a way out of this dilemma and into the future. America's soldiers found unacceptable any suggestion that they had failed on the battlefield, but they were willing to admit that policy had been badly made and that they had misunderstood their role in making it.

Perhaps the most important in-house military study in the immediate post-Vietnam era was Colonel Harry Summers's seminal *On Strategy: A Critical Analysis of the Vietnam War.* An explicitly Clausewitzian analysis originating in an official U.S. Army War College study first published in 1981, *On Strategy* expressed the Army's most fundamental "lessons learned" from that conflict.[32] Summers's work is reminiscent of F. B. Maurice's *British Strategy: A Study of the Appliction of the Principles of War* (1929) in that it analyzes the problem in terms of both grand military theory and the traditional "principles of war" as divined by J. F. C. Fuller. Summers's book is much more narrowly Clausewitzian and thus a good deal more consistent and coherent. His use of Clausewitz's concepts is brilliant, although his estimation of the character of the Vietnam War is debatable.

Summers's argument was tremendously influential both inside and outside the armed forces. It underlies important subsequent statements of national policy, most notably the "Weinberger Doctrine" expressed by Secretary of Defense Caspar Weinberger in 1984. Frequently quoted during the many debates over military action against Iraq in 1990/91, the Weinberger Doctrine explicitly cites Clausewitz in the third of its six points: "As Clausewitz wrote, 'No one starts a war—or rather, no one in his senses ought to do so—without first being clear in his mind what he intends to achieve by that war, and how he intends to conduct it."[33] Other reactions to Vietnam and subsequent military embarrassments, such as the army's "total-force" policy and the 1986 Goldwater–Nichols reforms of the Joint Chiefs of Staff, are similarly intended to correct civil-military imbalances in policymaking.

Once the uniformed thinkers had seriously delved into *On War*, they found a great deal more that was worthy of their attention. For the first time, Clausewitz truly came to dominate the official American military doctrinal debate: *On War* was adopted as a key text at the Naval War College in 1976, the Air War College in 1978, and the Army War College in 1981. It has always been central at the U.S. Army's School for Advanced Military Studies at Leavenworth (founded in 1983). The U.S. Marine Corps's brilliant little philosophical field manual *FMFM 1: Warfighting* (1989) is essentially a distillation.[34]

U.S. Army doctrine, especially that of "AirLand Battle" enunciated in *FM 100-5: Operations* starting in 1982, has been expounded in Clausewitzian terms.[35] It also provides some classic examples of the manner in which Clausewitz's ideas can mutate in others' hands. For instance, *FM 100-5* and *FMFM 1* use the term "center of gravity" to denote an enemy's key weaknesses rather than the source of his main strength. The concept they express is a good one, but there is no real reason to put Clausewitz's imprimatur on it. The result has been a doctrinal tempest-in-a-teapot over the proper semantics.[36]

There has also been considerable Clausewitzian ferment in the U.S. Air Force, although its impact on official doctrine is less clear. The individual who has done the most to proselytize Clausewitz in all of the upper-level military schools is probably the historian David MacIsaac. Although MacIsaac has published relatively little on the subject himself,[37] many military educators—including Summers—trace their introduction to the philosopher to his guidance. Lieutenant Colonel Barry Watts based his 1984 study of the air force's doctrine almost entirely on the Clausewitzian concept of friction. Major Mark Clodfelter, then a professor at the Air Force Academy, called his important critique of U.S. air doctrine, *The Limits of Airpower: The American Bombing of North Vietnam*, a "Clausewitzian analysis."[38]

Perhaps the most thoroughgoing example of American military Clausewitzianism is the new basic U.S. Marine Corps doctrinal manual, *FMFM 1*. Fundamentally a condensation of Clausewitz, *Warfighting* is heavily spiced with Sun Tzu and salted with concepts from a great many other military thinkers. A product of the era of Marine Corps revitalization under commandant General Al Gray, it is a uniquely philosophical document rather than the usual Jominian cookbook. In some respects it represents Clausewitz's revenge on his persecutors: Of fifty-nine source citations, nineteen refer to Clausewitz, just one to Liddell Hart.

Along with the enthusiasm for Clausewitz in the army, marine corps, and air force, the navy has revived the study of Corbett. In the post-Soviet era, Corbett's work, because of its emphasis on joint and littoral operations, seems likely to eclipse Mahan's as the navy's theoretical keystone.

Curiously, it is *On War*'s connection between national policy and military policy, along with various operational concepts, that have attracted most of the new doctrinal attention. "Moral forces," long a focus of Clausewitz's students, are not at all central to the current fad. Doctrinal discussions on maintaining troop morale still tend to center on keeping the soldiers well fed and on resolving issues of personal leadership rather than on enhancing the troops' moral and political will to fight. This probably derives from the U.S. military's particular professional ethic and the awkwardness of political indoctrination in a democratic society. Nonetheless, it marks a real weakness. Military institutions persist in seeing war as belonging to the domain of either art or science, rather than to the social sphere. Hence the American services' continuing (though diminishing) emphasis on educating officers in engineering and the hard sciences rather than in the social disciplines.[39]

The Influence of Scholars

The new prominence of Clausewitzian concepts in Anglo-American military thought has not been the product of historical circumstances alone, of course. There has also been a concerted and sustained effort by British and American scholars. The appearance of Michael Howard and Peter Paret's magnificent new English translation of *Vom Kriege* in 1976 coincided happily with the soul-searching of American soldiers in the wake of Vietnam, but it was the culmination of a project conceived in the very early 1960s when Vietnam was only a small cloud on the horizon. Its origins could be traced fairly directly to Edward Mead Earle's seminars at Princeton in the early 1940s.

For the most part, the new Anglo-American interest in military theory became the province of a new brand of civilian military theorist. These new civilian military thinkers were similar in some ways to pre–World War I British thinkers like Wilkinson, Corbett, and Thursfield. At first, however, they were mostly political scientists (like Osgood and Huntington) rather than historians, and their understanding of Clausewitz was rooted in the work of German expatriates like Rothfels, Rosinski, and Paret, not in the work of their Anglo-Saxon predecessors.

American historians were relatively slow to pick up on the historical implications of Clausewitz's theories. In 1959, however, two years after Kissinger, Osgood, and Huntington had introduced Clausewitz prominently into their discussions of contemporary policy problems, a solid and positive view of Clausewitz appeared in a work that many in the United States regard as seminal in the development of a body of truly professional military historical literature there. Theodore Ropp's *War in the Modern World* was the only important book that Ropp (1911–) ever published,[40] largely because he put his energies so thoroughly into teaching. He was, however, the mentor of a great percentage of the recipients of military history doctorates in the United States after World War II (forty-eight of them).[41] His positive view of Clausewitz had much to do with damping down the lingering impact of Liddell Hart's fulminations. Ropp's emphasis on the social and political context of war, an approach first highly developed by Delbrück, gave great impetus to the growth of the "new" military history, with its focus on the interaction between armies and societies.

This is not to say that Clausewitz was well known even among the general run of American military historians. For example, in a survey of fifteen of S. L. A. Marshall's books written between 1940 and 1979, there is only one mention of Clausewitz, a comment largely irrelevant and clearly derived from Fuller.[42] Of course, Marshall's rejection of political or ideological factors in soldiers' combat motivation—his basic argument was that soldiers fight primarily for their buddies, the "primary group"—made much of Clausewitz irrelevant. Perhaps this is a reason that Marshall's work, so bitingly critical of the U.S. Army, nonetheless proved so appealing to the American military before Vietnam.

Bernard Brodie was a key figure in alerting other scholars to the importance of Clausewitz. As Rosinski liked to point out, however, Brodie himself tended to fixate on technology as the driving factor in strategy and history.[43] Brodie's "comparative disinterest in the niceties of Clausewitz's theorymaking" has been commented on by other analysts.[44] Although he had been aware of Clausewitz and especially Corbett since the 1930s and was the first major scholar to discuss the political and strategic implications of nuclear weapons,[45] the atomic bomb caused him to lose faith—at first—in Clausewitz. He never was able to discover a practical political use for nuclear weapons. It was the invention of the hydrogen bomb that led him to return energetically to the philosophy of *On War*.[46] Brodie's two essays in the 1976 Howard/Paret edition were probably his most sophisticated contributions in the field.

Much more important to military historians, particularly in England, has been Sir Michael Eliot Howard (1922–). Howard, whose education was interrupted by World War II, served as a captain in the Coldstream Guards and won the Military Cross in 1943. He began teaching history in 1947 at King's College, London. He first read Clausewitz (in the Graham translation) in 1953 when he was appointed lecturer in war studies.

> I was initially most impressed by his concept of "friction," and the importance of moral forces as a means to overcome it. This related very directly to my own wartime experiences, and made me realize that what I had been through was a universal phenomenon in military affairs. Only very much later did I become interested in his teaching about the connection between war and politics. Fundamentally he appealed to me, and still does, because of his success in explaining the limitations of intellectualizing about war. It is an aspect of his teaching that I find still goes down very well in lecturing to the Services, and quite often leads them actually to read him.[47]

Howard moved to Oxford in 1968 and was appointed to the Chichele chair in 1977, serving as Spenser Wilkinson's successor as professor of the history of war until 1980. Howard has been particularly successful at implanting a respect for Clausewitz in his students, who have come to dominate British military studies. A number of his protégés have contributed to the English-language literature specifically on Clausewitz.[48] In 1980, Howard moved up to the even more prestigious Regius Professorship of Modern History and thence to Yale in 1989, as the first Robert A. Lovett Professor of Military and Naval History. From Yale, he has moved on to the Institute for Advanced Study at Princeton.

Unquestionably the outstanding American scholar on Clausewitz today is Peter Paret. Born in Berlin in 1924 of Jewish family, Paret arrived in the United States (after repeated displacements) in 1942. He received his doctorate in history under Howard at the University of London in 1960. He has taught at Princeton and the University of California at Davis and is a member of the Institute for Advanced Study at Princeton. From 1968 to 1989, he was associated with Stanford University. He now lives in Princeton, although he remains a senior fellow at the Hoover Institute.

Paret is not primarily a military historian, despite his many works in that field. Rather, his main interests are in intellectual and aesthetic history rather than military affairs. His exegesis of Clausewitz's thought is brilliant and, were this book focused on the period after World War II or on an analysis of Clausewitz's own meaning, Paret and his views would certainly dominate the story. Although he was still quite junior as an academician, Paret early became the driving force behind scholarly studies of Clausewitz in the United States. In 1962 he helped launch what came to be called the "Clausewitz Project" at Princeton. A conference on Clausewitz was held in Berlin on 12–13 June 1964; Princeton's Center of International Studies had already announced the creation of the project in April.[49] The participants were Paret, Howard, Brodie, Gordon Craig, Klaus Knorr, and John Shy; Germany was represented by Werner Hahlweg and Karl Dietrich Erdmann. Liddell Hart had some nominal connections with the project, and he assisted Paret in attempts to obtain funding from the Social Science Research Council.

The goal of the project was to produce a large collection of Clausewitz's work in English translation. Each of the participants was assigned a particular piece: Howard and Brodie agreed to work on *Vom Kriege*; Craig drew a set of political writings. Howard engaged the services of a retired member of the British Foreign Office, Angus Malcolm, who had translated other works in German. Malcolm was "an agreeable and civilized man with a gift for languages but not an intellectual."[50] He died after completing only a rough draft, which then served as the basis for Paret and Howard's 1976 English edition. This version looks to be the definitive translation for the foreseeable future.[51]

Unfortunately, probably owing to funding constraints (and possibly Princeton University Press's loss of interest in military subjects in the antiwar environment of the later 1960s), relatively little of the project's ambitious agenda ever reached fruition. Only the Howard/Paret edition of *On War*, Paret's intellectual biography *Clausewitz and the State* (both published by Princeton in 1976), and some other translations by Paret (some with the assistance of Daniel Moran) ever reached the publication stage. Paret and Moran published another volume of Clausewitz's historical and political writings in 1992, including such interesting pieces as Clausewitz's "Observations on Prussia in Its Great Catastrophe." *On War* has been a tremendous success, arriving on the market just as the Vietnam War became history and the subject of military and political postmortems.

There have, of course, been a number of other important works specifically on Clausewitz published in English since 1945. Aside from a plethora of articles (largely in the military press), a number of condensations, and a popular biography,[52] perhaps the most noteworthy are the Frenchman Raymond Aron's *Clausewitz: Philosopher of War*,[53] the Israeli Jehuda Wallach's *The Dogma of the Battle of Annihilation: The Theories of Clausewitz and Schlieffen and Their Impact on the German Conduct of Two World Wars*, and—another Israeli—Azar Gat's *The Origins of Military Thought: From the Enlightenment to Clausewitz.*

By 1992, Clausewitz's theories and concepts had thoroughly penetrated Anglo-American military writing, theoretical, doctrinal, and historical. On the eve of the American-led United Nations war against Iraq's Saddam Hussein, Harry Summers noted the thoroughness with which Clausewitz had penetrated American thinking: "Clausewitzian theory is going to define and determine the conflict in Iraq."[54] In the wake of the collapse of the Soviet Union, theorists seeking a new basis for European military organization in the concept of "non-offensive defense" (NOD) find their philosophical bases in the "benign side of Clausewitz," especially his emphasis on the power of the defense.[55] Nonmilitary academia has responded to the trend: For instance, MIT has offered a summer seminar on Clausewitz since 1989. Clausewitz is even beginning to appear in the popular press, something that last happened in Britain before World War I.

It has, in fact, become difficult to find a recent book on any military subject that does not make some reference to the philosopher. "Clausewitzian analyses" of this and that military problem are omnipresent. Writers on the American Civil War increasingly cite Clausewitz, following a bitter debate in the mid-1970s on the merits of following the German writer instead of Jomini (see Chapter 4). The 1988 *Elements of Confederate Defeat* discusses Clausewitz on at least fifty of its pages.[56] Charles Roland's 1991 *An American Iliad* is structured around the Clausewitzian concepts of chance and friction in war.[57]

As Howard's and Paret's participation indicates, the trend is trans-Atlantic. One of the most ambitious recent works in military history is a collaboration between the American Eliot Cohen and the Briton John Gooch, *Military Misfortunes: The Anatomy of Failure in War*. In a model of military scholarship, Cohen and Gooch tried consciously to apply Clausewitz's concept of "critical analysis" to a set of military debacles. Focusing on the interrelationships among the various levels of war, their analyses located the sources of failure in the complex interaction of organizational culture, structure, and practices, rather than in the failings of individuals.[58]

Thus the musings of General Carl Philipp Gottlieb von Clausewitz, a Prussian soldier who fought against Napoleon and who died over 160 years ago, have come to dominate military thinking and writing in English.

Contrary Currents

The fashion for Clausewitz has its downside, of course, and all of the usual abuses are in evidence. Some authors have gone beyond merely selectively quoting the philosopher to the wholesale recasting of his approach to theory in support of their own. For example, Colonel (USA, retired) Trevor Nevitt Dupuy (1916–) is well known for his attempts to apply quantitative methods to the understanding of war. He seeks to use mathematics both to interpret historical experience and to provide predictive military models. Whatever the value of Dupuy's methods, it would be hard to find a military theoretical approach more alien to that of Clausewitz. Nonetheless, Dupuy insists that his numerical methods "can lead to a new, forward-looking theory of combat essentially based upon Clausewitz's deterministic, predictive, mathematically based theoretical concept (*sic*)."[59] Concepts like "Lanchester's number theory" and the "unaimed fire equation" are supported throughout the book by the frequent—and generally pointless—invocation of Clausewitz.[60] "Just as Newton's physics can be summarized by the simple formula, $F = MA$, so too can Clausewitz's theory of combat be summarized in an equally simple formula: $P = NVQ$."[61]

There are some small signs that this fashion is beginning to subside.

Over the years Clausewitz has periodically been declared obsolete, only to reemerge more influential than ever. Such arguments often focus on nuclear wars, but it seems increasingly likely that it is the nuclear theorists, not Clausewitz, who have been rendered obsolescent.[62] There have also been complaints by military traditionalists about the excessive influence of "Clausewitz nuts" and by theoretical purists of "the prostitution of Clausewitz since 1981, particularly in FM 100-5 and its various degenerate offspring."[63] Both complaints have some justification. The eclecticism of Anglo-Saxon military thought is rooted in the same spirit as the Latin warning, *Cave ab homine unius libri* ("Beware the man of one book"): A narrow reliance on Clausewitz is inconsistent with the philosopher's own teaching. On the other hand, using *On War* as a mere stockpile of juicy quotations in support of this or that doctrinal position is also an abuse.

In part, however, criticism of the new Clausewitzians is simply reaction; would-be competitors have little choice but to seek to dislodge the philosopher from his post-Vietnam primacy. And, of course, some people are simply tired of hearing about this long-dead genius. As David Chandler has put it, "Clausewitz's airy Kantian generalizations have held sway long enough."[64] Martin van Creveld attempted in his 1991 *Transformation of War* "to construct a different, non-Clausewitzian and non-strategic, framework for thinking about war." He argues that war in the post–Cold War era is driven by forces outside the nation-state system and beyond the rational boundaries allegedly emphasized in *On War*. The pattern of conflict in the post-1945 world no longer yields to the "Clausewitzian assumption that war is rational." "To put it in a nutshell, I no longer consider war to be a means to an end. Instead, fighting is the one occasion in which the distinction between means and ends is abolished."[65] In this view, the "Clausewitzian universe" is obsolete because it is centered on war making by the "state"; Clausewitz's trinity of government, army, and people is therefore not applicable to Europe before the Treaty of Westphalia or to the world emerging from the Cold War era.

Why this should be so is unclear: The "state" existed long before Westphalia, and a great many of the present-day conflicts that Creveld describes are waged by groups who represent would-be states. Stateless and antistate terrorism existed in the classical and medieval worlds, as well as in Europe in the heyday of nationalism. Clausewitz's own Prussia was a dynastic state radically different in conception from the nation-states that fought the great wars of the twentieth century.

If we fall into the error of believing that Clausewitz's war was merely "a continuation of [rational] policy by other means," then it might not in fact apply to the recent spate of blatantly irrational ethnic conflicts. It is also possible that in a world seemingly freed of fundamental ideological conflict, in a period in which some would seriously suppose an "end to history," Clausewitz's strife-driven worldview might come to seem less relevant. Chandler's suggestion that "Baron Antoine-Jomini's rival (and more prosaic) approach . . . is under serious reconsideration" may be a symptom of such a trend, further encouraged by what seems to some—in forgetful retrospect—to have been the "simplicity" of the Persian Gulf War.

Nonetheless, if Clausewitz's works at some point become relegated to the same dusty bookshelves as those of most of his contemporaries, it will probably be because, at long last, his key insights will have been thoroughly absorbed and his own expression of them superseded.[66] If not, we can look forward to another Clausewitzian revival after the next military disaster.

22

Some Final Thoughts

Is it possible to see any particular or distinctive patterns in the development of Clausewitz studies in English over the period between 1815 and 1945? How does reviewing the historical reception of Clausewitz contribute to an understanding of his theories and of his significance as a military theorist? Are there any larger lessons to be derived concerning the value of military theory or the manner in which military concepts are transmitted and received?

It is certainly possible to find some patterns in the Anglo-American study of Clausewitz between 1815 and 1945. For example, Clausewitz's admirers were generally military reformers, or at least persons seriously dissatisfied with the status quo in their national military institutions. In itself, this is hardly surprising: Anyone dedicated enough to read *On War* is likely to be dissatisfied with any status quo. With the exception of the duke of Wellington, however, whose interest in Clausewitz's work on the campaigns of 1812 and 1815 was essentially personal in nature, almost all the nineteenth century Britons who commented on the philosopher were social reformers as well. The anonymous 1835 reviewer, John Mitchell, Charles Chesney, John Frederick Maurice, J. J. Graham, and Spenser Wilkinson all called energetically for social reform in the army. Some of them had a great deal of influence (Maurice, Wilkinson); some of them very little (Mitchell, Graham).

As individuals, Clausewitz's serious readers have often been "maverick" personalities, except during those rare periods—generally brought on by severe military embarrassments—when military reform was in fashion.

That this should be so is also perhaps to be expected: The tendency toward philosophical hairsplitting necessary in the application of Clausewitz's methods is rather alien to the spirit of military organizational culture.

In the twentieth century the social reform component seems to drop out, perhaps because the reforms of late Victorian Britain and the triumph of nationalism throughout the West made the "popular" elements of Clausewitz's thought less controversial. The more narrowly military reform element remained. Clausewitz temporarily entered the British mainstream after the Boer War, a period of major military reform, but lost popularity during the interwar era of retrenchment. Nonetheless, the most vociferous British military reformers of the interwar era, Fuller and Liddell Hart, were both very much aware of Clausewitz and to some degree influenced by him; Fuller eventually acknowledged this and became a proponent of the philosopher's ideas. Because they persisted in connecting Clausewitz to the errors of the Great War that they wished to extirpate, it was difficult for them to tie him into their reform arguments. More than anything else, however, it was these two men's egotistical reluctance to be "followers" of anyone else that led them to reject Clausewitz in public. Less egocentric thinkers like Frederick Maurice's son Frederick Barton Maurice and Cyril Falls made no bones about acknowledging the Prussian thinker's influence, although they were also less clearly "reformers."

This pattern continued in America with many peculiarities. Robert M. Johnston and Hoffman Nickerson were certainly maverick personalities, and military reformers in a technical sense. Their social ideas, however, were not terribly progressive, and they were not attracted by Clausewitz's stance on popular warfare. John McAuley Palmer fits the reform pattern much better with his suspicion of the officer corps as a class and his vision of a "citizen army." His willingness to flaunt the official army line after World War I also marks him as a maverick.

One should not push this pattern too far. The German expatriates who did so much to advance Clausewitz studies in America were, by definition, social outcasts from their own country, but this was usually less a function of personality than of ethnicity. With the exception of the highly individualistic Alfred Vagts, their social views are not prominent in their discussions of the philosopher. The U.S. Army's most important Clausewitzian, Dwight Eisenhower, cannot be characterized as either a reformer or a maverick. True, his progressive 1920 article on tank warfare angered his infantry superiors and jeopardized his career. This might be taken as a sign of reformist inclinations, but it can be more easily called a misstep in the career of a quintessential (and extremely shrewd) organization man. Eisenhower, however, was a practitioner, rather than a commentator like most of the other subjects of this study.

There are some other common and distinct patterns in the British and American reception of Clausewitz. Both British and American military writers were more likely to consume ink in discussions of the morality of war or military policy than were their German counterparts. Clausewitz himself largely ignored the issue, and his brief discussion of "moderation" in war was easily (and frequently) misconstrued as a lack of ethical concern or as actual incitement to atrocity. Nonetheless, Anglo-Saxon writers were much more likely than Frenchmen or Germans to find a moral (i.e., ethical) imperative in Clausewitz's message. Nickerson's rejection of "Douhetism" and Cyril Falls's concern with the "barbarization of war" are relevant examples. One of Wilkinson's major concerns was the strategic value of the moral high ground. He argued that policy must be morally defensible if it is to be expected to win popular support, and public opinion was one of Clausewitz's major objectives in war. Other Clausewitzians— Oliver Prescott Robinson, for example—made the same argument.

One of the most prominent of modern American military historians, Russell F. Weigley, perhaps typifies the opposing view. Weigley, discussed at points throughout this book, long exhibited blind spots when dealing with the Prussian philosopher of war. At first apparently under the spell of Liddell Hart's interpretation, he briefly adopted a consciously Clausewitzian approach during the early 1970s. Over the long haul, however, and despite a good understanding of some elements of *On War*, Weigley consistently attacked what he considered to be Clausewitz's main thesis, that war is "a mere continuation of policy." He persistently accepted the translation of *Politik* as "policy"—ignoring the fundamental difference between "policy" and "politics"—and interpreted Clausewitz's famous description of war as a pure prescription leading to a disastrous routiniza-tion of aggression. He noted, correctly enough, that the political ascen-dency of military leaders always tends to grow in proportion to the severity of a military crisis, and complained that the civilian leadership "tends to sacrifice policy to the exigencies of war."[1] But Weigley seemed not to grasp that individual leaders and individual states are unable to control the domestic and international political environment in which they operate (i.e., what Clausewitz called the "spirit of the age") or that governments do not conceive their policies "rationally" in blithe indifference to one another's actions. As a historian, Weigley committed a sin that Clausewitz roundly condemned: He let his own fundamental decency and horror of war distort his perception of the dynamics of social interaction, of which war is a typical manifestation.

Gradually, however, Weigley has come to believe that his earlier views of Clausewitz were erroneous. In 1991 he chose once again to attack the notion of war as a continuation of policy: "War in the age of battles was not an effective extension of policy by other means . . . but the bankruptcy of policy." This time, however, he left out Clausewitz's name. He tells me that this was because he has come recognize that this phrase in English is so misleading in regard to *On War*'s actual argument.[2]

A concern like Weigley's over the morality of war is probably the most distinctive single element in the Anglo-Saxon interpretation of *On War* before 1945. It can be found in both *On War*'s proponents, who—like

Wilkinson, Falls, and Nickerson—saw an (implied) positive moral message in it, and its opponents, who did not.

The positive moral interpretation was largely forgotten, however, in the age when nuclear weapons made "thinking the unthinkable" a dominant feature of Anglo-American strategic thought. A more detached—not to say amoral—interpretation of Clausewitz became the norm in the English-speaking world as in the German, driven in part by the circumstances of the Cold War, in part by the influence of German expatriates, and in part by Clausewitz's own style of expression.

Both British and American theorists were more likely to accept Clausewitz's assessment of the dynamic relationship between the attack and the defense than were German military writers. (As theorists, Caemmerer and Ritter von Leeb were exceptions, but the German army often showed in practice a remarkable appreciation for the underlying truth, at the tactical and operational levels if not the strategic.) Neither the British nor the American armies, as institutions, were able to do the same, persistently misunderstanding the point and determined to produce an all-purpose and offensive doctrinal prescription. Nonetheless, the British army's pre–World War I internal debate on this point seems to have been more lively than the German army's.

On another and related point, both British and American writers were more likely than Germans to be sensitive to the essentially conservative balance-of-power views expressed in *On War*. This sensitivity derived from their moral concerns, from their greater willingness to accept a balanced view of the defense, and from the realities of coalition warfare against a formidable and aggressive Germany. The balance-of-power factor was stressed in the first "American" translation of *Vom Kriege*, admittedly the product of a German expatriate, but one whose familiarity with Clausewitz and whose motive for writing were rooted in an American context. F. B. Maurice and H. Rowan-Robinson also connected Clausewitz to their balance-of-power discussions. There is, of course, a significant element of predisposition in this: The Anglo-Saxon powers have always been great manipulators of the balance of power in pursuit of their own ends.

There is no such continuity between the British and the Americans on another important aspect of Clausewitz's thought. The British never showed any propensity for rejecting Clausewitz's connection between war and politics (although it was a focus of their suspicions of Germany). They were not much interested in this aspect of *On War* in the nineteenth century, largely because—as Wellington's remarks show—they were quite aware of the connection. Further, the British tradition of military subordination to the civil power, which dates back at least to the upheavals of the seventeenth century, made most unlikely the kind of opposition to this idea that surfaced in Germany. Such opposition as did surface in Britain was generally based on a contrary consideration, the reluctance of soldiers to intrude on the prerogatives of politicians. British soldiers accepted—if often morosely, like G. F. R. Henderson—that politics was indeed going to influence strategy no matter how this might derange military operations. The experience of World War I, and quite possibly a reading of *On War*, certainly influenced British soldiers like William Robertson to seek a more balanced interaction between military and political leaders, but the principle that policy and politicians guide strategy was seldom questioned.

In America, professional soldiers bitterly resisted the idea that politics had any relevance to military strategy or operations. Even the undeniably political nature of the Civil War—especially Lincoln's war policies and Grant's and Sherman's loyal execution of them—failed to win the officer corps's concession on this theoretical point. In practice, the principle of civilian control nevertheless prevailed, probably owing to the Anglo-American constitutional tradition and the force of George Washington's example. McClellan, despite his contempt for Lincoln and for politicians in general, attempted no coup d'état.

Even so, the U.S. Army as an institution continued to argue that politics ceased when war began, that the management of war was a business for professionals alone, and that there was no substitute for victory (i.e., the Moltkean idea that war best serves policy through the total destruction of the enemy's ability to fight). The Truman–MacArthur crisis over Korea settled this issue in a practical sense, but it was undoubtedly the Vietnam experience that finally drove home to the army as an institution the inherent interaction of war, politics, and policy.[3] The Vietnam war had a similar impact on the army's offspring service, the U.S. Air Force, although it is not clear that this lesson has been entirely accepted by the air force as an institution. Most writing on Clausewitz by air force officers is critical of the air force.[4]

The pattern of Clausewitz's reception in Great Britain and the United States correlates well with Samuel Huntington's analysis of the professionalization of armies. Huntington suggested that military professionalization in the leading Anglo-Saxon countries had been delayed by uncertainties as to the location of civilian authority over their military institutions.[5]

In Britain the contest was between Crown and Parliament. It was not resolved until 1904 (when the last commander of the army was replaced by a chief of the general staff). The first widespread adoption of Clausewitz in Britain coincided perfectly with the professionalization of the British army.

In America, the much more mature attitude toward politics and war that has been evidenced by the U.S. military since Vietnam, and the faith in Clausewitz evidenced in Harry Summers's semiofficial work and in the 1984 Weinberger Doctrine, correlates well with Huntington's description of the professional military ethic. The same period has seen the official adoption of Clausewitz as a guiding light in most of the American armed services.

The sources of American soldiers' long-standing failure to accept the political implications of war are hard to determine; it is always difficult to account for a nonevent. Possibly the "total" nature of America's great wars, in which political and military goals were essentially compatible, made them overlook the impact of political guidance on strategy. Or perhaps they failed to appreciate the intrinsic connections between "policy," the influence of which they accepted, and "politics," a term they associated with partisanship, discord, and corruption.

Conversely, perhaps it was the social and political insecurity of the army that made its officers so vociferously resentful of politicians. The long persistence of the "militia myth" made career officers instinctively suspicious of any proponent of popular warfare. Perhaps, as John M. Palmer implied, they simply never gave much thought to the political sphere, out of complacency, naiveté, a very narrow view of "professionalism," or simple anti-intellectualism. The "Prussianism" of the American army, which one might date back to Steuben but which was certainly evident after 1870, might also be a factor.

The American navy, more British in its traditions, produced in A. T. Mahan a theorist who argued that "diplomacy" (i.e., external politics) drove naval policy in both peace and war. Mahan evinced no great interest in Clausewitz, but neither did he see any great contradictions between their views. The interwar American naval theorist George Meyers had no problem in reconciling Mahan and Clausewitz, and the very experience of navy men in accepting one set of theories may have made them more willing to consider another.

Among Anglo-Saxon soldiers, however, such willingness was generally rare. What were the sources of the frequently noted Anglo-Saxon aversion to military theory? Azar Gat finds it in the Enlightenment tradition (of which Jomini was a representative), as opposed to that of the German *Aufklärung* and the various philosophical currents that underlay Clausewitz's own writing. Others would find it in such nebulous concepts as "national character" or the "military mind" (what Liddell Hart called its "essential concreteness").

The fact that many of Clausewitz's key concepts were ignored or rejected even in Germany and that a number of British military writers demonstrated an intelligent grasp of the arguments in *On War*—demonstrated, in fact, a greater willingness to accept important ideas like the subordination of military to political considerations, the power of the defense and, especially in Corbett's case, the possibility of limited war—tends to cast doubt on all these theories.

In this connection, we might consider the nonlinear characteristics of Clausewitz's thought. These infuriated would-be "scientists" of war like the young Fuller. *On War* might indeed have puzzled generations of Liddell Hart's "essentially concrete-minded soldiers" if they were in fact seeking concrete doctrinal guidance. On the other hand, such soldiers were probably equally befuddled by Fuller's attempts to provide a "scientific" (i.e., linear) theory of war, and his occasional escape from the scientific approach took the even more unacceptable form of mysticism.

Britain's soldiers, particularly in the Victorian period, had more practical experience of war than just about anyone. This experience was gained generally in colonial or imperialist wars which varied wildly in their character and conduct, both from one another and from continental conflicts. Most British soldiers thus seem to have grasped intuitively that a linear approach—with which they naturally identified the word *theory*—was inappropriate, rendering it suspect or worse. Wellington's comments (via Ellesmere) on the "pompous charlatanerie" of Jomini typify this attitude. Such skepticism may seem reprehensible—a symptom of mere anti-intellectualism—when directed toward *On War*, but it seems rather more perceptive and laudable when directed at the work of most other theorists.

The key factor among uniformed military thinkers may have been a matter of military professionalism, as Huntington suggested. The Germans produced in the elder Moltke a powerful, self-professed Clausewitzian, but the Moltkean tradition stands opposed to Clausewitz in crucial respects. Despite the vaunted but narrow professional competence of the German officer corps, the German army tended to represent a social class rather than the nation. It thus failed Huntington's key test of professionalism. Many of Germany's strategic errors were the result.

The slow professionalization of the British—and even more so the American—officer corps was due to more complex factors and had different consequences. The British produced no Moltke, much to their own frequently expressed regret, but important elements of the British military leadership were equally progressive. The "Wolseley ring," for instance, was an intelligent, energetic, and reformist clique, and in its key theorist Frederick Maurice we find an important Clausewitzian influence. Many of the most important British military writers of the pre–World War I era, including G. F. R. Henderson, Julian Corbett, and Spenser Wilkinson, were heavily influenced by Clausewitz, although few of them drew great attention to the fact.

One might argue, in fact, that many of Clausewitz's ideas were received more favorably in pre–World War I Britain than in Germany: It was simply not in the Anglo-Saxon writers' character to express obeisance to a single dominating theorist, regardless of how much they may have found useful or intriguing in his writings. The German military writers, on the other hand, were quick to express their adoration of "the master" (as Goltz and Bernhardi, among others, were wont to call Clausewitz), regardless of how much of his argument they preferred quietly to ignore.

Thus, what was lacking in British military literature was largely the self-consciously "Clausewitzian" terminology to which German writers were addicted. The use of this terminology was not unimportant. It meant that bits and pieces of Clausewitz's ideas and method were transmitted much further via German writers than by British. In terms of the direct transmission of certain key ideas, however, the most influential British military thinkers were generally more receptive. Both the Chichele chair at Oxford and the key post of *Times* military correspondent have generally been held by writers intensely aware of Clausewitz and, with the questionable exception of Liddell Hart, heavily influenced by him.

In any case, it is much easier to attribute British and American military failings and German successes (and vice versa) to factors external to the armies themselves rather than to any failings in the area of military theory. The peacetime dispersion, penury, small mobilization bases of the Anglo-Saxon armies between 1815 and 1945, and the lack of military sophistication among the political classes do much more to explain their wartime behavior than does any alleged intellectual poverty among soldiers.

Even less answerable is another question: Was the Anglo-Saxon aversion to theory a good thing or not? In practice, the German tendency toward what Rosinski in a laudatory tone called "systematic thinking" resulted in a rigid political logic that drove the German nation to destruction. (One could argue endlessly whether that logic was Clausewitz's, depending on whether one emphasizes its rational or its romantic aspects.) The more pragmatic, empirical—or, to be more pejorative, the bumbling, "muddling-through"—Anglo-Saxon approach has paid greater dividends in the long run.

The implications of this argument are somewhat elusive. Perhaps we should take into account Clausewitz's discussion of war as an art or a science. Tactics is largely in the realm of science; what Clausewitz called "strategy" (and we call "operations") is in the province of art. The German military thinkers' conscious military intellectualism, their propensity for "systematic thought," thus may account for their widely conceded excellence at the tactical and operational levels of war.

War as a whole, however, falls within the domain of neither art nor science. The nearer we come to the level of policy, the more the essentially social character—the political logic—of war asserts itself. Clearly, the strategic success of the Anglo-Saxons has not been derived from the study of Clausewitz (which is not to say that it would not help). Rather, their success has been to a large degree conditioned by the fact that their historical evolution created institutions that simply assumed, without the need for a great deal of conscious thought, the supremacy of political over military considerations and the dangers inherent in resorting to violence in pursuit of policy. Further, by their nature, democratic institutions breed a feel for the workings of the balance of power; monarchies and dictatorships cannot be expected to excel at integrating competing domestic concerns, at building coalitions, and at combining strategies. That the Anglo-Saxon powers should be consistently superior at the level of state policy and grand strategy is thus not too surprising. In the terms of Clausewitz's discussion of military genius, what we have here is the triumph of character over intellect.

Insofar as this is a study in the transmission of ideas, however, perhaps the greatest lesson to be found in this survey of the Anglo-American reception of Clausewitz is the prosaic one that it helps to actually read a book before embracing or rejecting its argument and that other writers' summaries—including, it should be noted again, the one included in this book—are not a trustworthy basis for judgment.

Another lesson that is probably uncomfortable to intellectuals, who like to imagine that their books can alter the pattern of human events, is that complex ideas do not easily make the jump from one mind to another, no matter how carefully or eloquently expressed. It cannot be demonstrated that any of the writers discussed in this study ever changed course merely because of reading the most brilliant of all writers on war. In many cases, the lessons they drew from Clausewitz were obviously lessons to which they were already predisposed. For example, John Mitchell had clearly formulated his reform program before he found in Clausewitz a theoretical justification for it. The pedagogical ideas that the elder Frederick Maurice derived from Clausewitz were highly compatible with those of his educational reformer father. Liddell Hart saw confirmed those ideas on the power of the defense that he drew from his experience in World War I. Eisenhower's attitude toward ends and means is as clear in his fiscal as in his military policies. Writers with views as diametrically opposite as John M. Palmer's and Hoffmann Nickerson's could express them in Clausewitzian terms. At best, a reading of *On War* has enabled Clausewitz's students to interpret the lessons of their own experiences: William Robertson's turnaround on the issue of civil–military relations is a useful example.

To say that readers accept (or even perceive) only what they are able to recognize as restatements of their own views or experiences is almost certainly going too far, but not by much. *On War* is often less a window into reality than a mirror for its reader, perhaps necessarily so. This has been my own experience with it. When I first read it as an undergraduate at the College of William and Mary, it was the abstract discussion of "absolute war" and the idea of war as a rational continuation of policy that seemed to me to be its essence. When I read it during my military service, it was the discussion of friction, chance, and moral factors that most struck me. Today, when I work as a historian, it is Clausewitz's historicist philosophy that provides the key to understanding. Every time I have read it, it has seemed a different book, but it is only myself who has changed.

Thus it is little wonder that survivors of the trench warfare of 1914–18 saw their experiences in *On War*'s pages, just as Vietnam veterans tend to see in it a textbook on what went wrong in their war. That this is the case would not have surprised Clausewitz, who insisted that personal experience was essential to any understanding of the phenomenon of war.

This problem of experience and perception connects to a difficulty that might serve as another warning to writers. Once printed, thoughts are cast in stone, and later generations have little concern for the nuances of a writer's personality or intellectual evolution. It is true that scholars with a taste for intellectual history, like Rothfels, Rosinski, Paret, and Gat, have come to some intriguing conclusions, ferreting out the meaning of

On War by analyzing its author's personality and the manner in which its concepts developed. So did Caemmerer and Delbrück earlier. Of course, their conclusions often differ radically, as is shown in Rosinski's and Caemmerer's attacks on Delbrück and Paret's critique of Rothfels. Other examples can be found in Gat's criticisms of Paret—which are often absurd and reminiscent of Rosinski—and of Raymond Aron: "Paret . . . totally misinterprets the essence of Clausewitz's military teaching throughout his life. . . . Aron's theoretical *naïveté* is astonishing."[6]

On the other hand, most soldiers and military analysts have accepted *On War* as a self-contained philosophy of war, often impervious even to its own internal contradictions. Many assumed that the "Instruction for the Crown Prince" was a mere summary of the larger and later work. In any case most have tended to read both books without considering their original historical context, as when Fuller among others blithely assumed that Clausewitz sought to represent the ideas of Napoleon.

As a further depressant for would-be theorists, it seems that although *On War* was well enough understood by those who read it for themselves, its author's ideas rarely survived repeated retransmission. Progressively simplified and modified by friend and foe alike, his subtle descriptive dualities became brutally simple prescriptions. Even otherwise sophisticated historians have often interpreted Clausewitz in narrowly tactical or strategic terms, seeking to find his influence in adherence to some allegedly "Clausewitzian" prescription. As a result, they have found his influence where there was none and missed it where there was. Thus Clausewitz's reputation mutated effortlessly from that of the "apostle of total war" into that of "the preeminent military and political strategist of limited war in modern times." His most clever formulations were most easily turned on their heads, usually not by writers working directly from a reading of *On War*, but by those deriving their knowledge at second hand.

Ironically, all of this goes to confirm one of the most basic of Clausewitz's historicist ideas, that the nature of war is determined by a complex of social forces, by the "spirit of the age," rather than by the conscious desires of individual actors or theorists.

These lessons certainly do not mean (as many academics and soldiers have privately complained to me) that Clausewitz's theories are valueless because they are so endlessly flexible.[7] The record of Clausewitz's historical reception and rejection clearly indicates the value of his descriptive approach to war, history, and military theory. It demonstrates as well the dangers of attempting to apply military theory prescriptively in predicting the nature of the next war, as Goltz did before World War I and Liddell Hart did before World War II. Like the finest tools available to artists, scientists, or soldiers, the product of a Clausewitzian approach is very much dependent on the peculiarities of the mind that wields it. However the predispositions of the reader may affect his or her view of war, the lens offered by Clausewitz provides for a much more distinct vision.

One question that we need to ask is simply, Is military theory really very useful?[8] Obviously, the great bulk of military theory that has been promulgated over the ages has been of very limited value. Although it has served the indispensable purpose of transmitting basic military concepts and knowledge to generations of soldiers (who, owing to the very nature of the profession, can have only a very limited base of practical experience), it has also led in practice to many rigidities and absurdities. Even the most sophisticated and useful theory (which is to say Clausewitz's) serves at best to define the bases for debate and is easily manipulated to serve prescriptive functions alien to its descriptive nature.

If military theory does in fact have any great utility, the next question must be For whom? Scholars? Politicians? Writers of military doctrine? Soldiers themselves? It was Clausewitz's great goal—and to some extent his achievement—to bridge the gap between theory and practice. Unfortunately, his work has often fallen into the crack it sought to span, perceived as being too concrete and pragmatic for the intellectual, too complex and ambiguous for the active politician, and too ethereal for the practical soldier. Too many people on all sides of the chasm have simply failed to read *On War*.[9] More fundamentally, the gap represents a real dichotomy between the values and perceptions of scholars and soldiers, and their sometimes well-founded suspicions of one another. Perhaps inevitably, perhaps as the result of correctable failings in their education, practical soldiers and—to a similar extent, political scientists like Lebow— tend to lack the broad historical understanding needed to internalize Clausewitz's historicist argument and to distinguish the practical utility of his concepts and method.

Clausewitz himself was skeptical of the role of theory in forming the character of military leaders, although he hoped it could educate their judgment, and *On War*'s intended audience is unclear. Clausewitz wrote essentially for the "military analyst." In practice, that probably means staff officers and military historians rather than commanders. Certainly, the historian's work benefits from Clausewitz's descriptive theory. The individual historian is almost inherently more flexible, creative, and consistent than any committee of military textbook writers and is much more likely to study Clausewitz's work in its historical context. Good historical writings benefit both the soldier and the policymaker. However, the most sophisticated attempts to apply the lessons of *On War* have generally been made by historical scholars with both political and military connections (Corbett, Wilkinson) who were thus able to temper their contemporary-oriented ideas with both the historian's long-range perspective and some understanding of political and military organizational realities.

Unfortunately, indirect transmissions of Clausewitz's theory, however much more convenient they may be to read than his own complex writings, have proved to be unreliable if not downright dangerous. Historians, political scientists, military analysts, and doctrinal compilers seem to have little trouble understanding Clausewitz's arguments when they read them for themselves. No matter how devoted they may be to transmitting his insights in their own works, however, they unavoidably simplify, rephrase, "clarify," and select among them.[10] Driven by transient concerns and the ever-evolving spirit of their own times, most give in to their own creative urges and expand, modify, and even recast them wholesale, rejecting certain aspects of *On War* and promoting their own views.

There is nothing intrinsically wrong with this. Indeed, it is inherent and vital to the intellectual process, and most of the writers we have examined were quite honest about what they were doing. It appears, however, that many of their readers have been unable to derive from the resulting amalgam much sense of Clausewitz's original argument. This is just as true for scholars as for soldiers; political scientists and historians who have experienced Clausewitz only through the eyes of Bernard Brodie or Robert Osgood express images of him just as skewed as those expressed by soldiers who have experienced him only through the eyes of Colmar von der Goltz.

And that original argument is very important, not only for its own sake but because of the role that Clausewitz's theories have come to play in the American national security community. *On War* gave shape to the most important formulations of the final "lessons learned" from the Vietnam experience, as expressed in Harry Summers's work and in the Weinberger Doctrine. The impressive "jointness" with which the American armed forces and connected agencies waged the Persian Gulf War in 1990/91 can be traced to a significant, if unquantifiable, extent to the common conceptual base that this study has engendered. Clausewitz has provided the intellectual common ground that formal doctrine has always sought but—because of its unavoidably narrow focus, single-service orientation, and prescriptive intent—failed to provide. The value of that common ground lies in the very flexibility of Clausewitzian theory that many have found so frustrating: It provides a common set of concepts and intellectual tools that greatly facilitate analysis and discussion while leaving the conclusions to be reached as open as ever to creativity and to differing goals and points of view. It is probably necessary, therefore, that military leaders be schooled directly in the works of Clausewitz. Otherwise, that vital common ground will be eroded as secondary and derivative treatments, as always, drift further and further from the original and from each other.

It is certainly outside the scope of this book to do more than to raise such fundamental and practical issues of military education. They are nonetheless questions that inexorably arise from any contemplation of Clausewitz's reception in Great Britain and in the United States.

Notes

Chapter 1

1. Bernard Brodie, "Clausewitz: a Passion for War," *World Politics* 25 (January 1973), 228–308, referring to Carl [Phillip Gottlieb] von Clausewitz, *Hinterlassene Werke, Vom Kriege*, vols 1–3 (Berlin: Dümmlers Verlag, 1832).

2. Carl von Clausewitz, *On War*, eds. and trans. Michael Howard and Peter Paret (Princeton, NJ: Princeton University Press, 1976). Sales figures are courtesy of Princeton University Press, letter from Deborah Tegarden to Bassford, 24 July 1989.

3. For a useful survey see Michael I. Handel, ed., *Clausewitz and Modern Strategy* (London: Frank Cass, 1986). This includes essays on Clausewitz in France, Italy, and Germany, but the discussion on England is limited to the works of J. F. C. Fuller and Liddell Hart. See also Jehuda L. Wallach, *The Dogma of the Battle of Annihilation: The Theories of Clausewitz and Schlieffen and Their Impact on the German Conduct of Two World Wars* (Westport, CT: Greenwood Press, 1986). *Vom Kriege*'s modern editor, Werner Hahlweg, included a broad survey of the international literature on Clausewitz in the nineteenth German edition (Bonn: Ferdinand Dümmlers Verlag, 1980); see especially "Clausewitz und die angelsächsische Welt," 138–53.

4. The first term is one used frequently by Liddell Hart. The second is from Robert Endicott Osgood, *Limited War Revisited* (Boulder, CO: Westview Press, 1979), 2.

5. Peter Novick, *That Noble Dream: The "Objectivity Question" and the American Historical Profession* (Cambridge: Cambridge University Press, 1988), 7.

Chapter 2

1. Quotations from *On War* given in this section are in most cases taken from the translation by Michael Howard and Peter Paret (Princeton, NJ:

Princeton University Press, 1976), since that is the version most accessible to most readers.

2. The false conception of Clausewitz as an ivory tower intellectual with little practical experience is often repeated, even by writers whose view of Clausewitz's philosophy is quite positive; for example, see Philip B. Davidson, *Vietnam at War* (Novato, CA: Presidio Press, 1988), 15.

3. A chronology of Clausewitz's writings appears in Peter Paret's *Clausewitz and the State: The Man, His Theories, and His Times* (Princeton, NJ: Princeton University Press, 1976), 330.

4. *On War*, bk. 2, chap. 2, sec. 15.

5. Clausewitz's approach has connections to Kant, Hegel, and Fichte. See especially Paret, *Clausewitz and the State*; and W. B. Gallie, *Philosophers of Peace and War: Kant, Clausewitz, Marx, Engels and Tolstoy* (Cambridge: Cambridge University Press, 1978). Azar Gat, *The Origins of Military Thought: From the Enlightenment to Clausewitz* (Oxford: Oxford University Press, 1989), emphasizes the differing influences of the Enlightenment, *Aufklärung*, and Romantic intellectual movements. These connections are real but should not be overstressed. Clausewitz was well (if self-) educated and was certainly familiar with these writers, but the only philosopher to whom he made direct reference in discussing *On War* was Montesquieu. Although some of *On War*'s abstractions sound vaguely dialectical, actual elements of Hegel's formal dialectic rarely appear. Clausewitz's philosophical methods are his own and appear to be empirical in origin.

6. See Stephen J. Cimbala, *Clausewitz and Escalation: Classical Perspective on Nuclear Strategy* (London: Frank Cass, 1992), 1–12.

7. See especially bk. 8, chap. 5, "Closer Definition of the Military Objective—Continued: Limited Aims."

8. For example, *On War*, bk. 3, chap. 16.

9. This view of Clausewitz's use of history is not universally held. See, for example, John Gooch, "Clio and Mars: The Use and Abuse of History," *Journal of Strategic Studies* 3 (1980): 21–36. Gooch argued (although his points were somewhat inconsistent) that Clausewitz had used history to support his theories, rather than deriving his theories from history. In fact, Clausewitz did neither: He derived his theories from experience (both his own and historical) and then tested them against history. What makes Clausewitz remarkable as a military theorist is that he actually allowed the test results to modify his argument, sometimes in a radical manner. Gooch's view seems to be based on a rather purist idea of the historian's mission. This aspect of *On War* will no doubt remain a source of controversy, involving as it does fundamental disputes over the nature of history as a discipline and the values of professional historians.

10. See particularly bk. 2, chaps. 5 ("Critical Analysis") and 6 ("On Historical Examples"), and bk. 8, chap. 3.B. ("Scale of the Military Objective and of the Effort To Be Made").

11. "Operational" is a modern construction encompassing much of what Clausewitz discussed as "strategic."

12. Sun Tzu has been translated into English many times. Sun Tzu, *The Art of War*, trans. Samuel B. Griffith [Brigadier General, USMC] (Oxford: Oxford University Press, 1963), provides much of the basis for my discussion. See also Sun Tzu, *The Art of Warfare*, trans. Roger T. Amers (New York: Ballantine, 1993), an authoritative new translation based on ancient texts recovered by archaeologists.

13. A detailed comparison of Clausewitz and Sun Tzu is outside the boundaries of this study. See, however, Michael I. Handel, *Sun Tzu and Clausewitz: The Art of War and On War Compared* (Carlisle Barracks, PA: Strategic Studies Institute, U.S. Army War College, 1991), which generally accords with my argument, or Handel's *Masters of War: Sun Tzu, Clausewitz and Jomini* (London: Frank Cass, 1992). John E. Tashjean, "The Cannon in the Swimming Pool: Clausewitzian Studies and Strategic Ethnocentrism," *Journal of the Royal United Services Institute*, June 1983, 54–57, looks at some possibly fundamental dichotomies between strategic thinking east and west.

14. Jean Joseph Marie Amiot, *Art militaire des Chinois* (Paris: Didot l'aîné, 1772).

15. Henri Jomini, *Traité de grande tactique* (Paris: Giguet et Michaud, 1805). On Jomini, see Crane Brinton, Gordon A. Craig, and Felix Gilbert, "Jomini," in *Makers of Modern Strategy: Military Thought from Machiavelli to Hitler*, ed. Edward Mead Earle (Princeton, NJ: Princeton University Press, 1943), 77–92; Michael Howard, "Jomini and the Classical Tradition," in *The Theory and Practice of War*, ed. Michael Howard (New York: Praeger, 1966), 3–20; John Shy, "Jomini," in *Makers of Modern Strategy: From Machiavelli to the Nuclear Age*, ed. Peter Paret (Princeton: Princeton University Press, 1986), 143–185. The best English-language discussion of Jomini's military career can be found in John R. Elting, "Jomini: Disciple of Napoleon?" *Military Affairs*, Spring 1964, 17–26. Unlike most biographical discussions of the Swiss, which are based on his own highly colored reminiscences to people he wished to impress, Elting's study is based on Xavier de Courville, *Jomini, ou de le Devin de Napoleon* (Paris: Plon, 1935): "Written by Jomini's descendants, from his personal papers, it is the most impartial of his biographies."

16. Elting, "Jomini"; Robert M. Johnston, *Clausewitz to Date* (Cambridge, MA: The Military Historian and Economist, 1917), 9–11.

17. *On War*, bk. 2, chap. 2.

18. For Jomini's theoretical writings in English translation, see Antoine-Henri Jomini, *Treatise on Grand Military Operations: or A Critical and Military History of the Wars of Frederick the Great as Contrasted with the Modern System*, trans. Col. S. B. Holabird, 2 vols. (New York: D. Van Nostrand, 1865); Baron de Jomini, *The Art of War*, trans. Major O. F. Winship and Lieut. E. E. McLean, (New York: G.P. Putnam, 1854). Important derivative works include Dennis Hart Mahan's instructional works for West Point; Henry Wager Halleck, *Elements of Military Art and Science* (New York: D. Appleton, 1846); Edward Bruce Hamley (1824–93), *The Operations of War Explained and Illustrated* (London: William Blackwood and Sons, 1866).

19. Most discussions of Jomini compare him with Clausewitz. For explicit efforts to do so, see U.S. Military Academy, Department of Military Art and Engineering, *Clausewitz, Jomini, Schlieffen* (West Point, NY, USMA, 1951) (rewritten, in part, by Colonel [USA] John R. Elting, 1964); J. E. Edmonds, "Jomini and Clausewitz" [a treatment extremely hostile to the German], *Canadian Army Journal* 5 (May 1951), 64–69; Joseph L. Harsh, "Battlesword and Rapier: Clausewitz, Jomini, and the American Civil War," *Military Affairs*, December 1974, 133–38; Major [USAF] Francis S. Jones, "Analysis and Comparison of the Ideas and Later Influences of Henri Jomini and Carl von Clausewitz," Unpublished paper, Maxwell Air Force Base, AL: Air Command and Staff College, April 1985; Colonel [USA] Richard M. Swain, "'The Hedgehog and the Fox': Jomini, Clausewitz, and History," *Naval War College Review*, Autumn 1990, 98–109.

20. These points are most easily found in the bibliographical essay that opened the original French edition of the *Summary*, "*Notice: Sur la théorie actuelle de la guerre et sur son utilité*" (On the present theory of war and of its utility). This essay is missing from (or severely edited in) most English-language editions, although it is present in the 1854 American translation.

21. On Moltke, see Gunther E. Rothenberg, "Moltke, Schlieffen, and the Doctrine of Strategic Envelopment," in Paret, ed., *Makers of Modern Strategy*, 296–325; Lieut.-Colonel F. E. Whitton, *Moltke* (New York: H. Holt, 1921). Daniel J. Hughes [USAF School for Advanced Airpower Studies, Maxwell Field, Al.], has prepared a translation, as yet unpublished, of several of Moltke's works.

22. Grand [German] General Staff, *Moltke's Military Works: Precepts of War*, trans. Commander (USN) A. G. Zimmerman, (Newport, RI: Department of Intelligence and Research, U.S. Naval War College, 1935), pt. 2, p. 1.

23. Quoted in Otto Pflanze, *Bismarck and the Development of Germany*, vol. 1 (Princeton, NJ: Princeton University Press, 1990), 479.

24. For example, see William Manchester, *The Last Lion: Winston Spencer Churchill* (Boston: Little, Brown, 1988), vol. 2, 135: "If Clausewitz saw war as a science, the chancellor [Neville Chamberlain] saw it as a business."

25. Carl von Clausewitz, *The Campaign of 1812 in Russia* (London: John Murray, 1843), 185.

26. *On War*, bk. 6, chap. 1.

27. My definitions; Clausewitz does not distinguish the two concepts.

28. For an example of the latter interpretation, see David Kaiser, *Politics and War: European Conflict from Philip II to Hitler* (Cambridge, MA: Harvard University Press, 1990), 415.

29. See, for example Burton I. Kaufman, *The Korean War: Challenges in Crisis, Credibility, and Command* (New York: Knopf, 1986), 150.

30. See Howard and Paret, eds., *On War*, note on p. 608.

31. For example, see Arnold H. Price, "Clausewitz," *Encyclopædia Britannica*, 15th ed. (1985).

32. Carl von Clausewitz, "Betrachtungen über einen künftigen Kriegsplan gegen Frankreich" (written c. 1830), first published by the Historical Section of the General Staff as an appendix to *Moltkes Militärische Werke, Teil I: Militärische Korrespondenz, Teil 4* (Berlin, 1902), 181–97; reprinted in Carl von Clausewitz, *Verstreute kleine Schriften*, ed. Werner Hahlweg, (Osnabrück: Biblio Verlag, 1979), 547.

33. *On War*, bk. 8, chap. 2.

34. Russell F. Weigley, "Military Strategy and Civilian Leadership," in *Historical Dimensions of National Security Problems*, ed. Klaus Knorr, (Lawrence: University Press of Kansas, 1976), 70, citing Gerhard Ritter, *The Sword and the Scepter* (Coral Gables, FL: University of Miami Press, 1969–73), vol. 1; compare *On War*, bk. 1, chap. 2.

35. *On War*, bk. 8, chap. 2.

36. *On War*, bk. 1, chap. 7.

37. *On War*, bk. 1, chap. 4.

38. For example, see Colonel T. N. Dupuy [USA, ret.], *Understanding War: History and Theory of Combat* (New York: Paragon House, 1987).

39. Alan D. Beyerchen of Ohio State University was kind enough to let me read his then-unpublished paper, "Chance and Complexity in the Real World:

Clausewitz on the Nonlinear Nature of War," *International Security,* Winter 1992/1993, 59–90. My treatment accordingly reflects some of his insights.

40. James Gleick, *Chaos: Making a New Science* (New York: Penguin Books, 1987), 8.

41. See Randolph Roth, "Is History a Process? Revitalization Theory, Nonlinearity, and the Central Metaphor of Social Science History," *Social Science History,* Summer 1992.

42. Most natural phenomena are nonlinear. Dividing them along linear and nonlinear lines is similar to dividing the animal world into elephants and "non-elephant animals." See Beyerchen, "Chance and Complexity in the Real World."

43. *On War,* author's preface.

44. *On War,* bk. 8, chap. 4.

45. See *On War,* bk. 1, chap. 2, "Purpose and Means in War," and bk. 3, chap. 1.

46. My example, not Clausewitz's.

47. *On War,* bk. 1, chap. 2.

48. *On War,* bk. 4, chap. 11.

49. See especially "On the Basic Question of Germany's Existence," in Carl von Clausewitz, *Historical and Political Writings,* ed. and trans. Peter Paret and Daniel Moran (Princeton, NJ: Princeton University Press), 377–84.

50. *On War,* bk. 3, chap. 3.

51. As is pointed out by Jehuda L. Wallach, *The Dogma of the Batle of Annihilation: The Theories of Clausewitz and Schlieffen and Their Impact on the German Conduct of Two World Wars* (Westport, CT: Greenwood Press, 1986).

52. I owe this observation to Alan Beyerchen. For a creative misperception based on the use of the word *duel,* see Michael Walzer, *Just and Unjust Wars: A Moral Argument with Historical Illustrations* (New York: Basic Books, 1977), note on p. 25.

53. *On War,* bk. 3, chap. 8 (from the 1908 Graham/Maude version).

54. *On War,* bk. 3, chap. 9, and bk. 4, chap. 8.

55. William McElwee, *The Art of War from Waterloo to Mons* (Bloomington: Indiana University Press, 1974), 29: "Essentially their work was imitative, based on the profound studies of Carl von Clausewitz into the system and methods which had enabled Napoleon almost to subjugate the whole of Europe." McElwee was speaking of Scharnhorst and Gneisenau, Clausewitz's mentors, not his disciples.

56. Bradley S. Klein, "The Politics of the Unstable Balance of Power in Machiavelli, Frederick the Great, and Clausewitz: Citizenship as Armed Virtue and the Evolution of Warfare" (Ph.D. diss. [political science]: University of Massachusetts at Amherst, 1984), sees the balance-of-power mechanism and the nation-state system as inevitably sources of war, a model "intolerable" given the total war experience and the existence of nuclear weapons.

57. *On War,* bk. 6, chap. 1.

58. Clausewitz, *Historical and Political Writings,* ed. Paret and Moran, 231.

59. Moran's treatment of Clausewitz's politics is excellent. See also C. B. A. Behrens, "Which Side Was Clausewitz On?" *New York Review of Books,* 14 October 1976, 41–44.

Part I

1. Hew Strachan, *From Waterloo to Balaclava: Tactics, Technology, and the British Army, 1815–1854* (Cambridge: Cambridge University Press, 1985), 8; Peter

Paret, "Clausewitz: A Bibliographical Survey," *World Politics* 17 (1965): 272–285; Joseph L. Harsh, "Battlesword and Rapier: Clausewitz, Jomini, and the American Civil War," *Military Affairs*, December 1974, 133–38. Werner Hahlweg's "Clausewitz und die angelsächsische Welt" listed no item in English predating 1873 save the anonymous 1843 translation of *The Campaign of 1812 in Russia*.

2. As Strachan himself (somewhat inconsistently) goes on to demonstrate in a brief discussion of references to Clausewitz in the British military literature of the period in *From Waterloo to Balaclava*, 8–11.

Chapter 3

1. J. E. Marston, *The Life and Campaigns of Field Marshal Prince Blücher* (London: Sherwood, Neely, and Jones, 1815); Carl von Clausewitz, "Der Feldzug von 1813 bis zum Waffenstillstand" (Glatz, 1813); Peter Paret, *Clausewitz and the State: The Man, His Theories, and His Times* (Princeton, NJ: Princeton University Press, 1976), 240, n. 46.

2. Peter Paret, "'A Proposition not a Solution'—Clausewitz's Attempt to Become Prussian Minister at the Court of St. James," in Peter Paret, *Understanding War: Essays on Clausewitz and the History of Military Power* (Princeton, NJ: Princeton University Press, 1992), 178–90.

3. Unsigned review of Clausewitz, "On War," *Metropolitan Magazine* (London) 13 (May–June 1835): 64–71, 166–76; *Military and Naval Magazine of the United States* 5 and 6 (August–September 1835): 426–36, 50–63.

4. North Ludlow Beamish, *History of the King's German Legion*, 2 vols. (London, 1832–37); Friedrich Wilhelm Bismark, *Lectures on the Tactics of Cavalry*, trans. North Ludlow Beamish (London, 1827).

5. Friedrich Wilhelm Bismark, *On the Uses and Application of Cavalry in War*, trans. North Ludlow Beamish, (London: T. and W. Boone, 1855).

6. John Mitchell, postscript to "Military Science and the Late Disasters in Affghanistan" [*sic*], *United Service Gazette*, 14 May 1842, 4; Leonhard Schmidtz, "Memoir of the Author" in John Mitchell, *Biographies of Eminent Soldiers of the Last Four Centuries* (Edinburgh: William Blackwood and Sons, 1865). See Hew Strachan, *From Waterloo to Balaclava: Tactics, Technology and the British Army, 1815–1854* (Cambridge: Cambridge University Press, 1985), 8–11. Jay Luvaas devoted a chapter to Mitchell in his *The Education of an Army: British Military Thought, 1815–1940* (Chicago: University of Chicago Press, 1964).

7. See John Mitchell's unsigned "Review of the British Army, and of the Present State of Military Science," *Monthly Chronicle* (London) 1 (March–June 1838): 317–30.

8. John Mitchell, *Thoughts on Tactics and Military Organization* (London: Longman, Orme, Brown, Green, and Longmans, 1838), 7–8.

9. John Mitchell, *The Fall of Napoleon*, 3 vols. (London: G. W. Nickerson, 1845), esp. vol. 1, xxii–xxiii; vol. 3, 164, 190, 220–21, 281, 331; John Mitchell, "The Vulnerability of Russia," *United Service Gazette* 3 (June 1854): 4.

10. Mitchell, "Late Disasters in Affghanistan." Mitchell was fully aware of the 1835 review of *On War*.

11. See *On War*, bk. 2, chap. 5, "Critical Analysis." Clausewitz's discussion of this approach is ambivalent.

12. Mitchell, *Thoughts on Tactics*, x–xi; Mitchell, "Late Disasters in Affghanistan."

13. Carl von Clausewitz, *Der Feldzug von 1815 in Frankreich* (Berlin: Ferdinand Dümmlers Verlag, 1835).

14. K. A. Schimmer, *The Sieges of Vienna by the Turks*, trans. Francis Egerton, 1847; Francis Egerton, *National Defences; Letters of Lord Ellesmere*, 1848; Unsigned [Wilhelm Meyer, 1797–1877], *Military Events in Italy*, trans. earl of Ellesmere (London: John Murray, 1851); and Earl of Ellesmere, *The War in the Crimea: A Discourse* (London: John Murray, 1855). Egerton's unsigned 1842 review of a life of Blücher (Raushnick's *Marschall Vorwàrts: Oder Leben, Thaten, und Character des Fürsten Blücher von Wahlstadt, Quarterly Review* 70 [June and September 1842]: 446–85) draws on a memorandum from Wellington, makes reference to Clausewitz, and shows a familiarity with the Prussian writer's *Campaign of 1815*. *Quarterly Review*, v.XC, no.CLXXIX, December 1851, 1–34. So did his unsigned review essay, "Memoirs on Russian and German Campaigns—by Müffling, Müller, Wolzogen, Cathcart, &c."

15. Liverpool to Wellington, 10 September 1840, Papers of the first duke of Wellington, University of Southampton (WP2/71/28).

16. Wellington to Liverpool, 14 September 1840, Papers of the third earl of Liverpool (Add MSS 38196, f 143), British Library.

17. Wellington Papers 8/1 contains Liverpool's translation of Clausewitz's *Campaign of 1815*, together with correspondence and memoranda about it dating from 1842.

18. Clausewitz, *Der Feldzug von 1815 in Frankreich*, 30.

19. See Gurwood to Wellington on Liverpool's translation of Clausewitz, 12 September 1840 (WP2/71/36–7); Gurwood to Wellington, 22 September 1840 (WP2/71/71–2). Egerton then ordered a copy of Clausewitz's collected works. Letter, Egerton to John Murray, 11 November 1840, archives, John Murray Publishing Company.

20. Wellington's memorandum appears (dated 24 September 1842) in Field Marshal Arthur Duke of Wellington, K. G. "Memorandum on the Battle of Waterloo," in *Supplementary Despatches, Correspondence, and Memoranda of Field Marshal Arthur Duke of Wellington*. Edited by [his son] the Duke of Wellington, K.G. (London: John Murray, 1863), vol. 10, 513–31. It is discussed in Alice, Countess of Strafford, *Personal Reminiscences of the Duke of Wellington by Francis, the First Earl of Ellesmere*, ed. Francis Egerton (London: John Murray, 1904), 90. Egerton's editor (82) characterized the duke's memorandum as "famous." Mitchell's *Fall of Napoleon* (esp. vol. 3, 55–56) seems to draw on it, although it is not specifically cited among the duke's dispatches. See also G. R. Gleig, *The Life of Arthur Duke of Wellington* (London: Longmans, Green, Reader, and Dyer, 1865), 382; E. L. S. Horsburgh, *Waterloo: A Narrative and a Criticism* (London: Methuen, 1895).

21. For example, see letter, Michael Howard to me, 6 February 1990. John Keegan, *The Face of Battle* (New York: Viking-Penquin, 1976), makes no reference. David Chandler mentions Clausewitz in *Waterloo: The Hundred Days* (London: Osprey, 1980) only in general reference to the theories of *On War*, so does Paddy Griffith, ed., *Wellington as Commander: The Iron Duke's Generalship* (Sussex: Antony Bird Publications, 1985). Neville Thompson, *Wellington After Waterloo* (London: Routledge & Kegan Paul, 1986) makes no reference.

22. Jac Weller, *Wellington at Waterloo* (New York: Crowell, 1967), 71, n. 1.

23. Wellington to Sir John Sinclair, 13 April 1816, *Supplementary Despatches*, 507.

24. Wellington, "Memorandum."

25. Keegan, *Face of Battle*, 117.

26. Unsigned, "Marmont, Siborne, and Alison," *Quarterly Review* 76 (June–September 1845): 204–47. This article was apparently a joint venture of Gurwood, Egerton, and Wellington himself. See Archives of the John Murray Company, manuscript index to vol. 76, *Quarterly Review*; J. H. Stocqueler (pseud.), *The Life of Field Marshal the Duke of Wellington* (London: Ingram, Cooke, and Company, 1853), vol. 2, 330. Egerton's vociferous attacks on Archibald Alison concerning his discussion of Waterloo were made with the duke's "approbation and assistance." Egerton, *Personal Reminiscences*, 58. Alison, in his massive *History of Europe from the Commencement of the French Revolution in 1789 to the Battle of Waterloo in 1815* (London, 1843–44), also briefly discussed Clausewitz; he received about the same billing as Jomini did. Both Egerton and the American general Henry Halleck (in his *Elements of Military Art and Science*), concluded that Allison's work was "utterly worthless" to the military man.

27. Especially Colonel Charles C. Chesney, R.E., discussed later.

28. Carl von Clausewitz, *Der Feldzug von 1812 in Rußland* (Berlin: Ferdinand Dümmlers Verlag, 1835); Carl von Clausewitz, *The Campaign of 1812 in Russia* (London: John Murray, 1843).

29. Wellington, letter 18 October 1842, in Egerton's *Personal Reminiscences*, 238–39.

30. Clausewitz, *Campaign of 1812 in Russia*, 185, 193.

31. C. E. Watson, "The German Campaigns of Gustavus Adolphus," *United Service Magazine*, pt. 3 (1852): 557–70; Carl von Clausewitz, "Gustav Adolphs Feldzüge von 1630–1632," *Hinterlassene Werke* (Berlin, 1832–37), vol. 9, 1–106, written c. 1814–15.

32. Karl von Clausewitz, *La campagne de 1796 en Italie*, trans. J. Colin, (Paris: L. Baudoin, 1899).

33. Charles de Clausewitz, *De la guerre*, trans. Major d'Artillerie Neuens (Paris: J. Corrârd, 1849–51); General de Clausewitz, *Theorie de la grande guerre*, trans. Lieutenant-Colonel de Vatry, 3 vols. (Paris: L. Baudoin, 1886–87).

34. Nicolas Édouard Delabarre Duparcq, *Commentaires sur le traité de la guerre de Clausewitz* (Paris, 1853).

35. Unsigned, "De la Barre Duparcq's Commentaries on Clausewitz," review in the *United Service Magazine*, pt. 1 (1854): 26–36.

36. See other British references to Clausewitz in an unsigned review of a translation of M. Brialmont's *History of the Life of Arthur Duke of Wellington*, appearing in *Edinburgh Review* 110 (July 1859): 208; *Aide-Mémoire to the Military Sciences* [a collection edited by a committee of the Royal Corps of Engineers] (London: J. Weale, 1846–52), vol. 1, 6. The aide-mémoire has a single unilluminating mention of "Klausewitz."

37. Duparcq's *Eléments d'art et d'histoire militaires* (Paris: C. Tanera, 1858) shows no influence by Clausewitz, save one irrelevant footnote reference to his own *Commentaire*.

38. See Jomini's *Summary*, chap. 1.

39. Luvaas, *Education of an Army*, 18, quoting a British officer in the same period, citing "The Regeneration of the Army," *United Service Magazine*, no. 1 (1849).

40. Edward Bruce Hamley (1824–93), *The Operations of War Explained and Illustrated* (London: William Blackwood and Sons, 1866).

41. Lieut.-Colonel Charles C.[Cornwallis] Chesney, R. E., *Waterloo Lectures: A Study of the Campaign of 1815* (London: Longmans, Green, 1868).

42. Ibid., v–vi, 18, 80.

43. He denied Clausewitz's view of the use of forests in the defense, based on American Civil War experience. See Chesney, *Waterloo Lectures*, 190.

44. Ibid, 18, 190. On Chesney's teaching, see Brian Bond, *The Victorian Army and the Staff College, 1854–1914* (London: Eyre Methuen, 1972), 89.

45. Lieutenant-Colonel Charles C. Chesney, R. E., "The Study of Military Science in Time of Peace," *Journal of the Royal United Service Institution* 15 (1871). Although there is no reference to Clausewitz, Chesney's influence may be reflected in the Staff College prize essay for 1872, "The Battle of Wörth," by Lieut. E. H. H. Collen, R. A., *Journal of the Royal United Service Institution* 17 (1873), which opened with a discussion of the relationship between strategy and politics.

46. *Aufstragstaktik* ("mission tactics") is a word with post–World War II origins and dubious historical validity; it is more widely used by American admirers of the German army than by Germans. Nonetheless, it conveys the essential idea, though its relationship to Clausewitz's ideas is subtle. It best relates to his emphasis on the specific: If events are so dependent on individual actions, individual actors must be given the responsibility and freedom to take positive action at all levels. If victory is instead dependent on general causes, then such decentralization is less important.

Chapter 4

1. Baron de Jomini, trans. Capt. G. H. Mendell and Lieut. W. P. Craighill [USA], *The Art of War* (Philadelphia: J. B. Lippincott, 1862; reprinted, Westport, CT: Greenwood Press, 1971). Overt references to Clausewitz appear on pages 166 and 178.

2. Jomini, Baron de. *Summary of the Art of War*, trans. Major O. F. Winship and Lieut. E. E. McLean (New York: Putnam, 1854). The copy I examined had been owned by Philip St. George Cooke, J. E. B. Stuart's father-in-law.

3. Henri Jomini, *The Life of Napoleon*, trans. H. W. Halleck (New York: D. Van Nostrand; London: N. Trübner, 1864).

4. Henry Wager Halleck, *Elements of International Law and Laws of War* (Philadelphia: Lippincott, 1872).

5. Henry Wager Halleck, *Elements of Military Art and Science* (New York: D. Appleton, 1846). I am uncertain whether Halleck read German, but he cited many German works.

6. Nicolas Édouard Delabarre-Duparcq, *Elements of Military Art and History*, trans. and ed. Brigadier General George W. Cullum (New York: D. Van Nostrand, 1863).

7. Halleck, *Elements of Military Art and Science*, 136.

8. Thomas E. Griess, "Dennis Hart Mahan: West Point Professor and Advocate of Military Professionalism, 1830–1871" (Ph.D. diss., Duke University, 1968), 317–26.

9. Nathaniel Wright Stephenson, *Lincoln: An Account of His Personal Life* (Indianapolis: Bobbs-Merrill, 1922), 286; Carl Sandburg, *Abraham Lincoln: The War Years* (New York: Harcourt Brace, 1939), vol. 3, 187; Gore Vidal, *Lincoln: A Novel* (New York: Ballantine, 1984), 248. For reasons I cannot quite fathom, Russell Weigley, "Military Strategy and Civilian Leadership," in *Historical Dimen-*

sions of National Security Problems, ed. Klaus Knorr (Lawrence: University Press of Kansas, 1976), 38–77, disagrees about the compatibility between Clausewitz's ideas and Lincoln's conduct of the war.

10. See, for example, G. F. R. Henderson, *Stonewall Jackson and the American Civil War* (London: Longmans, Green, 1898), 309. Henderson was being sarcastic about a Lincoln he despised; it is unclear whether he was actually suggesting that the president had read Clausewitz.

11. See T. Harry Williams, "The Return of Jomini: Some Thoughts on Recent Civil War Writing," *Military Affairs,* December 1975, 204–6. He cited no specific instances but was probably talking about J. F. C. Fuller, among others. Williams may also have been referring to articles like Errol MacGregor Clauss's, "Sherman's Failure at Atlanta," *Georgia Historical Quarterly* 53 (1969): 321–29. Clauss suggested that Sherman's campaign was a failure because it did not meet the standards that Clausewitz set forth in his *Principles of War.* See also Archer Jones, "Jomini and the Strategy of the American Civil War: A Reinterpretation," *Military Affairs* 34 (December 1970): 127–31.

12. [General USA] John McAuley Palmer, *Washington, Lincoln, Wilson: Three War Statesmen* (Garden City, NY: Doubleday, 1930), 233, states that Lincoln had, in fact, "made some study of German" but doubts that he could have read "so abstruse a book in the original."

13. Carl Schurz, *The Reminiscences of Carl Schurz,* ed. Carl L. [Lincoln] Schurz, vol. 2 (New York: McClure, 1907), 273.

14. Schurz to Lincoln, 13 August 1862, Abraham Lincoln Papers (Library of Congress). Schurz's advice to Lincoln contains no specific references or any particularly suggestive lines. Schurz was profoundly aware of political factors (see especially Schurz to Lincoln, 5 April 1861), but then Schurz, like Lincoln, was a politician.

15. Letter, F. N. Maude to Palmer, 10 December 1928, John McAuley Palmer Papers (Library of Congress). Palmer developed the idea in *Washington, Lincoln, Wilson,* 233–48, 257–58. Palmer also discussed the idea with British General Colin R. Ballard, who had published *The Military Genius of Abraham Lincoln* (London, 1926; reprinted New York: World, 1952). Ballard rejected the notion, however. Ballard to Palmer, 26 January 1929.

16. Brooks Simpson, *Let Us Have Peace: Ulysses S. Grant and the Politics of War and Reconstruction, 1861–1868* (Chaper Hill: University of North Carolina Press, 1991), xv–xvii, 266.

17. Jay Luvaas, "Clausewitz and the American Experience," lecture delivered at the U.S. Army War College, Carlisle, PA, from 1982 to 1987.

18. For example, Charles Royster, *The Destructive War: William Tecumseh Sherman, Stonewall Jackson, and the Americans* (New York: Alfred A. Knopf, 1991), 353–54.

19. Basil H. Liddell Hart, *Sherman: Soldier, Realist, American* (New York: Dodd, Mead, 1929).

20. John G. Nicolay and John Hay, *Abraham Lincoln: A History* (New York: Century, 1890), vol. 4, 359–60.

Chapter 5

1. Carl von Clausewitz, *On War,* trans. J. J. Graham (London: N. Trübner, 1873). I have been unable to locate Graham's or Trübner's papers. (Trübner's

business records still exist but include no correspondence.) The archives of Clausewitz's German publisher, Dümmlers Verlag, were unfortunately destroyed during the Second World War II.

2. William Douglas (1826–95), "General Carl von Clausewitz on War," *United Service Magazine*, August 1873, 469–82, and October 1873, 164–77. Charles Chesney, however, whose interest pre-dated Moltke's victories, did directly connect Moltke's successes with the latter's study of Clausewitz. See Unsigned, "Studies of the Recent War," *Edinburgh Review* 133 (April 1871): 545–86.

3. British army lists covering the years 1824 to 1884; supplement to the *London Gazette*, 2 March 1858; Graham's obituary in *Illustrated London News*, 21 July 1883.

4. J. J. Graham, *Elementary History of the Progress of the Art of War* (London: R. Bentley, 1858).

5. Archives of Kegan Paul, Trench, Trübner and Henry S. King, 1858–1912, microfilm (Bishops Stortford: Chadwyck-Healey, 1974), J5, 50.

6. See Edmund H. Fellowes, *The Military Knights of Windsor, 1352–1944* (Windsor: Oxley and Son, 1944).

7. Peter Paret, "Clausewitz: A Bibliographical Survey," citing the unsigned book review of *On War* (taken from a list of publications examined by the British general staff), *Journal of the Royal United Service Institution* 52 (1908): 584–85.

8. Paret might have done better to cite Frederick Maurice's brief bibliographical comment: "*On War.* By General Carl von Clausewitz. Translated (very badly) by Colonel S. S. (*sic*) Graham." Colonel F. Maurice, *War* (London: Macmillan, 1891), 136. On the other hand, Spenser Wilkinson, whose papers contain a detailed abstract he had made of *On War*, recommended Graham's translation as "excellent." See Wilkinson's paper (kept by the Army Museums Ogilby Trust), 13/57; "Note" to Stewart L. Murray, *The Reality of War: An Introduction to Clausewitz* (London: Hugh Rees, 1909), x. No criticism of Graham's work appears in the early reviews. When Karl von Donat produced a translation of Rudolf von Caemmerer's *The Development of Strategical Science During the 19th Century* (London: Hugh Rees, 1905), he used Graham's translation for the excerpts from *On War*. A 1918 review of Major-General T.D. Pilcher's abridgment compared Pilcher's work unfavorably with both the German original and Graham's translation; see *Times Literary Supplement*, 18 April 1918, 179. Most specific criticisms of the 1873 Graham edition that predate 1965 concern typography, for example, the review in *United Service Magazine*, April 1908. Hans Rothfels made some specific—and damaging—linguistic criticisms in his essay "Clausewitz," in *Makers of Modern Strategy: Military Thought from Machiavelli to Hitler*, ed. Edward Mead Earle (Princeton, NJ: Princeton University Press, 1943), 95, n. 9.

9. For favorable comparison of the Graham translation with the Howard/Paret version, see Victor M. Rosello [Major, USA], "Clausewitz's Contempt for Intelligence," *Parameters*, Spring 1991, 103–14. Many of my correspondents have privately indicated a preference for the Graham version, which is probably a reflection of their long familiarity with it.

10. The ambitious if idiosyncratic Graham index sought to provide a guide to Clausewitz's theoretical discussions. It was dropped from the first Maude edition but was later (and somewhat hastily) revised to fit the new pagination. The Howard/Paret translation was reissued in 1984 with a new index, but this—despite Paret's statement that it is modeled on Werner Hahlweg's concep-

tual index in the 1980 German edition—is merely a list of names, places, battles, and wars, not a guide to ideas.

11. See, for instance, the next to last paragraph in bk. 1, chap. 2, of the Graham translation: "Still we must require him to remember that he only travels on forbidden tracks, where the God of War may surprise him; that he ought always to keep his eye on the enemy, in order that he may not have to defend himself with a dress rapier if the enemy takes up a sharp sword." *Vom Kriege*: "Aber wir müssen doch immer von ihm fordern, daß er sich bewußt bleibe, nur Schleichwege zu gehen, auf denen ihn der Kriegsgott ertappen kann, daß er den Gegner immer im Auge behalte, damit er nicht, wenn dieser zum scharfen Schwert greift, ihm mit einem Galanteriedegen entgegentrete." Howard/Paret: "But he must never forget that he is moving on devious paths where the god of war may catch him unawares. He must keep his eye on the enemy in order to be adequately prepared should he suddenly be attacked with massive force."

12. Carl von Clausewitz, *General Carl von Clausewitz on War*, trans. A. M. E. Maguire, with notes by T. [Thomas] Miller Maguire, (London: William Clowes and Sons, 1909).

13. Howard to me, 6 February 1990.

14. "Preface," in Carl von Clausewitz, *Historical and Political Writings*, ed. and trans. Peter Paret and Daniel Moran (Princeton, NJ: Princeton University Press, 1992), xii.

15. Roger Ashley Leonard, *A Short Guide to Clausewitz On War* (New York: Putnam, 1967); Carl von Clausewitz, *On War*, ed. Anatol Rapoport (Baltimore: Penguin Books, 1968).

Chapter 6

1. Translator's preface to Unsigned [William Meyer, 1797–1877], *Military Events in Italy*, trans. the earl of Ellesmere (London: John Murray, 1851), v.

2. *Aide-Mémoire to the Military Sciences* [a collection edited by a committee of the Royal Corps of Engineers] (London: J. Weale, 1846–52), vol. 1, 1.

3. Antoine-Henri Jomini, *The Art of War*, trans. Major O. F. Winship and Lieut. E. E. McClean (New York: Putnam, 1854), 183, rejected Napoleon's criticism of Wellington's choice of battlefield.

4. [Francis Egerton], "Marmont, Siborne, and Alison." *Quarterly Review*, 76 (June and September 1845), 204–247; John Mitchell, *The Fall of Napoleon* (London: G. W. Nickerson, 1845), vol. 2, 203.

5. Jay Luvaas, *The Military Legacy of the Civil War* (Chicago: University of Chicago Press, 1959), 229.

6. John Mitchell, *United Service Gazette*, 20 June 1840, 4.

7. Michael Howard, "The Influence of Clausewitz," in Carl von Clausewitz, *On War*, ed. and trans. Michael Howard and Peter Paret (Princeton, NJ: Princeton University Press, 1976), 27.

8. John Shy, "Jomini," in *Makers of Modern Strategy: From Machiavelli to the Nuclear Age*, ed. Peter Paret (Princeton, NJ: Princeton University Press, 1986), 178.

9. Otto Pflanze, *Bismarck and the Development of Germany: The Period of Unification, 1815–1871* (Princeton, NJ: Princeton University Press, 1963), 458, citing Lucius von Ballhausen, *Bismarck-Erinnerungen* (Stuttgart, 1921), 502. Whether Bismarck is to be believed is another matter.

Part II

1. Azar Gat, *The Origins of Military Thought: From the Enlightenment to Clausewitz* (Oxford University Press, 1989), 130, citing Spenser Wilkinson (one of the greatest proponents of Clausewitz studies in this period), *The French Army Before Napoleon* (Oxford: Clarendon Press, 1915), 15. On the same page, Wilkinson launched into a discussion of Clausewitz. In his "Note" to Stewart L. Murray's *The Reality of War: An Introduction to Clausewitz with a Note by Spenser Wilkinson* (London: Hugh Rees, 1909), viii, Wilkinson said "When Clausewitz died, the two books on war which were thought the best were those of the Archduke Charles of Austria and General Jomini. To-day the book of Clausewitz, 'On War,' easily holds the first place."

2. Russell F. Weigley, *The American Way of War: A History of United States Military Strategy and Policy* (New York: Macmillan, 1973), 210.

3. Basil H. Liddell Hart, *The British Way of Warfare* (London: Faber & Faber, 1932; New York: Macmillan, 1933), 17.

4. Russell F. Weigley, review of the 1976 Howard/Paret translation of *On War*, date uncertain. This review (from the files of Princeton University Press) appears to be a book club advertisement.

5. Russel F. Weigley, in his *History of the United States Army* (Bloomington: Indiana University Press, 1967; enlarged ed., 1984), 273, states: "Clausewitz was translated into English in 1873, and a general awareness at least of his main ideas spread among American officers soon thereafter." He cites no evidence for this, and I have found none.

Chapter 7

1. For example, General Bronsart von Schellendorf (1832–91), *Duties of the General Staff* [Der Dienst des Generalstabes (Berlin: E. S. Mittler)]. Its publishing history contrasts with *On War*'s. The first German edition appeared in 1875/76; it was published in London by C. K. Paul in 1877–80. The third edition appeared in both German and English in 1893 (trans. Intelligence Division, War Office, publisher HMSO). The fourth edition got the same treatment in 1905.

2. Evidently no English translation was made of Moltke's essays on strategy (1871) or his *Instructions for the Senior Troop Commanders* (1869). Many of Moltke's other works were translated but usually somewhat later, in the 1890s or 1900s. Even those had little theoretical significance.

3. Wilhelm von Blume (1835–1919), *Campaign 1870–71*, trans. E. M. Jones (London: H. S. King, 1872); Wilhelm von Blume, *Strategie: Eine studie* (Berlin: E. S. Mittler, 1882).

4. F. N. Maude, *Military Letters and Essays* (Kansas City, MO: Hudson-Kimberly, 1895), 100–1. Phil Sheridan was an observer with the German army. William Hazen's *The School and the Army in Germany and France* (New York: Harper and Brothers, 1872), makes no reference to military theory.

5. Archives of Kegan Paul, Trench, Trébner, and Henry S. King, J5, 50; E1, 594.

6. Colonel J. F. Maurice, R. A., "War,"; Colonel Charles Chesney, R.E., "Battle," *Encyclopædia Britannica*, 9th ed. (New York: Scribner, 1878–88).

7. Brian Bond, *The Victorian Army and the Staff College, 1854–1914* (London: Eyre Methuem, 1972), 306, provides statistics.

8. Unsigned, "The Battle of Dorking: Reminiscences of a Volunteer," *Blackwood's Edinburgh Magazine* 109 (May 1871).

9. Hamley's book is listed as one of nine on the 1934 Naval War College's supplementary reading list. U. S. Naval War College Archives, RG4/1805.

10. Jay Luvaas, *The Education of an Army: British Military Thought, 1815–1940* (Chicago: University of Chicago Press, 1964), 170, 174. Chapter 6 is devoted to Maurice.

11. On Maurice, see Bond, *Victorian Army*, 136–38; Spenser Wilkinson, *Thirty-five Years, 1874–1909* (London: Constable, 1933), 135. Wolseley to Lady Wolseley, 12 September 1897, cited in Luvaas, *Education of an Army*, 191.

12. Lieutenant F. Maurice (Edinburgh: William Blackwood and Sons, 1872), 84–98.

13. Colonel F. Maurice, *War* (London: Macmillan, 1891); Lieutenant-Colonel F. Maurice (Maurice's son, Frederick Barton Maurice), ed., *Sir Frederick Maurice: A Record of His Work and Opinions* (London: Edward Arnold, 1913), 76; Luvaas, *Education of an Army*, 438.

14. Maurice, *War*, 13–22.

15. Ibid., 136–37.

16. See Bond, *Victorian Army*, 136–37.

17. Maurice, *His Work and Opinions*, 121. Compare *On War*, bk. 2, chap. 5.

Chapter 8

1. Clausewitz's chief proponents at the time, Henderson, Maude, and Spenser Wilkinson, thought so. See Wilkinson's critique, "Puzzles of the War," *Monthly Review*, October 1900, 87–97, does not name Clausewitz but refers to specifically Clausewitzian ideas, including "centres of gravity" and the need to "estimate the character of the war." Spenser Wilkinson Papers, 13/47.

2. Michael Howard (citing Hahlweg's introduction to the 16th German ed., 52), introductory essay to *On War*, ed. and trans. Michael Howard and Peter Paret (Princeton, NJ: Princeton University Press, 1976), 37–38. A Japanese translation of the *Principles of War* was made, based on a French translation: *Taisen gakuri*, published by the Gunji Kyoiku Kai (Association for military education) in 1903. *On War* itself was translated by Mori Ogai (a medical officer in the Imperial Army, better known by his personal name, Ogai, as a novelist and poet) as *Senso ron* beginning in 1899. It appears in Ogai's collected works. See also Yoichi Hirama, "Sun Tzü's Influence on the Japanese Imperial Navy," which also discusses Clausewitz and Mahan.

3. *Times* Military Correspondent, "À la Clausewitz," *Times*, 23 March 1905. See also Military Correspondent of the *Times*, "Clausewitz in Manchuria," *The Times History of the War in the Far East* (London, 1905). Mori Ogai translated Repington's *Times* reports and published them in the newspaper *Jiji shimpo*.

4. Spenser Wilkinson, *Thirty-five Years, 1874–1909* (London: Constable, 1933), 237; Brian Bond, *The Victorian Army and the Staff College, 1854–1914* (London: Eyre Methuen, 1972), 141; Jay Luvaas, *The Education of an Army: British Military Thought, 1815–1940* (Chicago: University of Chicago Press, 1964), 291–330; J. E. Edmonds's article on Repington, in *Dictionary of National Biography*. W. Michael Ryan defends Repington, whose reputation is rather odi-

ous, in *Lieutenant-Colonel Charles à Court Repington: A Study in the Interaction of Personality, the Press, and Power* (New York: Garland Press, 1987).

5. See *Times* Military Correspondent [Repington], *Imperial Strategy* (London: John Murray, 1906), especially "1806 and 1906—A Parallel"; *The Foundations of Reform* (London: Simpkin, Marshall, 1908); and (Repington's memoirs) *Vestigia* (London: Constable, 1919), 293.

6. T. E. Lawrence, "Evolution of a Revolt" (October 1920), in *Evolution of a Revolt: Early Postwar Writings of T. E. Lawrence,* ed. Stanley Weintraub and Rodelle Weintraub (University Park: Pennsylvania State University Press, 1968), 103–4; Basil H. Liddell Hart, *T. E. Lawrence to His Biographer* (New York: Doubleday, 1938), 50; Basil H. Liddell Hart, *Colonel Lawrence: The Man Behind the Legend* (New York: Dodd, Meade, 1934), 128.

7. Field-Marshal Sir Claude Auchinleck to B. H. Liddell Hart, 20 November 1950. B. H. Liddell Hart Papers, I/30/30, Liddell Hart Centre for Military Archives, King's College London.

8. Archives of Kegan Paul, Trench, Trübner and Henry S. King, C33, 151.

9. Review of Captain E. F. Calthrop's translation of Sun Tzu, *The Book of War,* in *United Service Magazine,* December 1908, 332–33.

10. Advertisement, "War Maps and War Books," *Times,* 7 August 1914, 2.

11. Haig Papers, National Library of Scotland, *Report on a Conference of General Staff Officers at the Staff College, 7–10 January 1908,* MS ACC 3155, no. 81, 36–37.

12. L. E. Kiggel, as editor of Hamley's *Operations of War,* inserted the single reference to Clausewitz, which appeared only in editions after 1907.

13. Bond, *Victorian Army,* 266.

14. William Robertson (1860–1933), *Soldiers and Statesmen, 1914–1918* (New York: Charles Scribner, 1926), 300–303; William Robertson, *From Private to Field-Marshal* (London: Constable, 1921), 255.

15. See also Robertson, *Soldiers and Statesmen,* vol. 2, 299–304.

16. "Clausewitz, vol. 1," William R. Robertson Papers I/3/6, Liddell Hart Centre for Military Archives, King's College London. Corrections in Robertson's hand.

17. For Robertson's later willingness to criticize government policy, see his "Wasting Our Army: Objectionable Military Commitments," *Morning Post,* 1 March 1923, 7–8.

18. J. E. Edmonds, "Clausewitz and the Downfall of Prussia in 1806," *Army Review,* April 1914, 403–16.

19. Walter Haweis James, *Modern Strategy* (London: Blackwood, 1903, 1904; rev. ed., 1908), 172 in the revised edition. James sought to balance Jomini and Clausewitz.

20. See bibliographical essay for "Men Against Fire: The Doctrine of the Offensive in 1914," in *Makers of Modern Strategy: From Marchiavelli to the Nuclear Age,* ed. Peter Paret (Princeton, NJ: Princeton University Press, 1986), 909.

21. Edward A. Altham, *The Principles of War Historically Illustrated* (London: Macmillan, 1914).

22. John Gooch, *The Plans of War: The General Staff and British Military Strategy c. 1900–1916* (New York: Wiley, 1974), 124, says ambiguously that "Haig . . . was deeply critical of the failure [of the general staff's educational policy] to encourage and develop what Clausewitz had called 'skill in sagacious calculation,' and suggested new and broader-based policies to overcome what was likely to be

a factor of very serious consequence in the field." Tim Travers, in "Technology, Tactics, and Morale: Jean de Bloch, the Boer War, and British Military Theory, 1900–1914," *Journal of Modern History* 51 (June 1979), characterized Haig (along with F. N. Maude and Stewart Murray) as a "supporter of Clausewitz." See also Tim Travers, *The Killing Ground: The British Army, The Western Front and the Emergence of Modern Warfare, 1900–1918* (London: Allen & Unwin, 1987), 49, citing references to Clausewitz in Haig's *Cavalry Studies, Strategic and Tactical* (London, 1907), 142, 174–75. Haig's emphasis throughout was on "moral[e]."

23. See, for example, F. N. Maude, *Military Letters and Essays* (Kansas City, MO: Hudson-Kimberley, 1895), 40; G. F. R. Henderson, *The Battle of Spicheren* (London: Gale and Polden, 1891), 287–91. Henderson strongly stressed junior officer initiative in his articles "War" and "Strategy," *Encyclopædia Britannica,* Supplement for 1902.

24. Jehuda L. Wallach, *The Dogma of the Battle of Annihilation: The Theories of Clausewitz and Schlieffen and Their Impact on the German Conduct of Two World Wars* (Westport, CT: Greenwood Press, 1986), 9.

25. [Wilhelm Leopold] Colmar von der Goltz, *The Nation in Arms,* trans. Philip A. Ashworth (London: W. H. Allen and Company, 1887; rev. eds., Hugh Rees, 1903, 1906, 1913); Colmar von der Goltz, *The Conduct of War: A Brief Study of its Most Important Principles and Forms,* trans. Joseph T. Dickman (Kansas City, MO: Franklin Hudson, 1896).

26. John Bigelow, *The Principles of Strategy: Illustrated Mainly from American Campaigns,* 2nd ed. (Philadelphia: Lippincott, 1894; reprinted Westport, CT: Greenwood Press, 1968). "Jominian" is Weigley's characterization of Bigelow's argument. See Russell F. Weigley, *Towards an American Army: Military Thought from Washington to Marshall* (New York: Columbia University Press, 1962), 94–95; Carol Reardon, *Soldiers and Scholars: The U.S. Army and the Uses of Military History, 1865–1920* (Lawrence: University Press of Kansas, 1990), 96, says that Bigelow "relied upon some of the more sophisticated ideas of Prussian theorist Karl von Clausewitz" but offers no evidence.

27. I. B. Holley, Jr., *General John M. Palmer, Citizen Soldiers, and the Army of a Democracy* (Westport, CT: Greenwood Press, 1982), 66.

28. Steve E. Dietrich, "The Professional Reading of General George S. Patton, Jr.," *Journal of Military History* 53 (October 1989): 387–418. The West Point Library special collection contains Patton's copies of *On War.*

29. Martin Blumenson, *The Patton Papers, 1885–1940* (Boston: Houghton Mifflin, 1972), 210.

Chapter 9

1. See Field Marshal Earl Roberts, "Memoir," in G. F. R. Henderson, *The Science of War* (London: Longmans, Greene, 1906); Major David A. Fastabend, "G. F. R. Henderson and the Challenge of Change," *Military Review,* October 1989. The best discussion of Henderson is by Jay Luvaas, *The Military Legacy of the Civil War* (Chicago University Press, 1959), 170–90.

2. See especially G. F. R. Henderson, *The Campaign of Fredericksburg, November–December 1862: A Study for Officers of Volunteers* (London: K. Paul, Trench, 1886).

3. Peter Paret, "Clausewitz: A Bibliographical Survey," *World Politics* 17

(1965); 272–85. See also Peter Paret, "Clausewitz and the Nineteenth Century," in *The Theory and Practice of War*, ed. Michael Howard (New York: Praeger, 1966).

4. Henderson's criticism (*Science of War*, 169) of Hamley specifically attacked the paragraph in which his book dismissed "moral factors," the very point at which Kiggell inserted a reference to Clausewitz.

5. Michael Howard, "The Influence of Clausewitz," in Carl von Clausewitz, *On War*, ed. and trans. Michael Howard and Peter Paret (Princeton, NJ: Princeton University Press, 1976), 38, citing Henderson, *Science of War*, 173. Actually, Clausewitz did say (*On War*, bk. 2, chap. 2, sec. 15), "Everyone knows the moral effects of a surprise, of an attack in flank or rear. . . . What could we do with any theory which should leave them out of consideration?" (Graham translation).

6. *On War*, bk. 2, chap. 2.

7. See especially Henderson's "War." Henderson's contempt for Lincoln pervades his *Stonewall Jackson and the American Civil War* (London: Longmans, Green, 1898).

8. For example, see G. F. R. Henderson, *Battle of Spicheren* (London: Gale and Polden, 1891), 288, 295: "But what says Clausewitz, first of military writers?"

9. Henderson, *Science of War*, 42.

10. Henderson, *Spicheren*, 299.

11. Tim Travers, "Technology, Tactics, and Morale: Jean de Bloch, the Boer War, and British Military Theory, 1900–1914," *Journal of Modern History* 51 (June 1979).

12. A True Reformer [Maude], *Letters on Tactics and Organization* (Calcutta, 1888).

13. F. N. Maude, *Military Letters and Essays* (Kansas City, MO: Hudson-Kimberley, 1895), 100.

14. Ibid., 266.

15. See, for example, F. N. Maude, *The Jena Campaign* (London: Swan Sonnenheim and Company, 1909), 81, n. 1. David Chandler, *The Campaigns of Napoleon* (New York: Macmillan, 1966), noted that Clausewitz "completely misunderstood the *manouevre sur les derrières*." His view seems to be derived from Maude's. See also Colonel Camon (French army), who made the same argument in his *Clausewitz* (Paris: Chapelot, 1911). Compare Peter Paret: Clausewitz's "earliest surviving essay, written a year before Austerlitz, demonstrates the sureness with which he already grasped the essentials of Napoleonic strategy"; Paret, "Clausewitz and the Nineteenth Century," 25.

16. Brian Holden Reid, *J. F. C. Fuller: Military Thinker* (New York: St. Martin's Press, 1987), 20.

17. There are some hints of such an attitude in *On War*, for example, the last paragraphs in bk. 3, chap. 6.

18. Carl von Clausewitz, *General Carl von Clausewitz on War*, trans. A. M. E. Maguire, with notes by T. Miller Maguire (London: William Clowes and Sons, 1909).

19. See also comments on Maguire in Paret, "Bibliographical Survey," 275, n. 17.

20. Stewart L. [Lygon] Murray (1863–?), *The Reality of War: An Introduction to Clausewitz with a note by Spenser Wilkinson* (London: Hugh Rees, 1909), in my view the best condensation of *On War*, albeit very reflective of its period.

21. Ibid., xiv.
22. Ibid., 114–15.
23. Basil H. Liddell Hart, *The British Way of Warfare* (London: Faber & Faber, 1932; New York: Macmillan, 1933), 44–45.
24. Letter, Wilkinson to Admiral Lord Charles Beresford, 9 October 1894, Spenser Wilkinson Papers, 13/21.
25. Spenser Wilkinson, *Thirty-five Years, 1874–1909*, (London: Constable, 1933), chap. 10.
26. For example, John Gooch, *The Plans of War: The General Staff and British Military Strategy c. 1900–1916* (New York: Wiley, 1974), 15.
27. In his autobiography, which avoided intellectual issues and rarely mentioned Clausewitz, Wilkinson recalled (298) advising Lord Milner (governor, South Africa), to read *On War* in 1898. Also (314) Foster Cunliffe, later the first lecturer in military history at Oxford.
28. Spenser Wilkinson Papers, 13/57.
29. Letter, Dilke to Balfour, 21 December 1893; reprinted in Stephen Gwynn and Gertrude M. Tuckwell, *The Life of the Rt. Hon. Sir Charles W. Dilke* (London: John Murray, 1917), 451–54.
30. For example, see the review of Wilkinson's *Government and the War* (London: Constable, 1918), in *Punch*, 25 June 1918.
31. See John B. Hattendorf, "The Study of War History at Oxford, 1862–1990," unpublished manuscript, to be published as part of John B. Hattendorf and Malcolm H. Murfett, eds., *The Limitations of Military Power: Essays Presented to Norman Gibbs on His Eightieth Birthday* (New York: St. Martin's Press, 1990); notice of Wilkinson's appointment in *United Service Magazine*, January 1910; Repington, "A Plea for History," *Times*, 10 September 1904.
32. Spenser Wilkinson, *The University and the Study of War: An Inaugural Lecture Delivered Before the University of Oxford, November 27, 1909* (Oxford: Clarendon Press, 1909).
33. Letter, Michael Howard to me, 23 September 1989.
34. In Spenser Wilkinson, *The Brain of an Army: A Popular Account of the German General Staff* (Westminster: A. Constable, 1895), Wilkinson includes a brief but prominent discussion (176–78) of *On War*. Root's letter is quoted in Wilkinson's *Thirty-five Years*, 260–61. See also Russell F. Weigley, *History of the United States Army* (Bloomington: Indiana University Press, 1967; enlarged ed., 1984), 315–317.

Chapter 10

1. Rudolph von Caemmerer, *The Development of Strategical Science During the Nineteenth Century* (London: Hugh Rees, 1905; reprinted Carlisle, PA: U. S. Army War College, 1983, and Iowa City: University of Iowa Press, 1985).
2. Friedrich von Bernhardi, *On War of Today*, 2 vols., trans. Karl von Donat (London: Hugh Rees, 1912–13); reviewed (unfavorably in comparison with Clausewitz and Goltz), in *Times Literary Supplement*, 8 August 1912, 314.
3. Apparently the only work by Delbrück to appear in English in this period was *Numbers in History: Two Lectures Delivered Before the University of London* ["How the Greeks Defeated the Persians, the Romans Conquered the World, the Teutons Overthrew the Roman Empire, and William the Norman Took Possession

of England"] (London: University of London Press, 1913). The lectures were given on 6 and 7 October 1913.

4. On Meckel, see Ernst L. Presseisen, *Before Aggression: Europeans Prepare the Japanese Army* (Tucson: University of Arizona Press [for the Association for Asian Studies], 1965), 79–88.

5. Cited in Stewart L. Murray, *The Reality of War: An Introduction to Clausewitz with a Note by Spenser Wilkinson* (London: Hugh Rees, 1909), 6.

6. Caemmerer, *The Development of Strategical Science*, 32–33.

7. Ibid., 29, 42–47.

8. Ibid., 42–47; Carl von Clausewitz, "Betrachtungen über den künftigen Kriegsplan gegen Frankreich" (1830), in *Verstreute kleine Schriften*, ed. Werner Hahlweg (Osnabrück: Biblio Verlag, 1979), 533–63.

9. This is also the view of Azar Gat in *The Origins of Military Thought: From the Enlightenment to Clausewitz* (Oxford University Press, 1989), 251–52.

10. Murray, *Reality of War*, 42–44.

11. Meckel was among the most extreme in his offensive-mindedness, extremely suspicious of popular warfare and of the extended order in tactics, motivated by distrust of the individual soldier based on his experiences in the Franco-Prussian War.

12. Caemmerer, *The Development of Strategical Science*, 36.

13. See Jehuda L. Wallach, *The Dogma of the Battle of Annihilation: The Theories of Clausewitz and Schlieffen and Their Impact on the German Conduct of Two World Wars* (Westport, CT: Greenwood Press, 1986), 49–50, 75–76.

14. Karl von Clausewitz, *Vom Kriege*, ed. W. von Scherff (Berlin: Dümmlers Verlag, 1880), 312.

15. Caemmerer, *The Development of Strategical Science*, 38.

16. See Repington, *Imperial Strategy* (London: John Murray, 1906), 52, and "The War Day by Day: Clausewitz and the Moderns," *Times*, 11 March 1915, 6.

17. Murray, *Reality of War*, 96–98.

18. Haig to Kiggell, 14 July 1910, cited in E. K. G. Sixsmith, *Douglas Haig* (London: Weidenfeld and Nicolson, 1976), 60.

19. John Terraine, *Douglas Haig: The Educated Soldier* (London: Hutchinson, 1963).

20. Douglas Haig, *Cavalry Studies, Strategical and Tactical* (London: Hugh Rees, 1907), 142.

21. Tim Travers, *The Killing Ground: The British Army, the Western Front and the Emergence of Modern Warfare, 1900–1918* (London: Allen & Unwin, 1987), 87; Captain Charteris, "The Relative Advantages of Offensive and Defensive Strategy," Public Record Office, WO 79/61.

22. Spenser Wilkinson, *The University and the Study of War: An Inaugural Lecture Delivered Before the University of Oxford, November 27, 1909* (Oxford: Clarendon Press, 1909, 20.

23. Tim Travers, "Technology, Tactics, and Morale: Jean de Bloch, the Boer War, and British Military Theory, 1900–1914," *Journal of Modern History* 15 (June 1979): 277.

24. Caemmerer, cited in Murray, *Reality of War*, 97.

25. One exception: Lt.-General Sir Gerald Ellison (1861–1947), *The Perils of Amateur Strategy* (London: Longmans, Green, 1926), thought the idea preposterous, an attitude highly colored by Gallipoli and hostility to Churchill. His prewar views are unknown.

26. Murray, *Reality of War*, 66.

27. Ferdinand Foch, *Des principes de la guerre* (Paris, 1903); trans. J. de Morinni [Major, Canadian Expeditionary Force], *The Principles of War* (New York: H. K. Fly, 1918). For arguments on Foch and H. W. Wilson, see Bernard Ash, *The Lost Dictator: A Biography of Field Marshal Sir Henry Wilson* (London: Cassell, 1968); Brian Bond, *The Victorian Army and the Staff College, 1854–1914* (London: Eyre Methuen, 1972); Basil H. Liddell Hart, *The Ghost of Napoleon* (London: Faber, 1933), 138.

28. Peter Paret, "Napoleon," in *Makers of Modern Strategy: From Machiavelli to the Nuclear Age*, ed. Peter Paret (Princeton, NJ: Princeton University Press, 1986), 127.

29. Jean Lambert Alphonse Colin, *The Transformations of War*, trans. L. H. R. Pope-Hennessy (London: Hugh Rees, 1912; reprinted Westport, CT: Greenwood Press, 1977). See also Jean Colin, *The Great Battles of History*, translated "under the supervision of Spenser Wilkinson" (London: Hugh Rees, 1915).

30. Ibid., 304.

31. Ibid., 341.

32. Colin, *Transformations*, 334.

33. Cited in ibid., 334–35.

34. Ibid., 71–72.

Chapter 11

1. For knowledge of Maltzahn's work I am indebted to Professor Jon Sumida of the University of Maryland. Admiral von Maltzahn, *What Lesson Has General von Clausewitz's Work, "On War," for the Naval Officer?* trans. W. H. Hancock (Portsmouth: War College, November 1906), no. 4 (Naval Library P806); originally *Marine Rundschau*, June 1905. See also Curt Freiherr von Maltzahn, *Naval Warfare*, trans. John Combe Miller (London: Longmans, Green, 1908; Leipzig, 1906). Maltzahn frequently cited Julian Corbett's historical works.

2. Vice Admiral S. O. Makarov, Imperial Russian Navy, *Discussion of Questions in Naval Tactics*, trans. Lieutenant [USN] John B. Bernadou (Washington, DC: Office of Naval Intelligence, 1898; reprinted Annapolis: United States Naval Institute, 1990). Compare Carl von Clausewitz, *Principles of War*, trans. Hans W. Gatske (Harrisburg, PA: Military Service Publishing Company, 1942), 13.

3. Naval War College Archives, RG8/UNT 1894.

4. Ronald Spector, *Professors of War: The Naval War College and the Development of the Naval Profession* (Newport, RI: Naval War College Press, 1977), 117.

5. William Dillworth Puleston, *Mahan: The Life and Work of Captain Alfred Thayer Mahan, U.S.N.* (New Haven, CT: Yale University Press, 1939), 295; Spector, *Professors of War*, 121. Robert Seager, ed., *Alfred Thayer Mahan: The Man and his Letters* (Annapolis, MD: U.S. Naval Institute Press, 1978), 552, 683, n. 11, is not sure that Mahan ever read Clausewitz; if so, he places it around 1910. Mahan may nonetheless have known the broad outlines of *On War* earlier.

6. Mahan's copy has been lost; his marginal notes were transcribed into a copy donated to the Naval War College by Puleston.

7. Alfred Thayer Mahan, *Naval Strategy Compared and Contrasted with the Principles and Practice of Military Operations on Land: Lectures Delivered at the*

Naval War College, Newport, R.I., Between the Years 1887 and 1911 (Boston: Little, Brown, 1911), contains two explicit references to Clausewitz: a footnote on p. 120, to Clausewitz's sarcastic discussion of "keys to the country" (bk. 6, chap. 23, of *On War*); and p. 279, where Mahan refers to Clausewitz as "one of the first of authorities." He also discusses Corbett citing *On War* on the relationship of defense and offense. Mahan is comparing the naval and land aspects of strategy, clearly referring to the Clausewitzian interpretation without identifying it as such. See also his discussion of some naval war plans in a letter to Raymond P. Rogers, 4 March 1911, in Alfred Thayer Mahan, *Letters and Papers of Alfred Thayer Mahan*, eds. Robert Seager II and Doris D. Maguire (Annapolis, MD: U.S. Naval Institute Press, 1975), vol. 2, 389–94. Mahan also talks about "ends and means" at some length (especially on p. 5), in a manner strongly reminiscent of Clausewitz.

8. See Puleston, *Mahan*, 295; Spector, *Professors of War*, 121.

9. Julian S. Corbett, *Drake and the Tudor Navy* (London: Longmans, Green, 1898).

10. Donald M. Schurman, *Julian S. Corbett, 1854–1922: Historian of British Maritime Policy from Drake to Jellicoe* (London: Royal Historical Society, 1981), 36–37.

11. Barry D. Hunt, "The Strategic Thought of Sir Julian S. Corbett," in *Maritime Strategy and the Balance of Power*, ed. John B. Hattendorf and Robert S. Jordan (New York: Macmillan, 1989), 112.

12. So suggests Eric J. Grove, "Introduction," in Julian S. Corbett, *Some Principles of Maritime Strategy* (Annapolis, MD: U.S. Naval Institute Press, 1988; originally published London: Longmans, Green, 1911), xli.

13. Hunt, "Strategic Thought of Sir Julian S. Corbett," 112.

14. Mahan to John P. Merrell, 20 December 1908; Mahan to Raymond P. Rogers, 4 March 1911, in *Letters and Papers of Alred Theyer Mahan*. See also John B. Hattendorf, "Sir Julian Corbett on the Significance of Naval History," *American Neptune*, 31 (1971): 275–85.

15. Schurman, *Corbett*, 51.

16. Corbett's lectures are preserved in "Lectures on Naval Strategy by Sir Julian Corbett," in Julian S. Corbett Papers, "Deed Box," MS 81/143 in Britain's National Maritime Museum.

17. Corbett's "Notes on Strategy" (the "Green Pamphlet") is reproduced as an appendix to the 1988 edition of Corbett's *Some Principles*, 307–45.

18. Julian S. Corbett, *England in the Seven Years' War* (London: Longmans, Green, 1907).

19. Hunt, "Strategic Thought of Sir Julian S. Corbett," especially 124–25. See also Donald M. Schurman, *The Education of a Navy: The Development of British Naval Strategic Thought, 1867–1914* (Chicago: University of Chicago Press, 1965), 147–84.

20. William R. Hawkins, "The Man Who Invented Limited War," *Military History Quarterly* 4, no. 1 (Autumn 1991): 105–11, believes that Corbett somehow "broke" with Clausewitz over this issue.

21. Bernard Brodie, *Seapower in the Machine Age* (Princeton, NJ: Princeton University Press, 1941), cites a number of Corbett's works, including *Some Principles*.

22. Winston S. Churchill, *The World Crisis* (New York: Scribner, 1923), 93.

23. Reginal Esher, *Journals and Letters of Reginald Esher*, ed. Oliver, Vis-

count Esher, vol. 3 (1938), cited in Arthur J. Marder, *From the Dreadnought to Scapa Flow*, vol. 1 (Oxford: Oxford University Press, 1961), 404.

24. Schurman, *Education of a Navy*, 190, makes a similar argument about Churchill.

25. Professor Raymond Callahan (University of Delaware), "British Strategy in World War II," paper presented at the USMC Command and General Staff College, 9 October 1992.

26. See letter, Wilkinson to Beresford, 9 October 1894, Spenser Wilkinson Papers, 13/21.

27. Spenser Wilkinson, *The Command of the Sea* (Westminster: A. Constable, 1894); Spenser Wilkinson, *The Brain of the Navy* (Westminster: A. Constable, 1895).

28. Spenser Wilkinson, "Strategy in the Navy," *Morning Post*, 3 August 1909, referring to Lieutenant Fisher, RN, "The Command of the Sea: What Is It?" *Journal of the Royal United Service Institution* 53 (July 1909): 847–864, third place winner of the Royal United Service Institution's essay contest.

29. Spenser Wilkinson, "Strategy at Sea," a review of Corbett's *Some Principles of Maritime Strategy*, *Morning Post*, 19 February 1912, in Spenser Wilkinson Papers, 13/54.

30. Anonymous, "Great Britain, Germany, and Limited War," *Edinburgh Review*, April 1912, 485–514. L. H. R. (Ladislaus Herbert Richard) Pope-Hennessy is identified as the author in that journal's archives, University of Reading. See also Pope-Hennessy's "The British Army and Modern Conceptions of War," *Edinburg Review*, April 1911, 321–46, and "The Place of Doctrine in War," *Edinburgh Review*, January 1912, 1–30.

31. Julian S. Corbett Papers, Box 5, cited in Grove, "Introduction," in Corbett, *Some Principles*, xlii.

32. See especially Wilkinson, "Strategy at Sea."

33. For example, see John Gooch, *The Plans of War: The General Staff and British Military Strategy c. 1900–1916* (New York: Wiley, 1974), 15.

34. Keith M. Wilson, "Spenser Wilkinson at Bay: Calling the Tune at the *Morning Post*," *Publishing History* 19 (1986): 33–52.

35. Repington, *The Foundations of Reform* (London: Simpkin, Marshall, 1908), 1–12.

36. Julian S. Corbett Papers, Box 6. Much of its argument appears in *Some Principles*, chap. 4, pt. 1, "Defence Against Invasion," 233–61.

37. Simon Joseph Fraser, fourteenth Baron Lovat, later Major-General, 1871–1933; Public Record Office, Cab. 16/3A, *Report and Proceedings of a Sub-committee of Imperial Defense. Appointed by the Prime Minister to Reconsider the Question of Overseas Attack*, 22 October 1908. Lord Roberts's discussion of Clausewitz appears on pp. 3–4, Lord Lovat's on p. 101. This material is Crown copyright and is reproduced with the permission of the Controller of Her Majesty's Stationery Office.

38. *Militär-Wochenblatt*, 28 March 1883.

39. This argument appears several times in *On War* (e.g., bk. 6, chap. 24: "Instruction for the Crown Prince" [Graham/Maude vol. 3, 282–84]. On boldness as a part of military genius, see bk. 3, chap. 6.

40. Wilkinson also speaks of Colomb (1831–99) as a Clausewitzian. Colomb's forecast of the next European war, *The Great War of 189–* (London: William Heinemann, 1893), was a collaboration with F. N. Maude and J. F. Maurice.

41. Rear-Admiral Sir Charles Ottley's introduction to James R. Thursfield's *Naval Warfare* (Cambridge: Cambridge University Press, 1913), ix.

42. Thursfield, *Naval Warfare*, 1–5.

Chapter 12

1. Shelford Bidwell and Dominick Graham, *Fire-Power: British Army Weapons and Theories of War 1904–1945* (London: Allen & Unwin, 1982), 1.

2. Note that John Gooch's *The Plans of War: The General Staff and British Military Strategy c. 1900–1916* (New York: Wiley, 1974) makes almost no mention of Clausewitz, nor is there a single meaningful reference to the philosopher in Paul Kennedy, ed., *War Plans of the Great Powers, 1880–1914* (London: Allen & Unwin, 1979). Insofar as Bidwell and Graham's excellent *Fire-Power* deals with "theories of war," Clausewitz is conspicuous only by his absence.

3. Azar Gat, *The Origins of Military Thought: From the Enlightenment to Clausewitz* (Oxford: Oxford University Press, 1989), 130.

4. For example, see Curt Frieherr von Maltzahn, *Naval Warfare*, trans. John Combe Miller (London: Longmans, Green, 1908; Leipzig, 1906), 118; V. I. Lenin, "British Pacifism and British Dislike of Theory," *Collected Works* (Moscow: Progress Publishers, 1964), vol. 21, 260–69.

5. Basil H. Liddell Hart, *The British Way of Warfare* (London: Faber & Faber, 1932; New York: Macmillan, 1933), 17.

6. See Repington's column *The Times*, "The War Day by Day": "Forces Moral and Material," 8 March 1915, 6; "The Austro-German Offensive—Russian Tenacity," 9 March 1915, 6; and "Continuity in War—Clausewitz and the Moderns," 11 March 1915, 6.

7. Basil H. Liddell Hart, "Armed Forces and the Art of War: Armies," in *The Zenith of European Power, 1830–1870*, ed. J. P. T. Bury, vol. 10 of *The New Cambridge Modern History* (Cambridge: Cambridge University Press, 1960), 320.

8. John I. Alger, *The Quest for Victory: The History of the Principles of War* (Westport, CT: Greenwood Press, 1982), 186.

9. Michael Howard, "The Influence of Clausewitz," in Carl von Clausewitz, *On War*, ed. and trans. Michael Howard and Peter Paret (Princeton, NJ: Princeton University Press, 1976), 39.

10. See Spenser Wilkinson, *Government and the War* (London: Constable, 1918).

11. John Wheeler-Bennett, *Brest-Litovsk: The Forgotten Peace, March, 1918* (New York: W.W. Norton, 1971 [1938]); and Fritz Fischer's *Germany's Aims in the First World War* (New York: Norton, 1967), *War of Illusions* (New York: Norton, 1973), and *World Power or Decline: The Controversy over Germany's Aims in the First World War* (New York: 1974).

12. During the war, Hans Delbrück suggested alternative ideas for a German political–military strategy based explicitly on Clausewitz's argument. See Arden Bucholz, *Hans Delbrück and the German Military Establishment* (Iowa City: University of Iowa Press, 1985), 86–119.

13. C. E. Callwell, *Military Operations and Maritime Preponderance* (Edinburgh: Blackwood, 1905), 180.

14. Barry R. Posen, *The Sources of Military Doctrine: France, Britain, and Germany Between the World Wars* (Ithaca, NY: Cornell University Press, 1984), relates organizational factors and offensive strategies.

15. General Jakob Meckel, quoted in Stewart L. Murray, *The Reality of War: An Introduction to Clausewitz with a Note by Spenser Wilkinson* (London: Hugh Rees, 1909), 7.

Part III

1. Edward Mead Earle, ed., *Makers of Modern Strategy: Military Thought from Machiavelli to Hitler* (Princeton, NJ: Princeton University Press, 1943).
2. Karl von Clausewitz, *On War*, trans. O. J. Matthijs Jolles (New York: Random House, 1943; Washington, DC: Infantry Journal Press, 1950).

Chapter 13

1. Robert Matteson Johnston, *Clausewitz to Date* (Cambridge, MA: *Military Historian and Economist*, 1917).
2. Alexander Baltzley, "Robert Matteson Johnston and the Study of Military History," *Military Affairs*, Spring 1957, 26–30; Colonel Arthur Latham Conger, "Robert Matteson Johnston, 1867–1920," *Journal of the American Military History Foundation*, Summer 1937, 45–46.
3. Jurgen Herbst, *The German Historical School in American Scholarship: A Study in the Transfer of Culture* (Ithaca, NY: Cornell University Press, 1965), 1, 8–9. Herbst's book covers primarily the period from 1876 to 1914. Significantly, it, too, makes no reference to Clausewitz or Delbrück.
4. Carl Reardon, *Soldiers and Scholars: The U.S. Army and the Uses of Military History, 1865–1920* (Lawrence: University Press of Kansas, 1990), 67.
5. *Military Historian and Economist* 2 (April 1917): 261.
6. Reardon, *Soldiers and Scholars*, 146.
7. *Military Historian and Economist* 1 (January 1916): 80.
8. Russell F. Weigley, *Towards an American Army: Military Thought from Washington to Marshall* (New York: Columbia University Press, 1962), 179.
9. Johnston, *Clausewitz to Date*, 9–11.
10. Robert M. Johnston, *Bull Run: Its Strategy and Tactics* (Boston: Houghton Mifflin, 1913), ix.
11. Ibid., *Bull Run*, 269; Robert M. Johnston, "War and Peace, Limited or Unlimited?" *Nineteenth Century*, July 1919, 34–39.
12. For example, see *The Military Historian and Economist*: A. L. C. and R. M. J. [Conger and Johnston], "A Prospective Theory of the Conduct of War," April 1917, 133–39; Unsigned (presumably Conger or Johnston), Review of P. Roques, *Le Général de Clausewitz* (Paris, 1912), October 1917, 452–54; Unsigned "Comment," January 1918, 52–53; "General Palat" (pseud. for P. Lehautcourt), "German Military Theory at the Outbreak of the War," October 1917, 357–371; and Emile Laloy, "French Military Theory, 1871–1914," July 1917, 267.
13. Robert M. Johnston, "An Approach to the Study of Napoleon's Generalship," *Annual Report of the American Historical Association for the Year 1914* (Washington, DC, 1916), vol. 1, 223–27, and "Napoleonic Notes," *Military Historian and Economist*, January 1918, 55–64.
14. Johnston, "War and Peace"; Robert M. Johnston, *First Reflections on the Campaign of 1918* (New York: Henry Holt, 1920), 24. The 1830 campaign plan appears prominently in Johnston's "Germany and Belgium," *Military Historian and Economist*, April 1916, 153–165.

15. Johnston, *Clausewitz to Date*, 44.

16. Hoffman Nickerson, *The Armed Horde 1793–1939: A Study of the Rise, Survival and Decline of the Mass Army* (New York: G.P. Putnam, 1942), 337–40, first noted these divergences between Johnston and Clausewitz but implied no fundamental antagonism. Hans Rothfels evidently derived his view of Johnston from Nickerson, and then in "Clausewitz," in *Makers of Modern Strategy: Military Thought from Machiavelli to Hitler*, ed. Edward Mead Earle (Princeton, NJ: Princeton University Press, 1943) 94, he lumped Johnston with Liddell Hart as Clausewitz's Anglo-Saxon opponents.

17. *On War*, bk. 8, chap. 3.

18. Johnston, *First Reflections*, 34–35.

19. Johnston, *Bull Run* and *First Reflections*, 16.

20. Johnston, *First Reflections*, 68. Nickerson, *Armed Horde*, 337, compared Johnston's ideas with Hans von Seeckt's for the Reichswehr, but that force was always intended as the nucleus for a new mass army.

21. Johnston drew also on *On War*, the 1812–15 campaign studies, "other fragments," and commentaries on Clausewitz by writers like Blume and Mikhail Dragomiroff.

22. Johnston, "War and Peace," 34.

23. Of all the American military educators of the World War II era, Conger's approach to war, politics, military education, and military history seems the most "Clausewitzian." Circumstances suggest that Conger must have been exposed to Clausewitz: He studied with Delbrück in Berlin in 1910 and ran a seminar in military history at Harvard in 1915. There he cofounded and coedited *The Military Historian and Economist* with Johnston. This journal made frequent references to Clausewitz but never clearly under Conger's name. His "President Lincoln as War Statesman," State Historical Society of Wisconsin, *Proceedings* 64 (1916), takes a sophisticated look at the interrelationship of military and political strategy, sneers at Jomini, and uses the terms "friction" and "center of gravity" (albeit not in a clearly Clausewitzian manner). Its view of the inherent odds against a Union victory is rooted in a Clausewitz-like view of the interrelationship between attack and defense. There is, however, no direct mention of Clausewitz, thus no "smoking gun" to justify a larger discussion here of Conger's intellectual influence on the U.S. Army.

24. T. D. Pilcher, ed., *War According to Clausewitz* (London: Cassell, 1918).

25. Compare *On War*, bk. 1, chap. 1, sec. 9.

26. Review, "Clausewitz Abridged," *Times Literary Supplement*, 18 April 1918, 179.

27. Pilcher, ed., *War According to Clausewitz*, 256, 258.

Chapter 14

1. Certainly many German commentators believed that Clausewitz had been consistently ignored, misunderstood, or distorted by the German general staff. Herbert Rosinski, *The German Army* (New York: Frederick A. Praeger, 1966; original ed., 1939), 109–14, and Delbrück both thought the German army had entirely missed Clausewitz's key points. See also Field Marshal Paul von Kleist in Basil H. Liddell Hart, *The German Generals Talk* (New York: 1948), 194. J. E. Edmonds, "Jomini and Clausewitz," *Canadian Army Jounral* 5 (May 1951): 64–69, recalled asking at the Kriegsakademie in 1899 whether Clausewitz were

read there. The answer—he claimed—was no. See also the essays on Germany in Michael I. Handel, ed., *Clausewitz and Modern Strategy*, (London: Frank Cass, 1986), especially Jehuda L. Wallach, "Misperceptions of Clausewitz' *On War* by the German Military"; Klaus Jürgen Müller, "Clausewitz, Ludendorff and Beck"; and Williamson Murray, "Clausewitz: Some Thoughts on What the Germans Got Right." Murray, arguing that German soldiers paid little attention to Clausewitz, cites General Leo Geyer von Schweppenburg's comment to Liddell Hart: "You will be horrified to hear that I have never read Clausewitz or Delbrück or Haushofer. The opinion on Clausewitz in our general staff was that of a theoretician to be read by professors." This reflects perhaps a reaction to the overuse of Clausewitz before World War I. In 1917, Hans von Seeckt said to his wife and was quoted in Antulio J. Echevarria II, [Captain, USAR], "Neo-Clausewitzianism: Appropriations of Clausewitz by Freytag-Loringhoven and the General Staff, 1890–1914" (Ph.D. diss., Princeton University [in progress]): "The mere mention of the name is enough to make one sick." Nonetheless, Murray argues that German tactical and operational behavior was in fact highly "Clausewitzian." How it came to be that way is debatable.

2. Brigadier General J. D. Hittle, ed., *Jomini and His Summary of the Art of War* (Harrisburg, PA: Military Service Publishing, Company, 1947). Lynn Montross made the same point: "The Prussian writer's theories have endured to shape the warfare of a day which has forgotten the *Précis*"; *War Through the Ages* (New York: Harper Bros., 1944; revised and enlarged 1946, 1960), 583. In fact, Jomini's influence lived on in doctrinal publications, transmitted mainly via Hamley.

3. Joe Greene's condensation was republished in England, introduced by J. F. C. Fuller. See Joseph I. Greene, ed., *The Living Thoughts of Clausewitz* (London: Cassell, 1945).

4. Spenser Wilkinson, *Government and the War* (London: Constable, 1918), chap. 7.

5. Ernest Lavisse and Charles Andler, "The German Theory and Practice of War," trans. "L.S." *Studies and Documents on the War* (Paris: Librairie Armand Colin, 1915), especially 26, often cited in U.S. and British war propaganda.

6. F. J. C. Hearnshaw, *Germany the Aggressor Throughout the Ages* (New York: Dutton, 1942), 234.

7. *On War*, bk. 5, chap. 14.

8. [Brigadier General] J. H. (John Hartman) Morgan (1876–1955), *Assize of Arms: The Disarmament of Germany and Her Rearmament (1919–1939)* (New York: Oxford University Press, 1946), 98, n. 15, 313; n. 152, 148–49.

9. Morgan influenced John Wheeler-Bennett's *The Nemesis of Power: The German Army in Politics, 1918–1945* (London: Macmillan, 1964), but Wheeler-Bennett (like Morgan, an assistant at Nuremberg) also saw in Clausewitz's 1812 actions a positive precedent for German military resistance to Hitler.

10. Caroline E. Playne, *The Pre-War Mind in Britain: An Historical Review* (London: Allen & Unwin, 1928), 155–65.

11. Erich Ludendorff, *Meine Kriegserinnerungen* (Berlin, 1919), 10, cited in Hans Speier, "Ludendorff: The German Concept of Total War," in *Makers of Modern Strategy: Military Thought from Machiavelli to Hitler*, ed. Edward Mead Earle (Princeton, NJ: Princeton University Press, 1943), 306–321.

12. Part of a 1916 parliamentary debate containing this point is included in Ralph Haswell Lutz, *Fall of the German Empire, 1914–1918*, trans. David G.

Rempel and Gertrude Rendtorff (Stanford, CA: Hoover War Library Publication, 1934; New York: Octagon Books, 1969), vol. 1, 224–25.

13. See Ralph Haswell Lutz, ed., *The Causes of the German Collapse in 1918*, trans. W. L. Campbell (Stanford, CA: Stanford University Press, 1934), 200–21.

14. See also Edward A. Thibault, "War as a Collapse of Policy: A Critical Evaluation of Clausewitz," *Naval War College Review*, May-June 1973, 42–56.

15. *On War*, bk. 6, chap. 5.

16. Paul Birdsall, *Versailles Twenty Years After* (New York: Reynal and Hitchcock, 1941), 3, 304. For similar treatments, see Guenter Hans Reimann [an international economist], *Germany: World Empire or World Revolution* (London: Secker and Warburg, 1938), 24; George Sava (pseud. G. A. M. Milkomane), *School for War* (London: Faber, 1942), 24; Wyndham Lewis [a British artist and writer who flirted with fascism in the 1930s], *The Hitler Cult* (New York: Gordon Press, 1972; orig. London, 1939), 6. Lewis stated: "Nazi technique was acquired, it is important to recall, in putting into execution the precepts of Clausewitz—namely the maximum of terror as a law of nature, since it was a law of war."

17. *On War*, bk. 8, chap. 4), "Instruction for the Crown Prince," 209–210 in the Graham/Maude translation.

18. On that topic see Peter M. Baldwin, "Clausewitz in Nazi Germany," *Journal of Contemporary History* 16 (1981): 5–26: Albert T. Lauterbach, "Roots and Implications of the German Idea of Military Society," *Military Affairs* 5 (1941): 1–20.

19. Unsigned, "Clausewitz on the Defeat of Jena-Auerstädt," *Army Quarterly*, October 1941, 109–21; compare J. E. Edmonds, "Clausewitz and the Downfall of Prussia in 1806," *Army Review*, April 1914, 403–46.

20. Edmonds, "Jomini and Clausewitz."

21. T. E. Lawrence, *Revolt in the Desert* (New York: George H. Doran, 1927), 66.

22. T. E. Lawrence, *Evolution of a Revolt: Early Postwar Writings of T. E. Lawrence*, ed. Stanley Weintraub and Rodelle Weintraub (University Park: Pennsylvania State University Press, 1967), 105.

23. Cyril Falls, *A Hundred Years of War* (London: Duckworth, 1953, 1961), 280.

24. Basil H. Liddell Hart, ed., *T. E. Lawrence to His Biographer* (New York: Doubleday, 1938), 76.

25. Ibid., 4.

26. Liddell Hart's correspondents often sought to curry favor with him by joining his attack on Clausewitz, for example, Captain [Swedish army] G. E. F. Boldt-Christmas's letter, 20 November 1939 (B. H. Liddell Hart Papers I/87/2).

27. T. E. Lawrence, *Seven Pillars of Wisdom* (New York: Doubleday, 1926, 1935), Ch. 33, "Generalizing the military theory of our revolt."

Chapter 15

1. Jay Luvaas, "Clausewitz, Fuller and Liddell Hart," in *Clausewitz and Modern Strategy*, ed. Michael I. Handel (London: Frank Cass, 1986), 197–212; Captain [USAF] Kenneth L. Davison, Jr., "Clausewitz and the Indirect Approach—Misreading the Master," *Airpower Journal*, Winter 1988, 42–52. Michael Howard, "The Influence of Clausewitz," in Carl von Clausewitz, *On War*, ed. and trans. Michael Howard and Peter Paret (Princeton, NJ: Princeton University Press, 1976), 38–41, discusses Liddell Hart's interpretation.

2. Michael Howard, "The Liddell Hart Memoirs," *Journal of the Royal United Service Institution,* February 1966, 58–61.

3. Quoted in ibid.

4. On permutations in Liddell Hart's reputation, see John Mearsheimer, *Liddell Hart and the Weight of History* (Ithaca: Cornell University Press, 1988), 1–5. Mearsheimer's overall interpretation, however, is controversial.

5. See discussions of Clausewitz in Basil H. Liddell Hart, "The Napoleonic Fallacy," *Empire Review,* May 1925; *Foch: The Man of Orleans* (Boston: Little, Brown, 1932), 23–26, *Ghost of Napoleon,* especially pt. 3, chap. 2; and *Strategy* (New York: Praeger, 1954), 352–57. Liddell Hart's *British Way of Warfare* (London: Faber & Faber, 1932; New York: Macmillan, 1933), provides his substitute for "Clausewitzian" thinking, and *Strategy* provides the best statement of his strategic thought.

6. Carl von Clausewitz, *On War,* ed. and trans. J. J. Graham and F. N. Maude, new and rev. ed. (London: K. Paul, Trench, Trübner, 1908), vol. 1, xi.

7. Basil H. Liddell Hart, "Armed Forces and the Art of War: Armies," in *The Zenith of European Power, 1830–1870,* ed. J. P. T. Bury, vol. 10 of *The New Cambridge Modern History* (Cambridge: Cambridge University Press, 1960), 320.

8. Liddell Hart to radio commentator E. H. Carr, 22 August 1951. B. H. Liddell Hart Papers I/150/1.6

9. Liddell Hart, *Ghost of Napoleon,* 125–26.

10. Jehuda L. Wallach, *The Dogma of the Battle of Annihilation: The Theories of Clausewitz and Schlieffen and Their Impact on the German Conduct of Two World Wars* (Westport, CT: Greenwood Press, 1986), 15; 31, n. 28; 241–46, discusses contrasts between the two ideas. Albert T. Lauterbach, "Roots and Implications of the German Idea of Military Society," *Military Affairs* 5 (1941): 1–20, attempts to equate them. See also Peter R. Moody, Jr. "Clausewitz and the Fading Dialectic of War," *World Politics* 31 (1979): 417–33.

11. A point he made often; for example, see Basil H. Liddell Hart, *Colonel Lawrence: The Man Behind the Legend* (New York: Dodd, Mead, 1934), 30, 56.

12. Liddell Hart, *Ghost of Napoleon,* 123.

13. Howard, "Influence of Clausewitz," 40.

14. Basil H. Liddell Hart, *Memoirs* (London: Cassell, 1965), vol. 1, 142.

15. Basil H. Liddell Hart, *The Decisive Wars of History* (Boston: Little, Brown, 1929), 147.

16. Basil H. Liddell Hart, *Europe in Arms* (New York: Random House, 1937), 218–21. In his *The German Generals Talk* (New York: Morrow, 1948), 194, Liddell Hart passed on without comment General Kleist's regrets that the Nazis had not better understood Clausewitz, especially in regard to the relationship between war and politics and on the difficulties of conquering Russia.

17. Lynn Montross, *War Through the Ages* (New York: Harper Brots., 1944; revised and enlarged, 1946, 1960), 585. Listed on the Commandant's Reading List, ALMAR 127–89 (111500Z Jul89). Headquarters United States Marine Corps, *FMFM 1: Warfighting* (Washington, DC: U.S. Government Printing Office, 1989). See also André Beaufre [Foreword by Liddell Hart], *Introduction to Strategy,* trans. R. H. Barry (New York: Praeger, 1965 [Paris, 1963]), 20.

18. Barbara W. Tuchman, *The Guns of August* (New York: Macmillan, 1962), especially 36, 38, 350–51.

19. Griffith wondered whether Clausewitz had ever read Sun Tzu. He asked Werner Hahlweg if the 1772 Amiot translation had been in Clausewitz's personal

collection. Liddell Hart, seeing the letter, remarked, "It seems doubtful . . . for Clausewitz's own "On War" would have been better if he had." Liddell Hart to Griffith, 16 July 1959; letter, Griffith to Hahlweg, 13 July 1959. B. H. Liddell Hart Papers I/333/61,60b.

20. Field Marshal Viscount Montgomery of Alamein, *A History of Warfare* (New York: World, 1968), 20, 414–15.

21. Discussed in Liddell Hart's correspondence with Hahlweg, October 1958. Liddell Hart read no German, but Hahlweg translated the letters.

22. Liddell Hart to himself, "Thoughts on philosophy, politics & military matters," 7 June 1932. B. H. Liddell Hart Papers 11/1932/20.

23. Liddell Hart's *British Way of War*, probably owing to Wilkinson's criticisms, shows a subtle understanding of Clausewitz's approach.

24. Harold D. Kehm, "Review" (of Basil H. Liddell Hart's Strategy), *Army Combat Forces Journal* 5 (October 1955): 62–63; Liddell Hart to Major John H. Cushman (USA), 5 January 1955; reply, 6 March 1955. B. H. Liddell Hart Papers I/215/14, 15a.

25. Mearsheimer, *Liddell Hart and the Weight of History*. The discussion of Liddell Hart and Clausewitz is minimal.

26. Brian Bond, *Liddell Hart: A Study of His Military Thought* (New Brunswick, NJ: Rutgers University Press, 1977), especially 77, 113.

27. Bury, ed., *The Zenith of European Power*, 302–30.

28. Werner Hahlweg to Liddell Hart, 6 November 1958. B. H. Liddell Hart Papers I/342/10.

29. Michael Howard recalls Hahlweg as "being intensely deferential to Liddell Hart, as indeed all Germans were at that time." Howard to me, 26 September 1990. Hahlweg's letters to Liddell Hart are embarrassingly obsequious; for example, see Hahlweg to Liddell Hart, 30 October 1958.

30. Werner Hahlweg, "Clausewitz und die angelsächsische Welt," in Carl von Clausewtiz, *Vom Kriege*, 19th ed. (Bonn: Ferdinand Dümmlers Verlag, 1980), 138–53.

31. B. H. Liddell Hart Papers, Paret to Liddell Hart, 11 January 1962; reply, 19 January 1962, Liddell Hart Papers 1/566.

32. Letter, Fuller to William Sloane, Rutgers University Press, undated but in reply to letter, Sloane to Fuller, 30 January 1961. J. F. C. Fuller Papers, Liddell Hart Centre for Military Archives, King's College London, IV/6/5; IV/6/6a.

33. [J. E. Edmonds], review of Fuller's *Foundations of the Science of War* (London: Hutchinson, 1926), in *Army Quarterly*, 12 (1926): 165–66.

34. Brian Holden Reid, *J. F. C. Fuller: Military Thinker* (New York: St. Martin's Press, 1987); A. J. Trythall, *Boney Fuller: Soldier, Strategist, and Writer, 1878–1966* (New Brunswick, NJ: Rutgers University Press, 1977).

35. Fuller, *Foundations of the Science of War*, 20.

36. Fuller, *The Dragon's Teeth: A Study of War and Peace* (London: Constable, 1932), 66–67, 210–11, 255–56.

37. Michael Howard, *War and the Liberal Conscience* (London: Temple Smith, 1978), 131.

38. J. F. C. Fuller, *War and Western Civilization, 1832–1932: A Study of War as a Political Instrument and the Expression of Mass Democracy* (London: Duckworth, 1932), 46–49, 111. Basil H. Liddell Hart, *The Remaking of Modern Armies* (London: John Murray, 1927), 93.

39. J. F. C. Fuller, *Memoirs of an Unconventional Soldier* (London: I. Nicholson and Watson, 1936), 429.

40. J. F. C. Fuller, *Machine Warfare: An Inquiry into the Influence of Mechanics on the Art of War* (Washington, DC: Infantry Journal Press, 1943), 2–3.

41. Joseph I. Greene, ed., *The Living Thoughts of Clausewitz* (London: Cassell, 1945).

42. J. F. C. Fuller, *The Second World War, 1939–45: A Strategical and Tactical History* (New York: Duell, Sloan and Pearce, 1949), 32–33.

43. J. F. C. Fuller, *The Conduct of War, 1789–1961: A Study of the French, Industrial, and Russian Revolutions on War and Its Conduct* (London: Eyre and Spottiswoode, 1961), 12, 59–76.

44. Carl von Clausewitz, *On War*, ed. and trans. Michael Howard and Peter Paret (Princeton, NJ: Princeton University Press, 1976), bk. 2, chap. 2. Graham/Maude is obscure on this point, but the Jolles version is clear.

45. Michael Howard, "Clausewitz and His Misinterpreters," *Listener*, 22 March 1956, 279–80.

46. Letter, Fuller to Sloane, undated but in reply to letter, Sloane to Fuller, 30 January 1961, J. F. C. Fuller Papers IV/6/5; IV/6/6a.

47. Paul Kennedy, ed., *War Plans of the Great Powers, 1880–1914* (London: Allen & Unwin, 1979), made only one significant reference (17) to Clausewitz, citing Fuller. "After all, even Clausewitz had admitted that 'the subordination of the political point of view to the military would be contrary to common sense' because 'policy is the intelligent faculty, war only the instrument.'"

48. See Spenser Wilkinson, "Killing No Murder: An Examination of Some New Theories of War," *Army Quarterly*, October 1927, 14–27; Liddell Hart's response, January 1928, 396–401.

49. Wilkinson to Colonel (USA) Marius Scammell, 18 January 1928; 9 February 1932. Spenser Wilkinson Papers 13/68.

50. Liddell Hart, *Remaking of Modern Armies*.

51. A similar argument was made later by Lieutenant Colonel (USA) Marshall H. Armor to Major (USA) John H. Cushman and brought to Liddell Hart's attention. Letter, Cushman to Liddell Hart, 6 March 1955. B. H. Liddell Hart Papers I/215/14, 15a. Armor had criticized Liddell Hart's "deprecation of Clausewitz" in a review of Liddell Hart's *Strategy*, in *Military Review*, February 1955, 110. Armor explained to Cushman privately that he liked the book but thought Liddell Hart's arguments essentially the same as Clausewitz's. Others have perceived similarities between Liddell Hart's arguments and Clausewitz's, for example, Raymond B. Furlong [Lieutenant General, USAF], "Strategymaking for the 1980's," *Parameters*, March 1979, 9–16. Jehuda Wallach argued in *Dogma*, 7, that Liddell Hart's interpretation of military history, particularly the psychological nature of "victory," was the same as Clausewitz's. Liddell Hart was willing to acowledge that Sun Tzu had anticipated him, but not Clausewitz; see his "Foreword" to Griffith's translation.

52. Saxe, quoted in Liddell Hart, *Remaking of Modern Armies*, 95–96.

53. Liddell Hart *British Way of Warfare*, 21–22.

Chapter 16

1. George Orwell, "Perfide Albion" (review of Liddell Hart's *British Way of Warfare*), *New Statesman and Nation*, 21 November 1942, 342–43; Liddell Hart's reply, *New Statesman and Nation*, 19 December 1942, 409–10.

2. Hoffman Nickerson, *Arms and Policy, 1939–1944* (New York: G.P. Putnam, 1945), 54–57.

3. Robin Higham, *The Military Intellectuals in Britain, 1918–1939* (New Brunswick, NJ: Rutgers University Press, 1966), rather inconsistently characterized Rowan-Robinson as both a critic of Fuller and Liddell Hart (39) and a "Fullerite" (109).

4. See ibid., *39, 40, 109–10; H. Rowan-Robinson, Security?: A Study of Our Military Position* (London: Methuen, 1935), 46, 52, and *Imperial Defence: A Problem in Four Dimensions* (London: Frederick Muller, 1938), 3, 7, 64. Rowan-Robinson cited as a prominent source of inspiration A. S. Eddington, *Space, Time and Gravitation* (Cambridge: Cambridge University Press, 1920). Similar imagery appears in Harold W. Nelson, "Space and Time in *On War*," in *Clausewitz and Modern Strategy*, ed. Michael I. Handell (London: Frank Cass, 1986), 134–49, although Nelson acknowledged (134) that "Clausewitz did not see these factors as the central elements."

5. Rowan-Robinson, *Imperial Defence*, 7.

6. Cyril Falls, *The Nature of Modern Warfare* (New York: Oxford University Press, 1941), and *Ordeal by Battle* (London: Methuen, 1943).

7. Falls, *Ordeal by Battle*, 8.

8. Wilkinson discussed Bourcet frequently. See for example "The Soul of an Army," *Army Review*, July 1911, 173–78, and *The French Army before Napoleon* (Oxford: Clarendon Press, 1915). Wilkinson's *The Defence of Piedmont, 1742–1748: A Prelude to the Study of Napoleon* (Oxford: Clarendon Press, 1927), is largely a study of Bourcet's ideas.

9. Herbert Rosinski, "IMS: Captain Falls on Modern Warfare," *Infantry Journal* 50 (January 1942): 78–81.

10. Unsigned, "Strategy and Tactics: Lessons from Modern Methods," *Times Literary Supplement*, 16 October 1943, 496.

11. Cyril Falls, *The Place of War in History: An Inaugural Lecture* (Oxford: Clarendon Press, 1947).

12. Cyril Falls, *The Art of War: From the Age of Napoleon to the Present Day* (New York: Oxford University Press, 1961).

13. Ibid., 6–7, 44, 218–19, 157.

14. See F. B. Maurice's Foreword to Victor Wallace Germains, *The Mechanization of War* (London: Sifton Praed, 1927).

15. Major-General Sir F. [Frederick Barton] Maurice, *British Strategy: A Study of the Application of the Principles of War* (London: Constable, 1929), 48.

16. Maurice concluded (ibid., 39) that Clausewitz, Colin, Fuller, and the British *Field Service Regulations* agreed on only two "principles": that the object was the overthrow of the enemy's armed forces and that the most effective means to this end was concentrating superior physical and moral strength at the decisive point.

17. Ibid., 113.

18. Ibid., 44–47.

19. Ibid., 42–43.

20. Rowan-Robinson, *Imperial Defence*, 3–4.

21. W. J. Woodhouse, *King Agis of Sparta and His Campaign in Arkadia in 418 B.C.* (Oxford: Clarendon Press, 1933; New York: AMS Press, 1978), cites *On War* on virtually every page of the main narrative, referring to the translation by J. J. Gordon (*sic*). His approach is strikingly similar to Delbrück's, but his

single reference to him is critical. F. E. Adcock, *The Roman Art of War Under the Republic* (Cambridge, MA: Harvard University Press, 1940) drew on Clausewitz via Delbrück.

22. On Maude's correspondence with Ballard and Palmer, see Chapter 4. Maurice compared Clausewitz and Lincoln but drew no direct connection. Like Ballard, he viewed Lincoln much more positively than did Henderson, whom Maurice, *Statesmen and Soldiers of the Civil War: A Study of the Conduct of the War* (Boston: Little, Brown, 1926), vi, 152–61, criticized on this point.

23. Auchinleck to Liddell Hart, 20 November 1950; reply, 23 November 1950. B. H. Liddell Hart Papers I/30/30,31.

Chapter 17

1. Robin Higham, *The Military Intellectuals in Britain, 1918–1939* (New Brunswick, NJ: Rutgers Univrsity Press, 1966), 119; the air power theorists are discussed on pp119–234.

2. [Air Vice-Marshal, R.A.F.] E. J. Kingston-McCloughry, *Global Strategy* (New York: Praeger, 1957), 44, 196. Kingston-McCloughry's pre–World War II books make no reference to Clausewitz.

3. Basil H. Liddell Hart, "Argument for Airpower," *The Memoirs of Captain Liddell Hart* (London: Cassell, 1965), vol. 1, 137–58.

4. Giulio Douhet, *The Command of the Air*, trans. Dino Ferrari (New York: Coward-McCann, 1942).

5. Alexander de Seversky, *Air Power: Key to Survival* (New York: Simon & Schuster, 1950), 104, 206. De Seversky's *Victory through Air Power* (New York: Simon & Schuster, 1942), frequently mentions Mahan but never Clausewitz or Corbett.

6. See Edward Warner, "Douhet, Mitchell, Seversky: Theorists of Air Warfare," in *Makers of Modern Strategy: Military Thought from Machiavelli to Hitler*, ed. Edward Mead Earle (Princeton, NJ: Princeton University Press, 1943). David MacIsaac, "Voices from the Central Blue: The Air Power Theorists," in *Makers of Modern Strategy: From Machiavelli to the Nuclear Age*, ed. Peter Paret (Princeton, NJ: Princeton Universtiy Press, 1986). Neither writer found a need to make any significant mention of Clausewitz in his survey of interwar air power thinking. Neither did Robert Frank Futrell, *Ideas, Concepts, Doctrine: Basic Thinking in the United States Air Force, 1907–1960* (Maxwell AFB, AL: Air University Press, 1989).

7. Major [USAF] James B. Smith, "Some Thoughts on Clausewitz and Airplanes," *Air University Review*, May–June 1986, 52–59, provides the basis for this paragraph on Hansell and ACTS. He acknowledges that the theoretical basis for ACTS thinking was "at best, vague" but perceives a number of "distinct parallels" between *On War* and ACTS thinking on strategic bombardment. However, Haywood S. Hansell, Jr., *The Air Plan That Defeated Hitler* (Atlanta: Higgins-McArthur, 1972), does contain a substantial(if inconclusive) discussion of Clausewitz and quotes (32) a wartime lecture by Lieutenant General Harold L. George, director of the Department of Air Tactics and Strategy at ACTS, which translated Clausewitz's most famous statement as "War is the furtherance of national policy by other means."

8. Martin Kitchen, "The Political History of Clausewitz," *Journal of Strategic Studies* 11 (March 1988): 27–50, citing Norbert Krüger, "Adolf Hitlers Clausewitzkenntnis," *Wehrwissenschaftliche Rundschau*, 18 (1968).

Chapter 18

1. University of Pennsylvania, 1987, iv. Brower is now a professor at West Point.

2. Major Michael R. Matheny, "The Development of the Theory and Doctrine of Operational Art in the American Army, 1920–1940," paper, U.S. Army Command and General Staff College, School for Advanced Military Studies, Fort Leavenworth, KS 22 March 1988, 31.

3. Ibid., 26; Command and General Staff School, *Principles of Strategy for an Independent Corps or Army in a Theater of Operations* (Fort Leavenworth, KS: U.S. Army Command and General Staff School Press, 1936).

4. *Principles of Strategy for an Independent Corps or Army*, 19.

5. Martin Blumenson is aware of no other references by Patton to Clausewitz (letter, Blumenson to me, 25 June 1990) but stated that "a good case, I believe, can be made for Patton's having digested Clausewitzian thought in his methods of training and operational execution." Probably true, but such inferences are outside the scope of this study.

6. Excerpts appear in Keith E. Eiler, ed., *Wedemeyer on War and Peace* (Stanford, CA: Hoover Institution Press, 1987), 10–26.

7. Albert C. Wedemeyer, *Wedemeyer Reports* (New York: Henry Holt, 1958), 51, 60, 80, 81, 90. None of these references is revealing.

8. Williamson Murray, "Clausewitz: Some Thoughts on What the Germans Got Right," in *Clausewitz and Modern Strategy*, ed. Michael I. Handel (London: Frank Cass, 1986), 267–68, citing Albert C. Wedemeyer, "German General Staff School," Report 15,999 dated 7/11/38 from the military attaché, Berlin, 1kb 6/23/39, National Archives.

9. Foch, who used Clausewitz, became a major icon after the war. See Ferdinand Foch, *The Principles of War* (New York, 1918; reprinted New York: AMS Press, 1970). The required military history textbook at both West Point and the Command and General Staff School, from 1909 to the outbreak of World War II, was Matthew Steele's *American Campaigns* (Washington, DC: U.S. Infantry Association, 1909). Steele's book, hastily concocted from lectures he had put together at Leavenworth, contained no meaningful references to theory or Clausewitz and few to Jomini.

10. Harry P. Ball, *Of Responsible Command: A History of the U.S. Army War College* (Carlisle Barracks, PA: Alumni Association of the U.S. Army War College, 1983), 212–14; compare *On War*, bk. 2, chap. 2.

11. Unsigned review of Captain Kübler's *Clausewitz und der Gebirgskrieg, Review of Military Literature* 16 (March 1936), 105–6.

12. Colonel William K. Naylor, *Principles of Strategy: With Historical Illustrations* (Fort Leavenworth, KS: General Service Schools Press, 1921), 296. Clausewitz's "remarkable sympathy for the defensive" was discussed by Colonel René Altmayer, *Revue militaire française*, trans. J. S. Wood and appearing in "The German Military Doctrine," *Field Artillery Journal*, March–April 1935, 181–91, comparing the theories of Frederick the Great, Clausewitz, and Moltke.

13. Naylor, *Principles*, 58.

14. General Service Schools, *List of Books on Military History and Related Subjects*, [Colonel Conrad H. Lanza, FA, compiler] (Fort Leavenworth, KS: General Service Schools Press, 1923), Combined Arms Research Library, Fort Leavenworth, Special Collections 016.3550 09 L297L 1923, 7.

15. General Service Schools, *The Jena Campaign: Source Book*, [Colonel Conrad H. Lanza, FA, compiler] (Fort Leavenworth, KS: General Service Schools Press, 1922), 515–611.

16. D. K. R. Crosswell, "Aides, Adjutants, and Asses: The United States Army's Advanced Schools in the Inter-war Years," paper presented to the American Military Institute conference on military education, April 1989, 20.

17. Oliver Prescott Robinson, *The Fundamentals of Military Strategy* (Washington, DC: United States Infantry Association, 1928).

18. Ibid., viii–ix.

19. Ibid., viii–ix.

20. Ibid., 76.

22. Ibid., 4.

23. Ibid., 1–2.

23. Dwight D. Eisenhower, "A Tank Discussion," *Infantry Journal*, November 1920.

24. Charles H. Brown, draft article on Fox Conner, 27 May 1964, Composite File, 1, Eisenhower Papers.

25. Brown, Conner draft, 15–16.

26. Stephen E. Ambrose, *Soldier, General of the Army, President-Elect, 1890–1952*, vol. 1 of *Eisenhower (New York: Simon & Schuster, 1983). See also* Eisenhower Public Papers (EPP) in *Public Papers of the Presidents* and Eisenhower Papers, Dwight D. Eisenhower Library, Abilene KS.

27. This discussion of the historiography on Eisenhower is derived largely from Fred I. Greenstein, "Eisenhower as an Activist President: A Look at New Evidence," *Political Science Quarterly* 94 (Winter 1979–80), 575–99; and from lectures by John Lewis Gaddis at Ohio University, 1979–81.

28. Richard M. Nixon, *Six Crises* (Garden City, NY: Doubleday, 1962), 161, cited by Greenstein, "Eisenhower," 576.

29. Which does not prevent its occasional reappearance. See the treatment of Eisenhower in John M. Taylor, *General Maxwell Taylor: The Sword and the Pen* (Garden City, NY: Doubleday, 1989).

30. Quoted by Greenstein, "Eisenhower," 588.

31. Dwight D. Eisenhower, *At Ease: Stories I Tell My Friends* (Garden City, NY: Doubleday, 1967), 185.

32. Brown, Conner draft, 12.

33. None of the various Eisenhower collections includes a copy of *On War* in any version.

34. Course at the Army War College, 1927–28: Command Course No. 14, "Report of Committee No. 1, Subject: War and Its Principles, Methods and Doctrines," 27 February 1928. File 347–1, Army War College Curricular Archives, U.S. Army Military History Institute, Carlisle Barracks, PA.

35. Interview, Dr. Milton Eisenhower on behalf of Dr. Bela Kornitzer with Dwight D. Eisenhower, 17 March 1955. Whitman Diary Box 4, Ann C. Whitman Papers, March 1955 (4), Eisenhower Papers.

36. Letter, Dwight D. Eisenhower to Olive Ann Tambourelle, 2 March 1966. Eisenhower Post-presidential Papers, Special Name, Box 8.

37. *Public Papers of the Presidents: Dwight D. Eisenhower, 1955*, news conference of 12 January 1955, 57.

38. See, for example, David Eisenhower, *Eisenhower: At War, 1943–1945* (New York: Random House, 1986), 216, 438. William B. Pickett, "Eisenhower

as a Student of Clausewitz," *Military Review*, July 1985, 21–27, is an interesting article on Eisenhower that attempts to divine the impact of Clausewitz from his relationship with Conner and Marshall, but I think it goes beyond the evidence. It describes both Marshall and Eisenhower as "disciples of Clausewitz" (largely in terms of their ideas describing the perfect military commander), but neither Marshall's published papers nor Eisenhower's published correspondence with him make any reference to the philosopher.

39. John Lewis Gaddis, *Strategies of Containment: A Critical Appraisal of Postwar American National Security Policy* (New York: Oxford University Press, 1982), 127–97.

40. Based on Clausewitz's discussion in *On War*, "Ends [Purpose] and Means in War," bk. 1, chap. 2.

41. Gaddis, *Strategies of Containment*, 61, 355–56.

42. Ibid., 135, 188. Gaddis (35, n. 17) 135) cites as examples of Clausewitzian influence Eisenhower's remarks (*Public Papers of the Presidents*) to USIA staff, 10 November 1953, 74; Eisenhower press conference, 12 January 1955, 57; Eisenhower press conferences, 7 March and 23 May 1956, 292–93, 525.

43. *On War*, bk. 1, chap. 3, "The Genius for War"; "Instruction for the Crown Prince," p222 in the translation by J. J. Graham and F. N Maude (London: K. Paul, Trench, Trébner, 1908).

44. Commander (USN) A. G. Zimmerman's 1935 partial translation of *Moltke's Military Works: Precepts of War* contained significant discussions of Clausewitz as filtered through Moltke's organizational biases.

45. Correspondence with Sims, Spenser Wilkinson Papers 13/43.

46. The entire month of August in both the junior and senior class syllabi of 1931. Naval War College Archives, RG4, 1805, 1805–a.

47. The logistics course of 1928 suggested the reading of thirty-seven pages of *On War*. Two of Corbett's books were suggested for the Naval War College junior class of 1931. *On War* was not listed. Corbett's major work was the first required reading for the senior class of 1934, but only the first two chapters of Book 1 and eleven pages of Book 8 of *On War* were on the syllabus. Naval War College archives, RG4/1356; RG4/1616; RG4/1805, 1805–A.

48. Naval War College, "Books Recommended for a Course of Reading," Naval War College archives, RG8/UNT 1894.

49. Bernard Brodie's *A Layman's Guide to Naval Strategy* (Princeton, NJ: Princeton University Press, 1942) mentions Clausewitz and Corbett in the preface (viii–x) but not in the text. Brodie's manuscript had been closely critiqued by Herbert Rosinski; these references are probably a bow in his direction. Brodie's *Seapower in the Machine Age* (Princeton, NJ: Princeton University Press, 1941), had drawn frequently on Corbett, which was itself unusual, but his serious interest in Clausewitz probably dates from the 1950s.

50. George Julian Meyers, *Strategy* (Washington, DC: Byron S. Adams, 1928).

51. Ibid., 157–158.

52. On Corbett's *Some Principles of Maritime Strategy*, see Meyers, *Strategy*, 98.

53. Meyers, *Strategy*, 21–22.

54. One exception: Russell F. Weigley discussed Meyers's work in his *The American Way of War: A History of United States Military Strategy and Policy* (New York: Macmillan, 1973), 206, 210, 532, and in "Military Strategy and

Civilian Leadership," in *Historical Dimensions of National Security Problems*, ed. Klaus Knorr (Lawrence: University Press of Kansas, 1976), 38–77.

55. Review of Meyers's *Strategy*, Rear Admiral (ret.) Reginald R. Belknap, U.S. Naval Institute *Proceedings* 55 (April 1929): 357–60, which went on for four double-columned pages without noting Clausewitz's dominating influence in the book. Also reviewed by Major Kenna Eastham (U.S. Cavalry), *Cavalry Journal* 38 (1929): 297–98, who saw Meyers's treatment as "entirely new and original," because it did not depend on the "well known 'immutable' principles of war" of the "familiar authorities . . . Napoleon, Clausewitz, Moltke, and Foch."

56. See Nickerson's obituary, *New York Times*, 25 March 1965, 37.

57. Hoffman Nickerson, *The Armed Horde 1793–1939: A Study of the Rise, Survival and Decline of the Mass Army* (New York: Putnam, 1942), xvii; for Nickerson's treatment of Clausewitz, see especially 139–145.

58. Ibid., 338–39.

59. Hoffman Nickerson, *Arms and Policy, 1939–1944* (New York: Putnam, 1945), 54. See also his *Armed Horde*, 344.

60. Compare Carl von Clausewitz, *Principles of War*, trans. Hans Gatzke (Harrisburg, PA: Military Service Publishing, 1942), 45–46.

61. Nickerson frequently drew on Clausewitz's analysis of the offense and defense to illustrate his theories. Despite Liddell Hart's humiliation over the same issue, he later argued that the events of 1940 had not disproved that analysis and that the Battle of Britain had confirmed it. See Nickerson, *Arms and Policy*, 135.

62. Hoffman Nickerson, "Clausewitz: A Hundred Years After," *Army Quarterly*, July 1940, 274–84.

63. Hoffman Nickerson, *Can We Limit War?* (London: Arrowsmith, 1933), 124.

64. Nickerson, "Clausewitz: A Hundred Years After."

65. Nickerson, *Armed Horde*, 142.

66. *On War*, bk. 1, chap. 2.

67. Nickerson, *Armed Horde*, 140–41.

68. Political scientist Quincy Wright, *A Study of War*, 2 vols. (Chicago: University of Chicago Press, 1942), 279, 905, 1215, makes a number of references to Clausewitz. None of these shows any comprehension, and most appear to derive from Nickerson's work. Wright did not pick up on Nickerson's positive tone, however, and Nickerson also transmitted Fuller's early, negative views on Clausewitz's contribution to "democratic" wars. Wright also appears to have mistaken F. N. Maude's social Darwinist editorial comments for Clausewitz's own expressed views. He called Clausewitz an expounder of international violence. But Wright himself was no pacifist. He was a prominent signer of a petition demanding the immediate U.S. entry into the war against Nazi Germany. See *Chicago Daily Post*, 16 August 1941.

69. I. B. Holley, Jr., *General John M. Palmer, Citizen Soldiers, and the Army of a Democracy* (Westport, CT: Greenwood Press, 1982), 1.

70. Palmer's argument for the Swiss model is best developed in his *Statesmanship or War* (Garden City, NY: Doubleday, Page, 1927).

71. Cited in Russell F. Weigley, *Towards an American Army: Military Thought from Washington to Marsahll* (New York: Columbia University Press, 1962), 227.

72. Palmer's ideas are rather summarily dismissed as "silliness" in Allan R. Millett and Peter Maslowski's widely used textbook, *For the Common Defense: A*

Military History of the United States of America (New York: Free Press, 1984), 366.

73. See Michael S. Sherry, *Preparing for the Next War: American Plans for Postwar Defense, 1941–45* (New Haven, CT: Yale University Press, 1977), *passim*; Weigley, *Towards an American Army*, chap. 13, "John McAuley Palmer and George C. Marshall: Universal Military Training."

74. Holley, *Palmer*, 66. Holley, of Duke University, worked closely with his subject in turning Palmer's partially written manuscript into a comprehensive biography. "Unfortunately . . . the general died before I reached that part of my research where the question arose, so I never queried him directly on Clausewitz." Letter, Holley to me, 27 November 1989.

75. For such discussions, see especially Palmer's *Statesmanship or War*, 24–26; John M. Palmer, *Washington, Lincoln, Wilson: Three War Statesmen* (Garden City, NY: Doubleday, 1930), 224–39.

76. John McAuley Palmer Papers: "Memorandum for General Harbord, Subject: Mr. Millard's Papers on the Far Eastern Question," 13 October 1921.

77. U.S. Senate, *Reorganization of the Army: Hearings before the Subcommittee of the Committee on Military Affairs*, 65th Cong., 1st sess., S.2715, II, 1174–75.

78. In this focus, Palmer was taking a cue from Clausewitz similar to that taken by German historian Otto Hintze. See Otto Hintze, *The Historical Essays of Otto Hintze*, ed. Felix Gilbert (New York: Oxford University Press, 1975), especially "Military Organization and the Organization of the State"; Felix Gilbert, "From Clausewitz to Delbrück and Hintze: Achievements and Failures of Military History," *Journal of Strategic Studies* 3 (1980): 11–20.

79. Holley, *Palmer*, 89.

80. Holley, *Palmer*, 617. The book was *America in Arms: The Experience of the United States with Military Organization* (New Haven, CT: Yale University Press, 1941).

81. Palmer, *Statesmanship or War*, 239; Palmer, *Washington, Lincoln, Wilson*, 245–48. His Lincoln-related correspondence with Colin Ballard and F. N. Maude touched on some organizational observations that Clausewitz had made concerning the optimal number of divisions in a corps. See John McAuley Palmer Papers: Palmer to General Colin R. Ballard, 4 November 1928; reply, Ballard to Palmer, 26 January 1929; Palmer to Colonel F. N. Maude, 4 November 1928; reply, Maude to Palmer, 18 November 1928; Maude to Palmer, 10 December 1928.

82. Biographical information extracted from Greene's own editorial comments in the *Infantry Journal* or elsewhere; obituaries, *Combat Forces Journal*, August 1953, 12–15, and *New York Times*, 27 June 1953, 15; letter, L. James Binder (editor of *ARMY*) to me, 12 July 1990.

83. Greene was involved in the quest for a textbook on the psychology of men in combat: National Research Council, *Psychology for the Armed Services*, ed. Edwin G. Boring (Washington, DC: Infantry Journal Press, 1945, 1948). Greene wrote the foreword and published a version for the common soldier: National Research Council, *Psychology for the Fighting Man* (Washington, DC: Infantry Journal Press, 1943).

84. Correspondence in Herbert F. Rosinski Papers Series II, Box 2, Folder 21.

85. Greene's understanding of Clausewitz is criticized by Brodie in "A Guide to the Reading of *On War*," in *On War*, ed. Howard and Paret, 646.

86. Dallas Irvine, "The French Discovery of Clausewitz and Napoleon," *Journal of the American Military Institute* 4 (1940): 143–61. Irvine cited mostly French and German thinkers (and Wilkinson) and mentioned neither Fuller nor Liddell Hart.

87. Letter, Gilbert to me, 25 July 1990.

88. Felix Gilbert remembers DeWeerd (1902–79) as one American scholar who came to the seminars with a ready knowledge of Clausewitz. Gilbert to me, 25 July 1990. DeWeerd was editor of *Military Affairs* from 1937 to 1942 and associate editor of Joe Greene's *Infantry Journal* from 1942 to 1945. After the war, like Bernard Brodie, he became an important member of the RAND Corporation. All his published references to Clausewitz are ambiguous.

89. Possony (born in Vienna in 1913 and emigrated in 1940) became closely associated with the U.S. Air Force. Karl von Clausewitz, *War, Politics, and Power: Selections from On War, and I Believe and Profess,* ed. and trans. Colonel [USAF] Edward M. Collins (Chicago: Henry Regnery, 1962), was published by one of his students.

90. Gilbert to me, 13 July 1990.

91. Ibid.

92. Craig was drafted into the project by Gilbert and first became interested in Clausewitz at that time. Gilbert to me, 27 May 1990, 10 September 1990.

93. Rosinski's contribution was late and violated all of Earle's editorial guidance. Rosinski partially redeemed himself with an enthusiastic review of Earle's book in *Infantry Journal,* December 1943, 57–59, but criticized Earle's failure to include a discussion of the British school of sea power (Corbett went almost unmentioned). Earle accepted this criticism as valid. Earle to Rosinski, 26 November 1943, Herbert F. Rosinski Papers Series II, Box 2, Folder 12.

94. Rothfels was critical of Liddell Hart's treatment of Clausewitz in his article. "Irving M. Gibson" [pseud.], "Maginot and Liddell Hart: The Doctrine of Defense" (which also discussed Fuller) makes no mention of the topic.

95. Earle sent Eisenhower a copy of *Makers of Modern Strategy,* but it appears that Ike never read it. Letter, John Eisenhower to Robert E. Davison (acting superintendent, Gettysburg National Park), 14 April 1990.

96. Cited in Richard P. Stebbins, *The Career of Herbert Roskinski: An Intellectual Pilgrimage* (New York: Peter Lang, 1989), 60. Palmer's letters to Rosinski, 1941–46, appear in Herbert F. Rosinski Papers Series II, Box 3, Folder 5.

Chapter 19

1. See especially General Ritter von Leeb's (1876–1956) highly Clausewitzian tract on defense: *Defense,* trans. Dr. Stefan T. Possony and Daniel Vilfroy (Harrisburg, PA: Military Service Publishing, 1943).

2. Recounted in Hans Delbrück's Preface to vol. 4 of *History of the Art of War Within the Framework of Political History,* trans Walter J. Renfroe, Jr. (Westport, CT: Greenwood Press, 1985).

3. As Jehuda L. Wallach points out in *The Dogma of the Battle of Annihilation: The Theories of Clausewitz and Schlieffen and Their Impact on the German Conduct of Two World Wars* (Westport, CT: Greenwood Press, 1986), 42–44, Schlieffen's understanding of Delbrück's analysis was incomplete, and the basis for his strategic concept had been laid before he read about Cannae.

4. Spenser Wilkinson—writing to Colonel (US) Marius Scammell, 4 March

1928—was ambivalent: "Have you read Delbrück on numbers at Marathon? Worth reading though I think not trustworthy. Delbrück has written a history of war which [you] should perhaps look at." Spenser Wilkinson Papers 13/68.

5. Gordon A. Craig, "Delbrück: The Military Historian," in *Makers of Modern Strategy: Military Thought from Machiavelli to Hitler*, ed. Edward Mead Earle (Princeton, NJ: Princeton University Press, 1943); Peter Paret, ed., *Makers of Modern Strategy: From Machiavelli to the Nuclear Age* (Princeton, NJ: Princeton University Prss, 1986). Fuller's knowledge of Delbrück came from Craig's discussion. J. F. C. Fuller, *The Second World War, 1939–45: A Strategical and Tactical History* (New York: Duell, Sloan and Pearce, 1949), 32–33.

6. Little of Delbrück's work appeared in English. Some of his more inflammatory nationalist comments appeared in British and American Great War propaganda. An extended comment from the *Preussiche Jahrbücher* concerning Germany's colonial ambitions was reproduced in the London *Times* of 25 July 1917; it also appeared in Committee on Public Information, *Conquest and Kultur: Aims of the Germans in Their Own Words* (Washington, DC: Committee on Public Information, January 1918) and was quoted elsewhere. Delbrück's "The German Military System" appeared in Various German Writers, *Modern Germany in Relation to the Great War*, trans. William Wallace Whitelock (New York: Mitchell Kennerley, 1916) (originally *Deutschland und der Weltkrieg*, 1915), 169–83. Delbrück's magnum opus, *Geschichte der Kriegskunst im Rahmen der politischen Geschichte* (4 vols., 1900–20; a further 3 vols. in the series were completed by other writers by 1936), did not begin to appear in English until 1975: Hans Delbrück, *History of the Art of War within the Framework of Political History*, trans. [Brigadier General, USA] Walter J. Renfroe, Jr., 4 vols. (Westport, CT: Greenwood Press, 1975–85). The only writers I know to have used Delbrück's concept of "two poles" of war were classicists. See, for example, F. E. Adcock, *The Roman Art of War Under the Republic* (Cambridge, MA: Harvard University Press, 1940), 77–78.

7. Gordon A. Craig, *The Politics of the Prussian Army, 1640–1945* (Oxford: Clarendon Press, 1955).

8. Letter, Craig to me, 10 September 1990.

9. These ideas are discussed throughout Delbrück's *History of the Art of War*. See especially vol. 4, chap. 4, 293–318. Delbrück discussed the controversy over Frederick the Great on pp439–44.

10. Craig, "Delbrück," in Earle, ed., *Makers of Modern Strategy*, 261. Italics added.

11. Craig, "Delbrück," in Paret, ed., *Makers of Modern Strategy*, 327.

12. Craig, "Delbrück," in Earle, ed., *Makers of Modern Strategy*, 341.

13. Craig, "Delbrück," in Paret, ed., *Makers of Modern Strategy*, 341.

14. Delbrück's 1913 *Numbers in History* contained the Marathon study (without the supporting documentation in *Art of War*, vol. 1, 72–90), but it does not appear to have been widely read during the period under discussion.

15. See Alfred H. Burne's *The Agincourt War* (London: Eyre and Spottiswoode, 1956), 12, and *Strategy, as Exemplified in the Second World War* (Cambridge: Cambridge University Press, 1946), 14.

16. John Keegan, *The Face of Battle* (New York: Viking-Penguin, 1976), 34–35, 54. Keegan has expressed distinct hostility to Clausewitz (and to things German in general): See, John Keegan, "Peace by Other Means?: War, popular opinion and the politically incorrect Clausewitz," *Times Literary Supplement*, 11 December 1992: 3–4. In *The Face of Battle*, however, he said that Delbrück "had almost always

talked sense." He then went on to argue, unaccountably, that nuclear strategists like Herman Kahn were nothing but "Hans Delbrück writ large."

17. Gatzke's translation was based on the 1936 German edition edited by Luftwaffe General Friedrich von Cochenhausen.

18. Alfred Vagts, review of Carl von Clausewitz, *Principles of War*, trans. Hans W. Gatzke (Harrisburg, PA: Military Service Publishing, 1942), *New Republic*, 9 November 1942, 616.

19. *Cavalry Journal*, September–October 1942, 94.

20. As revealed in Phillips, ed., *Roots of Strategy* (Harrisburg, PA: Military Service Publishing, 1943).

21. Clive Garsia, "The War and Strategy," *International Affairs* 19 (1943): 676–77.

22. Alfred Vagts, review of Clausewitz, *Principles*.

23. Conversation with Detlev Vagts (his son), 12 October 1991.

24. Alfred Vagts, *A History of Militarism: Civilian and Military*, revised ed. (New York: Free Press, 1959), 13.

25. One frankly hostile treatment by an expatriate German was Albert T. Lauterbach's "Roots and Implications of the German Idea of Military Society," *Military Affairs* 5 (1941): 1–20. Lauterbach (1904–), an Austrian Jew and political economist who emigrated to the United States in 1938, saw Clausewitz's concept of "absolute war" as "clearly a forerunner of totalitarian warfare." Clausewitz saw "annihilation of the enemy as the real purpose of warfare (and therefore implicitly of politics!)." He denied any connection between the approaches to war of Clausewitz and Frederick the Great because "although [the latter's] ruthlessness and cynicism could hardly be exceeded, there is little reason to believe that he thought of totalitarian wars or annihilation strategy in their present-day meaning." Ludendorff's ideas were "just new formulas for the same way of thinking," and Hitler was a Clausewitzian.

26. It has been my own suggestion that Graham's translation of *On War* in 1873 was little connected to events and had virtually no short-term impact in Britain, an argument that would negate this particular theory. However, the post–South African War fashion for Clausewitz in Britain coincides well in time with the professionalization of the British army via the Haldane reforms.

27. Vagts credited this argument to Hans Rothfels, *Carl von Clausewitz; Politik und Krieg: Eine ideengeschichtliche Studie* (Berlin: F. Dümmler, 1920; reprinted 1980), 191.

28. Vagts, *History of Militarism*, 183–85.

29. Vagts's review of Gatzke, ed., *Principles*.

30. Jolles has been identified as Hungarian, Czech, and Dutch. Jay Luvaas, in his lecture "Clausewitz and the American Experience" (Carlisle, PA: U.S. Army War College, 1982) quoted an unidentified Israeli professor as saying "whereas the first English translation was by an Englishman who did not know German, the 1943 American translation was by a Hungarian who did not know English." There is little in the Jolles translation to warrant such a comment.

31. Letter, Prof. A. L. H. Rubin to (university president) Robert Hutchins, 17 November 1941. President's Papers, University of Chicago, 1925–45, 92/8.

32. Robert M. Hutchins, "Military Education and Research," 28 February 1941. President's Papers, University of Chicago, 1925–45, 92/10, 14–16.

33. Hutchins to Harvey H. Bundy (special assistant to the secretary of war), 10 June 1942. President's Papers, University of Chicago, 1925–45, 93/1.

34. O. J. Matthijs Jolles, "Introduction" to Carl von Clausewitz, *On War*, trans. O. J. Matthijs Jolles (New York: Random House, 1943; Washington, DC: Infantry Journal Press, 1950), xxvi. His math is suspect; Book 6 represents only one quarter of *On War* by page count.

35. Rothfels, *Clausewitz; Politik und Krieg*; Karl von Clausewitz, *Politische Schriften und Briefe*, ed. Hans Rothfels (München: Drei Masken Verlag, 1922).

36. Hans Rothfels, "Clausewitz," in *Makers of Modern Strategy: Military Thought from Machiavellit to Hitler*, ed. Edward Mead Earle (Princeton, NJ: Princeton University Press, 1944), 93–113. Letter, Howard to me, 26 September 1990.

37. He was also critical of R. M. Johnston, F. B. Maurice, and the Graham translation.

38. Peter Paret, *Clausewitz and the State: The Man, His Theories, and His times* (Princeton, NY: Princeton University Press, 1976), 129, n. 15; 134, 135, n. 32; 163, n. 31; 169, n. 1; 302–03, 432–35, 443.

39. Ibid., 433, citing Rothfels, Clausewitz; *Politik und Krieg*, 70.

40. See Barry H. Steiner, "On Strategy and Strategists," in his *Bernard Brodie and the Foundations of American Nuclear Strategy* (Lawrence, KS: University Press of Kansas, 1991).

41. Richard P. Stebbins, *The Career of Herbert Rosinski: An Intellectual Pilgrimage* (New York: Peter Lang, 1989).

42. Herbert Rosinski, *"Die Entwicklung von Clausewitz Werk "Vom Kriege" im Licht seiner 'Vorreden' und 'Nachrichten,'* "*Historische Zeitschrift* 151 (1935): 278–93.

43. An earlier paper, "Clausewitz als Lebensphilosoph," had appeared in *Der Volkswirt* 31 (1932): 56. An unpublished typescript exists in Rosinski's papers (7/1), "Ueber die Theorie des Kriegs," but this may date from much later (1953?).

44. Azar Gat's *The Origins of Military Thought: From the Enlightenment to Clausewitz* (Oxford: Oxford University Press, 1989), contains an argumentative but convincing appendix discussing this issue.

45. Herbert F. Rosinski, *The German Army* (New York: Praeger, 1966; original ed., 1939), 112.

46. Rosinski to Princeton University Press (Smith), 12 June 1942. Herbert F. Rosinski Papers, Series II, Box 3, Folder 7.

47. Herbert F. Rosinski, Review, "IMS: Captain Falls on Modern Warfare," of Cyril Falls, *Nature of Modern Warfare*, *Infantry Journal* 50 (January 1942): 78–81. Falls himself made much the same point, without the implied criticism, in his *The Art of War: From the Age of Napoleon to the Present Day* (New York: Oxford University Press, 1961), 6–7.

48. Herbert F. Rosinski Papers Series II, 3/4. The project is also discussed in Stebbins, *Rosinski*, 61–62.

49. Herbert Rosinski, *Power and Human Destiny* (New York: Praeger, 1965) and *The Development of Naval Thought*, ed. B. Mitchell Simpson III (Newport, RI: Naval War College Press, 1977).

50. Rosinski to his ex-wife, Maria-Luise Stebbins, around 1961, quoted in Stebbins, *Rosinski*, 165–66.

51. See Herbert F. Rosinski Papers, Series IV, 6/3, "The Role of Civilian Scholars in the Study of War."

52. Herbert F. Rosinski Papers, Series IV, 6/18, "Clausewitz," a lecture delivered at the U.S. Naval War College on 17 November 1953.

53. Cited in Stebbins, *Rosinski*, 149.

54. Raymond Aron (1905–83), *Clausewitz: Philosopher of War*, trans. Christine Booker and Norman Stone (Englewood Cliffs, NJ: Prentice-Hall, 1985), vii.

55. Lectures on Clausewitz given at Oxford exist in several versions in Herbert F. Rosinski Papers Series IV, 5/27.

56. Letter, Gilbert to me, 25 July 1990.

57. See Henry E. Eccles (Admiral, USN), *Military Concepts and Philosophy* (New Brunswick, NJ: Rutgers University Press, 1965).

58. See references to Rosinski in Bernard Brodie, "Clausewitz: A Passion for War," *World Politics* 25 (January 1973): 288–308.

59. See Stebbins, *Rosinski*, 155–56, and Rosinski's critique of Brodie's work in Herbert F. Rosinski Papers, Series II, 3/7, especially his letter of 15 May 1942.

60. Paret rarely mentions him. Perhaps most curious is Jehuda Wallach's failure in *The Dogma of the Battle of Annihilation: The Theories of Clausewitz and Schlieffen and Their Impact on the German Conduct of Two World Wars* (Westport, CT: Greenwood Press, 1986) to cite Rosinski's draft "Clausewitz and Schlieffen" (Herbert F. Rosinski Papers Series V, Box 7, Folder 2) or his published "Scharnhorst to Schlieffen: The Rise and Decline of German Military Thought," *United States Naval War College Review* 29 (Summer 1976): 83–103. Wallach does discuss *The German Army*.

Chapter 21

1. Forrest K. Kleinman, "The Pied Piper of Modern Military Thought," *Military Review* 37 (November 1957): 56–64. Although Kleinman referred repeatedly for support to intellectual figures like Arnold Toynbee, Friedrich Nietzsche, and the semanticist Alfred Korzybski, his argument is so shallow that it is not worth analyzing here. See also Forrest K. Kleinman and Robert S. Horowitz, *The Modern United States Army* (New York: D. Van Nostrand, 1964).

2. For example, chap. 13, "Employment of Secret Agents."

3. Carl von Clausewitz, *On War*, ed. Anatole Rapoport (Baltimore: Penguin Books, 1968).

4. See Anatol Rapoport, *Strategy and Conscience* (New York: Harper & Row, 1964), which describes Rapoport's relevant views.

5. Rapoport, ed., *On War*, 13, 54–80. The term was also picked up by Michael Howard in his Foreword to Roger Parkinson's *Clausewitz: A Biography* (Briarcliff Manor, NY: Stein & Day, 1971), 11. Howard, of course, meant it as a compliment.

6. Rapoport, ed., *On War*, 67; Herman Kahn, *On Thermonuclear War* (Princeton, NJ: Princeton University Press, 1961), 163.

7. Herman Kahn, *Thinking About the Unthinkable* (New York: Horizon Press, 1962).

8. Michael Howard, "The Military Philosopher," *Times Literary Supplement*, 25 June 1976, 754–55.

9. Clausewitz receives no mention in Kissinger's own *White House Years* (Boston: Little, Brown, 1979); it appears that the discussion in his *Nuclear Weapons and Foreign Policy* (New York: Harper Bros. 1957) was his only extended reference. Among Kissinger's biographers, only Bruce Mazlish, *Kissinger: The European Mind in American Policy* (New York: Basic Books, 1976), attempts to show him as a "disciple of Clausewitz" (233). Peter W. Dickson, *Kissinger and*

the Meaning of History (Cambridge: Cambridge University Press, 1978), 168, n. 3, specifically attacks this thesis, arguing that "there is no evidence that Kissinger had read either Metternich or Clausewitz before completing his undergraduate thesis," that is, before he turned twenty-seven. Even Mazlish (58) acknowledges that "Kissinger never became a scholar in relation to" Clausewitz.

10. Henry A. Kissinger, *A World Restored: Metternich, Castlereagh, and the Problems of Peace, 1812–1822* (Boston: Houghton Mifflin, 1957, 1973).

11. Kissinger, *Nuclear Weapons and Foreign Policy*, 340–44.

12. Kissinger cited Lenin's marginalia to Clausewitz in "Cahier de Lénine no. 18674 des Archives de l'Institut Lénine à Moscow," in *Les Fondements théoretiques de la guerre et de la paix en U.R.S.S.*, ed. Bertholdt C. Friedl (Paris: Éditions médicis, 1945), 47–90. For Lenin's relevant views in English, see also V. I. Lenin, *Collected Works*, "The Collapse of the Second International" (1915), vol. 21 (205–59, especially 219; "War and Revolution" (a lecture delivered on 14 May 1917), vol. 24, 398–421; "Left-Wing Childishness and the Petty-Bourgeois Mentality" (1918), vol. 27, 323–54, especially 32; "Speeches at a Meeting of Members of the German, Polish, Czechoslovak, Hungarian and Italian Delegations" (11 July 1921, speech no. 1), vol. 42, 324–27.

13. Henry A. Kissinger, *Years of Upheaval* (Boston: Little, Brown, 1982), 562–63, 989; Hans Morgenthau, *Politics Among Nations: The Struggle for Power and Peace*, 6th ed. (New York: Knopf, 1985), 379.

14. United States Military Academy, Department of Military Art and Engineering, *Clausewitz, Jomini, Schlieffen* (Westport, NY: USMA, 1951, 1964).

15. Edward Luttwak, *The Grand Strategy of the Roman Empire: From the First Century A.D. to the Third* (Baltimore: Johns Hopkins University Press, 1976), 61; compare Luttwak's review of *On War* and Paret's *Clausewitz and the State*, in *New Republic*, 14 May 1977, 36–37.

16. Michael Walzer, *Just and Unjust Wars: A Moral Argument with Historical Illustrations* (New York: Basic books, 1977), 22–25. Walzer based his argument on a reading of Collins's heavily abridged version of *On War*.

17. Joel Achenbach, "War and the Cult of Clausewitz," *Washington Post*, 6 December 1990, D1.

18. Manus A. Midlarsky, *On War: Political Violence in the International System* (New York: Free Press, 1975), 1.

19. U.S. Air Force Office of the Director of Intelligence, "Outlines of the Principles of Warfare from Clausewitz to the Present Time" ("An unclassified study, in outline form, dealing with the development of modern theories of warfare as propounded by Clausewitz, Ludendorff, Engels and Marx, Trotsky, Lenin and Stalin") (Maxwell Air Force Base, AL: Air University Press, 1949); Byron Dexter, "Clausewitz and Soviet Strategy," *Foreign Affairs* 29 (October 1950): 41–55; Werner Hahlweg, "Clausewitz, Lenin and Communist Military Attitudes Today," *Journal of the United Service Institutes* 105 (May 1960): 221–25; Donald E. Davis and Walter S. G. Kohn, "Lenin as Disciple of Clausewitz," *Military Review*, September 1971, 49–55; W. B. Gallie, *Philosophers of Peace and War: Kant, Clausewitz, Marx, Engels and Tolstoy* (Cambridge: Cambridge University Press, 1978); Jacob W. Kipp, "Lenin and Clausewitz: The Militarization of Marxism, 1914–1921," *Military Affairs*, October 1985, 184–91; Roman Kolkowicz, "On Limited War: Soviet Approaches," in *New Directions in Strategic Thinking*, ed. Robert O'Neill and D.M. Horner (London: Allen & Unwin, 1981), 75–88. See also sources for Lenin's views on Clausewitz, discussed in n. 12.

20. On Mao and Clausewitz, see W. O. Staudenmaier, "Vietnam, Mao and Clausewitz," *Parameters* 7 (1977): 79–89; R. Lynn Rylander, "Mao as a Clausewitzian Strategist," *Military Review* 61 (1981): 13–21; Alexander Atkinson, *Social Order and the General Theory of Strategy* (London: Routledge & Kegan Paul, 1981).

21. See William V. Murry, "Clausewitz and Limited Nuclear War," *Military Review* 55 (April 1975): 15–28; R. A. Mason (RAF), "Clausewitz in the Nuclear Age," *Journal of the Royal United Service Institution*, September 1977, 81–82; Jack H. Nunn, [Major USAR], "Termination: The Myth of the Short, Decisive Nuclear War," *Parameters*, December 1980, 36–41; Bruce R. Nardulli, "Clausewitz and the Reorientation of Nuclear Strategy," *Journal of Strategic Studies*, December 1982, 494–510; Nicholas H. Fritz, Jr., [Colonel, USAF], "Clausewitz and U.S. Nuclear Weapons Policy," *Air University Review*, November–December 1982, 18–28; Richard Ned Lebow, "Clausewitz and Nuclear Crisis Stability," *Political Science Quarterly*, Spring 1988, 89–110; Robert Endicott Osgood, *The Nuclear Dilemma in American Strategic Thought* (Boulder, CO: Westview Press, 1988); John E. Shephard, Jr. [Major, USA], *"On War: Is Clausewitz Still Relevant?" Parameters*, September 1990, 85–99; Stephen J. Cimbala, *Clausewitz and Escalation: Classical Perspective on Nuclear Strategy* (London: Frank Cass, 1991).

22. Basil H. Liddell Hart, "War, Limited," *Harper's Magazine*, March 1946, 193–203.

23. See, for example, Seymour J. Deitchman, *Limited War and American Defense Policy* (Cambridge, MA: MIT Press, 1964). The only contemporary discussion of which I am aware linking Clausewitz and the ongoing war in Korea was French: René Silvain, "Clausewitz et la guerre de Corée," *Revue politique et parlementaire*, October 1951, 165–72. Russell F. Weigley, *The American Way of War: A History of United States Military Strategy and Policy* (New York: Macmillan, 1973), managed to make almost no reference at all to Clausewitz in its long discussion of post–World War II U.S. military policy (although the book as a whole demonstrated a new appreciation of the philosopher). Morton H. Halperin, *Limited War: An Essay on the Development of the Theory and An Annotated Bibliography* (Cambridge: Center for International Affairs, Harvard University, 1962), makes no significant refrence to Clausewitz as originator of the concept. His description of "Clausewitzian war" there and in *Limited War in the Nuclear Age* (New York: John Wiley and Sons, 1963) betrays no reading in Clausewitz beyond Chapter 1 of *On War*. The connection was made in John W. Spanier, *The Truman–MacArthur Controversy and the Korean War* (New York: Norton, 1959, 1965); David Rees, *Korea: The Limited War* (New York: St. Martin's Press, 1964); and Robert McClintock, *The Meaning of Limited War* (Boston: Houghton Mifflin, 1967).

24. Robert Endicott Osgood, *Limited War: The Challenge to American Strategy* (Chicago: University of Chicago Press, 1957), especially 21–23, 123.

25. Robert Endicott Osgood, *Limited War Revisited* (Boulder, CO: Westview Press, 1979), 2.

26. Lebow, "Clausewitz and Nuclear Crisis Stability."

27. Samuel P. Huntington, *The Soldier and the State: The Theory and Politics of Civil–Military Relations* (Cambridge, MA: Harvard University Press, 1957), 55–58.

28. For prominent U.S. Navy treatments of Clausewitz in this period, see

Paul R. Schratz [Captain, USN], "Clausewitz, Cuba, and Command," *United States Naval Institute Proceedings*, August 1964, 24–33; Henry E. Eccles [Admiral, USN], *Military Concepts and Philosophy* (New Brunswick, NJ: Rutgers University Press, 1965); James E. King, "On Clausewitz: Master Theorist of War," *Naval War College Review*, Fall 1977, 3–36. King was director of strategic research at the Naval War College from 1972 to 1977.

29. Casyndekan, Inc., *The Clausewitz Casyndekan* (Colorado Springs: Casyndekan, Inc., 1969).

30. *On War*, bk. 1, chap. 1, sec. 25, trans. Michael Howard and Peter Paret (Princeton, NJ: Princeton University Press, 1976).

31. *On War*, bk. 8, chap. 6.

32. Harry G. Summers, Jr., *On Strategy: A Critical Analysis of the Vietnam War* (Novato, CA: Presidio Press, 1982).

33. Caspar Weinberger, "The Use of Force and the National Will," *Baltimore Sun*, 3 December 1984, 11; Major [USMC] John F. Otis, Jr., "Clausewitz: On Weinberger," *Marine Corps Gazette*, February 1988, 16–17; Alan Ned Sabrosky and Robert L. Sloane, eds., *The Recourse to War: An Appraisal of the "Weinberger Doctrine"* (Carlisle, PA: Strategic Studies Institute, 1988). Future chairman of the Joint Chiefs of Staff General (USA) Colin Powell was Weinberger's influential military assistant at the time.

34. Headquarters, U.S. Marine Corps, *FMFM 1: Warfighting* (Washington, DC: U.S. Government Printing Office, 1989).

35. Headquarters, Department of the Army, *FM 100–5 Operations* (Washington, DC: U.S. Government Printing Office, 1982, 1986); Colonel Huba Wass de Czege, "Clausewitz: Historical Studies Remain Sound Compass References; The Catch Is Staying on Course," *ARMY*, September 1988, 37–43. Wass de Czege wrote a detailed *Guide to the Study of Clausewitz, On War* for use in the Advanced Military Studies Program at Fort Leavenworth.

36. Steven J. Argersinger, "Karl von Clausewitz: Analysis of FM 100–5," *Military Review* 66 (February 1986): 68–75; Lieutenant Colonel [USA] Archie Galloway, "FM 100–5: Who Influenced Whom?" *Military Review*, March 1986, 46–51; James J. Schneider and Lawrence J. Izzo, "Clausewitz's Elusive Center of Gravity," *Parameters* 17 (September 1987): 46–57; Richard M. Swain [Colonel, USA], "Clausewitz, FM 100–5, and the Center of Gravity," *Military Review*, February 1988, 83; Steven Metz and Lieutenant [USA] Frederick M. Downey, "Centers of Gravity and Strategic Planning," *Military Review*, April 1988, 22–33. *FMFM 1*, chap. 2, n. 28, acknowledges the difference between its definition and Clausewitz's.

37. See Lieutenant Colonel [USAF] David MacIsaac, "Master at Arms: Clausewitz in Full View," *Air University Review*, January–February 1979, 83–79.

38. LTC (USAF) Barry D. Watts, *The Foundations of US Air Doctrine: The Problem of Friction in War* (Maxwell Air Force Base, AL: Air University Press, 1984). Mark A. Clodfelter, "The Air War Against North Vietnam, 1965–1972: A Clausewitzian Appraisal and Perception of Effectiveness," paper presented at the annual meeting of the American Historical Association at Cincinnati, 1988; Mark A. Clodfelter, *The Limits of Air Power: The American Bombing of North Vietnam* (New York: Free Press, 1989).

39. See Colonel (USA) Mitchell M. Zais, "West Point: Swordmaking or Swordsmanship?" *Armed Forces Journal International*, March 1990, 57–62. (The title is a reference to the metaphorical use of the sword in *On War*.) See also

Commander [USCG] James F. McEntire, "Engineers or Guardians?" *United States Naval Institute Proceedings*, December 1990, 74–76.

40. Theodore Ropp, *War in the Modern World* (Durham, NC: Duke University Press, 1959). See also Ropp, "Strategic Thinking Since 1945," in O'Neill and Horner, eds., *New Directions in Strategic Thinking*, 1–13.

41. A list of Ropp's Ph.D. students is given as an appendix to Ropp's *History & War* (Augusta, GA: Hamburg Press, 1984), 77–80.

42. S. L. A. Marshall, *Blitzkrieg: Its History, Strategy, Economics and the Challenge to America* (New York: Morrow, 1940), 19–20, 144.

43. See Bernard Brodie's "Technological Change, Strategic Doctrine, and Political Outcomes," in *Historical Dimensions of National Security Problems*, ed. Klaus Knorr (Lawrence: University Press of Kansas, 1976), 263–306. See also Rosinski's critique of Brodie's work in Herbert F. Rosinski Papers, Series II, 3/7, especially his letter of 15 May 1942.

44. See King's critique of Brodie in "On Clausewitz: Master Theorist of War."

45. Bernard Brodie, ed., *The Absolute Weapon: Atomic Power and World Order* (New York: Harcourt Brace, 1946).

46. Barry H. Steiner, "Using the Absolute Weapon: Early Ideas of Bernard Brodie on Atomic Strategy," *Journal of Strategic Studies*, December 1984, 365–393, and especially 387, n. 18.

47. Letter, Howard to me, 9 May 1990.

48. Aside from Peter Paret's work, see Parkinson, *Clausewitz: A Biography*; Roger Ashley Leonard, *A Short Guide to Clausewitz On War* (New York: Putnam, 1967). Azar Gat was Howard's student from 1984 to 1986.

49. Department of Public Information, Princeton University, news release, 10 April 1964.

50. Letter, Howard to me, 9 May 1990.

51. The Howard/Paret translation of *On War* is compared with others in Chapter 4.

52. Parkinson, *Clausewitz: A Biography*, which Paret—rather characteristically—referred to as "much inferior . . . a poor specimen of popular biography, full of factual errors, howlers, and references to non-existent works." See Peter Paret, *Clausewitz and the State: The Man, His Theories, and His Times* (Princeton, NJ: Princeton University Press, 1976), 443. Paret is, of course, quite right about the errors, mostly in historical background. On the other hand, as Bernard Brodie pointed out, Paret's own biography, though a marvelous work of scholarship, is rather narrowly intellectual in focus. Parkinson gives a vibrant portrait of Clausewitz the man and soldier. See reviews by Bernard Brodie, "Clausewitz: A Passion for War," *World Politics* 25 (January 1973): 288–308; Gordon A. Craig, "Nothing Like a Good War," *New York Times Book Review*, 23 May 1971, 4, 26; A. J. P. Taylor, "Rational Wars?" *New York Review of Books*, 4 November 1971, 36–37.

53. Raymond Aron, *Clausewitz: Philosopher of War*, trans. Christine Booker and Norman Stone. The translation has been criticized and the book, though receiving much praise for its erudition, does not appear to have been widely read or cited.

54. Quoted in Achenbach, "War and the Cult of Clausewitz."

55. See Bjørn Møller, *Resolving the Security Dilemma in Europe: The German Debate on Non-Offensive Defence* (London: Brassey's, 1991), especially 8, 39–40.

56. Richard E. Beringer, Herman Hattaway, Archer Jones, and William N. Still, Jr., *The Elements of Confederate Defeat: Nationalism, War Aims, and Religion* (Athens: University of Georgia Press, 1988).

57. Charles P. Roland, *An American Iliad: The Story of the Civil War* (Lexington: University Press of Kentucky, 1991).

58. Eliot A. Cohen and John Gooch, *Military Misfortunes: The Anatomy of Failure in War* (New York: Free Press, 1990).

59. T. N. Dupuy, *Understanding War: History and Theory of Combat* (New York: Paragon House, 1987), 21-22. Dupuy's earlier *Numbers, Predictions and War* (Indianapolis: Bobbs-Merrill, 1979), makes little reference to the philosopher.

60. For an excellent Clausewitzian critique of the notion of using mathematical models as the basis for assessing the military balance, see Eliot A. Cohen, "Toward Better Net Assessment," International Security, Summer 1988, 50-87.

61. Where P = combat power; N = numbers of troops; V = variable circumstances affecting a force in battle [!]; and Q = quality of force. Dupuy, *Understanding War*, 30.

62. Achenbach, "War and the Cult of Clausewitz," quoting Colonel (USA, retired) Arthur Lykke, a senior professor of strategy at the Army War College; Colonel Lloyd Matthews, editor of *Parameters*, letter 17 July 1989. One of the best critiques of *FM 100-5: Operations* from the Clausewitzian standpoint was made by Colonel (USA) Richard M. Swain in an unpublished letter to the editor of *ARMY*, 28 August 1988, which criticized Wass de Czege for an "intuitive" approach to history and doctrine.

63. John E. Shephard, Jr., makes a recent case for Clausewitz's partial obsolescence in "*On War*: Is Clausewitz Still Relevant?" See also Bruce R. Nardulli, "Clausewitz and the Reorientation of Nuclear Strategy," *Journal of Strategic Studies*, December 1982, 494-510.

64. David G. Chandler, in an enthusiastic review of Weigley's *Age of Battles*, *Journal of Military History*, April 1992, 294-95.

65. Martin van Creveld, *The Transformation of War* (New York: Free Press, 1991); letter, van Creveld to me, 7 November 1990.

66. Bernard Brodie often made puzzled references, for example, in "The Continuing Relevance of *On War*," in Carl von Clausewitz, *On War*, ed. and trans. Michael Howard and Peter Paret (Princeton, NJ: Princeton University Press, 1976), 50, to the failure of modern military thought to incorporate and supersede Clausewitz, in the manner in which, say, Adam Smith's contribution to economics has been.

Chapter 22

1. Russell F. Weigley, "Military Strategy and Civilian Leadership," in *Historical Dimensions of National Security Problems*, ed. Klaus Knorr (Lawrence: University Press of Kansas, 1976), 38-77.

2. Russell F. Weigley, *The Age of Battles: The Quest for Decisive Warfare from Breitenfeld to Waterloo* (Bloomington: Indiana University Press, 1991), 543; interview, Quantico, VA, 9 September 1992.

3. Truman closely supervised the preparation of his memoirs, and thus the rather interesting reference to Clausewitz therein may represent some actual familiarity on his part. The context was not MacArthur and Korea, but the subject

was the political control of war. *Year of Decisions,* vol. 1 of *Memoirs by Harry S. Truman* (New York: Doubleday, 1955), 210.

4. See Raymond B. Furlong [Lieutenant General, USAF and Commander, Air University], "Strategymaking for the 1980's," *Parameters,* March 1979, 9–16, and "*On War,* Political Objectives, and Military Strategy," *Parameters,* December 1983, 2–10.

5. Samuel P. Huntington, *The Soldier and the State: The Theory and Politics of Civil–Military Relations* (Cambridge, MA: Harvard University Press, 1957), chap. 2.

6. Azar Gat, *The Origins of Military Thought: From the Enlightenment to Clausewitz* (Oxford: Oxford University Press, 1989), 169–70.

7. A point also made frequently in print. See, for example, Joseph Caldwell Wylie [Rear Admiral, USN], *Military Strategy: A General Theory of Power Control* (New Brunswick, NJ: Rutgers University Press, 1967), 53.

8. On this topic, see Ian Clark, *Waging War: A Philosophical Introduction* (Oxford: Clarendon Press, 1988), which is somewhat inevitably an inconclusive exploration.

9. It is impossible, of course, to draw a truly accurate picture of Clausewitz's readership. People like William Sloane of Rutger's University Press, Robert Hutchins (president of the University of Chicago), and possibly George Orwell, Nathaniel Wright Stephenson, and Carl Sandburg seem to have had some familiarity with his work. They might be total aberrations or the tip of some significant iceberg.

10. The recent Clausewitz fad in U.S. military doctrine instills little confidence that Clausewitzian theory can easily and directly make the transition from description to prescription without suffering in the process the usual absurdities and rigidities. One example, certainly absurd from the historian's viewpoint: "One can argue that this campaign [Portugal, 1810] was fought between a Clausewitzian (Massena) and a follower of Sun Tzu (Wellington)." Syllabus, "The Historical Practice of Operational Art," School of Advanced Military Studies, Fort Leavenworth, KS, AY 1988/89, 4–4–1.

Select Bibliography

Archival Sources

Archives of the *Edinburgh Review*, University of Reading (UK).
Archives of the John Murray Company, London.
Archives of Kegan Paul, Trench, Trübner and Henry S. King, publishers.
Julian S. Corbett Papers, National Maritime Museum, Greenwich (UK).
Eisenhower Papers, Eisenhower Library.
J. F. C. Fuller Papers, Liddell Hart Centre for Military Archives, King's College London.
Haig Papers, National Library of Scotland.
B. H. Liddell Hart Papers, Liddell Hart Centre for Military Archives, King's College London.
Abraham Lincoln Papers, Library of Congress.
John McAuley Palmer Papers, Library of Congress.
Papers of the Duke of Wellington, University of Southampton (UK).
The President's Papers, 1925–45, University of Chicago.
Public Record Office, Kew (UK).
William R. Robertson Papers, Liddell Hart Centre for Military Archives, King's College London.
Herbert F. Rosinski Papers, U.S. Naval War College Naval Historical Collection.
U.S. Army Military History Institute, Carlisle Barracks.
Spenser Wilkinson Papers, Army Museum's Ogilby Trust (UK).

Books and Articles of Special Interest

Aron, Raymond. "Reason, Passion, and Power in the Thought of Clausewitz." *Social Research*, Winter 1972: 599–621.

Aron, Raymond. "Clausewitz' Conceptual System." *Armed Forces and Society* 1 (November 1974): 49–59.

————. *Clausewitz: Philosopher of War.* Trans. Christine Booker and Norman Stone. Englewood Cliffs, NJ: Prentice-Hall, 1985. Originally *Penser la guerre, Clausewitz.* Paris: Editions Gallimard, 1976.

Atkinson, Alexander. *Social Order and the General Theory of Strategy.* London: Routledge & Kegan Paul, 1981.

Baldwin, P. M. "Clausewitz in Nazi Germany." *Journal of Contemporary History* 16 (1981): 5–26.

Beyerchen, Alan D. "Chance and Complexity in the Real World: Clausewitz on the Nonlinear Nature of War." *International Security,* Winter 1992/93: 59–90.

Brodie, Bernard. "Clausewitz: A Passion for War." (Review of Roger Parkinson's *Clausewitz: A Biography*). *World Politics* 25 (January 1973): 288–308.

————. "The Continuing Relevance of *On War.*" In Carl von Clausewitz, *On War.* Ed. and trans. Michael Howard and Peter Paret, 45–58. Princeton, NJ: Princeton University Press, 1976.

————. "A Guide to the Reading of *On War.*" In Carl von Clausewitz, *On War.* Ed. and trans. Michael Howard and Peter Paret, 641–711. Princeton, NJ: Princeton University Press, 1976.

————. "In Quest of the Unknown Clausewitz." (Review of Peter Paret's *Clausewitz and the State*). *International Security* 1 (Winter 1977): 62–69.

Bucholz, Arden. *Hans Delbrück and the German Military Establishment.* Iowa City: University of Iowa Press, 1985.

Caemmerer, Rudolph von. *The Development of Strategical Science During the Nineteenth Century.* Trans. Karl von Donat. London: Hugh Rees, 1905; reprinted Carlisle, PA: U.S. Army War College, 1983.

Casyndekan, Inc. *The Clausewitz Casyndekan.* Colorado Springs: Casyndekan, Inc., 1969.

Cimbala, Stephen J. *Clausewitz and Escalation: Classical Perspective on Nuclear Strategy.* London: Frank Cass, 1991.

Clark, Ian. *Waging War: A Philosophical Introduction.* Oxford: Clarendon Press, 1988.

Clausewitz, Carl von. "On War." Trans. and ed. unknown. *Military and Naval Magazine of the United States,* 5 and 6 (August–September 1835). Originally appeared in *Metropolitan Magazine* (London) 13 (May–June 1835): 64–71, 166–176.

————. *The Campaign of 1812 in Russia.* Trans. Francis Egerton, Lord Ellesmere. London: John Murray, 1843; reprinted Hattiesburg, MS: Academic International, 1970; reprinted Westport, CT: Greenwood Press, 1977; reprinted, London: Greenhill Books, 1992.

————. *On War.* Trans. Colonel J. J. (James John) Graham. London: N. Trübner, 1873.

————. *On War.* New and rev. ed. 3 vols. Trans. Colonel J. J. Graham and ed. Colonel F. N. Maude. London: K. Paul, Trench, Trübner, and Company, 1908.

————. *General Carl von Clausewitz on War.* Trans. A. M. E. Maguire, with notes by T. (Thomas) Miller Maguire. London: William Clowes and Sons, 1909. Originally ran as a serial in *United Service Magazine,* March 1907– March 1909.

————. "[Extracts from] Notes on Prussia During the Catastrophe of 1806." Trans. Colonel [USA] Conrad H. Lanza. In *Jena Campaign Sourcebook,* 515–603. Fort Leavenworth, KS: The General Service Schools Press, 1922.

———. "Prince August's Battalion in the Battle of Prenzlau." Trans. Colonel [USA] Conrad H. Lanza. In *Jena Campaign Sourcebook*, 604–11. Fort Leavenworth, KS: General Service Schools Press, 1922.

———. *Principles of War*. Trans. Hans W. Gatzke. Harrisburg, PA: Military Service Publishing, 1942; reprinted in Stackpole Books, *Roots of Strategy: Book 2, 3 Military Classics*, 301–86. Harrisburg, PA: Stackpole Books, 1987. Originally "Die wichtigsten Grundsätze des Kriegführens zur Ergänzung meines Unterrichts bei Sr. Königlichen Hoheit dem Kronprinzen" (1812; trans. from the 1936 German ed.), Clausewitz's memorandum for the crown prince. Another translation appears as an appendix to J. J. Graham's translation of *On War*.

———. *On War*. Trans. O. J. (Otto Jolle) Matthijs Jolles. New York: Random House, 1943; Washington, DC: Infantry Journal Press, 1950.

———. *The Living Thoughts of Clausewitz*. Presented by Joseph I. Greene. New York: Longmans, Green, 1943. Based on the Graham translation.

———. *The Living Thoughts of Clausewitz*. Ed. Joseph I. Greene, with an introduction by J. F. C. Fuller. London: Cassell, 1945.

———. *Vom Kriege*. 19th ed. Ed. Werner Hahlweg. Bonn: Ferdinand Dümmlers Verlag, 1952, 1980.

———. *War, Politics, and Power: Selections from On War, and I Believe and Profess*. Ed. and trans. Edward M. Collins [Colonel, USAF]. Chicago: Henry Regnery, 1962.

———. *On War*. Ed. Anatole Rapoport. Baltimore: Penguin Books, 1968. Based on the Graham translation.

———. *On War*. Ed. and trans. Michael Howard and Peter Paret. Princeton, NJ: Princeton University Press, 1976.

———. *Two Letters on Strategy*. Ed. and trans. Peter Paret and Daniel Moran. Carlisle, PA: Army War College Foundation, 1984.

———. *Historical and Political Writings*. Ed. and trans. Peter Paret and Daniel Moran. Princeton, NJ: Princeton University Press, 1992. Includes "Some Comments on the War of the Spanish Succession After Reading the Letters of Madame de Maintenon to the Princess des Ursins"; "Observations on the Wars of the Austrian Succession"; excerpts from "Observations on Prussia in Her Great Catastrophe"; "On the Life and Character of Scharnhorst"; excerpts from "The Campaign of 1812 in Russia"; excerpts from "Strategic Critique of the Campaign of 1814 in France"; "The Germans and the French"; excerpts from the "Political Declaration" of 1812; "Our Military Institutions"; "On the Political Advantages and Disadvantages of the Prussian *Landwehr*"; "Agitation"; "Europe Since the Polish Partitions"; and "On the Basic Question of Germany's Existence."

Clausewitz, Carl von, and the Duke of Wellington. *On Waterloo*. Ed. Christopher Bassford. Boulder, CO: Westview Press, in press.

Clodfelter, Mark A. "The Air War Against North Vietnam, 1965–1972: A Clausewitzian Appraisal and Perception of Effectiveness." Paper presented at the annual meeting of the American Historical Association, Cincinnati, 1988.

Cohen, Eliot A. "Toward Better Net Assessment." *International Security* 13 (Summer 1988): 50–87.

Cohen, Eliot A., and John Gooch. *Military Misfortunes: The Anatomy of Failure in War*. New York: Free Press, 1990.

Colin, Jean Lambert Alphonse. *The Transformations of War*. Trans. L. H. K.

Pope-Hennessy. London: Hugh Rees, 1912; reprinted Westport, CT: Greenwood Press, 1977.

Committee of Imperial Defence. *Report and Proceedings of a Sub-committee of Imperial Defense. Appointed by the Prime Minister to Reconsider the Question of Overseas Attack.* 22 October 1908. London: Public Record Office, Cab. 16/3A.

Corbett, Julian S. *Some Principles of Maritime Strategy.* Annapolis, MD: Naval Institute Press, 1988; originally London: Longmans, Green, 1911.

Craig, Gordon A. "Delbrück: The Military Historian." In *Makers of Modern Strategy: Military Thought from Machiavelli to Hitler.* Ed. Edward Mead Earle, 260–85. Princeton, NJ: Princeton University Press, 1943.

———. "Delbrück: The Military Historian." In *Makers of Modern Strategy: Military Thought from Machiavelli to the Nuclear Age.* Ed. Peter Paret, 326–53. Princeton, NJ: Princeton University Press, 1986.

Creveld, Martin van. "The Eternal Clausewitz." In *Clausewitz and Modern Strategy.* Ed. Michael I. Handell, 35–50. London: Frank Cass, 1986.

———. *The Transformation of War.* New York: Free Press, 1991.

———. "the Clausewitzian Universe and the Law of War." *Journal of Contemporary History,* 26 (1991): 403–429.

Davis, Donald E., and Walter S. G. Kohn. "Lenin as Disciple of Clausewitz." *Military Review,* September 1971, 49–55.

Delbrück, Hans. *History of the Art of War within the Framework of Political History.* Trans. [Brigadier General, USA] Walter J. Renfroe, Jr. 4 vols. Westport, CT: Greenwood Press, 1975–85.

Dexter, Byron. "Clausewitz and Soviet Strategy." *Foreign Affairs* 29 (October 1950): 41–55.

Douglas, William. Review of *On War. United Service Magazine,* August 1873, 469–83; October 1873, 164–76.

Earle, Edward Mead, ed. *Makers of Modern Strategy: Military Thought from Machiavelli to Hitler.* Princeton, NJ: Princeton University Press, 1943.

Echevarria, Antulio J. II [Captain, USAR]. "Clausewitzianism, Freytag-Loringhoven, and German Military Thought, 1890–1914." Ph.D. diss., Princeton University (in progress).

Editors of *Military Affairs,* with an introduction by T. Harry Williams. *Military Analysis of the Civil War: An Anthology.* Millwood, NY: KTO Press, 1977.

Edmonds, Colonel J. E. "Clausewitz and the Downfall of Prussia in 1806." *Army Review,* April 1914: 403–416.

[Edmonds, J. E. (?)]. "Clausewitz on the Defeat of Jena-Auerstädt." *Army Quarterly,* October 1941, 109–21.

———. "Jomini and Clausewitz." *Canadian Army Journal* 5 (May 1951): 64–69.

Egerton, Francis. *Personal Reminiscences of the Duke of Wellington by Francis, the First Earl of Ellesmere.* Edited by Alice, Countess of Strafford. London: John Murray, 1904.

Etzold, T. H. "Clausewitzian Lessons for Modern Strategists." *Air University Review,* May-June 1980: 24–28.

Falls, Cyril. *The Nature of Modern Warfare.* New York: Oxford University Press, 1941.

———. *Ordeal by Battle.* London: Methuen, 1943.

Fisher, Lieutenant T., R.N. "Command of the Sea: What Is It?" *The Journal of the Royal United Service Institution* 53 (July 1909): 847–64.

Frankland, Noble. "Philosophies of War." *Books and Bookmen,* December 1977: 38–39.

Franz, Wallace P. "Two Letters on Strategy: Clausewitz' Contributions to the Operational Level of War." In *Clausewitz and Modern Strategy*. Ed. Michael I. Handel, 171–96. London: Frank Cass, 1986.

Fritz, Nicholas H., Jr. [Colonel, USAF]. "Clausewitz and U.S. Nuclear Weapons Policy." *Air University Review*, November–December 1982: 18–28.

Fuller, J. F. C. *The Foundations of the Science of War*. London: Hutchinson, 1926.

———. *The Dragon's Teeth: A Study of War and Peace*. London: Constable, 1932.

———. *War and Western Civilization, 1832–1932: A Study of War as a Political Instrument and the Expression of Mass Democracy*. London: Duckworth, 1932.

———. *The Conduct of War, 1789–1961: A Study of the French, Industrial, and Russian Revolutions on War and Its Conduct*. London: Eyre and Spottiswoode, 1961.

Furlong, Raymond B. [Lieutenant General, USAF, ret.]. "*On War*, Political Objectives, and Military Strategy." *Parameters*, December 1983: 2–10.

———. "The Validity of Clausewitz's Judgments for the Sphere of Air and Space War." In *Freiheit ohne Krieg: Beiträge zur Strategie-Diskussion der Gegenwart im Spiegel der Theorie von Carl von Clausewitz*. Ed. Ulrich de Maizière, 221–28. Bonn: Ferdinand Dümmlers Verlag, 1980.

Gaddis, John Lewis. *Strategies of Containment: A Critical Appraisal of Postwar American National Security Policy*. Oxford: Oxford University Press, 1982.

Gallie, W. B. "Clausewitz Today." *European Journal of Sociology* 19 (1978): 143–67.

———. *Philosophers of Peace and War: Kant, Clausewitz, Marx, Engels and Tolstoy*. Cambridge: Cambridge University Press, 1978.

Gat, Azar. *The Origins of Military Thought: From the Enlightenment to Clausewitz*. Oxford: Oxford University Press, 1989.

Gat, Azar. "Clausewitz's Final Notes." *Militärgeschichtliche Mitteilungen*, 1 (1989): 45–50.

Gat, Azar. "Clausewitz and the Marxists: Yet Another Look." *Journal of contemporary History*, 27 (1992): 363–382.

General Staff (British army). *Report on a Conference of General Staff Officers at the Staff College, 7–10 January, 1908*. Haig Papers, National Library of Scotland, MS ACC 3155, no. 81.

Gibbs, Norman H. "War. Part A: The Western Theory of War." *Marxism, Communism and Western Society: A Comparative Encyclopedia*. Ed. C. D. Kernig. New York: Herder and Herder, 1972–1973.

———. "Clausewitz on the Moral Forces in War." *Naval War College Review*, January–February 1975: 15–22.

Gilbert, Felix. "From Clausewitz to Delbrück and Hintze: Achievements and Failures of Military History." *Journal of Strategic Studies* 3 (1980): 11–20.

Glenn, Major [USA] Russell W. "The Clausewitz Posthumous Analysis of the Gulf War." *British Army Review*, April 1992, 21–23; *Australian Defence Force Journal*, March–April 1992, 7–9.

Gooch, John. "Clio and Mars: The Use and Abuse of History." *Journal of Strategic Studies* 3 (1980): 21–36.

Hahlweg, Werner. "Clausewitz, Lenin and Communist Military Attitudes Today." *Journal of the United Service Institutes* 105 (May 1960): 221–225.

———. "Clausewitz und die angelsächsische Welt." In Carl von Clausewitz, *Vom Kriege*, 19th ed., 138–53. Bonn: Ferdinand Dümmlers Verlag, 1980.

———. "Clausewitz and Guerrilla Warfare." In *Clausewitz and Modern Strategy*. Ed. Michael I. Handell, 127–33. London: Frank Cass, 1986.

Handel, Michael I., ed. *Clausewitz and Modern Strategy.* London: Frank Cass, 1986.

Handel, Michael I. *Sun Tzu and Clausewitz: The Art of War and On War Compared.* Carlisle Barracks, PA: Strategic Studies Institute, U.S. Army War College, 1991.

Harsh, Joseph L. "Battlesword and Rapier: Clausewitz, Jomini, and the American Civil War." *Military Affairs,* December 1974: 133–138.

Hattendorf, John B. "Sir Julian Corbett on the Significance of Naval History." *American Neptune* 31 (1971): 275–285.

———. "The Study of War History at Oxford, 1862–1990." Manuscript to be published as part of John B. Hattendorf and Malcolm H. Murfett, eds., *The Limitations of Military Power: Essays Presented to Norman Gibbs on His Eightieth Birthday* (New York: St. Martin's Press, 1990).

Headquarters United States Marine Corps. *FMFM 1: Warfighting.* Washington, DC: U.S. Government Printing Office, 1989.

Henderson, G. F. R. *The Science of War.* London: Longmans, Greene, 1905.

Holley, I. B., Jr. *General John M. Palmer, Citizen Soldiers, and the Army of a Democracy.* Westport, CT: Greenwood Press, 1982.

Howard, Michael. "Clausewitz and His Misinterpreters." *The Listener,* 22 March 1956: 279–80.

———. "The Influence of Clausewitz." In Carl von Clausewitz, *On War.* Ed. and trans. Michael Howard and Peter Paret, 27–44. Princeton, NJ: Princeton University Press, 1976., 27–44.

———. "The Military Philosopher." (Review of Paret, *Clausewitz and the State,* and Aron, *Penser la guerre*). *Times Literary Supplement,* 25 June 1976: 754–55.

———. "The Forgotten Dimensions of Strategy." *Foreign Affairs,* Summer 1979: 975–86.

———. *Clausewitz.* Oxford: Oxford University Press, 1983.

Hunt, Barry D. "The Strategic Thought of Sir Julian S. Corbett." In *Maritime Strategy and the Balance of Power.* Ed. John B. Hattendorf and Robert S. Jordan. London: Macmillan, 1989: 110–35.

Huntington, Samuel P. *The Soldier and the State: The Theory and Politics of Civil–Military Relations.* Cambridge, MA: Harvard University Press, 1957.

Irvine, Dallas D. "The French Discovery of Clausewitz and Napoleon." *Journal of the American Military Institute* 4 (1940): 143–61.

Johnston, Robert Matteson. *Clausewitz to Date.* Cambridge, MA: *Military Historian and Economist,* 1917.

———. "War and Peace, Limited or Unlimited?" *The Nineteenth Century,* July 1919: 34–39.

Jomini, Baron de. *The Art of War.* Trans. Major O. F. Winship and Lieut. E. E. McLean. New York: Putnam, 1854.

King, James E. "On Clausewitz: Master Theorist of War." *Naval War College Review,* Fall 1977, 3–36. The much longer manuscript from which this article was derived is currently in the hands of Westview Press, Boulder, CO.

Kipp, Jacob W. "Lenin and Clausewitz: The Militarization of Marxism, 1914–1921." *Military Affairs,* October 1985: 184–91.

Kissinger, Henry A. *Nuclear Weapons and Foreign Policy.* New York: Harper Bros., 1957.

Kitchen, Martin. "The Political History of Clausewitz." *Journal of Strategic Studies* 11 (March 1988): 27–50.

Kleinman, [Master Sergeant, USA] Forrest K. "The Pied Piper of Modern Military Thought." *Military Review* 37 (November 1957): 56–64.

Lavisse, Ernest, and Charles Andler. *German Theory and Practice of War.* Trans. L. S. Studies and Documents on the War Series. Paris: Librairie Armand Colin, 1915.

Liddell Hart, Basil. H. "The Napoleonic Fallacy." *Empire Review*, May 1925.

———. Response to Wilkinson's "Killing No Murder." *Army Quarterly* 15 (January 1928): 396–401.

———. *The Decisive Wars of History.* Boston: Little, Brown, 1929.

———. *The British Way of Warfare.* London: Faber & Faber, 1932; New York: Macmillan, 1933.

———. *The Ghost of Napoleon.* London: Faber, 1933; reprinted Westport, CT: Greenwood Press, 1980.

———. "War, Limited." *Harper's Magazine*, March 1946: 193–203.

———. *Strategy.* Rev. ed. New York: Praeger, 1954, 1967.

———. "Armed Forces and the Art of War: Armies." In *The Zenith of European Power, 1830–1870.* Ed. J. P. T. Bury, 302–30. Vol 10 of *New Cambridge Modern History.* Cambridge: Cambridge University Press, 1960.

———. *The Memoirs of Captain Liddell Hart.* 2 vols. London: Cassell, 1965.

Lund, Robert R. *The Middle East: Employment of U.S. Military Forces from a Clausewitzian Perspective.* Washington, DC: Defense Technical Information Center, 1988. U.S. Government Document AD-B134 004.

Luvaas, Jay. "Student as Teacher: Clausewitz on Frederick the Great and Napoleon." In *Clausewitz and Modern Strategy.* Ed. Michael I. Handell, 150–70. London: Frank Cass, 1986.

———. "Clausewitz, Fuller and Liddell Hart." In *Clausewitz and Modern Strategy.* Ed. Michael I. Handel, 197–12. London: Frank Cass, 1986.

MacIsaac, Lieutenant Colonel [USAF] David. "Master at Arms: Clausewitz in Full View." *Air University Review*, January–February 1979, 83–79.

Maltzahn, Admiral [Curt Freiherr] von. *What Lesson Has General von Clausewitz's Work "On War" for the Naval Officer?* Trans. W. H. Hancock. Portsmouth: Naval War College, November 1906. From the *Marine Rundschau*, June 1905.

Marston, J. E. *The Life and Campaigns of Field Marshal Prince Blücher.* London: Sherwood, Neely, and Jones, 1815. Contains a loose translation of Clausewitz's "Campaign of 1813."

Matthews, Col. Lloyd J. "On Clausewitz." *ARMY*, February 1988: 20–24.

Maurice, Major-General Sir Frederick Barton. *British Strategy: A Study of the Application of the Principles of War.* London: Constable, 1929.

Maurice, Colonel J. F. "War." *Encyclopædia Britannica*, vol. 24, 9th ed., 343–63. New York: Scribner, 1878.

———. *War.* London: Macmillan, 1891.

Metz, Steven and Lieutenant [USA] Frederick M. Downey. "Centers of Gravity and Strategic Planning." *Military Review*, April 1988: 22–33.

Meyers, [Captain, USN] George Julian. *Strategy.* Washington, DC: Byron S. Adams, 1928.

Military Correspondent of the *Times* [Repington]. "À la Clausewitz." *The Times* (London), 23 March 1905.

———. *Imperial Strategy.* London: John Murray, 1906.

———. "The War Day by Day: Clausewitz and the Moderns." *The Times*, 11 March 1915: 6.

———. "Forces Moral and Material." *The Times*, 8 March 1915: 6.

Mitchell, John. *Thoughts on Tactics and Military Organization*. London: Longman, Orme, Brown, Green, and Longmans, 1838.

———. "Review of the British Army, and of the Present State of Military Science." *Monthly Chronicle* (London), v.1, March–June 1838: 317–30.

———. "Military Science and the Late Disasters in Affghanistan" (*sic*). *United Service Gazette*, 14 May 1842: 4.

———. *The Fall of Napoleon*, 3 vols. London: G. W. Nickerson, 1845.

———. "The Vulnerability of Russia." *United Service Gazette*, 3 June 1854: 4.

Møller, Bjørn. *Resolving the Security Dilemma in Europe: The German Debate on Non-Offensive Defence*. London: Brassey's, 1991.

Moody, Peter R., Jr. "Clausewitz and the Fading Dialectic of War." *World Politics* 31 (1979): 417–32.

Moran, Daniel. "Clausewitz and the Revolution." *Central European History*, 22 (June 1989): 183–99.

Müller, Klaus Jürgen. "Clausewitz, Ludendorff and Beck: Some Remarks on Clausewitz' Influence on German Military Thinking in the 1930s and 1940s." In *Clausewitz and Modern Strategy*. Ed. Michael I. Handel, 240–66. London: Frank Cass, 1986.

Murray, Major Stewart L. [Lygon]. *The Reality of War: An Introduction to Clausewitz with a Note by Spenser Wilkinson*. London: Hugh Rees, 1909.

Murray, Williamson. "Clausewitz: Some Thought on What the Germans Got Right." In *Clausewitz and Modern Strategy*. Ed. Michael I. Handel, 267–86. London: Frank Cass, 1986.

Naylor, Colonel [USA] William K. *Principles of Strategy: With Historical Illustrations*. Fort Leavenworth, KS: The General Service Schools Press, 1921.

Nelson, Harold [Colonel, USA]. "Space and Time in *On War*." In *Clausewitz and Modern Strategy*. Ed. Michael I. Handel, 134–49. London: Frank Cass, 1986.

Nickerson, Hoffman. *Can We Limit War?* New York: Frederick A. Stokes, 1934; reprinted Port Washington, NY: Kennikat Press, 1973.

———. "Clausewitz: A Hundred Years After." *Army Quarterly*, July 1940: 274–84.

———. *The Armed Horde 1793–1939: A Study of the Rise, Survival and Decline of the Mass Army*. New York: Putnam, 1942.

Orwell, George. "Perfide Albion." *The New Statesman and Nation*, 21 November 1942: 342–43.

Osgood, Robert Endicott. *Limited War: The Challenge to American Strategy*. Chicago: University of Chicago Press, 1957.

Otis, Major [USMC] John F., Jr. "Clausewitz: On Weinberger." *Marine Corps Gazette*, February 1988: 16–17.

Palmer, John McAuley [Brigadier General, USA]. *Statesmanship or War*. Garden City, NY: Doubleday, Page, 1927.

———. *Washington, Lincoln, Wilson: Three War Statesmen*. Garden City, NY: Doubleday, 1930.

Paret, Peter. "Clausewitz: A Bibliographical Survey." *World Politics* 17 (1965): 272–85.

———. "Clausewitz and the Nineteenth Century." In *The Theory and Practice of War*. Ed. Michael Howard, 21–41. New York: Praeger, 1966.

————. "Hans Delbrück on Military Critics and Military Historians." *Military Affairs* 30 (1966): 148–52.

————. Review of Werner Hahlweg, *Schriften—Aufsätze—Studien—Briefe: Dokumente aus dem Clausewitz-, Scharnhorst- und Gneisenau-nachlass sowie aus offentlichen und privaten Sammlungen.* Vol. 1, *American Historical Review* 72 (April 1967): 1011.

————. "Education, Politics, and War in the Life of Clausewitz." *Journal of the History of Ideas* 29 (1968): 394–408.

————. "An Anonymous Letter by Clausewitz on the Polish Insurrection of 1830–1831." *Journal of Modern History*, no. 2 (1970): 184–90.

————. "The Genesis of *On War.*" In Carl von Clausewitz, *On War.* Ed. and trans. Michael Howard and Peter Paret, 3–25. Princeton, NJ: Princeton University Press, 1976.

————. *Clausewitz and the State: The Man, His Theories, and His Times.* Princeton, NJ: Princeton University Press, 1976.

————. "Clausewitz." In *Makers of Modern Strategy: From Machiavelli to the Nuclear Age.* Ed. Peter Paret, 186–213. Princeton, NJ: Princeton University Press, 1986.

————. "Continuity and Discontinuity in Some Interpretations by Toqueville and Clausewitz." *Journal of the History of Ideas* 49 (January–March 1988): 161–69.

————. "An Unknown Letter by Clausewitz." *Journal of Military History*, April 1991: 143–51.

————. *Understanding War: Essays on Clausewitz and the History of Military Power.* Princeton, NJ: Princeton University Press, 1992.

Parkinson, Roger. *Clausewitz: A Biography.* Briarcliff Manor, NY: Stein & Day, 1971.

Pickett, William B. "Eisenhower as a Student of Clausewitz," *Military Review*, July 1985: 21–27.

Pilcher, T. D. [Major-General, British Army]. *War According to Clausewitz.* London: Cassell, 1918. Based on the Graham translation and 4th German ed.

[Pope-Hennessy, Major L. H. R.] "Great Britain, Germany and Limited War." *Edinburgh Review* 215 (April 1912): 485–514.

Renn, Ludwig (pseud. for Arnold F. Vieth von Grolssenau). *Warfare: The Relation of Warfare to Society.* New York: Oxford University Press, 1939.

Reynolds, Charles. "Carl von Clausewitz and Strategic Theory." *British Journal of International Studies* 4 (1978): 178–90.

Robinson, Oliver Prescott. *The Fundamentals of Military Strategy.* Washington, DC: United States Infantry Association, 1928.

Rosinski, Herbert. "IMS: Captain Falls on Modern Warfare." (Review of Cyril Falls's, *The Nature of Modern Warfare*). *Infantry Journal* 50 (January 1942): 78–81.

Rosinski, Herbert. "Clausewitz Today." (Review of Joseph I. Greene, ed., *The Living Thoughts of Clausewitz*). *Infantry Journal*, October 1943: 59–65.

————. "Scharnhorst to Schlieffen: The Rise and Decline of German Military Thought." *United States Naval War College Review*, Summer 1976: 83–103.

————. *The Development of Naval Thought.* Newport, RI: Naval War College Press, 1977.

Rothfels, Hans. "Clausewitz." In *Makers of Modern Strategy: Military Thought from Machiavelli to Hitler.* Ed. Edward Mead Earle, 93–115. Princeton, NJ: Princeton University Press, 1943.

Roth, Günter. "The Thought of Annihilation in the Military Doctrine of Carl von Clausewitz and Count Alfred von Schlieffen." In *Operatonal Thinking in Clausewitz, Moltke, Schlieffen and Manstein*. Ed. Militärgeschichtliches Forschungsamt. Bonn: E. S. Mittler and Son, 1988: 11–20.

Rylander, R. Lynn. "Mao as a Clausewitzian Strategist." *Military Review* 61 (1981): 13–21.

Schneider, James J., and Lawrence J. Izzo. "Clausewitz's Elusive Center of Gravity." *Parameters* 17 (September 1987): 46–57.

———. *The Education of a Navy: The Development of British Naval Strategic Thought, 1867–1914*. Chicago: University of Chicago Press, 1965.

Schurman, Donald M. *Julian S. Corbett, 1854–1922: Historian of British Maritime Policy from Drake to Jellicoe*. London: Royal Historical Society, 1981.

Speier, Hans. "Ludendorff: The German Concept of Total War." In *Makers of Modern Strategy: Military Thought from Machiavelli to Hitler*. Ed. Edward Mead Earle, 306–321. Princeton, NJ: Princeton University Press, 1943.

Staudenmaier, Lieutenant Colonel [USA] William O. "Vietnam: Mao vs. Clausewitz." Unpublished paper. Carlisle, PA: U.S. Army War College, 1976.

———. "Vietnam, Mao and Clausewitz." *Parameters* 7 (1977): 79–89.

Steiner, Barry H. *Bernard Brodie and the Foundations of American Nuclear Strategy*. Lawrence, KS: University Press of Kansas, 1991.

Summers, Harry G., Jr. [Colonel USA]. *On Strategy: A Critical Analysis of the Vietnam War*. Novato, CA: Presidio Press, 1982.

———. "Clausewitz and Strategy Today." *Naval War College Review*, March–April 1983: 40–46.

———. "Clausewitz: Eastern and Western Approaches to War." *Air University Review*, March–April 1986: 62–71.

———. *On Strategy II: A Critical Analysis of the Gulf War*. New York: Dell, 1992.

Swain, Richard M. [Colonel, USA]. "Clausewitz, FM100–5, and the Center of Gravity." *Military Review*, February 1988: 83.

Tashjean, John E. "The Cannon in the Swimming Pool: Clausewitzian Studies and Strategic Ethnocentrism." *Journal of the Royal United Services Institute*, June 1983: 54–57.

Thibault, Edward A. "War as a Collapse of Policy: A Critical Evaluation of Clausewitz." *Naval War College Review*, May-June 1973: 42–56.

U.S. Military Academy. Department of Military Art and Engineering. *Clausewitz, Jomini, Schlieffen*. West Point, NY: U.S. Military Academy, 1951. Rewritten, in part by Colonel [USA] John R. Elting, 1964.

Unsigned. "De La Barre Duparcq's Commentaries on Clausewitz." (Review of Nicolas Édouard Delabarre Duparcq's *Commentaires sur le traité de la guerre de Clausewitz* [Paris, 1853]). *United Service Magazine*, pt. 1, 1854: 26–36.

Wallach, Jehuda L. *The Dogma of the Battle of Annihilation: The Theories of Clausewitz and Schlieffen and Their Impact on the German Conduct of Two World Wars*. Westport, CT: Greenwood Press, 1986.

———. "Misperceptions of Clausewitz' *On War* by the German Military." In *Clausewitz and Modern Strategy*. Ed. Michael I. Handel, 213–239. London: Frank Cass, 1986.

Wass de Czege, Colonel [USA] Huba. "Clausewitz: Historical Studies Remain Sound Compass References; the Catch Is Staying on Course." *Army*, September 1988: 37–43.

Watts, LTC (USAF) Barry D. *The Foundations of US Air Doctrine: The Problem of Friction in War.* Maxwell Air Force Base, AL: Air University Press, 1984.

Weigley, Russell F. *The American Way of War: A History of United States Military Strategy and Policy.* New York: Macmillan, 1973.

————. "Military Strategy and Civilian Leadership." In *Historical Dimensions of National Security Problems.* Ed. Klaus Knorr, 38–77. Lawrence: University Press of Kansas, 1976.

Wellesley, Arthur. "Memorandum on the Battle of Waterloo." In *Supplementary Despatches, Correspondence, and Memoranda of Field Marshal Arthur Duke of Wellington.* Vol. 10, 513–31. London: John Murray, 1863.

White, Charles Edward [Grad. USMA, currently Command Historian, U.S. Army Infantry School, Fort Benning]. *The Enlightened Soldier: Scharnhorst and the Military Gesellschaft in Berlin, 1801–1805.* New York: Praeger, 1989.

Wilkinson, Spenser. *The Brain of an Army: A Popular Account of the German General Staff.* Westminster: A. Constable, 1890.

————. *The Brain of the Navy.* Westminster: A. Constable, 1895.

————. "Strategy in the Navy." *Morning Post,* 3 August 1909.

————. *The University and the Study of War: An Inaugural Lecture Delivered Before the University of Oxford, November 27, 1909.* Oxford: Clarendon Press, 1909.

————. "Strategy at Sea." (Review of Julian S. Corbett's *Some Principles of Maritime Strategy*). *Morning Post,* 19 February 1912.

————. *The French Army Before Napoleon.* Oxford: Clarendon Press, 1915.

————. "Killing No Murder: An Examination of Some New Theories of War." *Army Quarterly* 14 (October 1927): 14–27.

Williams, T. Harry. "The Return of Jomini: Some Thoughts on Recent Civil War Writing." *Military Affairs,* December 1975: 204–6.

Woodhouse, W. J. *King Agis of Sparta and His Campaign in Arkadia in 418 B.C.* Oxford: Clarendon Press, 1933; New York: AMS Press, 1978.

Zais, [Colonel, USA] Mitchell M. "West Point: Swordmaking or Swordsmanship?" *Armed Forces Journal International,* March 1990: 57–62.

Index